THOMAS MIFFLIN
From the Collections of the Historical Society of Pennsylvania

The Republicans and Federalists in Pennsylvania
1790-1801

•

A Study in National Stimulus and Local Response

•

By HARRY MARLIN TINKCOM

COMMONWEALTH OF PENNSYLVANIA

PENNSYLVANIA HISTORICAL AND MUSEUM
COMMISSION
·HARRISBURG·1950

THE PENNSYLVANIA HISTORICAL AND MUSEUM COMMISSION

CHARLES J. BIDDLE, *Chairman*

FRANCES DORRANCE

A. ATWATER KENT, JR.

THOMAS MURPHY

JOHN W. OLIVER

EDGAR T. STEVENSON

CHARLES G. WEBB

RICHARD NORRIS WILLIAMS, 2D

FRANCIS B. HAAS, *ex officio*
    Superintendent of Public Instruction

DONALD A. CADZOW, *Executive Director*

SYLVESTER K. STEVENS, *State Historian*

TRUSTEES—EX OFFICIO

JAMES H. DUFF,
    Governor of the Commonwealth

WELDON B. HEYBURN, *Auditor General*

CHARLES R. BARBER, *State Treasurer*

FOREWORD

The Pennsylvania Historical and Museum Commission is pleased to add this volume to its series of studies on the political history of the Commonwealth. In 1942 the Pennsylvania Historical Commission* published *The Counter-Revolution in Pennsylvania, 1776-1790*, by Robert L. Brunhouse. This earlier volume and the present work are the result of research completed at the University of Pennsylvania, under the direction of Dr. Roy F. Nichols, outstanding authority in the field of political history. A third volume covering succeeding years is already scheduled for publication.

The Commission, therefore, is continuing the policy of publishing such noteworthy contributions to Pennsylvania history, which might not otherwise find their way into print. Unfortunately, it is not the common practice today to publish doctoral dissertations. Many splendid contributions to history gather dust in manuscript form on the library shelves of the particular university where they were completed. It has been a policy of the Commission for some years to rescue certain distinguished works of this character from possible oblivion and to present them as additions to the historical literature of the Commonwealth. This plan, the Commission believes, has been greeted with enthusiasm by all students of Pennsylvania history. As a result of this program, many glaring gaps in the story of Pennsylvania's development are being filled.

Through the generosity of the Governor of the Commonwealth, James H. Duff, and of the General Assembly, this particular Commission was the recipient of unusually liberal appropriations for historical research and publications. This publication is one of several which will continue to appear, and which were made possible by these appropriations. The Pennsylvania Historical and Museum Commission is grateful to the Governor, to the members of the General Assembly, and to the people of the Commonwealth, who have combined to make possible this and other worthy additions to the growing number of books and research projects which add to our store of knowledge about Pennsylvania's past.

CHARLES J. BIDDLE, Chairman
Pennsylvania Historical and Museum Commission

February 2, 1950

---

* The Pennsylvania Historical and Museum Commission was created in 1945 by combining and consolidating the functions of the State Museum, the State Archives, and the former Pennsylvania Historical Commission.

TABLE OF CONTENTS

Chapter	Page
FOREWORD	iii
PREFACE	vii

Section I
POLITICAL NEBULAE, 1790-1792

I.	REVOLUTIONS AND CONSTITUTIONS, 1776-1790	1
II.	THE STATE AND THE UNION, 1790	19
III.	COMPROMISE CONFIRMED, 1790	33
IV.	CONGRESSIONAL ELECTIONS OF 1791 AND 1792	45

Section II
NATIONAL STIMULUS AND LOCAL RESPONSE, 1793-1795

V.	EVENTS AND OPINIONS	75
VI.	WHISKEY AND POLITICS	91
VII.	PRESQUE ISLE	113
VIII.	POLITICAL OPINIONS AND ELECTIONS, 1793-1795	135

Section III
THE TRIUMPH OF REPUBLICANISM, 1796-1801

IX.	SIGNS OF A RISING REPUBLICANISM	159
X.	ELECTIONS, ISSUES AND LABELS	175
XI.	PARTY GROWTH IN THE PENNSYLVANIA HOUSE OF REPRESENTATIVES, 1795-1798	199
XII.	REPUBLICAN VICTORY	215
XIII.	VICTORY AFFIRMED AND REAFFIRMED	243
XIV.	MCKEAN AND THE PATRONAGE POWER	263
XV.	CONCLUSION	269
NOTES		275
BIBLIOGRAPHY		329
INDEX		339

PREFACE

The evolutionary development of Pennsylvania's political parties during the first twelve years of the Federal period was characterized primarily by the State's intensive reaction to national and international issues. Prior to the formation of the Federal government political controversy stemmed principally from the remarkable Constitution of 1776; but with the appearance of the Federal Constitution and the State Constitution of 1790 a realignment of affiliations and a reinterpretation of ideologies were made necessary. It was in this latter year that the shifting political structure was remarked upon by numerous contemporary politicians. They were convinced that the old patterns had changed and that the operation of new and powerful stimuli would greatly alter current alignments and give a new direction to political forces. They were right. Future partisan organizations would find their *raison d'etre* in the necessity of expressing opinions arising from action taken by the national administrations.

The amorphousness of party groupings was well illustrated by the election of Thomas Mifflin to the governorship in 1790. With the destruction of the Constitution of 1776 the old Constitutionalist and Anti-Constitutionalist groups had lost their chief cohesive impellant. Mifflin, who had been popular with both factions, was elected as a compromise governor by an overwhelming majority. The old lines were rapidly disappearing.

During the next eight years the cumulative effect of state and national forces produced two determined political groups known as the Republican and Federalist parties. By 1798 the existence of these organizations was recognized by outstanding leaders such as Thomas Jefferson, William Duane, Thomas Mifflin and Thomas McKean. It was in 1799 that the Republicans, through superior organization and effective exploitation of unpopular Federalist legislation—particularly the direct property tax—were enabled to elect Thomas McKean to the governorship. In the following two years this victory was affirmed and emphatically reaffirmed. By 1801 the Republicans were in complete control of the State.

With deep gratitude I wish to thank the following institutions whose collections I utilized in the preparation of this volume: the Western Pennsylvania Historical Society, the Darlington Memorial Library of the University of Pittsburgh, the Library Company of Philadelphia, the American Philosophical Society, the Pennsylvania State Library, the University of Pennsylvania Library, Girard College, the Free Library of Philadelphia, the Library of Congress and the New-York Historical Society. The staffs of these institutions were unfailingly courteous and helpful in making available the sources under their care.

To the Director and staff of the Historical Society of Pennsylvania a special note of appreciation. My path to the riches in that institution was often straightened and smoothed by those ever-cooperative staff members who assisted my research with knowledge, wisdom and kindness.

With pleasure I acknowledge a debt of gratitude to the Pennsylvania Historical and Museum Commission, whose financial assistance made the publication of this volume possible; to Dr. S. K. Stevens for reading the manuscript, and to Mr. Donald Kent and Mrs. Elva Hamilton for excellent editorial advice and assistance.

Finally, I should like to express my deepest thanks to Professor Roy F. Nichols of the University of Pennsylvania for aid and encouragement, always freely given.

HARRY M. TINKCOM.

SECTION I

POLITICAL NEBULAE, 1790-1792

I will not pretend to define or describe an Aristocrat, a Democrat, a Jacobin, a Sans-culot, a Frenchman, an Anarchist, a Revolutionist, a Leveller, a Disorganiser, a Regicide, a Liberticide, etc. etc. etc. or even a Federal, an Antifederal, or a Friend of Government; for I am utterly unable to fix their boundary lines, or trace their shades of difference; and I make perpetual blunders when I attempt to apply them to my neighbors . . . All I can find out with certainty on this subject is, that whatever the true meaning of these names may be, the most hotheaded, the most ignorant, the most interested, and those who have been suddenly raised from indigence to opulence, are the most ready to apply them. . . .

. . . if a man be a good citizen, a good American, a good Republican, working his farm, supporting his family, obeying the laws, paying his taxes, and drinking his glass of whisky in good humor with all the world, should he be hunted down as Aristocrat, or sneered at as a Tory, or kicked out of company as a Jacobin, or have some of these hard favoured *Isms* thrown at his head if he cannot subscribe to the infallibility of his opponent?

THOMAS COOPER

CHAPTER I

REVOLUTIONS AND CONSTITUTIONS, 1776-1790

IN 1790, PENNSYLVANIA produced a Constitution that terminated more than fourteen years of struggle between the State's liberal and conservative elements. Destined to last for almost half a century, this Constitution put a documentary period to years of bitter strife and experiment. It concluded a political era and defined the total of the democratic processes that characterized the State in its most critical and formative years. But in its solemn and precise phraseology there is little indication of the turmoil and experimentation that preceded the convention which brought it into existence. In its almost complacent definition of what was considered proper and just government there is no hint of the wrangles and broils which made such a calm exposition possible. For during this formative period, from the Declaration of Independence to 1790, the democratic elements, after proclaiming the remarkably advanced Constitution of 1776 and an ultrademocratic conception of representative government, had seen their power and influence gradually whittled away by the conservative interests. Yet the Constitution of 1790, whose very existence was a result of a conservative victory, was not, in the light of historical evaluation or contemporary judgment, regarded as a seriously retrogressive or reactionary document.

In view of these considerations it is obvious that an understanding of the Constitution of 1790—and more important still, a knowledge of the political atmosphere it expressed—must be dependent on a general review of the circumstances which produced it. These were an outgrowth of the organic instrument which it replaced, the Constitution of 1776.

THE CONSTITUTION OF 1776

That revolutionary document was born of numerous quarrels and conflicting opinions, and their sources can be traced back to the charter under which Pennsylvania operated when under the control of William Penn. In the early assemblies many bitter controversies arose over the question of just representation for all parts of the colony.

When the population expanded beyond Philadelphia and its immediate environs, many of the inhabitants of that area evinced a strong desire to continue their control of the government. Since this could best be effected by controlling representation in the General Assembly, the Philadelphia group consistently apportioned the representatives in a manner that would best perpetuate its dominance. Their success is attested to by the fact that as late as 1764, when Pennsylvania had eight counties and thirty-six members in the Assembly, the little section in the southeastern part of the State, comprising the counties of Philadelphia, Bucks and Chester, had twenty-six of them. By the year 1776, these three counties, with only about one-third of the population, had twenty-four members in the Assembly in comparison to a total of fourteen for the counties to the westward.[1] In addition to the complaint of under representation the westerners also suffered restrictions which disfranchised large numbers of potential voters. This narrow suffrage, however, was imposed not only on those residing beyond the orbit of Philadelphia's control but upon the city itself. On the basis of population Philadelphia had only one-quarter of the representation to which it was entitled. A great many people failed to meet a voting qualification requiring the ownership of fifty acres or fifty pounds. Further, naturalization rules excluded many of German descent.[2] This accumulation of combustibles of a sectional, cultural and political nature generated a body of protest that needed only a spark to set it aflame. This was provided by the American Revolution.

When the conflict with Britain began the eastern aristocratic group, still exercising a control far out of proportion to its numbers, found its supremacy challenged by a combination of western farmers and Philadelphia artisans and mechanics. They were aided and strengthened by many able members of the middle class who saw an opportunity to participate more actively in the government and to bring the colony squarely into the fight against the mother country.

To both of these aims the conservative Assembly was flatly opposed, and the battle was joined. In 1776, after insistent pressure, the conservatives reluctantly permitted an extension in general representation which increased the number in that body by seventeen. Now with a total membership of fifty-eight the eastern section was represented by thirty members and the western counties by twenty-eight.[3] But this concession was unsatisfactory to the liberals.

As the struggle over the control of Pennsylvania continued it became so intense that placed against the wider background of the fight for independence it took on all the aspects of a "revolution within a revolution."[4] Indeed, it has been said that the grievances of the Pennsylvania patriots against the English were of less importance to them than their complaints against the eastern aristocracy.[5]

At a critical time—the State had remained conservative in an election of May 1, 1776—the Second Continental Congress provided an opportunity for the liberals to make another attempt. On May 10, of that year Congress recommended the creation of new state governments. Losing no time, the Philadelphia City Committee set in motion a series of events which resulted in a general conference at Philadelphia on June 18, 1776. Here arrangements were made for a Provincial Convention in which each county and the city of Philadelphia would be represented by an equal number of elected delegates.

The Convention met on July 15, 1776, and although created to form a Constitution it assumed complete control of the State in spite of the Assembly. This latter body, now rendered impotent by the Revolutionary Convention, met for the last time on September 26.[6]

When the Provincial Convention finished its work it proclaimed a Constitution which was to remain the organic law of Pennsylvania until 1790. As a revolutionary instrument it broke with the past and made Pennsylvania one of the most democratic of all the states. Fearing the power of a governor its framers made no provisions for such an office. Instead, an Executive Council was created with a president as the presiding officer. The supreme legislative power resided in an Assembly whose members were selected by an electorate no longer hampered by property qualifications. Assemblymen could be voted for by any tax-paying freeman who had reached the age of twenty-one and had lived in the State one year. All counties were entitled to legislative representation according to the number of taxable residents therein. The loyalty and good faith of the legislators were to be assured by the application of oaths of allegiance which required them to swear or affirm a belief in one God and acknowledge the divine inspiration of the Scriptures. Further, all State officeholders had to swear or affirm faithfulness to the Commonwealth and declare that they would "not directly or indirectly do any act or thing prejudicial or injurious to the constitution or government thereof, as established by the convention."[7]

The Constitution also introduced a new and unusual body known as the Council of Censors. This Council, whose members were to be elected every seven years, was charged with the responsibility of keeping the Constitution inviolate and determining whether or not it should be amended. Provision was made for a declaration of rights which guaranteed free and equal elections, trial by jury, freedom of speech and press, and right of assembly.

Since the new Constitution was a radical innovation and a frank attempt to efface the past, it was only natural that it should arouse a storm of opposition from the conservative groups which had so long administered the government. They saw it for what it was intended to be, an instrument of protest and revolt; they knew its guarantee of greater and fuller representation for the segments of the population hitherto politically underprivileged would threaten, even destroy their dominance; they feared it as a charter of privilege to the uneducated and lowly born; they were afraid that it would unleash forces which would overthrow the comfortable *status quo* and expose Pennsylvania to the ravages of mob violence and internecine strife. So, despite the threat of the British invasion, they fought the new order with such vigor and unrelenting bitterness that Congress had to intervene twice to preserve order.

The hatreds engendered in that strife were long remembered, and for years after the disappointed British had retired to their island the memories of that conflict still inflamed the passions and played no unimportant part in determining political behavior. Fundamentally, it was a fight between classes, between the "haves and have nots"; the mechanics, artisans and farmers against the aristocracy.[8]

STRUGGLE TO ABOLISH THE CONSTITUTION

In the quarrel over the Constitution and the governmental acts of the group that sponsored it and conducted the State's affairs, it was almost inevitable that factions would arise to give strength and force to those who supported opposing ideologies and methods. Logically enough, those who favored the Constitution became known as Constitutionalists and those who opposed it were labelled Anti-Constitutionalists, although members of the latter group generally preferred to call themselves Republicans.

The principal leaders of the Constitutionalists were the forceful George Bryan, Timothy Matlack, Benjamin Franklin, and two politically astute westerners, William Findley and John Smilie. On the opposing side were such capable and influential figures as George Clymer, James Wilson, Robert Morris and Thomas Mifflin.

The political struggle that ensued during the fourteen years after 1776 was centered primarily around the revolutionary Constitution. Several objections were voiced against it: the people had not ratified it, there was no check on the unicameral legislature, and it demanded that officeholders take an oath to support the government.

Many attempts were made to discard it, but they all met with failure until 1790. One of the most serious and interesting efforts was made in 1783-84 when the Council of Censors met. That "singular Political body," as William Findley termed it,[9] was created by the provincial Convention to determine every seven years whether or not the Constitution had been preserved and to inquire into the performance of the legislative and executive branches of the government. If this body decided that the Constitution required amendment it could, by a two-thirds vote, call a constitutional convention. Any amendments it proposed had to be announced at least six months before the election of a convention. The Council's membership, selected by a popular vote, was composed of two men from each county and from the city of Philadelphia.[10] This was democratic innovation to an advanced degree, for it submitted directly to elected representatives, and not to an appointed body of judges, the privilege of evaluating and interpreting the organic law.

Both contesting factions were looking forward with great expectations to the meeting of the Council in 1783, for it was recognized that the constitutional question was reaching a crisis.[11] When the Censors met in November, it was soon evident that the Anti-Constitutionalists had a majority. Subsequent record votes revealed this to be a majority of three, but slight as it was it enabled them to select Frederick A. Muhlenberg as chairman and to dominate the various committees during the first session.

On January 2, 1784, a committee, heavily weighted with Anti-Constitutionalists, reported that some parts of the Constitution required amendment. A resolution favoring the report was passed by a vote of twelve to ten and a committee composed of Arthur St. Clair, Thomas Fitzsimons, Samuel Miles, Thomas Hartley and John Arndt was appointed to list the articles in need of alteration.[12]

The recommendations of this committee practically demolished the Constitution of 1776. The Council of Censors was to be abolished, the Executive Council replaced by a governor, and the unicameral legislature discarded in favor of a legislative council and assembly. It was recommended that representation in the Assembly should be based on the number of taxables: 1250 for each assemblyman and 2500 for each member of the legislative council. Further, the committee suggested that the legislative council of twenty-nine members be elected in such a proportion that the five newer counties of Bedford, Northumberland, Westmoreland, Washington and Fayette would have four members and the other sections of the State twenty-five. This representation proposal was a direct blow at the less populous counties, for under the existing constitution each county, despite its population, had one representative in the Executive Council of thirteen.

To this report the minority entered a vigorous dissent, but since it was obvious that a two-thirds vote (the fraction necessary to call a convention) could not be obtained, the Republicans ended the deadlock in January, 1784, by adjourning the meetings until the following June. It was their hope that in the intervening months the citizens would convince the Constitutionalist Censors of the error of their position.

But when the Council reconvened in June, 1784, it was found that the situation which had prevailed during the first session had been reversed. Because of a resignation and a death among the Republicans their opponents had acquired two new members. These, in addition to the presence of two others who had not attended regularly in the preceding session, gave them a fairly consistent majority of fourteen to nine.

Now the dominant group, the Constitutionalists experienced no trouble in finding that the Constitution, although not a perfect instrument, was a valuable and worthy document. The Censors finally concluded their labors on September 16, 1784, by resolving that there was "no absolute necessity to call a convention to alter[,] explain or amend the Constitution."[13]

Although the Constitutionalists had won their fight in the Council of Censors, they were to experience several defeats in the Assembly during the next five years, as a brief review will indicate.

During the fight for independence the Constitutionalists had kept Pennsylvania true to the patriot cause. Faced by the British army and obstructed by Tories and lukewarm patriots, they fully appreciated the significance of Franklin's apt observation on the choice of hanging together or separately. To avert the latter, they enacted laws designed to unify their efforts which, when the war ended, were declared extreme by an ever increasing number of persons. The test laws fell within this category. Calculated to disfranchise those considered not in complete accord with the revolutionary government they excluded, at least according to the Anti-Constitutionalists, almost one-half of the people from the rights of full citizenship.[14] After the Revolution several attempts were made to abolish them. Then after their strictures had gradually been mitigated over a period of years, they were eliminated in 1789, when the oath of allegiance to the State was abandoned. It was a defeat for the Constitutionalists but not a serious one, for by that time the question was almost a dead issue.

They were also defeated in the Assembly on the bank issue in 1787, when, by a vote of thirty-five to twenty-eight, they failed to prevent the rechartering of the Bank of North America.[15]

A far more serious setback occurred when the Constitutionalists failed to prevent the ratification of the Constitution of the United States. Just nine days after that document had been submitted to the public in September, 1787, the Assembly called for a ratifying convention by a vote of forty-three to nineteen. But before all the necessary arrangements could be made nineteen Constitutionalists absented themselves from the Assembly, thus preventing a quorum. As the session was about to end an Anti-Constitutionalist mob captured two of the absent members and forced them into the Assembly hall. As a result of this kidnapping a quorum was secured and a date set for the opening of the ratifying convention. At the election for delegates to the convention the Constitutionalists lost again by a large majority, and the ratification of the Federal document (without a bill of rights) was a foregone conclusion.[16]

But the final and most decisive defeat of the Constitutionalists occurred when the Assembly decided to ignore the Council of Censors and call a constitutional convention. By 1789, the conservatives had unquestionable control of the Assembly, and they planned to exploit their numerical superiority to accomplish an object for which they had long contended. On March 24, 1789, a series of resolutions were passed by a vote of forty-one to seventeen. These repeated many old charges and declared that the people of the State had a right to alter the organic law by any means they thought desirable and proper.[17] In other words, if the people wished a change it merely remained for them to so notify the assemblymen during the summer recess and the legislators would promptly call a convention. That such action was unconstitutional the minority did not have to point out. Everyone knew it, and the Executive Council by a close vote refused to agree to the unlawful action.

When the Assembly met again in September, 1789, the Anti-Constitutionalists announced that while mingling with their constituents during the summer they had learned that the people wanted a convention. Their opponents, of course, denied this. Not more than one-seventh of the people, they said, had approved of the resolutions of the preceding session.[18] Nevertheless, those who were determined to destroy the Constitution would not be balked, and capitalizing upon their majority they passed resolutions which called for a convention, the members of which were to be elected in the same manner as the assemblymen. It was to meet in the following November.

The above succession of Constitutionalist defeats would seem to indicate that the group had lost its force and strength. But such a conclusion would be superficial. It should be pointed out that many of the setbacks suffered by the party of William Findley and George Bryan had been reversals on policies that were born during Revolutionary days. The war was over and the motives prompting many of these policies had disappeared. Further, the Anti-Constitutionalists did not have such a complete superiority in the State as Assembly votes indicated. In fact, as late as 1787, Thomas McKean reckoned the two chief opposing groups to be almost equal in numbers.[19] Granting that McKean's estimate was reasonably correct, it is clear that the Anti-Constitutionalists could not be so contemptuous of their opponents as to disregard them totally when the proposed convention would meet to create a new constitution. In addition, they must have realized that the groups for and against the ratification of the United States Constitution had been "almost equally balanced."[20]

Constitutional Convention of 1790

When the Constitutional Convention met at Philadelphia on November 24, 1789, it numbered among its members some of the most distinguished men of the times. It was probably the most capable and talented body of Pennsylvanians that had ever been gathered together to perform a public function. The electorate had shown wisdom in its selection of some of the best political and legal talent, from both factions, that the State afforded, and that was considerable. The conservatives were well represented by James Wilson, William Lewis, Thomas McKean and Samuel Sitgreaves. The Constitutionalists had chosen some of their best leaders in the persons of William Findley, John Smilie and Albert Gallatin.

Many of these leaders had played a prominent part in the State's history. Wilson, a member of the Federal Constitutional Convention and acknowledged to be one of the ablest lawyers in the country, lent to the discussions a profound body of legal knowledge. Lewis, a lawyer of wide reputation and a former member of the Assembly, took a prominent part in the debates. Sitgreaves and Gallatin were young men, and the latter had yet to demonstrate fully his outstanding ability as a political organizer and debater. Thomas McKean had already distinguished himself as a jurist and leader. As one of Delaware's representatives he had served with enthusiasm in the Stamp Act Congress and in the First Continental Congress. He was returned to Congress from Delaware again in 1775, despite the fact that he had, in the meantime, moved to Philadelphia.[21] Although disapproving of the Constitution of 1776, he had refused to join many Pennsylvania lawyers in boycotting the Constitutionalist government and had been made Chief Justice of the State. Strongly in favor of the Federal Constitution, he was now to work assiduously to revise the State document.

The chief figure in the Constitutionalist ranks was William Findley, from Westmoreland County. Born in Ulster, he had arrived in Pennsylvania in 1763. After a varied career as teacher, soldier in the Revolution and farmer, he had been elected a member of the Council of Censors in 1783. This was the first public body in whose work he had participated and he regarded it as the best possible training school for political affairs.[22] With ability unusual in one so inexperienced, he was of material aid in opposing the conservatives' demand for a convention. His constituents later rewarded him by sending him to the Assembly, where he developed into an able spokesman for his section.

The Constitutional Convention met in Philadelphia on November 24, 1789, but as no quorum was available it adjourned until the following day. Then enough members answered the roll call to begin the business at hand. The temper of the delegates was signified in their selection of Thomas Mifflin as president.[23] Although they may have been inclined to honor him as President of the Executive Council, their choice indicates the spirit of cooperation that generally marked the proceedings of the convention in the days that followed. Mifflin, an amiable, fair and tolerant man could be depended upon to conduct matters in an impartial manner. As to his political affiliations, there was some doubt about them even then. By 1789, the strongly pervasive influence of the United States Government was beginning to make itself felt in the State's councils, and Mifflin, although listed on the side of those who opposed the Constitution of 1776, was suspected of having been at odds with Washington during the Revolution. His selection, therefore, as presiding officer of the Convention, could not have been displeasing to those who voiced apprehensions as to the real nature and interest of the national administration. As presiding officer he was permitted to speak and vote in the committee of the whole, "yet his voice was seldom heard. His suffrages were always on the popular side."[24]

Alexander Graydon, a delegate, declared that "a panic terror of the power of the Union under the new Constitution prevailed in the convention."[25] The "consolidation" of national government dismayed "many federalists no less than . . . the anti-federalists," and much energy was expended there to discover methods whereby to resist its "encroachments." The compelling presence then of a superimposed authority on the functions of a State government that at various times had been almost unaware of the existence of an impotent Congress, constituted a determining factor that cannot be ignored in evaluating the convention's work.

The calmness with which the delegates began their labors was in sharp contrast to the acrimony and bitterness that had characterized the steps taken to bring them together. However, in the western counties especially, some men were of the opinion that since the convention had been called hastily and unconstitutionally, no delegates should be elected. Albert Gallatin had been one of those most actively engaged in preventing the sending of delegations from the four western counties. But ironically enough he himself had been chosen by Fayette County.[26]

The Convention had been in session only a short time when it became clear that the Constitutionalists were not going to resort to obstructionist tactics, as they had when the Assembly called for a convention to ratify the Federal Constitution. Instead, they participated wholeheartedly in the proceedings. Why did they now cooperate so effectively?

According to Alexander Graydon, a staunch conservative, the repudiation of the Constitutionalists had resulted in their discomfiture, and their acquiescence was purely a matter of necessity. As a result, he thought, they had worked diligently in the election for delegates so as to insure as large a representation as possible. And in numbers their membership was "not very inferior to that of their adversaries."[27] Graydon further attributed their cooperation to the fact that their opposition to the Federal Constitution had resulted in the complete defeat of the Constitutionalist party and had attached to it the stigma of anti-federalism, an embarrassment they were wisely trying to live down in order to restore their former prestige.

There is much to be said for the validity of Graydon's analysis of the Constitutionalists' position, and especially pertinent was his reference to the near equality of representation. But if they displayed a conciliatory attitude, so did their Republican opponents. They, too, must have realized that their position was not impregnable and their continued supremacy uncertain. As a matter of fact, Thomas Fitzsimons, member of Congress from Philadelphia and one of their most important leaders, believed that they could not long maintain control of the State.[28] Perhaps it was that conviction, as much as anything else, that inclined him toward the advisability of seeking an accommodation with the opposing group on the Constitutional issue. Shortly before the Assembly met in September, 1789—the Assembly which had called the Convention—he had written Benjamin Rush that a "change of Government" would redound not to the Republican party alone but to both "partys." Therefore he had proposed that George Bryan, firm champion of the document of 1776, "should be consulted and his assistance required to bring it about."[29]

So, although the conservatives had a majority, it was not of sufficient numerical strength to permit them to ride roughshod over their opponents, even if there had been complete unanimity in their ranks as to the desirability of such methods. Had it been their intention to exploit their present supremacy in the State by reverting to outmoded colonial concepts of government, the battle would have been fierce indeed. But they were too wise and sensible to do so. The lessons learned in the Revolution and in the years following that struggle were too emphatic to be ignored. To have turned back the clock would have been to flout reality; and no one could deny that men like Wilson, McKean and Mifflin were realists.

Fundamentally then, the stage was set for constructive compromise. It was merely a matter of recognizing that fact and acting accordingly. The man who had the good sense to analyze properly the general sentiment was shrewd William Findley. During the first days of the Convention he sat quietly by and listened to speeches that were strongly motivated by old factional quarrels and jealousies. After much profitless time had been spent in inveighing against and roundly damning the Constitution, Findley decided to act. Selecting James Wilson as the ablest member of the conservative group (and as it turned out he could have made no better choice) he took him aside to talk matters over. He began the discussion by assuring Wilson that he had never approved of the principles of the Constitution and that all his friends knew it. He had supported it only through the dictates of expediency. But intemperate denunciation of the document, he told the great jurist, would only "irritate the Spirit of party and make things worse instead of better."[30] Many men had favored the colonial charter because the Colony had been prosperous under it, but many more had an attachment for the present instrument because it had "carried them through the war." These men, he advised, should be instructed, not irritated.

Wilson agreed and asked Findley to make suggestions as to the best procedure to follow. The latter had a ready answer: amendatory resolutions should be presented before the Convention as a basis of discussion, but in the resultant debates the Constitution should be handled "with a delicacy approaching to reverence." Wilson again approved and declared that he would support such resolutions. But would Findley present them? Findley declined but offered to prepare the way for their reception by addressing the Convention. He thought this would "go further to reconcile the parties" than for him to offer the resolutions personally.[31]

Findley was as good as his word. In a long address he reviewed the Constitution, pointing out its excellences as well as its defects. However good in theory, it was no longer supported in confidence by the people. It had been a storm center for many years; it had often been violated and subjected to revision by the election of the Convention. He was certain, therefore, that "it was vain to think of restoring its energy without essential alterations."

Findley was pleased with the effect of his speech and thought it had "the greatest influence in reconciling parties of any I ever made." To its conciliatory tone he attributed the promptness with which the Convention agreed to a two-house legislature, veto power for the State's chief executive and a more independent judiciary.[32]

In preparing the rules of the Convention it had been decided to consider the various subjects to be discussed in the committee of the whole so as to allow greater freedom of debate. Thomas McKean was made chairman of this committee, a position he held until he resigned it on January 30, 1790. The delegates were forbidden to speak more than twice before the general Convention unless special permission to speak oftener had been secured.[33]

On December 10, 1789, William Lewis had moved that a committee of nine members be chosen by ballot to prepare a draft of a "proposed" constitution.[34] Then Findley, ever aware of the problem of representation, moved to postpone consideration of Lewis' resolution in order to introduce one which would determine voting qualifications for both branches of the legislature. This was a delicate issue, but the Convention neatly side-stepped it for the moment by refusing to postpone by a vote of thirty-four to twenty-nine. They also decided to elect the drafting committee later.

On that same day, a busy one indeed, the Convention in a series of important resolutions and votes laid the groundwork of a new Constitution. By a vote of fifty-six to five it was determined that Pennsylvania should have a legislature of more than one branch. Further, it was unanimously resolved that the chief executive authority should be vested in one person. Only four men opposed the granting of veto power to the executive. A majority of fifty-six to eight approved a resolution which permitted certain members of the judiciary to hold commission during good behavior "and be independent as to their salaries."[35] All members favored a more accurate definition of that section of the existing Constitution known as the "declaration of rights." Thus it was determined along what lines the Constitution should be revised.

The celerity with which these points were disposed of spoke well for the conciliatory efforts of Findley and Wilson. Both men kept their promises to each other and supported the resolutions previously agreed to. These resolutions were prepared and offered by Wilson at the insistence of Findley and others because "Wilson had prepared a draft of a constitution."[36]

On December 11, 1789, when the Convention elected the committee of nine to bring in a constitutional draft, it was found that Findley had won every vote but his own. Other prominent figures selected were Alexander Addison, William Lewis and, of course, James Wilson.

The committee lost no time in setting to work, and although its members often disagreed on details, progress was steady and continuous. It reported on December 21, 1789, and again two days later. From this time on to February 5, 1790, its proposals were considered in the committee of the whole.

The question of representation brought a sharp division of opinion. Section Four recommended limiting the membership of the House of Representatives to no less than sixty and no more than one hundred. Gallatin, seconded by Findley, tried to increase the latter figure by twenty, but this motion was decisively defeated. McKean, who had resigned as chairman of the committee of the whole in order to participate more freely in the debate, wanted to lower the minimum

House membership from sixty to forty-five. When the qualifications of members in the House were being discussed Samuel Ogden offered an amendment to a resolution which would have limited membership to those who held a freehold estate to the value of one hundred pounds. Apparently he lacked support for this amendment, for he withdrew it the day after it was offered.[37]

On the question of representation in Congress, Gallatin offered a resolution which, if accepted, would have saved future Assemblies much trouble. On February 1, 1790, he moved that the State be divided into districts for the purpose of electing national representatives. But for some unexplained reason he withdrew his motion the next day.

On the subject of the Governor's authority Findley attempted to have that official share his power with a council. The vote on this question marked the final defeat of the issue which he had championed in the drafting committee. He attributed his failure to the disgust, shared even by the old Whigs, with which the Executive Council was regarded. In addition he was thwarted by the generally held belief in the personal responsibility of a chief executive. James Ross was the only man who had assisted him in the committee debate on the matter.[38]

Although Ross sided with his western colleague on the desirability of curtailing the Governor's powers, he was in complete opposition to him on the method of selecting State Senators. This issue had also caused considerable difficulty in the drafting committee, and when the committee reported to the Convention it recommended that State Senators should be elected by the lower house. Then occurred the greatest storm of the entire Convention.

William Lewis maintained that a Senate elected by the Representatives would be wiser, more respectable than one chosen by the electorate. He was opposed by Wilson, who urged that Senators should be selected in the same manner as Representatives, except that they should be fewer in number and thus responsible to larger areas. The opposition said that the real purpose of a divided legislature was to permit the two houses to correct each other; if they were both selected in almost the same manner their homogeneity would defeat that purpose. To this objection Wilson replied that since the terms varied in length each house would develop a separate individuality.

Alexander Graydon remarked that much heat was engendered in the debating because the opposing principles of aristocracy and democracy were evident in the decisions. Wilson, "hitherto deemed an aristocrat, a monarchist and a despot, as all the Federalists were, found his adherents on this occasion, with a few exceptions, on the democratic or anti-federal side of the house."[39]

The proponents of popular election of Senators won, and Graydon gave Wilson chief credit for that victory. Russel J. Ferguson is in complete disagreement with this. He says that "Gallatin led the opposition to this proposal [that Senators be elected by the House of Representatives] and urged that State Senators be chosen by popular vote, and he was successful in having his idea accepted."[40]

Unsuccessful in their scheme to take the selection of Senators out of hands of the voters, the ultra-conservatives attempted to apportion the number of Senators from any one district according to a combination of wealth and population. In short, the wealth of the district would, along with its number of inhabitants, determine its representation in the Senate. Obviously such a plan would favor the eastern sections of the State. This proposal also failed in the Convention. Graydon, although a confirmed federalist, disapproved of "so invidious and sordid a principle." While the Convention was in session he jotted down some observations that seem to be at variance with the popular conception of an eighteenth-century federalist's views. "Whatever advantages may, for a time, be given to the poor by a state of turbulence and confusion, as soon as order is restored, the predominance of wealth returns. It seems unnecessary to protect local wealth. It is not probable, that the local distinctions now prevailing will continue, but rather that wealthy individuals will make common cause."[41]

McKean, who at this time certainly gave no indication of his later democratic protestations, desired to prevent any man from becoming a Senator unless he owned personal property to the value of five hundred pounds or possessed at least five hundred acres of land.[42]

Until February 5, 1790, the committee of the whole worked steadily on the proposals that had been presented by the drafting committee. Then it declared that a plan of government had been prepared. This was presented to the general Convention where it was discussed in minute detail. After many votes on phraseology the Convention announced that the document was ready for submission to the people. On February 26, 1790, it adjourned, after deciding to meet again in five months. In the meantime the people would have an opportunity to express their views on the Constitution.

The Convention reconvened on August 9, 1790. Apparently the Constitution had not created much of a stir, for the only group request to alter the document came from the Quakers. They objected to paying a sum of money in lieu of serving in the armed forces. Their request was refused. With that exception apparently no serious protests had been made to the proposed Constitution. For after again considering it section by section and clause by clause, no fundamental changes were made by the Convention. After ordering the document to be engrossed the group rose *sine die* on September 2, 1790.

Pennsylvania's new organic law created a government that was vastly different from that provided by the outmoded document of 1776. Full legislative power was vested in a legislature composed of a Senate and a House of Representatives. Members of the former, representative of districts, were to serve a four-year term, and those of the latter were to be elected annually from the counties and the city of Philadelphia. Supreme executive authority resided in a popularly elected Governor who, in addition to holding a veto power over the legislature and large appointive privileges, was commander-in-chief of the armed forces when they were not in the service of the United States. Given a three-year term, he could not serve more than nine of any twelve years. Liberal franchise privileges allowed any white freeman to vote who had resided in the Commonwealth for two years preceding an election and paid State or county taxes assessed at least six months before exercising the suffrage. A judiciary system was established which permitted judges of the supreme and common pleas courts to hold office during good behavior. Article IX, consisting of twenty-six sections, carefully outlined a bill of rights.[43]

The Constitution also contained a schedule of operation to ease the transition from the old order to the new. All laws not inconsistent with the new instrument of government were to remain in force; the president and the Executive Council were to hold office until December, 1790; with the exception of judges, who were to serve out their commissions, all officials appointed by the executive authority were to function only until September 1, 1791, unless their commissions expired or they were reappointed by the Governor; until a new enumeration could be made the same number of Representatives was to be elected "as is now prescribed by law." Special provisions were made for the election of the first Senate.[44]

That the Pennsylvania Constitution owed much to the Federal plan of government cannot be doubted. Not only did they reveal similarity in general outline and philosophy, but they both owed their very existence to a conflict of opposing circumstances and ideologies that could be resolved only by compromise and adjustment. In the contests between those who held liberal as opposed to conservative views on governmental principles both sides were forced to grant concessions.

The result was a liberal document. Indeed it has been called "the most liberal of all state governments which used the national Constitution" as its model.[45] And it in turn served as a guide for other constitutional conventions. For example, nearly three-fourths of the provisions of the Kentucky Constitution of 1792 "were taken directly from the Pennsylvania Constitution...."[46] Furthermore, it was not unknown among European scholars. In a study on individual and collective rights, as set forth in American organic law, Dietrich Hermann Hegewisch, a German scholar, cited the declaration of rights in the Pennsylvania Constitution as a model of liberalism.[47] In such fashion then did the conservatives affirm their victory.

The procedures followed at the Convention and over the State generally were completely democratic. Nowhere did a partisan band await a call to hurry to the Convention for the purpose of settling issues by armed intervention. The only compulsions exerted were those of argument and expediency. And although neither group was completely satisfied with the result, no organized protests or mass demonstrations greeted the published document. Fears that the conservatives would fortify their position by erecting a bulwark of stubborn retrogression were not born out in fact. And in no sense of the word did the new constitution express sharp sectional or group cleavages. Instead it represented the concerted effort of all groups and sections.

As a compromise instrument it was not calculated to provoke outraged dismay or wild enthusiasm. Unhampered by intransigent factionalism the assembled delegates, able and practical men as they were, forged a body of law that was fully cognizant of existing political realities. Neither iconoclastic nor unreasonably reactionary, it was a composite of many years of political experience. It did not ignore the many strides taken toward democracy during the exuberant Revolutionary era, but it did recognize that the great leveling impetus had been lost. The frenzies and rages of a people fighting for their rights and their lives had subsided in the quieter days of peace. And this new stability was now expressed in solid documentary form. In short, the Pennsylvania Constitution of 1790 placed a period stamp of finality on a phase of political ferment that was and is peculiar to American history.

CHAPTER II

THE STATE AND THE UNION, 1790

The State in 1790

A GENERAL VIEW of Pennsylvania in the year 1790 reveals it as an excellent field for the study of American democracy. Broad enough in area and so geographically constituted as to allow opportunities for the development of sectional tendencies, it nevertheless contained an assortment of elements so variegated as to preclude convenient generalizations. In searching for points of difference between the eastern and western sections, for example, constant attention must be paid not only to territorial demarcations but to political and economic factors as well.

Obviously, there were differences between the frontier regions, North and West, and a great urban development like Philadelphia, but at all times they experienced a political and economic interdependence. If the people dwelling beyond the crest of the Alleghenies evinced a strong interest in trade to the westward, they were certainly not disposed to ignore trading possibilities with the East. At least the value they placed upon their eastern trading outlets was to be violently demonstrated in an opposition to excise laws which hampered such economic intercourse. The Philadelphia merchant, in turn, could not afford to be insensitive to conditions anywhere in the State which affected his business. Furthermore, a predominantly agricultural economy forced a kinship between farmers, for whether they lived on the Schuylkill, Susquehanna or Allegheny, they shared many interests in common.

The barrier created by the Alleghenies, by no means insurmountable, tended to retard passage from one end of the State to the other, but it did not cause sectional isolation. At no time during the period under consideration could one, even by the most arbitrary means, have divided the State in such a manner as to produce a "solid" East or West. The transmontane area was preponderantly agricultural, but it also contained commercial interests of no mean influence. While generally manifesting a fondness for the more advanced principles of democratic government the western counties—Allegheny in particular—were not without their distinctly conservative groups.

By the year 1790, four counties had been organized in western Pennsylvania: Allegheny, Fayette, Westmoreland and Washington. According to the census of that year they had a population of 63,566.[1] Pittsburgh, later to develop into a mighty industrial center, had only 376 residents. The western region in general contained approximately 75,000 people. Racially the two dominant groups were the English and Scotch-Irish. It is difficult to determine which of the two was the larger, but it is probable that those of English stock were in the majority.[2]

East of the mountains the same lack of uniformity prevailed. Although most of the inhabitants of that region were engaged in agriculture a large number were devoted to commercial pursuits. The latter were located for the most part in Philadelphia and the immediate vicinity. Here were concentrated the wealthiest groups in the State. Although generally conservative in their political behavior the easternmost counties exhibited a heterogeneity that was conducive to intense rivalry. In their midst, for example, was Philadelphia County, one of the first counties in the East to embrace Democratic-Republicanism.

Comprising twenty-one counties, the State had a total population of 434,373, in 1790.[3] Of this total 211,000 were located in the eastern and southeastern counties of Philadelphia, Bucks, Chester, Berks, York and Lancaster. This area contained a wide diversity of cultural stocks, the most numerous being the English and German.

During the seven years following the formal end of the Revolution, a trying and critical period, the citizens of Pennsylvania had conducted themselves creditably. Disorder had been at a minimum, and no Daniel Shays had arisen to terrorize government officials. As a matter of fact crime had been steadily decreasing.[4] Under the ultra-democratic Constitution of 1776, the people had demonstrated a capability of governing themselves without engaging in sanguinary strife. Democracy could function in Pennsylvania without degenerating into anarchy. That was an incontestable fact.

The year 1790 saw the end of the "counter-revolution," the peaceful demise of one governmental experiment and the beginning of another. It had been accomplished not by mob violence, rifles and bayonets but by scratching pens and nods of compromise. In that year of confirmatory change the State actually experienced less crime than usual. Half the counties recorded no convictions "for any capital or other offence commonly prosecuted in our Courts of Oyer and Terminer and general

Goal [*sic*] delivery."⁵ In the other counties the number of such prosecutions was less than in former years.

The year was indeed an auspicious one. While politicians had been documenting both innovation and past experience the rest of the citizens also had been productively engaged. The population had increased "considerably," industry had flourished, new soil had been broken by the plow and crops were better than ever before.⁶ The generally pleasant state of affairs so favorably impressed the Supreme Court Justices that they thought it safe to conclude that the people were "actuated by a just regard for industry, frugality, order, morality and religion...." They were "contented with their present Constitution, Laws and magistrates" and enjoyed "civil, political & religious liberty and happiness."⁷ It was a blessed state.

But there were little clouds in the sky. They had been formed with the creation of the Federal government, and within a space of four years that government was to mobilize an army of 15,000 men to teach some of Pennsylvania's citizens a few lessons in obedience. Four years after that troops were to be called by that same government to discipline some of them once again.

After the Revolution they had worked out their own governmental problems peacefully enough, but they were to experience difficulty in adjusting themselves to a greater power, the United States government. Since their reaction to that government is a vital factor in this study of political behavior, it may be well to investigate the role played by the State in its origin.

Pennsylvania Joins the Union

From the time Pennsylvania became a state up until the establishment of the Federal government in 1789, her politicians were concerned with issues that were fundamentally local in nature. True, she had been a member of the Confederation, but that government was so ineffective that it never succeeded in really dominating its component parts. Thus the State's principal factions, often seemingly unaware of external conditions, fought their battles along local lines. This evident inclination to develop introspectively had been constantly strengthened by the ineptitude of a steadily declining Congress. But with the advent of the Federal union and the consequent broadening of political horizons the State had to adjust itself to an entirely new environment.

This adaptation was not effected without controversy, as the reception accorded to the proposed Federal Constitution of 1787 amply demonstrated. When the completed document was presented to the Pennsylvania Assembly on September 18, 1787,[8] opposition was immediate and definite. But since those favoring a strong Federal union were in the majority, they, by forcing a quorum on September 29, called a convention to consider the new frame of government.[9] In the election for delegates the Federalists won a decisive victory, and when they met in November, ratification was almost assured. Apprehensive that the Federal government would arrogate to itself too much of the State's sovereign power, the Anti-Federalists nevertheless had to bow to the inevitable. The Convention approved the Constitution by a vote of forty-six to twenty-three.[10]

Not only during the Convention but in the months that followed the Anti-Federalists — so designated by their opponents — expressed their views on what they considered to be the chief dangers and faults in the Constitution. Principally, they pointed out that the new instrument lacked a bill of rights, a deficiency that should be corrected.

Determined to rectify this omission they waited patiently until enough States had ratified the Constitution to make the organization of a national government almost a certainty. Then, on July 3, 1788, they issued a circular letter which asked the various counties to select delegates to attend a convention at Harrisburg on September 3, where proper amendatory action would be taken.[11] Further, since favorable action could best be obtained from a sympathetic Congress, it was suggested that the proposed convention should nominate congressional candidates who would be most likely to favor proper amendments.

In answer to the call thirteen counties sent thirty-three delegates, among whom were George Bryan and Albert Gallatin. With their deliberations carefully shrouded in secrecy they framed a petition to the Pennsylvania Assembly which, although never officially presented, listed the amendments to the Constitution that were considered necessary. Employing language so cautious that it bordered on timidity the petitioners assured the Assembly that their sentiments were "completely federal," and that they were firmly convinced that only a "confederacy of republican states" could "secure political liberty, happiness, and safety in the United States."[12] They were in complete agreement with the general system of government as prescribed by the Constitution, but they were confident that it would be quickly amended so as to "preserve certain rights and privileges . . . in the respective States."[13]

With reference to specific sections of the Constitution the suggested amendments would provide a stricter definition of the powers of Congress, clarify apportionment of national representation, permit any state legislature to recall its United States Senators if necessity arose, and forbid the existence of a peacetime standing army unless sanctioned by a two-thirds vote of both houses of Congress.[14]

The most apprehensive Federalists could hardly have placed a revolutionary construction on those recommendations. But they did insist, and undoubtedly with considerable justification, that the real purpose of the Convention was not to frame amendments but to prepare a list of congressional candidates for the coming elections.[15] But whether or not the Anti-Federalists attached more importance to election preparations than to the advocacy of amendments to the Constitution, they acknowledged and accomplished both, and in a spirit of harmony.[16]

In selecting congressional candidates the delegates at Harrisburg did not display much confidence in the strength of their following. Unwilling to risk a straight ticket, they compromised by choosing four Federalists and the same number of Anti-Federalists in order to divide their opponents. Hopeful of securing a part of the German vote they induced two Federalists, Daniel Hiester and Peter Muhlenberg, to run on the Anti-Federalist ticket.[17] After the list appeared in the *Neue Philadelphische Correspondenz* on November 11, the German interests added Frederick A. Muhlenberg's name to the Anti-Federal group.[18]

The Anti-Federalists had actually made definite arrangements for the election a month before the Pennsylvania Assembly made legislative provision for it. It was not until October 4, 1788, that a law appeared to regulate the selection of Congressmen and presidential electors. The eight national legislators and ten electors to which the State was entitled were to be selected at large by all voters qualified to elect assemblymen.[19]

By providing for an election-at-large the Assembly was attempting to exploit the Federalist majority in the State as a whole. Naturally, the election of all Congressmen on one ticket would assure a united Federalist representation in Congress. Elections by districts would have jeopardized that possibility. Consequently a state-wide campaign was necessary on the part of the factions, and the Anti-Federalists, with excellent foresight, had anticipated such a law by meeting in convention a month before it was passed.

Shortly after the passage of the Pennsylvania election law the Federalists, not to be outdone, also made arrangements for a general convention. They planned to meet at Lancaster, on November 3, 1788, to choose congressional candidates and presidential electors. Through the medium of letters of correspondence the various counties were urged to hold meetings and select delegates. Their efforts met with considerable success, for when the delegates gathered at Lancaster, all counties were represented but one. After deliberating a few days the Convention produced a congressional ticket that was completely Federal.[20]

But when it appeared, several politicians from Philadelphia and neighboring sections who were ever alert to the power of the German vote, noticed that it bore the name of only one man of German extraction, Frederick A. Muhlenberg. They thereupon added the names of Daniel Hiester and Peter Muhlenberg. Both the Federal and Anti-Federal tickets now carried those three men.[21]

When the congressional election was over and the results tabulated it was found that all the Federalists were successful. In the State at large they had triumphed by some 8,000 votes to 6,600 for their opponents.[22] Although the vote was small and the victory not by any means overwhelming it assured the State of a strong Federalist represensation in Congress. Six of the eight successful candidates had worked diligently in support of the Federal Constitution. Two of them, George Clymer and Thomas Fitzsimons, had been members of the Constitutional Convention; and four others, Thomas Hartley, Frederick A. Muhlenberg, Thomas Scott and Henry Wynkoop, had voted in favor of it in Pennsylvania's ratifying Convention.[23]

The election of 1788 introduced new election procedures. Since Pennsylvania's chief executive was appointed by the Executive Council and its representatives in Congress were selected by the Assembly, the electorate had never been called upon to take concerted action in the naming of individuals to represent the State as a unit. But because of the exigencies of participation in the Federal union (United States Representatives were to be chosen by the people) the politicians had to devise new electoral machinery. In its law of October 4, 1788, the Assembly had announced the date of election and the number of men to be chosen, but it was silent as to the method of screening the candidates in such a manner as to secure a limited selection at the polls. This problem was solved, as has been pointed out, by general nominating conventions which represented the State's two major factions.

Theoretically the State Conventions represented the people, but actually the delegates sitting in those bodies were chosen by very small minorities. A just and equitable choice of delegates would demand the participation of the voters in the districts—in this case, counties—which were represented by the delegates. Such participation could be obtained only by efficient intra-county organizations. And since no organizations of the kind existed the delegates actually spoke for only a very few interested persons.

The Pennsylvania Assembly in the fall of 1788 was strongly Anti-Constitutionalist and federalist, and when it selected two men to represent the State in the United States Senate its choice fell on Robert Morris and William Maclay. Both were considered to be staunch federalists. Before the matter was decided, however, much maneuvering was necessary.

Before the Assembly met in September, the Federalists were inclined to support George Clymer and William Maclay, while the Constitutionalists considered the possibility of electing Benjamin Franklin and William Irvine. A few days before the election, however, the Federalists shifted momentarily to Robert Morris and John Armstrong, Jr. That left Maclay temporarily out of the running, much to his regret.[24] The Constitutionalists then decided to capitalize on the situation by pairing their candidate Irvine with the disgruntled Maclay.[25] The Federalists countered this move by dropping Armstrong, retaining Morris and re-embracing Maclay. The latter's friends then deserted the hapless Irvine and the Morris-Maclay ticket was successful. Perhaps Irvine found some consolation in the assurance of David Redick that the Constitutionalists had loyally supported him. Had "your Republicans" not treacherously deserted, said Redick, "you would doubtless have been elected."[26] Judging from Redick's language, he certainly was not averse to planting seeds of suspicion in Irvine's mind on the conduct of "your Republicans, meaning Anti-Constitutionalists." Those seeds were destined to blossom luxuriantly.

The assemblymen who sent Robert Morris and Maclay to the United States Senate could hardly have known that the two men were to be poles apart on subsequent national policies. The Senators themselves could not have known, for all had yet to learn just what federalism was to mean in the adroit and powerful hands of an Alexander Hamilton.

Before his election to the United States Senate, William Maclay had engaged in a variety of pursuits as a surveyor, soldier in the Revolution, lawyer, judge and commissioner to investigate the navigation of the Susquehanna. As an assemblyman he represented Northumberland County from 1781 to 1785, and then served for two years in the Executive Council. He is principally remembered, however, as the author of a journal which he kept during his brief senatorial career. Shrewd, analytical and often bitter he subjected his contemporaries to incisive examination and appraisal.

The judgments on Maclay and his *Journal* have been varied. Because of his antagonism and opposition to the Hamiltonian program and to the centralization of national power he has been called "the father of the Democratic party."[27] Charles Beard sees some justification for calling him "the original Jeffersonian Democrat," and in evaluating the *Journal* he considered it "one of the most precious human documents for the study of American manners, morals, and intelligence, political and general."[28] Ellis P. Oberholtzer, however, in his highly laudatory biography of Robert Morris, is sure that Maclay went to the Senate to represent his own locality alone. A provincial Scotch frontiersman he was, says Oberholtzer, "a tattling, faultfinding person of ponderous conceit. He alone was entirely righteous. . . . The chief impression we receive of him is that he had a mean and censorious mind."[29] If Oberholtzer had Maclay's judgment of Morris in mind when he described him as "faultfinding" he was not far from wrong. For Maclay certainly did not spare his senatorial colleague.

Robert Morris, born in Liverpool in 1734, became a business partner of the Willings at the age of twenty. Combining a remarkable business ability with a patriotic desire to see the colonies achieve independence from England, he contributed mightily to the cause. As a member of the firm of Willing and Morris he imported supplies for the army while losing "no opportunity to make his profit in a deal" or to make "large profits in his capacity as middleman."[30] As Superintendent of Finance his efforts did much to bring success to American arms. Before accepting the office in 1781, he insisted that Congress recognize his rights to retain his commercial connections and that he be permitted to control the personnel of his department. After resigning in 1784, he was elected to the Pennsylvania Assembly in order to defend the Bank of North America. A firm believer in a strong central government, he served ably in the Federal Constitutional Convention.[31] As a member of the First Congress he was recognized as one of the principal leaders of the Pennsylvania delegation. But before his term ended he became heavily involved in land speculations which eventually brought personal disaster and a term of several years in debtor's prison.

Pennsylvanians in the First Congress

Since the creation of the national government had a profound effect on the political situation in Pennsylvania, an examination of the part her representatives played in its formation seems to be in order. When Congress met in the spring of 1789, the Constitution was merely a piece of paper. Its implementation would require much legislation, the soundness and practicability of which would do much to determine the continued acceptance of the Constitution's basic principles. In the establishment of this necessary legislation the Pennsylvanians played a large and important role.

At the very beginning, when the House of Representatives was considering a revenue bill, the manufacturing interests of Pennsylvania spoke through Thomas Hartley when he declared himself in favor of considering the revenue system as a protective instrument. Foreign countries, he said, had long encouraged the establishment of home manufactures by taxing imports. "All those manufactures which will tend to national utility" should be protected from foreign competition.[32]

George Clymer advocated the protection of unwrought steel, and spoke particularly of a furnace in Philadelphia which he was sure could supply the needs of the entire nation. These men were expressing the views of Philadelphia manufacturers such as those who had previously asked the old Congress for protective tariff legislation, and who were now constantly writing to Morris, Clymer and Fitzsimons. Maclay regretted that the Philadelphians did not keep him informed; but he did secure "a list of the Pennsylvania protecting duties" from Clymer and Fitzsimons, and the Speaker of the House, Frederick Muhlenberg, gave him information on the Philadelphia "sugar houses."[33] He complained that his efforts to speed the impost bill were counteracted by merchants who were delaying it in hope that their ships would dock before it went into effect. A Philadelphia merchant had said that Fitzsimons was among those so engaged in delaying maneuvers. Whereupon, Henry Wynkoop remarked that "Mr. Fitzsimons acted in a double capacity—as a merchant and as a representative."[34]

An event of great significance occurred when the Secretary of the Treasury's First Report on the Public Credit was presented to Congress on January 14, 1790. Maclay had been puzzled by an increase in "certificate" speculation, and he thought he saw the reason for it in Hamilton's funding proposals. The very articulate diarist was "so struck of an heap" that he could say nothing.[35] But that was only a temporary condition.

When the question of the assumption of state debts came up, he published many arguments in opposition to the measure. And in doing so he admitted that he placed his future in jeopardy. On April 2, 1790, he wrote: "I have put my political life in my hand in starting this opposition in the teeth of the Philadelphians. If I fail, my seat in Congress and disgrace in the public eye will follow."[36] When the fate of assumption hung in the balance, Fitzsimons and Clymer suggested that the Pennsylvania delegation support it in return for votes in favor of temporarily transferring Congress to Philadelphia. Maclay thought such bartering was unjustifiable.

He also reported on an overture made by Hamilton to Morris. When Tench Coxe, a Pennsylvanian who was serving as Assistant Secretary of the Treasury, discussed an assumption barter with Clymer and Fitzsimons, Morris heard about it. He then wrote to Hamilton that he would be strolling on the Battery at a certain time, and if Hamilton had anything to propose he might meet him there "as if by accident." When they met, Hamilton said "he wanted one vote in the Senate and five in the House of Representatives; that he was willing and would agree to place the permanent residence of Congress at Germantown or Falls of the Delaware, if he would procure him these votes."[37] Morris took the matter up with the Pennsylvania delegation, but the bargaining was later discontinued at Hamilton's request.

When the assumption bill was finally voted on, Fitzsimons, Wynkoop and Clymer supported it and Hartley, Peter Muhlenberg, Daniel Hiester and Thomas Scott voted in the negative. Clymer and Fitzsimons "were among the largest speculators and operators in securities in Philadelphia," but Wynkoop had none. The only security holder among those who voted against assumption was Daniel Hiester.[38]

The location of the national capital, either temporary or permanent, was naturally of great interest to Pennsylvania's Congressmen. Taking a long view on the subject, Benjamin Rush and Maclay had supported John Adams for the vice-presidency in the hope that he would influence the New England delegations in favor of Pennsylvania. But when the question arose in Congress, it became apparent that Adams had other views on the matter. The Vice-President consequently became the target for Maclay's choicer epithets, among which "fool" and "viper" were mild indeed.

The two Pennsylvania Senators were at odds on the permanent location of Congress. After Morris proposed the Falls of the Delaware (Trenton) to the Senate as the ideal location, Maclay, on August 25, 1789, presented the virtues of the Susquehanna region in a detailed description of Wright's Ferry, Yorktown, Carlisle, Harrisburg and Reading. He also included Germantown, a location later advocated by Morris. Before these suggestions were presented the Pennsylvania delegation had agreed to vote for every Pennsylvania site proposed in Congress.[39]

Four days after making his proposals in the Senate, Maclay heard "a terrible story" from a Maryland Congressman. According to his informant the Virginians and Pennsylvanians had consummated a general bargain to "fix the permanent residence on the Potomac, right or wrong, and the temporary residence was to be in Philadelphia."[40] Maclay refused to believe the tale, and all the Pennsylvanians he questioned as to its authenticity denied that any bargain had been made.

As the time went on the question became involved with other issues, principally that of assumption, as mentioned above. On May 24, 1790, Morris presented a resolution in the Senate which requested that Congress hold its next session in Philadelphia. When the men from New England insisted on remaining in New York, several Pennsylvanians met on May 28, 1790, and agreed to tell them flatly that if they persisted in voting for New York the Pennsylvanians would "agree to any other place whatever. . . ."[41]

In June, the question was reaching a climax. On the twenty-fourth the Pennsylvania delegation met again. Frederick Muhlenberg asked: "Shall we vote for a bill giving the temporary residence, ten years, to Philadelphia and the permanent residence to the Potomac?"[42] With the exception of Maclay all the men present voted in the affirmative. That decision was the forerunner of the one in Congress.

By the time the United States government had moved to Philadelphia in 1790, it had already manifested tendencies toward a centralization and concentration of power that were regarded with disapproval by many. It had already inspired a fear, in the mind of "Federalist" Senator Maclay at least, that the Constitution would become a trap to "ensnare the freedom of unsuspecting."[43] He was also sure that many men were interested in establishing an American monarchy. He viewed with great distaste the presidential levees which he thought smacked of royalty. He complained that "Republicans are borne down by fashion and a fear of being charged with a want of respect to General Washington." Then in an intemperate outburst he declared: "If there is treason in the wish I retract it, but would to God this same General Washington were in heaven. We would not then have him brought forward as the constant cover to every unconstitutional and irrepublican act."[44]

Maclay was certainly not alone in criticizing the administration, and as the Hamiltonian program unfolded that criticism was to grow. But in 1790, the policy-forming group was well entrenched. It had ridden to control on a dominant wave of Federalism and was well blessed with capable leaders. And although its policies had already met with opposition, neither their advocates nor opponents had yet united their efforts in adequate political organizations.

In Pennsylvania the political situation was similarly chaotic. Indeed, the loosely formed factions that had existed in the State during the past few years had all but disappeared. So nebulous had the situation become that it is almost impossible to discover any trace of general political organization whatever.

With the demise of the Constitution of 1776, the Constitutionalist party lost not only an invaluable symbol but its principal cohesive force as well. Thus, deprived of its great unifying compellant, it had to await the appearance of new issues to consolidate its loosely knit elements.

Months before the new document appeared in its final form, politicians had seen its effect on party formations. In February, 1790, William Bingham had predicted that the old party groups would merely take new names and divide on sectional lines, the east against the west.[45]

Thomas Fitzsimons, writing in August, 1789, when the calling of a Constitutional Convention was almost a certainty, was of the opinion that a "revolution" would occur "in our state Politicks . . . the Quakers and old Torys are better disposed to join the Constitutionalists than the Republicans, and I believe these together with the deserters from the later [*sic*] will rule the roost. If they do it well they have my consent—if they do not, we must endeavor to correct them."[46] Fitzsimons' observation is illuminating, not only for the light it throws on the current party fluctuations, but also for its intimations on the strength inherent in the Constitutionalists faction just preceding the call for a Constitutional Convention.

Jonathan Roberts, after observing that the old Whig and Tory groups had disappeared in 1783, distinguished the opposing groups in 1790 as "moderate" and "warm."[47] In his use of these indefinite terms —perfectly justifiable under the circumstances—he was referring respectively to the embryonic Federalist elements and to the men who were later to be identified as Republicans or Democratic-Republicans.

In 1787, issues engendered by the appearance of the Federal Constitution had blurred existing party alignments and created the federal and anti-federal groups. The word Anti-Federalist, however, as a motivation descriptive can be accurately applied only to those who disapproved of the Federal Constitution until it was supplied with a bill of rights. It cannot be emphasized too strongly that the men at the Harrisburg convention declared themselves decidedly in favor of a central government, requesting only that the Constitution be amended. Actually, Anti-Federalism was close to expiration when enough states had ratified the Constitution to make the organization of a national government a certainty.

It so happened that the Anti-Federalists of 1787 contained many men, a nucleus as it were, of the group that later became anti-Hamilton or anti-administration, but not anti-government. Certainly the former Anti-Federalists such as Gallatin, Smilie *et al.* did not hesitate to take an active part in the Federal government. In fact, they made every effort to do so. Maclay, one of the most rabid opponents of the administration's program, had no desire to destroy the government. Rather did he leave no stone unturned again to become a part of it as a Senator when his short term expired in 1791. As a Federalist in 1788, *i. e.*, one who favored a central government, he was elected to the Senate. But he was not a Federalist—one who supported the new administration—in 1790-91. In short the word Federalist meant one thing in 1788, and something else again in 1790. In the latter year it could be applied most accurately to those who supported Washington's administration and the Hamiltonian measures.

To those opposed to the administration the Federalists applied the term Anti-Federalist, a label of opprobrium and deeply resented. Historians have used it broadly, however, in an effort to generalize and distinguish between the two groups.

The absence of parties in the Pennsylvania of 1790 can be attributed to another contributing circumstance. There was no well-organized group of wealthy aristocrats capable of exerting an influence so powerful as to curb opposition. The old loyalists had migrated[48] and the Revolution had further weakened the Quaker influence. Bryan, Findley, Smilie, Franklin and other advocates of democracy had done their work well.

Although there were no general party organizations, men were, as has been pointed out, already beginning to take sides on issues involving the nature and functions of the national government. With the passage of time party lines were to become more closely drawn. And Pennsylvania, as host to the Federal government for ten years, was to react to national issues with a sensitivity so strong that her party groups were to arise primarily and fundamentally in response to them.

CHAPTER III

COMPROMISE CONFIRMED, 1790

THE AMORPHOUSNESS of Pennsylvania politics in 1790 was well illustrated by the gubernatorial election held in that year. The political dominance enjoyed by the conservatives on State issues since 1787 was not overwhelming; neither was their partisan majority. Those facts were emphasized by the constitutional convention, summoned at their behest, in a body of organic law which was frankly a compromise effort. The real test of their superiority would lie in their ability to install a man of their own choice in the Governor's chair. As it turned out they failed to do so, for the man eventually selected was as much of a compromise as the constitution itself.

The governorship of Pennsylvania was considered to be a very desirable position, and several men began setting their political caps for it long before the constitution which provided for the office had been proclaimed. In the nature of things the screening of those candidates was almost certain to be an unrepresentative and haphazard proceeding. Lacking a stimulating issue such as had marked the congressional nominating conventions of 1788, lacking also any organizational and selective machinery, and finally, without precedent to guide them, the leading politicians were forced to decide on candidates themselves, a task, incidentally, which they did not find distasteful.

It is little wonder then that some members of Pennsylvania's congressional delegation calmly assumed that the task of selecting a candidate would naturally fall upon them. For intimate information on the schemes and plans they concocted we are indebted to Senator Maclay. Nostalgic for his beloved Susquehanna, rheumatic and often only painfully mobile, he kept his sensitive ears to the ground and his vitriolic pen handy. Suspicious and distrustful of the group he referred to as the "Philadelphia junto," in which he included Fitzsimons, Morris and Clymer, he busied himself in ferreting out any schemes that might be afoot. On February 4, 1790, he confessed a doubt as to whom the junto would support. But he was certain that it would select someone who would "be their tool."[1]

As time went on, the plotting and conniving progressed. On February 8, 1790, Morris presented a memorial to the Senate requesting the appointment of commissioners "to inquire into his conduct while financier, and mentioning his unsettled accounts as a partner of Willing and Morris, which were in train of settlement."[2] Frederick Muhlenberg told Maclay the Philadelphians had agreed that Morris' memorial should be presented as the first step in clearing the way for his candidacy. Fitzsimons, who had informed Muhlenberg of the plan to boost Morris, was strongly opposed to Thomas Mifflin. As President of the Executive Council and a popular figure throughout the State, Mifflin would be a difficult man to defeat. But if he were elected, Fitzsimons declared, "they would be worse off than if no new constitution had been made."[3]

William Bingham, wealthy Philadelphia merchant, banker, and politician was also mentioned as a candidate. His accomplishments were many, not the least of which was his marriage to the beautiful Anne Willing. Under her genteel administration his home became one of the favorite centers for the political and social elite. He was later to become a United States Senator, but in 1790 he received little backing for the governorship.

Morris disapproved of Bingham as well as of Colonel Samuel Miles, a former Censor and Revolutionary patriot whose candidacy Maclay had heard advocated. But he was especially opposed to Mifflin. While discussing the latter with Maclay in the Senate, Morris deprecated Mifflin's appointments as President of the Executive Council. Then, with an oblique reference to Maclay's interest in public lands, he mentioned the Surveyor Generalship. "You should have had that office," he said.[4]

At the same time Morris spoke in favor of Arthur St. Clair as Governor. The latter had reason to be grateful not only for Morris' support, later openly given, but for a past favor. While serving as Superintendent of Finance during the Revolution, Morris had advanced sums of money from his own resources to certain needy army officers. St. Clair had been one of them.[5]

Frederick A. Muhlenberg, Speaker of the House, also with an eye on the Governor's chair, was much troubled by some news sent to him in April, 1790, by political friends. It seemed that the "aristocrats" in Philadelphia would support Mifflin instead of him. To Maclay he mournfully reflected on the inadequate return those "aristocrats had always made to him for his engaging the Germans to support their measures." He had wanted to be vendue master but they had not supported him, and although he was receiving "a share of the profits of the vendue office from Paton,"[6] these had amounted to little. An office was given to him in Montgomery County, but "it never paid him for the paper he spent for the Republican party."[7] Later he was to receive little encouragement from Fitzsimons when the latter took him aside to stress the "dignity of the Speaker's present place, and the certainty of his continuance in it."[8] To Maclay, it was clear that Fitzsimons wanted Muhlenberg to decline a possible nomination.

The Pennsylvania delegation to Congress had been in the habit of holding dinner meetings at Simon's tavern in New York to discuss current affairs. At one held early in May, 1790, Fitzsimons declared that it was expected that they should nominate a candidate for Governor. Maclay quickly interposed some remarks on the weather and succeeded in postponing a discussion. But after Scott, Hiester and Peter Muhlenberg left, Fitzsimons returned to his subject. Morris then made his wishes known by stating that although he was not unaware of the honor of his senatorial office he would, if elected Governor, discharge his duties impartially. Since Mifflin was a "very improper man," he hoped that "they would create opposition to him." After Muhlenberg declared himself in agreement with Morris, the group decided to unite in an effort to defeat Mifflin. "Mr. Morris, by way of finishing the business, addressed himself to the Speaker. 'May you or I be Governor.' "[9]

Judging from the repeated mention of Mifflin's name and the concerted effort made to defeat him, it is evident that the inner congressional circle of Pennsylvanians regarded his candidacy as a serious challenge. As a matter of fact, his supporters had not been idle. In June, 1790, James Hutchinson, a Philadelphia doctor who was later to take a leading part in the election of 1792, was quite confident of Mifflin's success. In a letter to Albert Gallatin he expressed great satisfaction at hearing that Washington and Fayette counties were so favorable to Mifflin. He made certain that the "aristocrats of this city" (Philadelphia) would oppose him. He had not yet learned who would be placed in opposition. But he did mention the possible candidacies of Frederick Muhlenberg and Morris, with the belief that Morris would be chosen.[10] It is to be noted that Muhlenberg's correspondents and Hutchinson conflicted in their opinions as to whom the "aristocrats" really favored.

Not all the self-appointed governor-makers were Congressmen. Samuel Bryan, office seeker, also decided to try his hand at the interesting game by advocating the candidacy of his father George, ardent defender of the Constitution of 1776, and a Judge of the State Supreme

Court. In May, 1790, he informed Albert Gallatin that although the "whigs" in eastern Pennsylvania had decided to support Mifflin because he was the best man they "could carry," they had but recently discovered that the "dormant spirit of the old whigs" was reviving so vigorously that there was a very good likelihood of electing a more acceptable man.[11] To sponsor Mifflin was "weakness itself," for there was "not a half-penny difference between Morris, Mifflin or Muhlenberg." His candidacy had inspired indifference and listlessness. Therefore they had decided to boost his father George, a proposal that was meeting with a fine response in Bucks, Montgomery, Chester and Northampton counties. An energetic campaign was being conducted in those counties with every promise of success. But they needed general support, Bryan concluded, and would Gallatin help the cause along by urging "every leading character" to exert himself?

It is difficult to say just what was the extent of the response evoked by Bryan's candidacy in the spring of 1790. It may have been encouraging, then, but future events did not bear out his son's optimism. Samuel undoubtedly underestimated Mifflin's appeal, for within a few weeks it became clear that he was the favored candidate. If the old Constitutionalists or "whigs," as the younger Bryan called them, deserted him, it was only momentary. (Samuel himself was later to find that Mifflin was acceptable after all, especially so when he wanted a job within the Governor's appointive power.) Bryan was widely known as a fiery Constitutionalist, as a positive and definite character, and as such he had no chance in 1790. He had been a leader in stirring Revolutionary times. Those days were gone, and when the contest reached the voters in October, 1790, he got no votes.

The name of the junto candidate was not publicly announced until September, 1790. Before the Constitutional Convention finally adjourned on the second of that month several of its members combined with a few assemblymen to select a candidate.[12] The results of this caucus were declared in an electioneering broadside a few days later. Over the signatures of Thomas Fitzsimons, George Clymer, Benjamin Rush, William Lewis, Robert Morris, James Wilson and Frederick A. Muhlenberg, the document warmly advocated the election of General Arthur St. Clair. After congratulating the citizens of Pennsylvania on its new constitution, the signers insisted that its promises could be made "real" if St. Clair were elected Governor. Mentioning no party names and unconcerned about specific issues, the broadside stressed the personal qualifications of St. Clair. He was patriotic, well-mannered, honest, informed and possessed of considerable military talent. After listing the candidate's estimable qualities, the signers struck a significant note when they pointed out that "he possesses the confidence of the President of the United States, and of course will not fail to use it for the important purpose of maintaining a constant harmony between the State of Pennsylvania and the Executive power of the National Government."[13]

As a candidate St. Clair was not nearly so well known as Mifflin. Born in Scotland in 1736, he had later become a lieutenant in the British army. After seeing service in Canada he resigned and settled in western Pennsylvania where he bought 4,000 acres of land in the Ligonier valley. As an officer in the American forces during the Revolution he was far from brilliant, once facing a court martial after evacuating Ticonderoga under circumstances that resulted in his recall from service in the field.[14] After the war he sided with the Anti-Constitutionalists and was elected to the Council of Censors in 1783. After two years' service in the Continental Congress he was appointed Governor of the Northwest Territory in 1787, a position he was to hold for many years.

Thomas Mifflin was born of Quaker parentage in Philadelphia in 1744. After graduating at the age of sixteen from the College of Philadelphia, he entered a business partnership with his brother George. As an ardent defender of colonial rights he opposed the Stamp Act, and subsequently took part in the First Continental Congress. Although he preferred active battle participation, in which he later displayed unusual personal bravery, he was appointed quartermaster general in 1775, a rank he held, with one brief interlude, until 1778. When his administration of the quartermaster's department was censured as being inefficient, he resigned from the army. He then served in the Continental Congress from 1782 to 1784. He was elected president of that body in 1783.[15]

For a connection between Mifflin's war record and his candidacy for the governorship reference should be made to the following. It will be recalled that the circular issued by the junto claimed that their candidate St. Clair possessed "the confidence of the President of the United States." Since St. Clair's sponsors had long recognized Mifflin as a formidable opponent, this phrase may have been a veiled allusion to the latter's supposed dislike of Washington. But any deeper interpretation of the phrase can rest only on the assumption that his contemporaries were aware of the historically alleged jealousy that he felt for the commander-in-chief. It has been said that as quartermaster general he aided General Horatio Gates in his plots.[16] Others say that he belonged to the group which attempted to have Washington removed as commander-in-chief, and that although he protested that "his action was dictated by the purest patriotism, it is impossible not to believe that his judgment was warped by jealousy excited by the preference Washington showed for others."[17] Speaking of Mifflin as Governor, Bernard Faÿ says that he "was not very fond of General Washington. . . ."[18] According to Bernhard Knollenberg there were contemporary rumors to the effect that Mifflin was hostile to Washington, but Mifflin "denied such hostility . . . and there is no substantial evidence in support of the charge."[19] William Rawle, the elder, a contemporary, was sure that Mifflin was completely innocent of any plot to remove Washington from command.[20]

Mifflin had the natural politician's ability to get along with a great variety of personalities and temperaments. Adept at social amenities and of an amiable disposition, he won friends easily. "In person," said William Rawle, "he was remarkably handsome, though his stature did not exceed five feet eight inches. His frame was athletic, and seemed capable of bearing much fatigue. His manners were cheerful and affable. His elocution open, fluent, and distinct."[21]

His name was placed before the electorate by a number of nominating meetings held in September and October. The *Pennsylvania Packet,* a Philadelphia newspaper, published the results of meetings held in the city and in Chester and Montgomery counties. The identity of these nominating groups from the standpoint of party affiliation past or future cannot be determined by their use of party labels, for none was announced. No mention was made of the old Constitutionalist or Anti-Constitutionalist groups or of the Federalists or Anti-Federalists. With what seemed to be a studied vagueness, the participants in those gatherings referred to them as meetings of "numerous" and "respectable" citizens or as "freeholders" and "electors."[22] At a Philadelphia meeting on October 9, 1790, presided over by Charles Biddle, Mifflin was nominated along with several candidates for the Assembly. The men selected were Jacob Hiltzheimer, Lawrence Seckle, Francis Gurney, Richard Wells and William Bingham.[23] All had been prominently identified with the Anti-Constitutionalist group, and a few were later to play conspicuous roles as Federalists. This was also true of the principals behind St. Clair's candidacy in Philadelphia.

When the junto came into the open with its candidate, the public response was not very satisfactory. Indeed, the electorate was so apathetic to St. Clair that in less than a week after the letter advocating his election appeared in the *Packet* on September 18, 1790, at least one of his supporters began to despair of success. This was no less a figure than Thomas Fitzsimons, an important leader in the campaign. On September 24 he mournfully observed that opposition to Mifflin was extremely feeble, and what little there was only served to make him stronger. He supposed therefore that "we must submit to the consequences."[24] Mifflin had associated himself "with the Constitutionalists" and Fitzsimons thought it likely that most of the State would fall into his hands. Such an outcome would be "vexatious" but not "as prejudicial" now as formerly. He was convinced that a Mifflin victory would "produce another combination."[25]

St. Clair also suspected that the "individuals who composed the Constitutional party" would rally behind Mifflin. "That party is not yet dissolved," he wrote to Fitzsimons on the eve of the election, "and will probably revive under a different name indeed, but with the same views."[26] The contradictions in St. Clair's observations on the existence of the Constitutionalist party are obvious. He speaks of it in the past tense and then conjectures on its revival, while declaring at the same time that it was "not yet dissolved." It seems likely that he thought the party was dead, but that the elements composing it would eventually reorganize.

The junto candidate was reluctant to run for the governorship, but he did so out of gratitude to his Philadelphia friends. He was happy, he told Fitzsimons, to have the approbation of "men who stand foremost in the community for wisdom probity and patriotism."[27] Admitting that Mifflin had made a large number of friends, St. Clair, nevertheless, discovered that his own candidacy was "relished in every part of the country I passed thro." He had learned from a political informant that William Findley was busily engaged in gathering votes for Mifflin in Westmoreland County. "They" planned to alter Findley's behavior though, by hinting that "they" had another person in mind for the next Congress. As to the success of their maneuver, St. Clair guessed that if Findley felt himself in danger he would "come round, if not—it will only make him more assiduous—I have however very little doubt that the counties on this side of the mountain will be divided in spite of the exertions he can make."[28]

But Findley, the shrewd prognosticator, had already made up his mind. He thought Mifflin would be the successful candidate.[29] He was right, but the extent of Mifflin's victory must have surprised the westerner, for he thought the contest would be close.

Far from being close, the election was a great triumph for Mifflin. In fact, his margin of victory was so overwhelming that it was virtually no contest.

When all the results were in it was found that he had won by a vote of 27,725 to a mere 2,802 for his opponent.[30] A third candidate, Charles Thomson, received two votes. Not one county gave a majority to St. Clair. He made his worst showing in Bucks County where he got thirteen votes to Mifflin's 2,286. He did best in Allegheny County where he lost by only four votes—354 to 350. The junto candidate, supported so strongly by prominent Philadelphians, actually made his best showing not in the east but in the western counties. The city of Philadelphia itself gave him only 91 votes to Mifflin's 1,761.[31] He was completely deluged in Philadelphia County by a vote of 18 to 1,424. The three eastern counties of Philadelphia, Bucks, Chester, and the City of Philadelphia gave Mifflin a majority of 6,333 out of a total vote of 6,536. In the four western counties of Allegheny, Washington, Fayette, and Westmoreland, with a total vote of 4,999, St. Clair received 1,354, less than a third.

In evaluating the election results, it would seem that the issue was determined not by party organization or alignments but by personalities. Mifflin, widely known and popular throughout the State, was more than a match for an opponent who was less familiar to the electorate. As a westerner, however, despite his backing by the "Morris" or junto clique, St. Clair made a relatively better showing in his section than in any other part of the State or in the State generally. It is certainly true that Mifflin must have received many votes from the old Constitutionalist party, but in view of his overwhelming majority the same would hold true for the former Anti-Constitutionalists. As a popular figure then, he transcended old party alignments and further blurred the already confused political picture. That he had the support of many of the old Constitutionalist leaders is undoubted. Findley, Gallatin, James Hutchinson and Samuel Bryan all favored him. Findley certainly enjoyed Mifflin's closest confidence, and he was to continue to do so for many years. Samuel Bryan was of the opinion that Mifflin had emancipated "himself from the servile thraldom of a junto" that would permit no "deviation from their monopolising dictates. . . ."

He referred of course to the Morris-Fitzsimons group. Mifflin had been elected, Bryan declared, through "the patronage and zealous support of the independent part of the Community, aided by a concurrence of highly favorable incidents."[32]

When Charles Biddle states in his *Autobiography* that St. Clair was a Republican or Anti-Constitutionalist candidate and Mifflin the Constitutionalist, he creates additional confusion.[33] He explained Mifflin's victory by saying that he was supported by all the Constitutionalists and many Republicans. Mifflin had been "Considered a staunch Republican [but] he had by some means given offence." Biddle did not mention the nature of the offense, but whatever it was it could not have been taken seriously by the voters in the three eastern counties and the city of Philadelphia, who favored him by a majority over thirty-one to one. Perhaps the alleged offense was felt most keenly by Morris, Fitzsimons and the other members of the clique who had endorsed St. Clair. Biddle, also a staunch Republican, had nevertheless worked assiduously in behalf of Mifflin's candidacy. But he wanted something.

For sometime he had been much interested in becoming the Secretary of the Commonwealth, a valuable and important job within the scope of the Governor's appointive powers. He was sure that his warm friendship with Mifflin (in the course of which Mifflin had often told him "there was no man in the world he loved and esteemed half so much") would guarantee his appointment.[34] Since many of the Constitutionalists had opposed the creation of the office, Biddle was of the opinion that "there would not have been such an office in the Constitution if it had not been for some of my friends in the convention." They knew he would have refused a mere private secretaryship, so they had worked to have the more important secretaryship created.[35]

But Biddle and his friends had miscalculated. Some time before his inauguration Mifflin had decided against Biddle's appointment, but he did not let him know about it until he had appointed Alexander James Dallas instead. Blaming Mifflin for want of candor, Biddle later brought the subject up and was informed by Mifflin that he had wanted to tell him, but was afraid that Biddle's hot temper would move him to "say something to affront him and that he would make any sacrifices rather than have a difference with me."[36]

The disappointed Biddle was indeed angry, and he told some of Mifflin's friends that he despised the Governor. Because of their estrangement he insisted that Mifflin pay back everything he owed him. Mifflin, usually in debt at that time, paid in full, and Biddle thought that the coolness between them was fortunate, for had they remained "on good terms" he never would have gotten his money. Later on, when the Governor made some appointments that pleased Biddle, the two men smoothed over their differences. But despite the many social invitations extended to Biddle he never quite forgave his erstwhile friend.

The office of Secretary of the Commonwealth also had its attractions for Samuel Bryan. When William Findley informed him that Biddle would not be appointed because he lacked "those talents and that fund of information" necessary for the secretaryship, Bryan became active in his own behalf. Findley had told him that, with the exception of James Hutchinson, Albert Gallatin and one other man, the information was to be kept secret.[37]

To secure the support of Hutchinson and Gallatin, Bryan wrote them letters on December 18, 1790. Since his letter to Gallatin was the fuller of the two, it alone will be quoted.

In choosing a Secretary of the Commonwealth, Bryan wrote, due regard should be given to "his connections, his natural weight in the country, the confidence and estimation in which he is held by the most respectable and leading persons throughout the State and particularly by the Whig interest, and Consequently the increased Confidence, estimation and support which the Governor would derive from the appointment."[38] Because Mifflin had thwarted the Morris-Fitzsimons or junto group, he should have a strong secretary who would aid in combatting the opposition which would surely come from that quarter. Bryan felt that he was just the man to satisfy those requirements.

As far as his literary ability was concerned, his efforts in that field had "received the plaudits of all America." He had written the minority dissent at the Pennsylvania convention which ratified the Federal Constitution, a statement that had been "highly celebrated throughout the United States, & occasioned more consternation among the friends of this [federal] government than anything that had preceded or followed it."

After this modest resumé of his talents he stressed the significance which his selection as secretary would have to the "Constitutional" interest.

> Such a decided measure as the appointment of me to this office would at once draw the line between the Aristocratic and Democratic interest, consolidate his [Mifflin's] and the interest of our Party, and ensure him from the wiles of the

other Party who will practice every finesse to alienate him from his present friends and views, which considering the Governor's former politics and connections may be otherwise not a very improbable event. The Governor's temper is such that in case of a thorough coalition and consequent despair of the other Party to gain him, that he would be the means of rendering our Party predominant through the state.

Bryan must have heard that Alexander James Dallas, a rising young attorney, was also interested in the secretaryship, for after dwelling at length on his own stellar qualifications he attacked him as a possible competitor. Dallas, with his "courtly flattering manners" would, if given the position, "ingratiate himself with the grandees of the Land and become instrumental to the alienation of the Governor from our Party." He "seems a decided democrat, but no dependence can be placed on professions made in his present circumstances." He is a "stranger in the country, without connections, and whose real principles cannot be satisfactorily known from the experience we have had of his conduct. . . . His appointment would give no weight to the Governor, but on the contrary disgust the community in general." Apparently Mifflin disagreed with Bryan's last sentence, for Dallas was the very man he eventually selected.

Alexander James Dallas, born in Jamaica in 1759, arrived at Philadelphia in 1783. Two years later he became a member of the Philadelphia bar, joining such luminaries as William Lewis, James Wilson, Jared Ingersoll and Jonathan D. Sergeant. The first five years of his legal practice were not lucrative, so he supplemented his income by editing for a brief period William Spotswood's *Pennsylvania Evening Herald* and *Columbian Magazine*. He also prepared a volume entitled *Reports of Cases Ruled and Adjudged in the Courts of Pennsylvania Before and Since the Revolution*. This much needed work was approved by the leading members of the bar. While trying to gain a foothold in the legal field Dallas lost no opportunities to advance himself socially as well as professionally. Tall, personable and easy in manner, he took part in Philadelphia society with commendable grace. Ably assisted by his young wife Maria, he entertained many important people at parties and suppers. Professionally he met many of Philadelphia's great lawyers through his editorial and legal activities. Fortunately enough, it was through the medium of his newspaper writing that his name was brought to the favorable attention of Mifflin when he was looking for a secretary.[39] By 1790 then, Dallas was fairly well known in Philadelphia as a young man of considerable talent.

When Mifflin named Dallas as Secretary of the Commonwealth, he displayed excellent political and executive judgment. Tactfully sidestepping the possible factional consequences of selecting either Bryan, the enthusiastic democrat, or Biddle, an avowed Federalist, he chose instead a man who had not engaged actively in politics, but who had already demonstrated abilities that would recommend him for the secretaryship. He was certainly aware that the tide of votes which elected him had overflowed old party lines. His political sense, if not his temporizing nature, suggested therefore the desirability of an appointment which would avoid the likelihood of the Governor's chair becoming the focal point of party broils. The prevention of a possible immediate revival of old animosities indicated a middle of the road policy. He adopted it.

When Samuel Bryan, marshalling arguments in favor of his own appointment to the secretaryship, had stressed the fact that his selection "would at once draw the line between the aristocratic and Democratic interest," he revealed an erroneous conception of the Governor's motives. Mifflin wanted no lines drawn. He preferred instead a neutralizing smudge, a political chiaroscuro designed to please many and alienate as few as possible.

According to the Constitution the Secretary of the Commonwealth was to keep a record of the Governor's official business, deliver necessary papers to the legislature and "perform such other duties as shall be enjoined him by law."[40] In practice Dallas expanded the position under the "such other duties" clause so as to make it one of real power and authority. He received reports from State officials and maintained a voluminous official correspondence. Mifflin, lacking literary talents and a comprehensive knowledge of law, came to lean more and more heavily upon his able secretary. It has been said that Dallas made himself, "next to the Governor, the most powerful official in the state government."[41] It is certain that throughout his nine years of office, particularly during the last three when Mifflin suffered very poor health, the Governor depended greatly on Dallas.

CHAPTER IV

CONGRESSIONAL ELECTIONS OF 1791 AND 1792

IN THE Pennsylvania Congressional elections of 1791 and 1792 the Federalists and Republicans shared several common aims: both had a profound respect for the sanctity of property, both desired a stable representative governent, and both wished to uphold the State and National Constitutions. The contest of 1792 was born of a curious mixture of divergent nominatory procedures, old political feuds and resentments, personal rivalries and ambitions. These were the principal ingredients in the political stew. The *pièce de resistance,* a burning issue which could inspire state-wide discussion and mold public opinion, was absent. Some issues there were, of course, but in the general scheme of things they played an unimportant part. Although two contesting groups appeared, neither was sufficiently strong nor confident enough to present two distinct congressional tickets to the public. Since both factions lacked state-wide organization, the principal work was done by small coteries of individuals in Philadelphia. Clear and definite party lines did not appear.

The Pennsylvania Congressional election law of October 4, 1788, applied only to the elections held in that year.[1] In the normal course of events Representatives to the Second Congress would have been selected in 1790, but on September 3, 1790, one day after the new constitution was adopted, the Assembly precipitately dissolved without making any provision for an election.[2] Consequently none was held in that year. Obviously, if the State were to be represented in the Second Congress, a special or off-year election would be necessary.

As a result, the subject was one of the earliest items of business to be considered by the first legislature under the new constitution. It had barely convened in December, 1790, when Cadwalader Evans, hardy conservative perennial from Montgomery County, urged the lower house to frame an election law. Then William Findley and Blair McClenachan, from Westmoreland and Philadelphia counties respectively, sought to delay the appointment of a committee to bring in a bill until the question could be discussed in the committee of the whole. It is certain that Findley had not forgotten the Federalist victory of 1788, when the State had elected Representatives on a general ticket. Under his leadership the westerners succeeded in precipitating a general discussion on the advisability of dividing the State into Congressional districts. On January 11, 1791, almost a month after the subject was first broached, the House resolved by a vote of thirty-two to thirty-one to have a bill brought in that would provide for a district election.[3]

Clearly revealed in the close vote were evidences of sectionalism. Dominated by members from the western counties, the majority of thirty-two in favor of a district election included all the Representatives from the transmontane region, one each from the counties of Philadelphia, Chester and Lancaster, and a majority from Berks and Northampton. The minority, on the other hand, obtained twenty-one votes from but four counties (Philadelphia, Bucks, Lancaster, York) and the city of Philadelphia.[4] Of course, the vote did not show pure sectionalism (Berks and Northampton were eastern counties), but it did indicate a marked preference on the part of the southeastern counties for an election method which would permit them to capitalize on their relatively large populations. The opposite was true of the four westernmost counties of Westmoreland, Fayette, Washington and Allegheny which, with 63,628 persons, comprised one-fifth of the counties but only one-seventh of the State's population.[5] They would patently benefit under a district system.

With this difficult problem disposed of, the committee, appointed by William Bingham, Speaker of the House, soon reported a bill, and on February 1, 1791, it was passed by a vote of thirty-three to twenty-eight.[6]

In the Senate the division produced by the general versus the district-election controversy was as sharp and close as it had been in the House. But there, too, the westerners had a slight advantage, and when the question of method came to a record vote the Senators usually split nine to eight.[7] That was the division on the law's passage there on March 10,[8] and its sectional characteristics were more evident than they were in the lower chamber. Of the State's twelve senatorial districts four contained the minority of eight in favor of a general election. Representing the counties of Philadelphia, Bucks, Chester, Lancaster, York and Delaware and the city of Philadelphia all in the southeastern section, those districts presented a solid front. The unanimity, however, was conspicuous only on the election law, and the reason for it—population advantage in a general election—is obvious. It did not demonstrate a persistent geographic or "interest" cleavage.

In addition to dividing the State into eight districts the election law, approved on March 16, 1791, further provided that Representatives could be taken from the State at large.[9] That is, a candidate for Congress was not required to live in the district in which he ran for office.

In comparison to the campaigns that preceded and followed it, the Congressional race of 1791 was dull and unexciting. Without the stimulus of an election-at-large no attempt was made at state-wide organization. Lacking county or district nominating machinery that was even partially representative of the majority of voters, candidates were placed before the public by small, influential groups or by single individuals. That this absence of a nominatory method would lead to confusion was to be expected. A case in point occurred in the district composed of Bucks and Philadelphia counties where Frederick Muhlenberg and Judge Henry Wynkoop found themselves in opposition. With that coyness common to many politicians with great but persistently disavowed ambitions Muhlenberg laid the problem before Thomas Fitzsimons for solution.[10] Muhlenberg wrote to Fitzsimons that in an effort to learn Wynkoop's intentions he paid him a visit. After the interview, in which Wynkoop had apparently hedged, Muhlenberg told his own supporters that although Wynkoop had not "positively declined" he had reason to believe that he would eventually do so. But Wynkoop had not been so obliging, and they were now, regrettably enough, pitted against each other in a race in which they would both probably come to grief. Muhlenberg was willing to let Fitzsimons decide the matter. "A line from you to him I know will have a decided effect—or if it is you [sic] opinion that I ought to give way, I will endeavour to prevail on my friends to take him up in my stead—more especially as I am not very anxious about the Business, & if I was I have offers from another District which bid fair to succeed."[11] Thus the reluctant aspirant to the political boss. Whatever Fitzsimons decided is not known, but the candidate who was "not very anxious" stayed in the race and won.

In some such haphazard fashion were most men placed before the public.[12]

When the results were in, it was found that the State was generally conservative. The Federalists had a majority in the State legislature and in the Congressional delegation. Of the eight men sent to Congress in 1788, only four—Thomas Fitzsimons, Thomas Hartley, Daniel Hiester, and Frederick Muhlenberg—were returned in 1791. The new Congressmen were William Findley, Israel Jacobs, John W. Kittera and

Andrew Gregg. Only two of these, Findley and Gregg, could be said to have had genuine Republican leanings. The latter considered himself a "staunch Whig and a sincere Republican. . . ."[13]

When Pennsylvania elected Congressmen again in 1792, her politicians were once more (as in 1788) faced with the necessity of conducting a state-wide campaign on a general election basis. That contest was centered in Philadelphia. Why did it occur there instead of in some other part of the State? The answer is to be found in the city's great importance as a cultural, economic and social center. One hundred years old in 1792, Philadelphia, America's principal city, already had a distinguished history as the birthplace of the Declaration of Independence and of the Federal Constitution.

Penn's "Greene Countrie Towne"

Prior to 1789, the year in which the city was given a new charter, the civic administration had very few democratic characteristics. Based on Penn's original charter, which made no provision for the popular election of city executives and councilmen, the administration was composed of a small number of self-perpetuating oligarchs. With little regard for civic welfare, the little group of leaders permitted the city to stagger along under a document that could repose nowhere so comfortably as in medieval Venice, an oligarchical republic whose spirit it reflected. When disease threatened the inhabitants, preventive measures to stop its spread were usually undertaken by public spirited citizens who operated on their own initiative. A further evidence of administrative ineptitude was the general prevalence of crime and sporadic riotings. At times, the criminal element was dominant, terrorizing the city at will.[14]

That the above conditions were recognized and condemned by the State's assemblymen is shown in the preamble to the Act of March 11, 1789, which gave Philadelphia a new charter. It declared that the city government was "inadequate to the suppression of vice and immorality, to the advancement of the public health and order, and to the promotion of trade, industry, and happiness; and in order to provide against the evils occasioned thereby, it is necessary to invest the inhabitants thereof with more speedy, vigorous, and effective powers of government than are at present established."[15]

A writer in the *Pennsylvania Packet* advocated the incorporation of Philadelphia under a new charter because such legislation would lower taxes, make it unnecessary for the State continually to legislate for the city, and (here the writer was looking ahead) provide the "means of inviting Congress and strangers of distinction to settle among us."[16]

The chartering Act of March 11, 1789, created a corporation to be known as "The Mayor, Aldermen and Citizens of Philadelphia." It provided for the election of fifteen aldermen and thirty common councilmen. These were to be elected by the freeholders and freemen respectively. The mayor was selected by the aldermen from their own number and the recorder was elected by the mayor and aldermen from the city's freemen. In the mayor, recorder, councilmen and aldermen were vested the power to make necessary ordinances and to enforce them.[17]

By virtue of her new charter Philadelphia ceased to be a closed corporation. Now that the city government was somewhat democratized it was no longer completely out of harmony with either the State or the nation.

With a city and suburban population of over 42,000 in 1790, Philadelphia proper ran from Vine to South Street and westward from the Delaware to Fifth Street. Beyond that the houses thinned out, and west of Twelfth Street the area was open pasture land. Well planned by William Penn and Thomas Holme, Philadelphia with its fine brick houses, raised sidewalks, public squares and imposing public buildings was considered by the far-ranging LaRochefoucauld-Liancourt as one of the world's most beautiful cities.[18] Its more imposing edifices included the State House, the Law Courts, where Congress held its deliberations, the City Hall, the American Philosophical Society and the Public Library. On High Street was located America's greatest public goods mart. As a port Philadelphia led New York in both imports and exports in 1792, and for many years after 1790 the city remained the nation's chief center of business and finance.[19]

The city's social life was noteworthy. The political and financial elite engaged in a continual round of entertainments in the homes of Washington, John Adams, Alexander Hamilton, William Bingham, Thomas Mifflin, John Penn, Samuel Powell, Benjamin Chew and others of prominence. Many had large country houses on the Schuylkill and, not to be outdone by Europeans, the Philadelphians patronized the watering places at Harrowgate and Yellow Springs.

Of the more than one hundred taverns in Philadelphia the best were Oeller's, the Indian Queen and the City Tavern.[20] These were often scenes of political gatherings and celebrations.

When the national government was moved to the dynamic city on the Delaware in 1790, it naturally became the most active political center in the United States. All roads led to the capital and it was there that factional broils became most intense. The political disputes that arose over national policies, already grown bitter in New York, were transplanted to Philadelphia, where the contestants unified their forces. It was inevitable therefore that the city influenced, and was influenced by, the issues and controversies that resulted in the formation of the Federalist and Republican parties. For ten years then, Philadelphia remained a political maelstrom.

As the State capital Philadelphia afforded an opportunity for Pennsylvania's legislators to rub shoulders with the nation's politically great and to view the sights of the big town. Attendance at the annual meetings of the legislature was an event of great importance not only to the lawmakers themselves but to their constituents. In those pilgrimages the legislators acted as links between affairs at the great metropolis and their back-country neighbors. As practical politicians they served their communities in a variety of ways. William Findley, for instance, who repeatedly represented his section in both the State and national legislatures, was not above attending to the humble requirements of his neighbors. When that able man rode forth to the capital in 1793, he carried with him a list of items to be purchased in Philadelphia's stores. "A good Gown Patren" for Mrs. Campbell, twelve yards of "middling light" calico for Nancy Bole, a copy of "fisher's Catticismes" for Mrs. Bole, a "quarter pound of bark" for Jenny Little, and black handkerchiefs for "the children's company coming in."[21] As a politician and as a friend Findley could not afford to ignore those requests.

Most of America's great political figures, as well as those with pretensions to that degree of quality, periodically dwelt in Philadelphia during the last decade of the eighteenth century. They were drawn there by State and national constitutional dicta, which called elections and legislatures with the inexorability of seasonal change. Arriving with section-born plans and schemes they created a pot-pourri from which emerged two dominant political groups. And the wherewithal for the creation of parties and the advancement of careers was bartered and exchanged with all the assiduity that characterized merchants in the country's greatest market on High Street.

Graced and dignified as it was by eminent visitors, the city also had in residence a number of extremely capable politicians who, regardless of legislative sessions, worked both in and out of season. And it was in the summer of 1792, when the legislators had returned to their constituents, that these men engaged in a strenuous Congressional campaign.

Congressional Election of 1792

In the spring of 1792 Congress, in preparation for the next Congressional election, dwelt at considerable length on a necessary apportionment bill. And although the Pennsylvania Assembly adjourned before the national lawmakers had decided on the number of Representatives to be returned by each State, its members did not retire until they had made some provision for the ensuing election.

Lacking information as to the number of Representatives to which Pennsylvania would be entitled, the Assembly, in an Act of April 7, 1792, arranged for another general election. An attempt was made to provide for a district election, but it was defeated by those who argued that the correct number of districts was undeterminable until it was definitely known how many men Pennsylvania would send to the next Congress.

It was a timely argument for those who favored a general election, and it may have enabled them to carry a point they had lost one year before. In the House of Representatives they won by a close vote of twenty-eight to twenty-six.[22] Similar to the vote on the same issue in 1791, it revealed a sectional distribution: the transmontane counties were wholly in favor of the district method while those in the southeastern section of the State were heavily opposed. When the bill finally passed in the House by a thirty-one to sixteen vote the southeastern counties had only one representative (James Boyd, Chester) listed in the minority.[23]

The Senate sustained the House, but only after an eight to eight tie was broken by Speaker Samuel Powell.[24] In 1791 John Hoge, from the Washington-Fayette district, had voted with the westerners, but this time he deserted his colleagues to favor the eastern group. In a year's time the Senate personnel had been altered slightly by resignations, but with the exception of Hoge, the geographic distribution of the vote on election methodology was the same as it had been in 1791.

The Act of April 7, 1792, required every voter merely to deliver "in writing on one ticket or piece of paper, the names of so many persons as this state is or may be entitled to as representatives in Congress . . ."[25] The national legislature did pass an apportionment bill on April 14, but it was then too late to affect procedure in Pennsylvania.[26]

The general election law thus forced the politicians once again to devise some sort of state-wide nominating machinery. And it was over the problem of nominatory devices that the outstanding episodes of the election occurred. Had there been two well-organized political parties with definite lines, disciplined ranks and efficient coercive machinery, it is quite likely that the nomination problems would have been settled within the parties themselves. But no such parties existed. Neither the Federalists nor their opponents—referred to by historians as Anti-Federalists, Republicans and Democratic-Republicans—had yet evolved tight organizations. This structural lack was the crux of the matter and the principal reason for the heated contest that enlivened the political atmosphere of Philadelphia and the State in general during the summer of 1792.

Although gradual evolutionary processes had not yet resulted in two disciplined organizations, they had proceeded so far as to reveal ideological distinctions. Such distinctions were in a state of flux, but the two sets of broadly divergent views had each reached a degree of coalescence which permitted the attachment of labels. Those in use were numerous, confusing and often applicable only to ephemeral or local conditions. In this study, be it noted, two terms will be used to denote the major contesting groups: Federalist and Republican. But up until 1796, when parties began to acquire recognizable borders, those names can be most accurately applied to opinion groups, to ideological "climates," as it were. Here they will be used in the opinion sense until evolutional crystallizing processes warrant their application to parties which in the mass designated themselves as Federalist or Republican.

While the issue of federalization was still in doubt, the terms Federalist and Anti-Federalist were fairly descriptive of those who respectively approved or disapproved of union under the Constitution. However, in solving the problems which arose with the administration of government, conflicting opinions began to produce divisions. Illustratively, the Federalists favored the national administration and a strong concentration of power in the national government. Their opponents, the Republicans, feared Federal concentration of power. At the risk of over-simplification, those may be considered as the major differences. There were others of course, some sincerely held, some exaggerated beyond their true significance for propaganda reasons. Broadly speaking, the Pennsylvania Federalists were the descendants of the former Anti-Constitutionalist party. Their opponents were, for the most part, formerly associated with the Constitutionalists. In 1792 the Pennsylvania Federalists, loosely led by the Morris-Fitzsimons group, had to meet a challenge. It was presented with vigor and cleverness by a group of Philadelphians led by Dallas, James Hutchinson, Jonathan D. Sergeant, Blair McClenachan and several westerners, notably Findley, Gallatin and Smilie. All these men were aggressive and shrewd.

Of the Philadelphians, Dr. James Hutchinson was probably the most enterprising and active. As an able physician with a large practice, and as a professor of chemistry at the University of Pennsylvania, the former Revolutionary surgeon was widely known and respected throughout the city. His rotund figure was a familiar sight on the busy streets. Wherever liberals gathered, there Dr. Hutchinson held forth with good-humored sagacity. Charles Biddle, who liked the jovial physician, described him as being "one of the best of men,"[27] and "fat enough to act the character of Falstaff without stuffing."[28] But the acerb Maclay who did not like him—indeed, he had few good words for anyone—thought Hutchinson as "greasy as a skin of oil. . . ."[29] Noted as a sprightly conversationalist, the good doctor's witticisms were to the lean and rheumatic Maclay nothing more than the "belchings of [a] bag of blubber."[30]

Since there is no cause to believe that Hutchinson entered politics for the sake of office or preferment, it seems reasonable to assume that he was prompted to do so by a combination of motives: a sincere desire to promote liberal democracy and a love of political activity for the pleasure and satisfaction it gave him. Certainly he was well endowed with those attributes which make for political success. He liked people and they liked him. He loved the intricacies, manipulations and bargainings consequent to political organization, and in those pursuits he was adept, particularly among the immigrants with whom he spent a great deal of time. But most important of all, Hutchinson had the gift of expression; he could write clear and trenchant prose. Eschewing the verbiage and sounding periods so common to many of his contemporaries he went directly to the core of any issue. His concise summaries of political situations and events always clarified and never confused. His western colleagues, absent from Philadelphia for the summer, were lucky to have Hutchinson as a source of political intelligence.

Had the gifted doctor lived and retained his interest in politics, he would have materially aided the growth of Republicanism. Unfortunately, however, he became one of the numerous victims of the yellow fever which raged with particular violence during the summer of 1793. Although a successful physician he died in straitened financial circumstances, leaving his family without adequate support. To provide for them Dallas, a warm friend of Hutchinson's, asked Albert Gallatin to assist him in raising a subscription "competent to the purchase of an annuity to protect his widow and orphans from want, or (what their natural protector detested above all things) servility and dependence."[31] It would seem that Hutchinson received no reward from his political activity other than the satisfaction it gave him.

Coupled with Dallas who, in his strategic position as Secretary of the Commonwealth could keep his fingers on the administrative pulse, Hutchinson was also greatly assisted by Jonathan Sergeant and Blair McClenachan. Both were fiery and enthusiastic Republicans. McClenachan, interested in commerce and banking, had an excellent record as a patriot during the Revolution. He combined a shrewd business sense with an active political interest.

Jonathan Dickinson Sergeant, born and raised in New Jersey, graduated from the College of New Jersey in 1762, and then took up the study of law. Twice chosen to represent his State in the Continental Congress, he was an ardent patriot in the Revolutionary movement. After his Princeton home was burned by the Hessians in December, 1776, he moved to Philadelphia. There he associated with the Constitutionalists, and in the following year he was appointed Attorney General, a position he held until 1780. He then devoted his attention to the practice of law.[32]

The western Republicans, led by Gallatin and Findley, were kept in touch with eastern developments by the Philadelphians. The most exciting phases of the election of 1792 occurred in Philadelphia, but the westerners were not idle. They could not afford to be. For although the counties beyond the mountains were preponderantly Republican they also contained small but influential Federalist groups. The strongest of these was located in Allegheny County where resided the powerful Neville family.

John Neville, born in Virginia in 1731, had fought with great credit in the Revolution, emerging at its conclusion with the rank of brevet brigadier general.[33] He had served as an Anti-Constitutionalist on the

Supreme Executive Council, and as a member of the Pennsylvania ratifying convention had voted for the Federal Constitution. As a large landholder he was, by 1792, a man of considerable wealth. Fortunate in his son, Presley, who was almost equal to his father in ability, John Neville headed a powerful little group that exerted great influence throughout the western country. This influence had its center in the Neville residence at Bower Hill, just outside of Pittsburgh. It was extended by the family itself and a group of able men with whom the family was intimately connected. These men were Abraham Kirkpatrick and Isaac Craig, brother-in-law and son-in-law respectively of John Neville, and George Woods, an attorney.[34] They were all Federalists.

Both the eastern and western parts of the State then, had able and opposing groups that were to struggle unceasingly for power throughout the last decade of the eighteenth century. The contest was to begin with the Congressional election of 1792.

On the evening of July 19, 1792, a group of Philadelphians, preponderantly Federalist in sentiment, met at the State House. The purpose of the meeting was to promote a state-wide conference of county commitees which would nominate thirteen Congressional candidates.[35] Through such a convention of committees it was hoped "that the opinions of all parts of the State could be obtained." Although Dallas and Hutchinson did not approve of the plan they were in attendance at the gathering. The meeting was poorly attended, however, and as a consequence nothing was accomplished beyond a resolution to meet again on July 25, 1792.

At the next meeting "a very numerous company" met and selected Mayor Matthew Clarkson as chairman.[36] "A motion was then made to select a committee, consisting of persons from each ward, to retire from the room, in order to report a number of names to be proposed as a Committee of Correspondence and a Committee of Conference."[37] The ward committee, headed by Robert Morris, recommended five men for each committee. The recommendation caused a heated discussion and when the hour grew late, the meeting was adjourned to Friday, July 27, 1792.

The July 27 meeting at the State House was hectic. Shortly after Samuel Powell had been placed in the chair, Dallas moved to erase from the record all mention of the previous meeting's committee report on the Committee of Conference. Considerable discussion then ensued and on a vote Dallas' motion was defeated. A vote was then taken on the question as to whether or not conferees should be appointed. After it was decided in the affirmative the meeting adjourned.[38] It ended precipitately without a division on the mooted conference question. The vote on the conferee motion had been taken by a show of hands and the chairman's decision in favor of the conference method was contested. Powell left the chair in great haste, ignoring a motion for division because of "the crowd in the room and the lateness of the hour (it being near 11 o'clock)."[39]

Since no date had been set for a future gathering, the Dallas-Hutchinson group decided to call one of their own on July 30, 1792.[40] In advertising it, they made a bid for the approval of the mechanics and tradesmen by pointedly stating that they would convene at seven o'clock in the evening, when the day's work was done.[41]

When the citizens arrived on the thirtieth it was found that their number was too great to be accommodated in the State House Assembly Room, and they had to retire to the Yard.[42] It was in fact the largest political gathering since the year 1779.[43] As to the attitude and opinions of the men in attendance, a writer in Bache's *General Advertiser* disavowed any intention on their part to injure the State or national governments. "It must have given pleasure to every candid mind," he declared, "to perceive, that notwithstanding the artful clamor that has been raised by the Stalking Horse of a Party, the cry of Federalism, no man who attended but was warmly attached to the support and prosperity of the Constitutions of the United States and of Pennsylvania, which are both happily founded upon the principles of representation, and to which every insidious attempt to new model and destroy the right of suffrage, is hostile and injurious."[44]

The proceedings in the State House Yard were begun on a highly respectable note with the selection of Chief Justice Thomas McKean as chairman. Then Dr. Hutchinson arose and reviewed the events of the past two days. He made it clear that he strongly opposed a State convention to select Congressional candidates. After the minutes of the disorderly meeting of July 27, 1792, were read, a resolution was passed which declared that Samuel Powell, chairman, must have misunderstood the result of the vote on the appointment of conferees. For, despite the chairman's decision, there were more men in opposition to the scheme than there were for it.[45] To settle the question, a motion was then passed to expunge from the record all that had been done at the meeting on July 27. That successful motion was followed by another which required the appointment of a seven-man committee of correspondence whose duty it would be to determine the opinion of the electors throughout Pennsylvania as to "persons to be nominated for Congress and as Presidential electors." The findings of the committee were to be submitted "to the consideration and choice of the citizens at a general meeting. . . ."[46]

The men appointed to serve as correspondents were McKean, Hutchinson, Dallas, James Wilson, John Barclay, Hilary Baker, and Jared Ingersoll. Wilson, however, did not approve of the correspondence method, so he later declined to serve.[47] Of the seven only one, Hilary Baker, had been appointed to serve on a committee at a previous meeting. That was on July 25, when Morris' ward committee had named him as a member of the conference committee.

Up to this point, after four meetings had been held to determine nominating procedure, only those favoring the correspondence method had succeeded in having a plan accepted in a meeting that had ended on a peaceful and moderately harmonious note. At least, the Conferees did not question the validity or decisiveness of the vote at the meeting on July 30, 1792. It had been their objective to have the conference plan sanctioned at a general and open meeting. Had their plan been successful it could have been publicized widely as having had the approval of the most densely settled section in the State. The plan had miscarried, however, through the vigilance and organizational ability of the Dallas-Hutchinson group.

But the Conferees were not at all willing to let the matter rest. On the morning of July 30, 1792, they notified the citizens of Philadelphia through several newspapers that another meeting would be held at the State House on the following afternoon at three o'clock. Consequently, many of this persuasion boycotted the Correspondents' gathering on the thirtieth.[48] The quarrel between the two factions was now becoming recognized and the gulf separating them was growing wider. The Correspondents, unwilling to let their opponents hold a general meeting without opposition, also decided to convene at the same time and place.

When the two groups met in the State House Garden on the afternoon of the thirty-first, they were, as the Conferees insisted, "absolutely independent of each other."[49] The stage was thus set for another hurly-burly similar to the one on the twenty-seventh.

When the milling crowd proceeded to business at half past three, both factions tried to select favorable chairmen. McKean was proposed by the Correspondents and Samuel Powell was brought forward by the Conferees. After a wild shouting of yeas and nays both men declined to serve. Other nominations were made, including Morris and John Barclay. James Wilson was then called upon to decide which man had received a majority. Three votes were taken, but the confusion and numbers present were so great that it was impossible to determine the successful nominee.[50] Finally, the Conferees "retired to the west part of the Yard and attempted to place Mr. Morris in the Chair, this being observed by the others occasioned a scene of confusion, they rushed forward, seized the chair and table and tore them to pieces, and it was with difficulty *violences of a more serious nature* were prevented."[51]

The Conferees had made their withdrawal move to install Morris because it had been observed that the number of men in favor of the correspondence scheme was increasing. As the tumultuous afternoon wore on the Correspondents' supporters became even more numerous and the Conferees, now discouraged, withdrew from the Yard.[52] The Correspondents also retired for they had accomplished their object on the preceding evening.

True to Hutchinson's prediction to Gallatin,[53] the Conferees made no further attempts to hold a general meeting in Philadelphia. Instead, they contented themselves in meeting behind closed doors with men in whom they "could confide."[54] At meetings held at Epple's Tavern on August 2 and 4, 1792, they appointed a committee to correspond with all parts of the State "to endeavor to obtain the sentiments of the inhabitants on the subject of a proper representation in Congress, and of Electors for a President and Vice President."[55] The committee was composed of George Latimer, Robert Waln, William Lewis, Israel Whelen, William Rawle, Richard Wells, Hilary Baker, John Wilcocks and Benjamin R. Morgan. George Latimer was its chairman. Shortly after the discussions at Epple's, the committee prepared a circular letter (frequently cited in this account) which reviewed the July events in Philadelphia and stated the case for the Conferees. In requesting suggestions from their correspondents in the country as to likely candidates, they gave assurance that after the men proposed had been investigated they would "no doubt meet the countenance and approbation of Pennsylvania."[56] By thus generalizing, they carefully avoided any commitment of the Philadelphians in particular to an acceptance of the names offered. In a postscript the committeemen observed that at a meeting in Montgomery County it had been proposed that a nominating convention be held in Lancaster on September 20, 1792.

So, in spite of the defeats administered by the Dallas-Hutchinson clique, the Philadelphia Conferees still favored a general conference. Hutchinson, who knew about the circular letter, feared that attempts would be made to appoint conferees in the various counties, but he hoped that "our friends in the country will take care that it is not done. . . ."[57]

The Correspondents were also busily soliciting support for their scheme. In a circular letter of August 3, 1792, their Committee of Correspondence, headed by McKean, enclosed the minutes of the meeting on July 30, 1792, and made a plea for cooperation. They assured the men to whom the letter was addressed that they had been delegated only to collect information and not to "deliberate upon the subject of election . . . to declare the sense of the people; or to frame a ticket." The committee was "authorized" only to collect the names of men "whom the citizens of every denomination and in every part of the State deem to be qualified" for Congress and for Presidential electors, "and to submit this list, without the influence of a selection, or a comment, to the deliberate consideration and unbiased suffrages of the People."[58] Promising to act with "impartiality," the Correspondents gave the impression that as public spirited citizens they were actuated only by the highest political motives, that their one aim was to secure the best possible representation in Congress regardless of party considerations.

But not all men were inclined to accept such high-minded professions at face value, whether made by the Correspondents or Conferees. The Correspondents, said "a Pennsylvanian," were Anti-Federalists and anarchists who, having failed to prevent the ratification of the United States Constitution, were now attempting to destroy the government itself. The conference plan on the other hand, if carried to a successful conclusion, would once again result in the election of men who were attached to Federal principles. He made a strong appeal to the farmers, merchants, manufacturers and mechanics to awaken from their lethargy and defeat the proponents of "antifederalism."[59]

In refutation "Sydney" assailed "a Pennsylvanian" for appealing to the voters as members of definite classes or occupational groups. It was wrong to discriminate, for there were no degrees of citizenship; all free men were citizens, untitled and uncategorized. The "cry of antifederalism" raised by the Conferees he labeled as a deception, "a hackneyed sound calculated to delude and alarm you—*men* and not *measures* are the object...." "Sydney" believed, and in this opinion he was not alone, that a nominating convention was nothing more than a body of electors, a device advocated by those who were inclined toward aristocratic principles.[60]

A broadside of October 9, 1792, made a similar charge, that a select few Conferees were attempting to usurp the right of popular selection by arrogating that privilege to themselves. William Lewis, a leader of the Conferees, was considered to be the principal offender.[61]

William Findley also considered the electoral system and the conference plan to be synonymous, both equally undemocratic. He thought James Wilson's refusal to serve on the committee of correspondence was inconsistent with his attack on "electors" during the constitutional convention of 1790.[62]

"Mentor," in an extravagant diatribe against the Conferees, declared them to be aristocrats, the logical descendants of "the Tories of 1776." He then proposed several candidates (generally approved by the Correspondents) who "ought to be forever dear to the Whigs and Republicans of Pennsylvania."[63]

But not all writers were partisan champions. "Common Sense Jun.," an independent, damned both groups impartially. Although the city was divided into two violently opposed parties, the situation would not be necessarily evil if they were both disinterested and patriotic. But they were not. Despite their claims of disinterestedness both groups were duping the people; both hatched secret plots; both were led by "aristocrats" who are "equally enemies to the Commonwealth." He exhorted the people to shun the struggling groups, vote as they wished, "and be free and independent."[64]

By far the most damaging attack against the Dallas-Hutchinson group was made by a well-informed Federalist who wrote over the pen name "Cerberus."[65] In an exposé, consisting of three letters to the *General Advertiser,* he accused the Correspondents of conniving to foist a list of Congressional candidates on the people that had been prepared by a very few men at a secret conference. In a detailed account "Cerberus" alleged that at the close of the spring session of the Pennsylvania legislature, after the law providing for the election of Congressmen had been passed, "a select number of country assembly-men, with a few *favored* citizens met at Anatomical Hall in fifth street, near the State House, and there formed a ticket."[66] The list included eleven names: William Findley, John Smilie, William Irvine, William Maclay, William

Montgomery, Andrew Gregg, Thomas Hartley, John W. Kittera, Frederick A. Muhlenberg, Daniel Hiester and Peter Muhlenberg. Two names were omitted, but these were to be filled in later with Philadelphians. The planners at Anatomical Hall, he declared, also named men in the different counties to serve as correspondents.

Challenged by a writer to prove his assertions "Cerberus" responded by printing a letter of August 5, 1792, from Ebenezer Bowman to William Lewis in which Bowman included the Correspondents' list of eleven candidates as well as all the county correspondents.[67] The Congressional ticket, said Bowman, had been handed to Jesse Fell of Luzerne County by a returning assemblyman. Although Bowman did not know who had prepared the list of candidates, he had heard that it was done by some assemblymen and Philadelphia citizens.

Another writer, "A Friend to Good Government," openly accused Dallas and Hutchinson of acting a "political farce" in their correspondence scheme. He declared that it had already been acknowledged that a ticket had been prepared at Anatomical Hall in the spring.[68]

Just how much truth was contained in the Federalists' allegations? An examination of two letters from Hutchinson to Gallatin indicates that their charges were not without considerable justification. On August 19, 1792, the doctor spoke of several candidates that had already been decided upon, but they were having considerable difficulty in selecting a suitable man from Philadelphia to place on the ticket. Further, he referred to an original list of candidates that had been prepared by men who sought to strike a geographic balance in the State, with the Susquehanna as the dividing line. William Maclay had been chosen as one of the seven men to represent the area east of the river, but Hutchinson felt that although Maclay actually resided in Harrisburg, his real "interest" lay to the west. Therefore, he should be dropped from the list, particularly so if there was any indication that Maclay would be preferred to William Montgomery.[69] Later the irascible ex-Senator was definitely excluded from the Correspondents' list of candidates.

By September 14, 1792, Dr. Hutchinson could report to Gallatin that "our ticket . . . is now completed and filled. . . ."[70] It consisted of Charles Thomson, William Findley, William Montgomery, Frederick A. Muhlenberg, Daniel Hiester, John Smilie, William Irvine, Jonathan D. Sergeant, Peter Muhlenberg, Thomas Hartley, Andrew Gregg, John W. Kittera and John Barclay.[71] It is significant to note that ten of the above thirteen had been mentioned in "Cerberus'" revelations. After

Maclay had been eliminated, Thomson, Sergeant and Barclay were added to complete the representation in eastern Pennsylvania.

Since the much publicized Committee of Correspondence, headed by McKean, had not yet reported on the names of candidates submitted (the report appeared on September 27), it seems clear that a small group of Republicans had agreed in advance on a Congressional ticket that was circulated surreptitiously among the party leaders. Further, it would appear that the real organizational work was not done by the widely discussed committee but by a few managers in Philadelphia who kept in close contact with leading politicians throughout the State. This is borne out evidentially by Hutchinson in a letter to Gallatin on September 14. When Gallatin replied to any letters sent by the Committee of Correspondence, he was advised to answer generally and "recommend either the whole ticket or those from your particular district, as you shall judge proper."[72] But if Gallatin had anything of a confidential nature to write, he was to send it by a reliable bearer to one of five men: Colonel Jacob Morgan, Colonel William Coats, Dr. Samuel Jackson, Dallas or Hutchinson. Apparently these five were the real campaign managers in Philadelphia.

As the summer of 1792 wore on into fall the politicians busied themselves with speculations, prophecies and reports on particular district activities. Hutchinson, usually optimistic and always enthusiastic, exulted in the opposition to the Conferee "aristocrats" in Philadelphia, and in "the regeneration of the Whig Spirit of the Citizens." He was confident of a "Whig" victory in Philadelphia city and county, Northampton, Montgomery, Berks and Dauphin. They would be defeated, he thought, in Delaware, Bucks, Chester, Lancaster, and York. The last mentioned county was "most to be dreaded, notwithstanding we have taken Hartley, who is by no means popular, yet he will have a unanimous vote [in York County, presumably], without being of the least use to our ticket."[73] Hartley noted on August 29, 1792, that electioneering had begun in Lancaster and that the citizens would favor a "truly liberal ticket."[74] From Carlisle, John Montgomery wrote William Irvine that he disapproved of all the Congressional tickets that had appeared, but that he was submitting one of his own which was the best he had seen! Nothing was being said in Carlisle about the election.[75] Even by September 17, 1792, there was no election "stir" in Montgomery's county, although he mentioned a proposed convention which would meet at Stoney Ridge that day.[76] According to John Wilkins, Jr., no election activity was noticeable in Pittsburgh, at least by August 31, 1792.⁷⁷ William Findley predicted success for the Correspondents in the western country, except in Pittsburgh. However, he had doubts as to Hartley's chances. With election day drawing near, he feared the influence of the army at Pittsburgh, but thought that "perhaps the sheriff candidates will watch one another against cheating."⁷⁸ Findley expected to be excluded from "the aristocratic Ticket," except in localities where expediency made it unwise to do so. From Penns Valley, Andrew Gregg reported that the zeal of the Philadelphians had reached his county, and caused many people to electioneer enthusiastically.⁷⁹

While concentrating on personalities, effective organization and the alleged aristocratic tendencies of their opponents, the Republicans made little effort to introduce the explosive excise question into the campaign. Since the passage of the excise law by Congress the year before, it had created resentment in Pennsylvania, particularly among the many western whiskey distillers who complained that the high tax on their product was ruinous. Several indignation meetings had been called beyond the mountains in 1791, but on August 21, 1792, one was held in Pittsburgh that induced decisive political repercussions.

The meeting, attended by men from four counties, approved a remonstrance to Congress requesting the law's repeal and resolutions that virtually ostracized anyone who served as an excise officer.⁸⁰ Two prominent Republicans, John Smilie and Albert Gallatin, were in attendance. Gallatin had served as clerk, signed the resolutions, and helped to write the remonstrance.⁸¹

Although politics had not been mentioned at the Pittsburgh meeting,⁸² reaction to the gathering was immediate and decisive. The Federalists recoiled with a mixture of horror and indignation at this attack on the Federal government. But their protestations did not conceal the obvious delight they experienced in exploiting a fine opportunity to make political capital at their opponents' expense.

By many Republicans, however, the action at the Pittsburgh meeting was thought to be nothing less than calamitous. Lamenting the affair, Hutchinson frankly told Gallatin that "your meeting and proceedings . . . have hurt us considerably in this part of the State, our adversaries who were effectually humbled rallied on reading your resolves, and I have no doubt they will loose [sic] us from 1,000 to 1,500 votes, and they will particularly injure our friend Smiley. . . ."⁸³ William Findley was sure that Smilie's presence at the meeting had done him harm . . . "but you know his temper," Findley wrote Irvine, "he could not resist importunity on that subject. . . ."[84]

Despite setbacks and Federalist attacks, the Committee of Correspondence plodded doggedly on at its appointed task. By September 27, 1792, when its findings were published, it had distributed 520 letters to selected individuals in twenty-one counties. The harvest of responses netted replies from eighteen counties which submitted a total of 44 candidates, Federalist and Republican together.[85] The names were then submitted to various county meetings for winnowing. The results were forwarded "to a Philadelphia committee. From these selections, a ticket was formed and published in the papers as the 'Rights of Man Ticket.'"[86] By a coincidence so unusual as to have been hardly accidental, the "Rights of Man" ticket was identical with the one sent by Hutchinson to Gallatin weeks before. However, despite its certain knowledge that a Congressional ticket had been long in circulation, the Committee of Correspondence brought its publicized labors to a conclusion with the pious observation that its main concern had been to "preserve the purity of the Right of Suffrage."[87]

While the Correspondents were busily describing their inner and outer circles, the Federalist Conferees were not idle. After their Philadelphia committee, headed by George Latimer, had indirectly endorsed a Montgomery County meeting's suggestion that a convention be held at Lancaster on September 20, 1792, this proposal was considered in several counties. In West Chester, Bethlehem, Harrisburg and other places, meetings were held at which delegates were appointed to attend the proposed Lancaster convention. That the men who attended these conclaves represented general opinion in their counties is extremely doubtful. Nevertheless, they appointed delegates on the assumption that they spoke for the county at large.

This assumption was not always permitted to go unchallenged by the Correspondence enthusiasts. For example, when a Montgomery County Federalist meeting of August 30, 1792, appointed delegates, it was repudiated eight days later by the Correspondents who claimed that the Conferees did not represent a majority in the county.[88] A similar affair also occurred in Harrisburg.[89] In no county, however, was the struggle between the two factions as lively as the one in Philadelphia.

Unresponsive as the counties appeared to be, the Federalists, nevertheless, went ahead with their plans to meet at Lancaster on September 20, 1792. When they convened there on the appointed day, it was found that only nine counties and the city of Philadelphia had sent delegates.⁹⁰ Of those west of the Susquehanna only York County had sent a delegation. With less than half the counties represented the convention, unabashed, proceeded to select Congressional candidates and Presidential electors for the entire State. For Congress they nominated William Findley, Frederick A. Muhlenberg, Daniel Hiester, William Irvine, Peter Muhlenberg, Thomas Hartley, John W. Kittera, Thomas Fitzsimons, Thomas Scott, James Armstrong, Henry Wynkoop, William Bingham, and Samuel Sitgreaves.⁹¹

To the Lancaster convention both Dallas and Hutchinson reacted vigorously. In a wave of letters to various parts of the State, they declared that the Conferees had no authority to meet, and that after engaging in some disputatious sessions they went home "dissatisfied and despondent." If "the Republican interest [loses] it will be our own fault not their [the Conferees'] ability."⁹² Hutchinson was especially incensed at Robert Waln and William Lewis for representing Philadelphia at the convention against the wishes of the majority of the citizens.⁹³

A comparison of the Conferee ticket with the one then being circulated by the Correspondents reveals that the first seven of the above men appeared on both tickets. So, despite the heated charges of anarchy, aristocracy and autocracy that the two groups hurled at each other, it would appear that the gulf between them was not so wide as to preclude the demands of expediency. The seven men they championed in common were too popular to be excluded by either side. Nor could either afford to ignore the German vote by dropping Hiester and the two Muhlenburgs. And the seven, if considered unobjectionable by the two factions for reasons of strategy and policy, also operated on a latitude of principle sufficiently wide as to permit a comfortable residence in "both your houses." If any one of them feared that the double sponsorship would jeopardize his political standing or prostitute his creed, he failed to show it by withdrawing from either ticket. Each was agile enough to stand with one foot in Lancaster and the other in Philadelphia without suffering undue strain. And, although the facile Findley might refer to his opponents as "aristocrats," he did not want to be omitted from their list. Hutchinson, too, found Hartley bearable because he was popular in York County.

The election, therefore, was not to be a contest involving thirteen candidates against thirteen, but of six against six—the six on each ticket over and above those both shared in common. It was a problem of seven and six to carry. For the Federalists the six were James Armstrong, Thomas Fitzsimons, William Bingham, Samuel Sitgreaves,

Thomas Scott and Henry Wynkoop. For the Republicans: John Smilie, Jonathan Sergeant, Andrew Gregg, John Barclay, William Montgomery and Charles Thomson.[94]

Both sides were determined to elect their entire ticket, but when election day (October 9) was over and the votes were counted, both experienced disappointment. The seven candidates the parties sponsored in common were easily elected, but of their other nominees each elected three only: the Federalists, James Armstrong, Thomas Fitzsimons, Thomas Scott; the Republicans, Andrew Gregg, William Montgomery, John Smilie.[95] In Philadelphia each of the seven polled over 2,100 votes, with a divergence of only twenty-four between the highest and lowest. The Federalists beat their opponents there by an average of over three hundred tallies, but they lost in Philadelphia County. In the State at large Findley, with a total of 33,158, was the leading candidate. Frederick A. Muhlenberg was second and Hiester third.

Commenting on the results, Hutchinson wrote Gallatin that "your Excise meeting lost us the majority in the counties of Berks and Dauphin, for the most of our ticket, the arts of our opponents, together with the President's proclamation,[96] and other circumstances too tedious to detail, detached many of our honest but credulous friends in the counties." The "Whigs" had many difficulties in Philadelphia, he said.[97]

In comparison to the stirring Congressional campaign the selection of Presidential electors was indeed a mild affair. Hutchinson had very little hope of a "Whig" electoral selection, but he felt that some effort should be made in Pennsylvania to assist "Whigs" in other states, particularly in the South, where an attempt would probably be made to elect a new Vice President. He sent Gallatin an electoral ticket proposed by the Correspondents for circulation. They would "be secret and silent in this business, but something may perhaps be done, tho I confess it will be difficult to induce the people to come out for an object they in general think of so little importance."[98]

Bache's *General Advertiser* paid little attention to the choice of electors. Commenting on the light November election in which they were selected, the paper felt that "the choice of an intermediate body appeared to remove from their attention the ultimate and important result of the election."[99] Washington's election was almost a foregone conclusion.

As to the significance of the Congressional election in general, certain conclusions may be drawn.

Party terminology and labels were confusedly varied. The Correspondents referred to themselves by that name or as Whigs and Republicans, and to their list of candidates as the "Rights of Man" ticket. They did not accept the Anti-Federalist label, disparagingly attached to them by their opponents. The Federalists, or Conferees, called "aristocrats" by the Republicans, described their list of candidates as the "Federal" ticket. All the terms were often loosely applied. Although there were some differences between the two groups, they were not uncompromisable.

As to nominating devices, neither the conference nor the correspondence plan was successful. The local county organizations that both needed for efficient operation were lacking. In the absence of such opinion-expressing organizations, the sentiment of any given area was perforce only a matter of inference. The knowledge the various sections had of the candidates in general was either non-existent or woefully inadequate.

Both Conferees and Correspondents tried to publicize their tickets, but bad transportation and communication facilities made the adequate dissemination of information a well-nigh impossible task. In a protest against general elections some citizens at Redstone Fort may well have spoken for all the voters when they declared that "to call such election free is an insult to common reason." They had not forgotten the lessons of 1788.[100] Truly, the election of 1792 was an equally convincing argument for district as opposed to general elections.

Since the candidates themselves did little or nothing to get acquainted with the electorate, the propaganda burden fell on the shoulders of a few enthusiastic workers. As a matter of fact, reticence on the part of seven of the aspirants was dictated by the peculiar circumstances of bipartisan sponsorship. For them a word of praise or blame in any direction might have been damaging. Silence meant success. But such a situation could hardly have been considered undesirable in that self-abnegating age when office supposedly sought the man. At least, that fiction was well preserved and cultivated.

The few issues that appeared in the campaign were, with the possible exception of the excise question, not clearly drawn. But although the excise tax was the cause of much agitation among interested westerners, their alarm was not proportionately shared throughout the State. The Federalists, however, exploited the western protests as attacks on the Federal government, and identified the Correspondents as promoters of such attacks. The real question at issue involved the dominance of small groups of politicians in a contest to control the selection of Pennsylvania's Congressional delegation. To Republicans such as Dallas and Hutchinson the election therefore served as a convenient opportunity to challenge Federalist supremacy and force a counting of heads to determine the extent of Republican strength. As politicians they were not satisfied with the indecisive results. For although they had tied three to three on the "partisan" candidates they must have been aware that many of the men they supported had been elected as Federalists in 1788 and 1791.

SECTION II

NATIONAL STIMULUS AND LOCAL RESPONSE, 1793-1795

Preview, 1793-1795

Insofar as definite party organization and alignments are concerned, political divisions had not crystallized in Pennsylvania by 1793. However, certain group characteristics were becoming more and more evident. Generally speaking, Pennsylvania inclined toward those individuals who proudly affiliated themselves with the "Federal interest." They supported the Hamiltonian program and the Washington administration, and approved additional Federal acquisitions of power. Many of them feared a possible resurgence of democracy that might oust the rich, well born and educated from the halls of government. Others regretted the enthusiasms of the French Revolution and later sympathized with the British in their war with France. Their ranks were principally composed of the old Anti-Constitutionalists who had risen to control in Pennsylvania at the expense of the waning democrats. Although republican in principle they were, by and large, representative of the State's more conservative element.

Their opponents, on the other hand, the men to be later designated as Republicans, were generally opposed to the above tenets of Federalism. They were to favor the French over the British and deplore the ever-increasing centralizing tendencies of the Federal government. In those tendencies and assumptions of power they saw manifestations of aristocracy that were considered incompatible with free government. They had a real and sincere dread of monarchy and feared its rise in the United States. Made up principally of the former Constitutionalist group and continually strengthened by disaffected Federalists and incoming immigrants, they were eventually to succeed in overthrowing the conservatives before the beginning of the nineteenth century. They were not wild-eyed propertyless radicals who sought to gain power through bloody revolution. They were businessmen, farmers, lawyers and physicians who were not any more averse to seizing the main economic or social chance than their more conservatively inclined brethren. They were, in fact, liberals who were to develop steadily under a gifted leadership that far exceeded that of the conservatives in winning votes. And their victory, when it came, was more negative than positive in that they rose primarily on the mistakes of the Federalists, not on any well integrated and formulated program of their own.

The State was to remain in the hands of the Federalists until 1799. They controlled both houses of legislature, received a majority of the appointive offices and selected, with one exception, all the United States Senators. Only once did the general electorate defeat a Federalist-sponsored candidate. That occurred in the presidential election of 1796, when Jefferson was favored over Adams by a narrow margin. No doubt the personality factor, always an indeterminant in political phenomena, played a large role in that decision.

Mifflin himself was supported by both Federalists and Republicans. And as such he defied party classification. As a popular figure with a consistent state-wide appeal, he was above parties, often decrying factional broils and antagonisms. He was friendly to both conservatives and liberals, often seeking the line of least resistance in exercising appointive power. He maintained peace with the legislature by avoiding controversial issues when possible; when such a course was not feasible, he moved slowly and deliberately. Adroit in the arts of appeasement and mollification, he steered a wavering course between extremes with such success that neither the conservatives nor liberals generally wished to replace him with a positive and aggressive personality. Neither group feared him; both received benefits and favors at his hands. Personable, agreeable, and an effective public speaker, he was so popular as to be almost unbeatable in a general election. He was challenged in 1793, but without success, and in 1796, after six years in office, the voters gave him a greater majority than they had in 1790. Truly, no conclusive struggle could occur between the two factions until Mifflin was no longer constitutionally available as a candidate for the governorship. As the Jeffersonians in the national arena had to wait until Washington declined a third term, so also were the Republicans in Pennsylvania compelled to avoid a trial of strength with their opponents until Mifflin had served three terms.

Had he declined to run in 1793 or 1796, or had Pennsylvania chosen to elect her Congressmen on a general ticket throughout the period, the liberals and conservatives would no doubt have split on more definite lines. But Mifflin wanted to stay in office as long as he could and, with the exception of the election of 1792, the State selected her Congressmen by the district method. As a result, the Republicans did not make an intensive bid for the governorship until 1799.

Within the next six years, however (1793-1799), the politicians were to see a plethora of issues. These arose from a series of events with which we are to be intimately concerned. Those to be considered from 1793 to 1799 are as follows: the Genêt affair and the pro-French enthusiasm in Pennsylvania, the rise of the Democratic Societies, the

Whiskey Rebellion, the Presque Isle development project, Jay's Treaty, the Alien and Sedition Acts and Fries' Rebellion. With exception of the last two named, all occurred prior to the year 1796, when Washington announced his retirement and Mifflin began his last term as Governor.

In the section under consideration, only the events occurring from 1793 to 1796 will be reviewed. In 1796, with Washington about to release the controls and with Mifflin unavailable for a fourth term, the State's politicians realized that the time for decisive and positive action had come. For the first time the Republicans made a serious effort to defeat the Federalists in a presidential election, and they succeeded. In this respect, the year 1796 was the end of an era and a proper dividing line in a study of party activities.

Considered over the entire period, that is from 1793 to 1799, the above events excited so much interest throughout the State that it was difficult for the most neutral-minded citizen to forbear partisanship. The reasons for Republican success at the end of the century, a victory so complete as to almost annihilate their opponents, are to be found in the cumulative and congealing effect these events had on party formation. The Republican victory was thus the end result of a long period of political action and reaction, of stimulus and response in which the Federal government acted as the principal center of stimulation. No political story of the period can be written unless due regard is paid to this continued interaction between the State and national government.

The following chapter will deal with three events that evoked a wide political response in Pennsylvania. They are (1) the Genêt affair, (2) the rise of the Democratic Societies and (3) Jay's Treaty. These will be followed by chapters on the Whiskey Rebellion and the Presque Isle development project.

CHAPTER V

EVENTS AND OPINIONS

Genêt Affair

THE FRENCH REVOLUTION met with the immediate approval of a great many people in the United States. This enthusiasm was shared by both the Federalists and their opponents. Such a reaction was hardly unnatural. Americans remembered with gratitude the assistance extended to the patriots during their own revolution. They gloried in doctrines that proclaimed the rights of man and the freedom of the individual. This political affinity was practically enhanced by French willingness to permit American traders to enter her island possessions, a privilege accorded by no other nation. And most important of all, Franco-American ties had been cemented by a treaty of formal alliance.[1]

In 1792 France's admirers in America rejoiced in her brilliant military victories as she courageously met the foes who had determined to encircle her and quench the new fires of democracy. She had indeed become the crusading champion of all those who embraced the stirring concepts of freedom and equality. The Philadelphia press recorded every shock of her clashing armies and reported fully on the latest ideas that emanated from Paris to shake the European continent. Public zeal made the month-old news vital and timely. And if newspaper content is any criterion, the Philadelphia citizenry was more interested in world affairs than in tavern brawls, vital statistics or the latest armed robbery on Market Street.

Three events caused a division in American opinion regarding France: the September massacres, the execution of Louis XVI, and the entrance of England into the war on the side of the monarchies. The first two combined to alienate many, principally Federalists, because of the implied threat to law and order. The last posed a very delicate and practical commercial problem. It was expected that the war would become a struggle for naval supremacy, which could vitally affect America's international position and commerce.

The French government, naturally anxious to maintain profitable and friendly relations with a country as commercially important as the United States, appointed Edmond Genêt as minister to Philadelphia. He was instructed to obtain supplies, promote American friendship and arrange for a new commercial treaty. But Genêt had other instructions which, if implemented according to the broad and reckless interpretation he gave them, probably would have drawn the United States into the war against England. It was his understanding that privateers were to be fitted out in American waters, and to effect this he came to the United States with two hundred and fifty letters of marque. In addition, he seemed to expect that prizes secured by these vessels would be received in American ports. The British, however, were not to be accorded the same privilege.[2]

Bursting with tactless enthusiasm, Citizen Genêt sailed into Charleston on April 6, 1793, to be greeted with open arms. Ostentatiously democratic, he was accessible to all, and he made a favorable impression. But not all his time was spent at public receptions. Shortly after his arrival, he sent out four privateers with a few American sailors on board and attempted to interest Americans in forming an expedition to attack Spanish settlements.[3] Then, on April 18, 1793, Genêt departed for the capital city.

While the Citizen was being blown northward over a sea of wine by winds of fervent oratory, an event occurred in Philadelphia which should have dampened his ardor. With the entire Cabinet in favor of taking a neutral position in the war, John Jay, at Hamilton's request, had drafted a statement of neutrality. This was presented to Washington, who, after he had heard of Genêt's joyous reception at Charleston, signed it on April 22, 1793.[4] Without mentioning the word neutrality, the proclamation made the administration's attitude quite clear. It requested all states "with sincerity and good faith [to] adopt and pursue a conduct friendly & impartial towards the Belligerent powers."[5] Thus was the official stage set for the French minister's debut.

The ardent French sympathizers in the capital were also preparing a welcome for Genêt. When he arrived on May 16, 1793, he was met at Gray's Ferry by a cheering throng and escorted in triumph to the heart of the city.[6] That night Charles Biddle, presiding over a meeting at the State House, appointed David Rittenhouse, Dallas, Hutchinson, Du Ponceau, Jonathan Sergeant and others as members of a committee to prepare a formal address to the personable young minister.[7] It was presented midst plaudits and smiles on the following day. On the evening of the eighteenth, a huge banquet in his honor was held at Oeller's tavern. The heavily-laden table, gaily decorated with French and American flags and liberty caps, was surrounded by some of Philadelphia's leading citizens.[8] On either side of the guest of honor sat Charles Biddle and Governor Mifflin.[9]

Each public appearance made by Genêt touched off new demonstrations in the responsive town. Crowds danced the *carmagnole* and lustily sang the *Ça Ira* as they surged through the streets. Philadelphia was stirred and excited as she had not been since the Revolution.

All this rampant enthusiasm was flaringly set forth in Benjamin Franklin Bache's *General Advertiser*. Young Bache, grandson of Benjamin Franklin, had founded his newspaper in 1790, with the encouragement of some members of the American Philosophical Society.[10] His interest in France and French ideas was not gained vicariously, for he had spent many years in that country with his grandfather.[11] Throughout his career as a newspaper man, his intense enthusiasm for France was reflected in his editorial policy. Bache and Genêt had much in common and the latter, on the day of his arrival, requested Bache to thank publicly all the people who had treated him with such kindness as he traveled to Philadelphia.[12] The *General Advertiser* thus early became the disseminator of many of Genêt's ideas. From that time on, the newspaper's anti-administration bias and its sympathy for the Republican cause became more pronounced. In time it became the country's leading Republican organ. Federalists must have smiled wryly indeed when the editor announced that his paper was "impartial."[13]

But not all the citizens greeted Monsieur Genêt with unbridled joy. To some the revels in the streets were vulgar and even fearsome, portents of violent revolution. In the opinion of John Adams, terror stalked the thoroughfares of the capital city "when ten thousand people . . . day after day *threatened to drag Washington* out of his house and effect a revolution in the government or compel it to declare war in favor of the French Revolution and against England."[14] Many stable Philadelphians believed that only the death of James Hutchinson and Jonathan Sergeant during the yellow fever epidemic prevented a revolution.[14a] Alexander Graydon, a sardonic, confirmed Federalist, reacted to the Genêt ovation in characteristic fashion. "What hugging and tugging!" he exclaimed, "What addressing and caressing! What mountebanking and chanting! with liberty-caps and the other wretched trumpery of *sans culotte* foolery! 'Give me an ounce of civet, good apothecary, to sweeten my imagination.' "[14b]

Truly the furor created by Genêt's arrival was as startling as it was unprecedented. The febrile "Genêtines" and purple oratory heralded something new,[15] and no one could be certain as to just what it was or what it meant. But if many were jubilant, others were dismayed and frightened.

The ecstatic Philadelphia welcome might well have turned the head of a more experienced and tactful diplomat than Genêt. But had his elation been tempered with sensitivity, he would have heeded warning signals in the reception tendered him by Washington on May 17, 1793. There was nothing ecstatic about the President as he received the Minister correctly and with high dignity.[16] The General's dignity could be awe-inspiring and at times frigid. There was no doubt that he was determined to keep the United States in a neutral position.

But when Genêt made it clear that he intended to arm and equip privateers in the United States and return prizes captured by them to American ports, the administration objected on the grounds that acquiescence in such action would make the United States a virtual ally of France. It was considered "incompatible with the territorial sovereignty of the U. S."[17] With this policy Genêt reluctantly complied during the month of June. On the sixth of July, however, Governor Mifflin was notified by the Philadelphia port warden that the *Little Sarah* (recently renamed the *Little Democrat*), a British vessel captured by the French *L'Embuscade,* had increased her armament in the port. Much concerned, Mifflin, to avoid the necessity of forcefully preventing the ship's departure, sent Dallas to Genêt with the request that it be kept in port.[18]

In angry and intemperate language the impetuous French Minister refused the request. Complaining of ill-treatment on the part of the United States government he "declared that 'he would appeal from the President to the people.' "[19] Any attempt to take possession of the vessel would be resisted by force.

Always the efficient secretary, Dallas hurried back to his superior and recounted the whole conversation. Mifflin duly reported it to Secretary of War Knox the next day, and on the day after that "confirmed" to Hamilton "the declaration with regard to appealing to the people."[20] Dallas also mentioned the matter to Jefferson. Genêt was then asked by Jefferson to detain the vessel until Washington could make a decision on the subject. But the request of the Secretary of State was likewise ignored, and before Washington, who had just returned from a trip, could make up his mind, the *Little Democrat* sailed defiantly away.

Monsieur Genêt had now gone too far. Thoroughly disgusted with his high-handed conduct Washington's Cabinet, on August 1, 1793, unanimously agreed to ask the French government for his recall.[21] He was to be permitted to remain as Minister though, until another could arrive to replace him.[22] Even Jefferson had concluded as early as August 3, 1793, that unless Genêt was abandoned he would "sink the republican interest."[23]

Knowing that Hamilton desired to carry the Minister's cavalier behavior to the public, Jefferson hoped to prevent it. But Hamilton was far too shrewd to miss the exploitative possibilities of Genêt's alleged intention of appealing his case directly to the people. In a letter of August 13, 1793, to Rufus King he indirectly suggested that the unwise threat, as well as other incidents surrounding the *Little Democrat*, be publicized.[24] King was willing to oblige, and later he told Hamilton that he and John Jay had decided to publish "an exact transcript" of Hamilton's letter.[25]

A storm broke over Dallas' head on December 2, 1793, when Jay and King accused him in the New York *Advertiser* of being on intimate terms with Genêt at least two months after the unsatisfactory interview in June.[26] As a leading Republican Dallas was, of course, given unwelcome credit for revealing Genêt's threatened appeal to the people. Self-defense prompted him to publish a statement in the *American Daily Advertiser* on December 9, 1793.[27] In this letter, a remarkable display of tortured obfuscation, the Secretary tried to wriggle out of his predicament. But he did not suceed in denying that he had used the word *appeal* when describing the interview to Mifflin.

The Genêt farce had certainly discomfited the Secretary, and as a result he was bitterly annoyed with its chief actor. He shared Gallatin's opinion that Genêt was only a nominal democrat, and believed that he was really inclined toward despotism. The French cause was dear to him, but it was regrettable that Genêt had ever been "deputed to support it."[28]

But Dallas was only one of the many that had been disappointed. All those who greeted Genêt openly—men like Rittenhouse, McKean, Sergeant, Hutchinson and Mifflin—had occasion to regret his rash conduct. Actually he was only a symbol of the new democracy, and although he disillusioned some in regard to his own character, the admiration for France and her struggle continued. Ideals similar to those being proclaimed in France were too firmly implanted in Pennsylvania to wither because of the ineptitude of their supposed champion.

The real damage, however, was suffered by the Republicans, for all over the State they had been generally identified with the pro-French enthusiasm. Although generally happy over their showing in the Congressional campaign of 1792, they must have realized that the cohesion evidenced in that election was so loosely integrated and delicate as to be little more than an organization in embryo. It needed the stimulus of an exciting issue to prosper. Coming at this most propitious time, the crusading zeal excited by the French Revolution and the European war was indeed a gift from the gods. This, coupled with an ever smouldering Anglophobic sentiment, afforded a positive coalescent that the Republican leaders seized upon as a golden opportunity to advance their "interest."

Of course, enthusiasm for France had been evident in Pennsylvania long before Genêt's appearance. But it was his opportune arrival that induced an outburst of feeling so intense and controversial that men were compelled to take sides and declare themselves.[29] As a political determinant this was one of the most significant aspects of the pro-French demonstrations. Jefferson, in steady contact with Philadelphia Republicans, was certain that the Proclamation of Neutrality had created two large groups of opinion and that an opportunity had arisen to test men's loyalty to Republican principles.[30] The war between England and France, he thought, had forced a distinction between "Republican and Monocrats in every state. . . ."[31]

The choosing of sides was indeed so general that Washington himself was not unaffected. Signs of cleavage were painfully evident in Congress and even among his most trusted advisers. Moderate and fair minded, he deplored the growing factionalism which he considered harmful to the nation. But the breach was widening, and in making a decision he chose Hamilton over Jefferson, the Federalists over the Republicans.[32] Aside from the broader aspects of the problem with its international complications, it is not unlikely that the milling crowds which surrounded his residence and shouted for aid to France had something to do with his decision. Such demonstrations were alien to his natural reserve and he recoiled from them. Throughout the remainder of his term Washington was at times almost driven to despair by the problems arising from the pro-French bias in the United States. In 1796 he wrote Charles Cotesworth Pinckney that the "greatest embarrassments" to his administration came from men who seemed more interested in promoting the interests of France than in establishing "a national character of their own."[33]

The President's attitude severely retarded the growth of the Republican party in Pennsylvania. Although he made no public declarations in favor of either of the major groups, his gradual inclination toward the Federalists was unmistakable. So great was his prestige and influence that open sponsorship was unnecessary. A few words at the right time would suffice, and at no time was this fact more dramatically illustrated than in his denunciation of the Democratic Societies in 1794. Since most of the societies—in Pennsylvania, at least—had their inception during the first great expression of pro-French sentiment, their growth was a definite reflection of that enthusiasm.

The Democratic Societies

The organization of politically conscious men into societies was of course not new in Pennsylvania. Antedating the democratic clubs by six years, the Society for Political Inquiries was started in Philadelphia in 1787 for the purpose of studying government and all aspects of political science. Non-partisan in object, its roster of members included such diverse persons as Mifflin, Franklin, James Wilson, Thomas Paine, Thomas Fitzsimons, Francis Hopkinson, Benjamin Franklin Bache and Robert Morris. Franklin was its guiding spirit and first president. Apparently the society aroused little interest, for its meetings were poorly attended. The last recorded one was held on May 9, 1789.[34]

Curiously enough, just as the Society for Political Inquiries died another organization of quite a different nature appeared. This new group, known as the Sons of Tammany, held its first parade in Philadelphia on May 1, 1789. It was formally organized by that date, preceding the New York Tammany Society by eleven days.[35] Although its original aims are obscure, it is quite possible that it shared the views of the New York group whose avowed purpose was opposition to the "aristocratic tendencies of the Federalists. . . ."[36] The Philadelphia organization existed for many years more, but it was never important politically.

Considered broadly the nine Democratic Societies formed in Pennsylvania during the 1790's revealed certain common characteristics.[37] Negatively, they opposed excise taxes and all supposed or actual centralizing, monarchical and Anglophile tendencies of the national government. Affirmatively they displayed strong democratic and Francophile sympathies. All, however, were vitally interested in disseminating political propaganda through their correspondence committees.

And although they showed no formal and material party connections,[38] their generally expressed beliefs inevitably would incline them toward the Republican group. Of the nine Pennsylvania societies, seven had their origin in 1793 and 1794.

The Federalist claim that the clubs were inspired by Genêt needs qualification.[39] Of the two that originated in 1793, only one, the Pennsylvania Democratic Society, could have owed its inception to him. The other, the German Republican Society, antedated his arrival in Philadelphia by several weeks. In 1794, when five more were organized, the discredited Genêt was hardly an inspiring democratic figure.

As to another Federalist contention—that they were direct imitations of the Parisian Jacobin Club—it should be remembered that the then defunct Society for Political Inquiries could equally have served as a model. Further, the Committee of Correspondence, the most important committee in each society, might well have traced its origin to Revolutionary days. Although it cannot be denied that the influence of the French Revolution on the origin of the societies was profound, it is equally undeniable that Americans in the 1790's did not have to depend on European models for political organization. American experience had already provided examples.

With men like Dallas, Sergeant and Hutchinson active in the club movement, it is almost certain that they considered them as likely instruments with which to build a more substantial party organization. Their association, both in the correspondence committee during the election of 1792, and in the Pennsylvania Democratic Society, was hardly coincidence.[40]

Although Jefferson had nothing to do with the organization of the Democratic Societies,[41] he heartily approved of them as forces indicative of new political alignments.[42] While Secretary of State, he declared in a Cabinet meeting of August 2, 1793, that the purpose of the Pennsylvania Democratic Society was to secure the re-election of Mifflin as Governor, and that when that object was effected it would expire unless stimulated by governmental opposition.[43] His observation had been occasioned by Secretary Hamilton's warm advocacy of a plan to expose the Genêt affair to the people by publishing all correspondence relative to it. Jefferson was sure that Hamilton's real object in appealing to the people was to injure the society, which had already caused alarm among the Federalists. It is possible, therefore, that he was less convinced of the society's immediate political object and autumnal demise than he was of the necessity of minimizing the alleged dangers inherent in the organization.

But whatever Jefferson's purpose may have been in ascribing party motive as the society's *raison d'être,* historians have generally accepted his opinion.[44] This conclusion seems to be warranted, despite the absence of confirmatory evidence in the club's proceedings or public declarations.

The first popular society to be formed in Pennsylvania was the German Republican Society. Its exact date of origin is unknown, but it probably held its initial meetings in March or the first part of April, 1793. On the thirteenth of the latter month its formation was noted in Philip Freneau's *National Gazette,*[45] and two days later Henry Kammerer, first president, publicly announced its objectives and purpose.[46] The German "character" had languished in America, said Kammerer, because the Germans had been inattentive to "the objects of government and education. . . ."[47] It was necessary, therefore, to awaken the political consciousness of this group and stimulate its interest in representative government. All the club's transactions were to be published in the German language, for many Pennsylvanians of that descent knew no other.

The men most actively engaged in the creation and development of the club were Peter Muhlenberg, Henry Kammerer, and Dr. Michael Leib. All were politically ambitious. Muhlenberg had served in the First Congress and had been selected for the Third in 1792. By this time, incidentally, he was leaning strongly toward Republicanism. Kammerer was to be a Philadelphia candidate for the Assembly on the anti-Treaty ticket (opposed to Jay's Treaty) in 1795. The secretary of the club, Michael Leib, a tireless and aggressive political organizer, had a long career ahead of him in both the State and the national legislatures.

In its beginnings the German group was dissimilar to the more influential Pennsylvania Democratic Society in two important respects: it could not have been inspired by Genêt, and its purpose was to educate and influence only one segment of the population. In this latter point of difference it may appear to have fitted more easily within the conceptual framework of the Society for Political Inquiries than of the Pennsylvania Democratic Society. But after the latter appeared the two clubs showed definite points of resemblance in their attitudes and principles. Both were pro-French and anti-British; both favored political education to promote intelligent participation in government;

both feared aristocratic tendencies in government and society. In addition, the leaders of both groups were of Republican persuasion.

If the exact date of origin of the German club is unknown, so too is that of the Pennsylvania Democratic Society. The first session of which there is any record was held on June 20, 1793. On the meetings held prior to that, there is no information because the first sixteen pages of the official minutes are missing.[48] Obscure also is the club's initial membership, but undoubtedly Dallas, Hutchinson and Jonathan Sergeant were among the first to become active participants. During the first year of existence the society's roster included the names of such prominent citizens as Samuel Bryan, Michael Leib, William Coats, Blair McClenachan, Israel Israel, Benjamin F. Bache, Jacob Morgan, Benjamin Rush and John Swanwick. The last three did not join until May, 1794.

Most industrious in promoting the work of the society were Dallas, Bache, Leib, Bryan, George Logan, Israel and McClenachan. The last two were secretary and president respectively. All the rest were members of the correspondence committee. Although David Rittenhouse was elected president on January 2, 1794,[49] there is some doubt as to whether he ever attended any meetings or was even a member.[50] His latest biographer[51] says he accepted the presidency. But if he did so, he quickly changed his mind, for in a letter of January 16, 1794, he refused the office because he did not expect to attend any of the society's meetings.[52] He was, however, in sympathy with its views. Some men, apparently, were elected to the club without their knowledge,[53] and Rittenhouse, then Director of the United States Mint, may have been one of them. This was certainly true of Charles Biddle, who was elected to the vice-presidency, also on January 2, 1794.[54]

The Federalists' reaction to the formation of the two Philadelphia societies was one of outraged indignation. One look at the membership roster of the Pennsylvania Democratic Society, however, should have convinced them that no plots subversive to government or injurious to property would be contrived in the opprobriously termed "demoniacal" societies. It may have been unwisely premature to publicize the mooted word "democratic," but certainly these were not dangerous radicals who sought to demolish the established political and economical norms. Rather was the opposite true. All the above named individuals were "sound" business or professional men. Leib, Rush, Logan and Hutchinson were physicians; Dallas was a lawyer and land speculator; McClenachan, Israel, Morgan and Swanwick were businessmen. Swanwick, indeed, was one of Philadelphia's richest merchants.

Why did Swanwick become a member of the Democratic Society? The answer to this question has value not only from the standpoint of one individual, but from that of other businessmen who affiliated themselves with the dynamic organization. It seems quite probable that he joined the club for business reasons—to use it in protest against British interference with American commerce and against any national legislation which would hinder the growth of American industry.

By way of explanation, it may be profitable to look ahead for a moment to his legislative career. While serving in the Fourth and Fifth Congresses, the little poet-merchant had many opportunities to utilize his wide business experience. There, his strong commercial sympathies found ample outlet in the work of the Committee of Commerce and Manufactures, of which he was chairman. His record clearly indicated a solicitude for the welfare of the American seaman,[55] a desire to strengthen the American navy,[56] and a willingness to procure government revenues by taxing land, dwellings and slaves instead of manufactured articles.[57] There is no doubt that he preferred direct taxes to those of the excise variety. In the light of his commercial predilections the above suggested motive for Swanwick's affiliation with the club is made even more credible by the fact that he joined shortly after it committed itself on current economic issues. On April 10, 1794, the society, in strongly worded resolutions, condemned Britain, our "implacable and unprincipled enemy" for waging "insidious and cowardly" naval war upon the United States.[58] Americans were urged to buy home products in order to encourage native manufactures and all *states* were asked to exclude British goods. Swanwick could certainly subscribe to those sentiments. Also, he may have regarded as a further inducement the society's anti-excise resolution on May 8, a protest against a tax on manufactured articles that was under consideration in Congress. Such a levy, said the resolution, would injure "infant manufactures" and impoverish the country.[59]

Significantly enough, on the same day the society declared for infant industries, a group of manufacturers met in Philadelphia and approved a strikingly similar resolution. The manufacturers had convened in response to a call put out by the Philadelphia "Tobacconists and Sugar Refiners."[60] It is impossible to believe that the coincidence of the two events was accidental.

As a matter of fact the society's resolution was perfectly timed. By thus offering itself as a propaganda instrument for the manufacturing interests, destined to become more and more influential, it increased its own membership and prestige. Shortly thereafter Swanwick became a member. So did Jacob Morgan, president of the manufacturers' meeting on May 8, 1794. Later, he was to become a director of the Bank of Pennsylvania and a force in Pennsylvania politics. The society had indeed become popular. During the two weeks following the appearance of its "infant industries" resolution, it obtained forty-three new members. The acquisition of a rich and successful man like Swanwick was a bright cockade in the society's cap. Others were sure to follow his lead, and many did so.

It is little wonder that the Federalists regarded the Pennsylvania Democratic Society with apprehension. Instead of dissolving after the gubernatorial election of 1793, as Jefferson had predicted, it was growing stronger. More alarming still, the club idea had spread, and groups were springing up in other parts of the country. In western Pennsylvania alone, three clubs had come into existence: the Mingo Creek Society, the Republican Society of the Yough and the Democratic Society in Washington. With the area already disturbed over the whiskey tax of 1791, the new societies were an additional source of uneasiness for the administration.

Near at hand the Pennsylvania Democratic Society was an especially large thorn in the administration's side. Almost every governmental suggestion produced an objection, every action brought an adverse reaction. The administration's fiscal policy would bring ruin, said the society, and its profession of neutrality in the European conflict was at least questionable. Government attempts to appease England and prevent our entrance into the war against her were described as "temporizing and pusilanimous." Such conduct would "bring contempt, disgrace and perhaps chains upon us."[61] Further, highly-placed individuals were being induced by the societies to voice opinions adverse to the administration.

At an outing on May 1, 1794, jointly sponsored by the two Philadelphia democratic clubs, a large crowd assembled at Israel Israel's country estate. There Governor Mifflin was heard to propose "Peace, on their own terms, to the French Republic."[62] Another toast was aimed directly at Washington and his administration: "Reason:—may it successfully counteract the baneful effects of Executive influence, expose the insidious acts of Judicial sophistry, and preserve inviolate the purity of legislation."⁶³ The eight hundred men in attendance had gathered to celebrate the success of the French Republic. At the gathering was Mifflin, the French Minister Fauchet, and several officials of the Federal and State governments. Peter Muhlenberg had helped to prepare the toasts.

The Anglophobic and Francophile sentiments that emanated from the Democratic Societies must have been very embarrassing to a professedly neutral government. This was particularly true at a time when the administration was trying to adjust its differences with the British. But of even greater concern was the fact that the societies had come into existence at all.

Factions were considered dangerous to national unity, and they were often criticized by Federalists and Republicans alike. Both sides, however, accused each other of encouraging partisan groups. Undoubtedly the Democratic Societies played an important role in creating party divisions. They publicized issues so forcefully that men were almost obliged to choose sides. In the opinion of Eugene P. Link, the historian who has delved most extensively into the work of these organizations, they "laid the groundwork for the Republican party."⁶⁴

That the Federalists recognized them as a threat to the administration is fully demonstrated by Hamilton's attitude and the repeated criticism in the Federalist press. Washington at last took public notice of the societies when he accused them in November, 1794, of fomenting the Whiskey Rebellion. Shallowly rooted, only embryonically organized and loosely coordinated one with the other, it was a blow from which they could not recover. Since Washington's denunciation was a result of the whiskey disturbance, the story of their decline in Pennsylvania properly belongs in the chapter devoted to that occurrence.

Jay's Treaty

Undoubtedly one of the strongest motivating factors behind the pro-French sentiment and the rise of the democratic clubs in Pennsylvania was a hatred for Britain. As a matter of fact, one is led to believe that dislike for that country was greater and more prevalent than love for France. This would apply especially after Americans heard of the execution of Louis XVI and the inception of the Reign of Terror. These events alienated many who abhorred violent changes in government. Aside from the enduring resentments born of the war for independence, Americans had many reasons to dislike and fear the British who, thought many, had never given up the idea of reacquiring the lost colonies. The main reasons were concerned primarily with freedom of trade and British retention of fortified places on American soil.

British trade policies were a bitter disappointment to the many Americans who had hoped that independence would bring rich commercial rewards. Anticipating a lucrative interchange of commodities with the British West Indies they were soon dismayed to find themselves virtually excluded from that trade by restrictive parliamentary measures. By an Act of 1788, a summary of previous acts already in force, only British ships could transport tobacco, naval stores and provisions to his majesty's possessions in the West Indies. Trade with Canada was also restricted to British vessels, and no American goods could be imported into that area except during specified times of emergency.[65] Because of these restrictions American traders were sorely harassed during the first ten years of independence. Seeking an outlet, they began to develop a thriving commerce with France and her possessions.

But this French trade was short lived. Determined to take drastic measures in her war with the French Republic, Britain, by an Order in Council on November 6, 1793, requested her naval commanders to seize all ships carrying goods to or from the French colonies. This had disastrous results for American shippers. Before the order was modified in the following year, it had ruined trade between the United States and the West Indies. The effect produced in the United States was sensational, and the administration was besieged with demands for relief and retaliation.[66]

Another great source of irritation was Britain's reluctance to give up several military posts on the northwest frontier. She had not evacuated the forts despite a promise made to the American Peace Commissioners at Paris in 1783. Consequently, Americans had to suffer the humiliating presence of a defeated nation's troops on American soil.

With the above problems weighing heavily upon his mind, Washington decided to submit them to negotiation with the British government in an effort to prevent an open break between the two countries. Accordingly, he sent Chief Justice John Jay to England on May 12, 1794, with the instructions to obtain a treaty which would secure, among other items, the evacuation of the northwest posts, compensation for shipping losses, and the right to trade with the British West Indies.

As it turned out, Jay's selection was not fortunate. He may have been a poor bargainer, or the disadvantages under which he labored may have been insurmountable—but whatever the reason for his poor showing the treaty he brought back was bad. By its terms England agreed to evacuate the northwest posts by June, 1796, submit to arbitration the disputes on boundaries, debts and shipping losses, and allow trade with the East Indies on certain conditions. But admittance to the West Indian trade was permitted only to American ships of seventy tons burden—and even this minor concession was hedged about with annoying restrictions.[67] No mention was made of reimbursement for slaves carried off during the Revolution or of British impressment of American sailors.

After the Senate had ratified the Treaty by a very close vote in June, 1795, Benjamin Bache secured a copy of the document and published it in the *Aurora*, on July 1. The anger it provoked in Pennsylvania and in Philadelphia, especially, was hotter than the temperature, and that was 91° in the shade. The Republicans pounced upon it with calculated fury. For here, in their opinion, was a perfect example of the Anglophilic bias of the administration, of its dislike for France, of its indifference to American international rights, and of its willingness to pay any price for peace. It was a concrete example of their predictions come true. If French Revolutionary excesses had dampened the republican ardor of some Americans, if the Whiskey Rebellion had undermined the democratic society movement, then here at last was a positive issue that could be fully exploited in a general appeal. And better yet it was an appeal to which many injured Federalists would lend a sympathetic ear. It was indeed an instrument that fitted neatly into their hands, and they took full advantage of the situation.

At a Philadelphia meeting on July 23, 1795, a committee composed of Dallas, McClenachan, Swanwick, McKean and other leading Republicans was appointed to memorialize Washington in severe disapproval of the Treaty.[68] Two days later, an even larger crowd, after listening to the fervid oratory of McClenachan, spilled out of the State House Yard and attacked the residence of William Bingham and the British Minister, George Hammond. Philadelphia was indeed overwrought.

But despite the febrile protest in Pennsylvania and the nation generally, Washington signed Jay's Treaty on August 14, 1795. When Bache heard of the President's action, he could not believe it was true.[69] But when the rumor was shortly confirmed, the columns of his gazette fairly blazed with protest. Bitter and unrelenting were his attacks, and they continued on through the winter and the following summer: the Treaty had widened the breach between the "aristocrats" and republicans,⁷⁰ Washington should be impeached for not taking the advice of the Senate in making the Treaty,⁷¹ it had made a war with France possible and probably created such a strong British influence in the country that only a second revolution could eradicate it.⁷² So spoke the powerful *Aurora*. With Bache's paper serving as their most effective publicizing agent, the Philadelphia Republicans prepared to use the Treaty issue with telling effect in the elections of 1795 and 1796.

CHAPTER VI

WHISKEY AND POLITICS

AFTER DEVELOPING his funding and assumption plans, Alexander Hamilton sought some means to increase governmental income. The measure eventually proposed was an excise tax. Never a popular revenue-raising device, the proposal met with considerable opposition in the national legislature. When the House of Representatives passed an excise bill on January 27, 1791, by a vote of thirty-five to twenty-one, the Pennsylvania delegation divided three to three.[1] The only Pennsylvanians who spoke for the bill were George Clymer and Thomas Fitzsimons. None spoke against it.

Two years before the bill became law, at least one Pennsylvanian had seen it coming. While Congress was debating a tariff measure in June, 1789, Senator Maclay suspected a design on the part of some men (including his colleague Morris) to lower tariff rates to such a point that a revenue deficiency would necessitate an excise.[2]

When the excise law was in its final stages in February, 1791, prophet Maclay, already justified in one prediction, made some others. He told the Senate that Pennsylvania's excise laws had been totally ineffective and that the Assembly "had been obliged to wink" at their violation in the western counties. Moreover, the United States would be able to enforce this Pandora's box, this "most execrable system" only by means of "a permanent military force."[3]

Maclay was not speaking for himself alone. While Congress was wrangling over the troublesome bill, the lower house of the Pennsylvania legislature, in resolutions of January 22, 1791, requested its United States Senators to "oppose any part of the excise bill . . . which shall militate against the just rights and liberties of the people."[4] Although the lower house passed its resolutions by a vote of forty-one to eighteen, the upper house refused to concur by one vote. This vote was not an expression of party opinion, said Brackenridge, for many of the strongest Federalists favored the resolution.[5] Eight months after Congress passed the excise law, the Pennsylvania legislature, responding to a disapproval of the measure which had already manifested itself, repealed all its own excise taxes on spirituous liquors.[6]

The national excise law, providing for the collection of a tax on whiskey, was a source of immediate dissatisfaction in western Pennsylvania.

There whiskey was one of the most readily marketable of all the farmers' products. The transportation of grain to distant markets was a long and expensive operation, but when corn was turned into spirits it could easily be handled. A uniform tax, aside from reducing profits, operated with unequal severity on the westerners: with whiskey worth say fifty cents west of the Alleghenies and twice that much on the eastern coast, a uniform tax would be twice as heavy in the west as in the east.[7]

Adverse reaction to the measure was immediate in the west, and the most important meeting to discuss the problem was held on September 7, 1791, at Pittsburgh, with representatives from the four western counties in attendance. In addition to deploring governmental tendencies in general, they laid special stress on the excise. It was declared to be an infringement on liberty of action, expensive and partial in operation, similar to the action of monarchial countries, and discouraging to agriculture. Further, it had been passed "to gratify men in their ambitious and interested measures."[8]

The following year the westerners became even more determined in their opposition.[9] At a Pittsburgh meeting on August 21, 1792,[10] attended by John Smilie, Albert Gallatin, David Bradford, James Marshall and many others, it was resolved that the enforcement of the excise law constituted a danger to civil rights and would bring ruin to the western country. Men who accepted an excise post were contemptible and "unworthy of our friendship." A remonstrance to Congress, which Gallatin helped to write, requested repeal of the obnoxious law.[11]

In the same month some rioters broke into a revenue collection office, tore down an excise notice and filled the "sign of the President's head" with bullet holes.[12]

Washington was not inclined to let such disorders and meetings pass without notice. In a proclamation of September 15, 1792, drafted by Hamilton, he warned all people concerned against obstruction of the law on pain of strict punishment. At the time he had no wish to preserve order by the use of troops except as a last resort.[13] To Hamilton the idea of the employment of the military to collect impost duties was to be regarded only "as a figure of rhetoric."[14]

The President's proclamation, along with a letter, was sent to the Governors of North and South Carolina, where disturbances had also occurred, and to Governor Mifflin.[15] In reply the latter, after citing the arrest and correction of rioters in Chester and Allegheny counties, assured Washington that every legal effort would be made to preserve the peace in Pennsylvania.[16] To effect this he alerted the judges of the common pleas and Supreme Court to the situation, especially emphasizing the duty of grand juries to examine offenses to which the proclamation referred. He also requested the judges to report carefully on every prosecution entered against whiskey rioters.

To ascertain public opinion in the affected areas, Mifflin requested information from persons who were interested in public reactions. William Findley, who received a letter of inquiry from the Governor, gave a candid report. There had been few instances of riotous opposition in his section, he said, and when disturbers of the peace had been tried in State courts they had been punished with "sufficient severity." Federal courts would not be interrupted unless attempts were made to transport accused persons out of their proper counties for trial. Should that be tried, he would "not undertake for the consequences." Findley did not expect the citizens to support the law's enforcement," "and however extraordinary this opinion may appear, I can assure you Sir, the earliest and most zealous friends to the government have generally been among those who have taken a lead from the beginning in expressing their disapprobation of the excise." From the first he had opposed the tax, and he would continue to do so in "a regular and orderly channel." It would therefore be "lost labour" for him to advise the people to continue to operate their stills and to pay the tax.[17]

Findley's view of the situation, although indeed gloomy, was no less so than that of the State's supervisor for excise collection, George Clymer. At the end of the year he concluded that the excise law had failed in Pennsylvania because of western opposition, and of the small fruit crop of the preceding year from which much liquor was ordinarily distilled. He was required to make a report to Hamilton on the tax collections in Pennsylvania and he found it a disagreeable task: Pennsylvania would make a poorer showing than any other state. When that fact was discovered, he feared "the sentiments that will be excited." To make his reportorial task less disagreeable, he asked General Edward Hand, a district excise surveyor, for additional reasons as to why Pennsylvania had performed so badly.[18]

When Mifflin addressed the legislature in December, he discussed the excise disturbances and the President's proclamation, which he thought the legislators would "peruse with pain." He had cooperated with the President in an effort to discharge the State's obligations to the Federal government, and although the spheres of jurisdiction in which the two operated were distinct, they were not adverse. Because of the Indian threat to the frontiers, suppression of domestic troubles was imperative. And since the Federal government had extended its jurisdiction there, it was duty bound to afford protection. The Governor was thus clear and rather adroit: if the national administration wished to try Pennsylvanians in Federal courts on excise charges, it must also protect the region against Indians. He was not saddling the national government with the full burden of protection however, for the legislature in its last session had shown its "liberality" by preparing to cooperate with national forces.[19] As to the seriousness of resistance in Pennsylvania to the excise, the Governor reported but few "instances of outrage," and most of the offenders had been prosecuted.[20]

For almost a year and a half after Washington's proclamation, there was a definite lull in opposition. But in the summer of 1794 new and even more serious outbreaks occurred in western Pennsylvania. Before outlining the July troubles in Allegheny County it may be well to summarize the general body of western protest which culminated in the series of events known as the Whiskey Insurrection. It is true that the disaffected westerner disapproved of the excise principle, that he feared a deprivation of his liberty, that he detested most of the tax collection officials and that he protested strenuously against trial in a distant Federal court. All those aspects of the law were sources of the irritation and anger which culminated in a number of riots and mass meetings in 1794. But the disturbances themselves were also symptomatic of a brooding discontent which began almost with the inception of the national government.

From the very first the concentration of large powers in a strong central government was suspected, and when Hamilton's funding and assumption plans were given the force of law many people thought they descried dangerous monarchical tendencies.[21] Many complained that the reward of victory against England was being given to the eastern wealthy classes to the exclusion of large numbers who had fought valiantly in the cause.[22] When the westerner wanted to buy land, he was often forced to deal with a speculator who owned thousands of acres on which he paid little or no tax. The government, over-solicitous of the large holder, permitted him to retain lands for an excessive profit.[23] The westerner also claimed that the government viewed with apparent unconcern the strictures placed on Mississippi navigation by the Spanish. Equally dilatory was the administration in its handling of the Indian menace which threatened his very existence at a time when he was plagued with busy officialdom intent on prying into his affairs to collect an unfair tax. He wanted the troublesome question of the frontier military posts cleared up.[24] He deplored the high interest of the public debt, the inequities of the funding system, exorbitant official salaries, and the National Bank law which permitted the management of millions of dollars by a few persons who might influence national officials "to evade the Constitution."[25] He resented the superior attitude of some easterners who looked with disdain on his humble abode and way of life, his manners and reputed lawlessness. He lived a hard and dangerous life on the fringe of civilization, beset by a multitude of ills. Now the excise brought them all to a head. He was ready to protest and he did so—vigorously.

In the summer of 1794, the succession of irritations attendant upon excise enforcement reached a crisis. It occurred when demands were made upon men who had defaulted in still registration to appear before a Federal court in Philadelphia. This requirement had always met with strenuous objection because of the time and expense involved. Congress responded to the protest by passing an act on June 5, 1794, which allowed State courts to hear cases arising from excise infractions.[26] But more than a month after its passage, John Neville, excise inspector in Allegheny County, and United States Marshal David Lenox served writs which demanded appearance before a Federal court in Philadelphia. In retaliation, an armed mob attacked Neville's house at Bower Hill on July 17, 1794, and burned it to the ground. One of the attackers, a Captain James MacFarland, was killed.[27] This was the most serious episode of the insurrection.

Shortly thereafter, David Bradford, James Marshall, John Canon and other active anti-excise leaders issued a circular calling for an armed meeting at Braddock's Field on August 1. The mails had been intercepted and secrets discovered that were "hostile to our interests. Here, Sir," said the exciting circular, "is an expedition proposed in which you will have an opportunity of displaying your military talents and of rendering service to your country."[28]

A large body of men met on the appointed day, listened to fervid speeches and discussed the situation. Then they all marched through Pittsburgh and dispersed. John Wilkins, brigadier general of militia in Allegheny County, thought there were seven or eight thousand men in the line of march.[29] The people of Pittsburgh expected the town to be burned. But their fears were groundless.

Official and unofficial observers who reported to State and national authorities took an alarming view of conditions in the west. General John Gibson was sure that a civil war was under way.[30] General John Wilkins shared a somewhat similar opinion and stated that the insurrectionists were so "respectable and powerfull [a] combination" that if government troops were sent against them very serious consequences would result.[31] He advised moderate measures on the part of the government, such as the sending of commissioners. When Dallas asked Wilkins to bring the rioters to justice, the general said that if he executed such orders his own property would be destroyed.[32]

H. H. Brackenridge thought that the excise law could not be enforced, and that if troops were sent over the mountain the middle counties would contest their passage westward. "Should an attempt be made to suppress these people," he predicted, "I am afraid the question will not be, whether you will march to Pittsburgh, but whether they will march to Philadelphia. . . ." Brackenridge, like Wilkins, also advised moderate measures. If troops were sent out, the disaffected, in self-defense, would organize "the three Virginia counties and those of Pennsylvania to the westward" into a new government. If the government did not resort to military force, such important questions as the navigation of the Mississippi and the ownership of the "western posts" might be favorably settled before Congress met. He proposed that the excise law be suspended as long as the Indian wars lasted.[33]

As soon as the State and national authorities heard about the Bower Hill incident, steps were taken to meet the situation. The news reached Philadelphia while Mifflin was out of town, so Dallas, acting in his stead, dispatched instructions to Attorney General Jared Ingersoll, judges of the court of common pleas, justices of the peace, sheriffs and other officers. He insisted that the rioters be found and brought to justice.[34] Dallas did not mention the possible use of militia.

Washington, much perturbed at the western riots, first placed all the pertinent documents he had received in the hands of Associate Supreme Court Justice James Wilson, with the request that he determine whether or not the courts were adequate to the exigencies of the situation. Then, before receiving Wilson's report, he invited the leading Pennsylvania officials to a discussion.

At the conference, held on August 2, 1794, the United States was represented by Washington, the Secretaries of State, War and Treasury, and the Attorney General. Appearing for Pennsylvania were Mifflin, Chief Justice McKean, Attorney General Jared Ingersoll and

Dallas. Washington began by stating that any action the Federal government took would depend on Wilson's report. Since that would not be delivered for some time, could not the State of Pennsylvania institute some "preliminary measures?"[35] Edmund Randolph, Secretary of State, made the same suggestion. To these proposals the wary Pennsylvanians made no comment. Apparently they were in doubt as to just what the suggested "preliminary measures" would involve. The United States Attorney General soon made that point clear, however, when he mentioned a Pennsylvania law of 1783, which authorized the use of militia in cases of emergency. To this Dallas, always well informed and resourceful, replied that it was his opinion that the act referred to had been repealed. Then, when Washington declared his intention of proceeding against the rioters, McKean had an answer to that: he was of the definite opinion "that the judiciary power was equal to the task of quelling and punishing the riots, and that the employment of a military force, at this period, would be as bad as anything that the Rioters had done—equally unconstitutional and illegal."[36] That ended the conference. The Pennsylvania authorities had refused to employ the militia and the State's Chief Justice had denied the legal right of the national government to do so.

Three days later, Mifflin, in the first of a series of letters to Washington, reaffirmed the stand taken at the conference and outlined the methods by which Pennsylvania intended to deal with the western disturbances.

In his opinion the Pennsylvania judiciary was still able to quell the disturbance, but should it become apparent that it was incompetent to do so, then he would cooperate vigorously "with the whole force which the Constitution and laws of the state entrust to me."[37] At present, however, circumstances dictated lenient methods. If Pennsylvanians were asked to fight each other without understanding the necessity for it, he could not assure their willingness to obey orders. A call to arms might increase existing opposition and alienate those peaceably opposed to the law. Finally, since there was reason to suspect that the British government was attempting to seduce the westerners away from their duty, severe measures might force them to ask for British protection.

He then told Washington of his plans to restore order. He would issue a proclamation to punish offenders, send three commissioners westward to reason with the disaffected persons and pledge forgiveness of past transgressions in return for a promise of submission, and call the legislature in special session if the above measures proved abortive. He closed by promising full support to Washington in "whatever duty you may impose in pursuance of your constitutional and legal powers."[38]

On August 4, 1794, one day before Mifflin sent his letter, Associate Justice Wilson reported to Washington that in his opinion the groups opposing the laws of the United States in Washington and Allegheny counties were too powerful to be dealt with by the marshal or by ordinary judicial proceedings.[39] Washington could now legally employ troops, for according to a law of 1792 the militia could not be called out until an associate justice or district judge had certified to the inadequacy of the courts to stem opposition to United States law.[40]

Although Mifflin had declared his willingness to cooperate, the President, if he gave credence to a report made by Hamilton on August 5, 1794, had reason to be dubious of the effectiveness of the cooperation Mifflin could command from the western peace officers. For Hamilton, in a long letter on excise disturbances, severely censured State officials in western Pennsylvania. They were, in his opinion, either "hostile or lukewarm" to the execution of the excise laws, and their unfriendly influence was the greatest obstacle the Federal officers had to face. The real object of the men in opposition was repeal of the excise law, and along with their reluctance to pay taxes "some persons of influence [wished] to embarass the Government." So Hamilton believed.[41]

Thus strengthened by reports from both Wilson and Hamilton, Washington, through Edmund Randolph, replied to Mifflin on August 7, 1794. Now resolved to take a firm hand, he set forth the administration's intention in a sharp and pointed manner that could not be misunderstood. The plan Mifflin suggested in his letter of August 5, 1794, "seems to have contemplated Pennsylvania in a light too separate and unconnected." Further, it would too long delay obedience to the law. His method of dealing with the insurrectionists would have been acceptable if there were no Federal government in existence, if national laws had not been violated for over three years, if excise officers had not been badly treated and if Wilson had not declared that ordinary judicial proceedings could no longer cope with the situation. When Mifflin feared the evil consequences of coercive measures, Washington concluded that the Governor disapproved of the administration's conduct. Nevertheless, the President expected the full cooperation of the Pennsylvania militia when called for and without any evidence of "a *passive* obedience to the *mandates* of government."[42]

When the Governor replied to Washington on August 12, 1794, he, too, went directly to the point. Recognizing Pennsylvania's subjection to national jurisdiction, he flatly denied that he contemplated "the state in a light too separate and unconnected."[43] At the conference on August 4, 1794, declared Mifflin, Washington had every intention to use militia, and when it was suggested that Pennsylvania take the initiative in calling troops (by authority of an act that had been repealed), such duplicate action would have resulted in confusion and useless expense. Further, Congress had given Washington guidance to handle such situations through the enactment of a positive law, whereas Mifflin, on the other hand, had no suitable legislation to direct his steps. He had perforce to act entirely on his own judgment. Hence his reluctance to use force until the State's judiciary had been fully tried. In his letter of August 5, 1794, he had, Mifflin said, cautiously excluded from view, "the case of the United States, whose Judiciary authority had in your opinion, proved inadequate to the execution of the laws and the preservation of order."[44]

By implication then, the national courts had failed, but those of the State at that time were still adequate. In such fashion did the Governor justify his confidence in the cooperativeness of the State officials in western Pennsylvania. But in that connection he must have suffered a rude shock indeed when he read Hamilton's August 5 report to Washington, in which the Secretary of the Treasury accused the officials in question of obstructing justice instead of aiding it. In a letter to Washington on August 22, 1794, he denied Hamilton's charges and asked for the evidence on which they were based so that he might punish the guilty officers. Without such evidence, he could no nothing at present, for the accusation was so "indiscriminate that those citizens who may be involved in its obloquy, do not enjoy a fair opportunity for defense, nor does the Government possess the means to discover the proper objects for its indignation and censure."[45]

In the above epistolary exchange, Mifflin had succeeded fairly well in justifying his determination to avoid using Pennsylvania militiamen to enforce a national law. If Pennsylvanians were to be mobilized to fight other Pennsylvanians, the call to arms would not be given by Mifflin without specific legislative sanction. He was adamant on that point. But if the Federal government chose to call troops, Mifflin would cooperate faithfully.[46]

While the two executives, national and State, were exchanging views on the functions and authority of their respective governments, Washington was taking decisive steps to bring the western disturbances to an end. Backed by Wilson's judgment that the courts had failed and by Hamilton's opinion (a reversal of his opinion of 1792)[47] that force should be used, the President had resolved on the employment of troops, but only as a last resort. Hamilton advised the calling of a body of militia large enough to discourage opposition and prevent general bloodshed.[48] He thought 12,000 men would be sufficient.

Accordingly, on August 7, 1794, Washington issued a proclamation in which he recapitulated the turbulence in western Pennsylvania, stated the need for forceful measures and declared his intention to call out the militia. All "insurgents" were commanded to "disperse" by September 1, 1794.[49]

On the same day Henry Knox, Secretary of War, sent a copy of the proclamation to Mifflin along with a request for 5,200 militiamen. The militia units were to be organized and equipped, ready "to march at a moment's warning." Requisitions for additional troops were also to be made on New Jersey, Maryland and Virginia to a total, including Pennsylvania's, of 12,950 men.[50]

Mifflin responded with alacrity. On the day he received the President's proclamation, he issued two of his own. The first announced his determination to support the President in punishing all unlawful combinations. In the second he asked the legislature to convene on September 1, 1794, to enact legislation suitable to the emergency.[51] On the following day he directed Adjutant General Josiah Harmar to order Pennsylvania's quota of militia into service.[52]

Although the whiskey rioters had been ordered to disperse by September 1, under threat of a militia call, Washington, in a final effort to restore peace without launching a military campaign, decided to send three commissioners westward with orders to confer with the disaffected persons. For this delicate mission he selected William Bradford, United States Attorney General, James Ross, Senator from Pennsylvania, and Jasper Yeates, Associate Justice of the Pennsylvania Supreme Court.[53]

The commissioners were instructed to inform the insurgents that Washington was reluctant to use force, but that he would enforce the excise law by that means if necessary. He would also grant amnesty, forget past acts and uncollected duties if the recalcitrants would guarantee compliance with the law during the year 1794. He refused to commit himself as to repeal, for that was the responsibility of Congress. On the critical question of trial in State or Federal courts,

Washington gave assurance that when convenient to the United States, Pennsylvania courts would be used if it appeared certain that they would not be frustrated by local opposition.[54]

Mifflin, who had decided to appoint State commissioners on August 5, 1794,[55] selected two men on the following day to go west with those named by Washington. Through his appointees, Thomas McKean and General William Irvine, Mifflin promised complete pardon for past transgressions if the westerners would guarantee future submission to the authorities.[56]

The commissioners were appointed by Mifflin and Washington in the knowledge that some inhabitants of the western counties had planned to hold a large meeting at Parkinson's Ferry on August 14, 1794.[57] Advised to hurry westward to confer with the leaders of that meeting, the commissioners lost no time in setting out.

At the Parkinson's Ferry meeting, attended by representatives from the counties of Westmoreland, Fayette, Allegheny, Washington, part of Bedford and Ohio County in Virginia, a committee was appointed to talk with the commissioners and report the result to a standing committee. The United States commissioners were informed of the meeting and they were so impressed with the determination of the men present that even before meeting with the conferees they reported to Randolph that conciliatory measures would be unavailing. Nothing less than the "physical strength of the nation" could enforce the law in western Pennsylvania.[58]

This was a gloomy opinion, but upon spending several days in the area the commissioners did not see fit to alter it. After discussing matters with two groups of conferees, appointed by meetings at Parkinson's Ferry and Redstone Old Fort, they decided that a satisfactory settlement could not be reached. As a result of this discouraging conclusion they left for Philadelphia on September 3, 1794.

Washington then decided to use force.

On September 9, 1794, he ordered Mifflin, through Hamilton, to assemble immediately the Pennsylvania militia. All western news was bad, said Hamilton, and since a peaceful settlement was unlikely and the military season was fast disappearing, the President thought the time for action was at hand.[59] Although Washington expected to meet "but a feeble opposition"[60] in the west, he did not decrease the original number of troops asked for in his letter to the Governor on August 7, 1794.

Now that troops were to be mobilized, Pennsylvania was unprepared to meet her full quota. Although Mifflin had ordered Harmar to organize the militia for instant movement one day after Washington's notification on August 7, 1794, he had allowed twenty days to elapse before inquiring into the progress of organization. Harmar himself had not followed up his organization order until prompted to do so by Mifflin on August 27, 1794.

So lax had been the brigade officers and so unresponsive were the militiamen themselves that when the call came on September 9, 1794, Mifflin had to admit that the State had failed to meet its quota. To supply the deficiency he asked for volunteers. In an address to the Philadelphia militia, he told the officers that unless they were willing to serve they should resign their commissions immediately.[61] Up to that time no returns had been submitted by the counties of Lancaster, Berks, York, Franklin, Northampton and the city of Philadelphia. Reports already received from Bucks, Montgomery, Chester, Delaware and Dauphin indicated that the officers in charge had very little hope of securing their quotas. In Bucks, the men objected to the poor pay; in Chester, militia officers were resigning; and from Dauphin came the news that the citizens were unwilling to march against fellow Pennsylvanians.[62]

That Mifflin was mortified and embarrassed by the dilatory militia he made quite evident. With almost frantic zeal he set off on a tour of several counties to inspire, coax and shame the reluctant militiamen into service. The government must stop "the tyranny that is attempted to be established by a few over the many," said the Governor at Lancaster. The organization of a standing army, feared by many, would be made unnecessary if the citizens would aid in suppressing the "seditious," "turbulent" and "treacherous" rebels in western Pennsylvania. "Will you save your Constitution?" he pleaded. "Will you defend your laws? Will you assist to rescue from anarchy, as you did from despotism, the freedom and Independence of America?"[63]

Mifflin thought that the unwillingness of the militia to serve was caused by a generally held suspicion that the insurgents had not been given an opportunity to "listen to reason." If the conciliatory efforts already made by the government to restore order were explained, he felt sure that the men would enroll with alacrity. To deliver such an explanation, he told the legislature, was his chief motive in making a tour of the counties.[64]

The Governor was an eloquent and persuasive speaker, and he was definitely alarmed and worried. Just a month before he and Dallas had opposed the calling of troops, and should Pennsylvania now fail to meet her obligations, the general knowledge of that opposition would do Mifflin no good politically. That fact could have been easily emphasized by his enemies, merely by pointing out that the governors of the other states from whom Washington had requisitioned troops were having little trouble in meeting their quotas.

With the legislature, which met according to request on September 1, 1794, Mifflin had no trouble. He explained that although he was once reluctant to use troops it was now necessary to do so, and he asked for the requisite legislation. The Assembly responded with a law on September 19, 1794, which authorized the Governor to draft for four month's service the number of militia requested by Washington and provided $120,000. for campaign expenses.[65]

When the people in western Pennsylvania learned that Washington had decided to send an army over the mountains, they experienced a decided change in attitude. In the several meetings that were held to reconsider their former position, the old incendiary oratory and belligerence were missing. A resolution to preserve peace and order was adopted at a Uniontown meeting of townships on September 17, 1794. At Pittsburgh, ten days later, a huge gathering decided that the western area was so orderly that military force would be unnecessary. At Parkinson's Ferry on October 2, 1794, several "delegates of Townships" met and declared that the people were now willing to obey the law. William Findley and David Redick, were delegated to report their peaceful resolutions to Washington "and detail such circumstances as may enable the President to judge whether an armed force be now necessary to support the civil authority in those counties."[66] At a final meeting on October 24, 1794, also at Parkinson's Ferry, representatives from all four western counties resolved that the law would be obeyed, and the representatives themselves promised to help capture any offenders.

Findley, H. H. Brackenridge and James Ross, all vitally concerned with public opinion and competent to evaluate it, were interested in two very important questions: were the westerners peacefully disposed (after Washington's proclamation of September 9), and was it necessary to dispatch troops to the troubled area?

Findley, who had attended some of the excise meetings but insisted that he was "no member," did not believe that the majority of the people were disgruntled.[67] By September 16, 1794, he noticed signs of returning order and a disposition everywhere, "except about the Monongahelea," to discuss all subjects but the excise law. "The salaries of office land jobbing and every description of oppression that they have heard named is brought into account, and those who are now turbulent with us with a few exceptions are the uninformed Germans. . . ."[68]

For predicting that the militia would march if called upon, Findley was threatened with "tarring and feathering." With regret, he told William Bradford that it was necessary to send troops into the western counties. For if they did not appear, "many here would never believe that they could have been brought." He thought "a very small force" would be sufficient, for the original intention of meeting the incoming army on the mountains had been abandoned.[69]

In Brackenridge's opinion the crisis passed when the United States commissioners had stated their proposals. The "pacific" measures taken by the government had broken the spirit of the insurrection, and if troops came they would "meet with nothing considerable to oppose them."[70]

James Ross also credited the commissioners with curbing the insurrection. But although they had severed the "Heads of the Hydra," he hoped that the army would "bury this pestiferous monster" when it arrived. And arrive it must, for without its presence "all will be lost" and a new rebellion would occur "more dangerous than the first & convince all the refractory that the arm of the United States was unable to reach them."[71] He hoped that "no representation will retard or stop this necessary measure."[72] It is evident that Ross had heard of the steps taken at Parkinson's Ferry on October 2, 1794, to stop the army's march by sending Findley and Redick to talk with Washington. Apparently Ross felt that the guilty would be punished only if the army arrived to do it.

If there was little likelihood that the army would be opposed, a possibility admitted by the above three men and Washington himself, the President, nevertheless, went ahead with his plans to send it over the mountains. After receiving Washington's order of September 9, 1794, the Governors of Pennsylvania, New Jersey and Virginia organized their quotas and moved toward Carlisle, the point of rendezvous. As they traveled, the militia looted, burned fences, and killed two civilians.[73]

On October 4, 1794, Washington arrived in Carlisle, where he viewed the troops and appointed Governor Lee as commander of the expedition with Governors Mifflin and Howell in the second and third positions of command. There he met Findley and Redick on their mission to obtain a cancellation of the marching orders.[74] Washington told them that he would pursue his original intention to convince the insurgents that they could not violate the laws with impunity. He thought the westerners were "scared."[75]

As the huge army of approximately 15,000 troops marched westward, Washington accompanied it as far as Bedford.[76] Then he returned to Philadelphia to be near Congress. When the army reached Parkinson's Ferry, Lee issued a proclamation on November 8, 1794, in which he scolded the insurgents and asked the "well-disposed" to take "an oath to support the Constitution and obey the laws."[77] Having met no resistance whatever, Lee rounded up all the suspects on November 13, 1794, and four days later issued orders to return eastward. But before leaving, Lee recruited an occupation force, many of whose members were obtained "from the very inhabitants against whom the larger body had marched but a few weeks before."[78]

The general apprehension of suspects on November 13, had been conducted in a rough manner. Twenty of those caught in the net were placed under guard and marched to Philadelphia where some were released on bail and others detained for months. None of the twenty was found guilty.[79] Of all the persons brought to trial for treason, only two received the death sentence. But both were pardoned by Washington when he was told that one was "insane" and the other a "simpleton."[80] In July of 1795 he pardoned all who were not then convicted or under indictment for offenses against the United States. Mifflin, a month later, pardoned those guilty of offenses committed in the Fourth Survey between July 11 and August 22, 1794. He excepted those who were still recalcitrant or those under indictment or conviction for offenses against Pennsylvania.[81]

Although the government was criticized for sending such a large army against a few rioters,[82] Washington could justify its size in more ways than one. Its very strength completely overawed the opposition to such an extent that not one rifle was turned against it. Thus the shedding of blood was averted, a fortunate outcome that might not have been effected by a small force whose weakness might have invited challenge. Then, too, the large numbers on the march demonstrated the government's ability to call upon and receive support when its laws were violently resisted by organized groups. This first serious resistance was thus completely squelched. That the government would not be trifled with was amply illustrated. The suppression of the "rebellion" or "insurrection" (two words that somewhat exaggerate the seriousness of the western protest) by the militia was not a victory in any true sense of the word. It was a lesson, a demonstration, the real significance of which was political, not military.

The action taken by the administration certainly emphasized the fact that any change in the national laws could be effected only by constitutional and legal means. Force would produce nothing but more force. The natural corollary, therefore, that seemed to follow this forcefully established rule of procedure involved an application of pressure on Congress, the originator of law, and not on the men selected to enforce it. Also, it would seem to urge the necessity of electing to Congress a sufficient number of men who would prove amenable to, and satisfy the demands of, the electorate. That the accomplishment of this latter object might be effected through a closer attention to party functions and organization could hardly have escaped the minds of contemporary politicians even in a day when many political leaders decried the spirit of factions. The solidification of opinion induced by the excise and the riotous response it provoked was unmistakable. Once again men had been forced to choose sides on a vital issue. Indeed, one writer, taking a retrospective view of the period from 1796 back to the American Revolution, thought it likely that the insurrection contributed more to party antagonisms in Pennsylvania than any other event.[83]

But however convincing the whiskey disturbance may have been as an argument for political organization, one of its immediate results was to discourage some of the organizational steps that had already been taken. This was peculiarly applicable in the case of the Democratic Societies.

The Insurrection and the Democratic Societies

The Federalist resentment engendered by the appearance of the Democratic Societies early in 1793 had increased with the passing months. In spite of heated attacks by the Federalist press—they had been accused of almost everything, including sedition[84]—they continued to flourish. But now they were to receive a blow that was to prove fatal. It came from the President himself on November 14, 1794, when he sent a message to Congress. Referring to the clubs as "self-created societies," the President specifically blamed them for causing the whiskey disturbances and of demonstrating a lack of respect for duly constituted government.[85]

In its reply to Washington, the Senate professed hearty agreement;[86] but the lower house was not so sure that the societies were responsible. Sharply divided, it spent several days in hot debate over the question of censuring the societies for misconduct.[87] The argument was begun on November 24, 1794, by Thomas Fitzsimons, while the House was considering an answer to Washington's message. Fitzsimons moved that the reply be amended to include a reprobation of the "self-created societies." By "disturbing the operations of the laws," said Fitzsimons, and "by deceiving and inflaming the ignorant and the weak [they] may naturally be supposed to have stimulated and urged the insurrection."[88] The next day, under heavy attack, he withdrew his amendment and substituted a milder one prepared by Benjamin Bourne, of Rhode Island. William Giles, thereupon, denied that all the clubs were blameworthy and successfully moved that "The Democratic societies of Philadelphia, New York and Pittsburg" be substituted for the more general term, "self-created societies."[89] Then on November 26, 1794, probably to obtain a record vote, the House approved a motion calling for reinstatement of "the obnoxious words," i.e., "self-created societies." Of the Pennsylvania delegation, Fitzsimons, Hartley, Kittera, Scott and Armstrong voted in the affirmative. In the negative were Findley, Gregg, Hiester, Peter Muhlenberg, Smilie and William Montgomery.[90] Irvine was absent. In spite of this vote, however, the sentiment of the House was clearly opposed to a condemnation of the clubs. This was shown shortly after when another vote was taken on an amendment which confined censure only to those "self-created societies" in the four counties of western Pennsylvania and "parts adjacent." Since only nineteen members voted in the affirmative, no further attempts were made to blame the societies for causing the insurrection. They were not mentioned at all in the House's answer to the President. Only two Pennsylvanians took part in the debate, Hartley and Fitzsimons. The latter, defeated for Congress a few weeks before by John Swanwick, was the chief opponent of the clubs.

Generally speaking, the Democratic Societies scattered over the country strongly disapproved of the violent methods employed against the excise in western Pennsylvania. Before Washington's proclamation of September 9, 1794, set the troops in motion four widely separated groups passed resolutions against those methods. They were the German Republican Society of Philadelphia, the Baltimore Republican Society, the Democratic Society of Canaan, New York, and the Democratic Society of Washington, North Carolina.[91]

Of the three societies in western Pennsylvania—the Democratic Society of Washington, the Republican Society of the Yough and the Mingo Creek Society—the last one was most active in the disturbances. It became, according to Brackenridge, "the cradle of the insurrection."[92] All of its known members were busy anti-excise agitators.[93] In cooperation with the Yough Society it planned to organize all the western counties into one group.

The Washington Society contained two men who became the most powerful leaders in the opposition to the excise: James Marshall, president, and David Bradford. It was unanimously opposed to the excise law and went so far in its opposition as to cause the resignation of David Redick, a member who favored only constitutional resistance. Bradford, on the other hand, advocated more severe measures. At Braddock's Field on August 12, 1794, he was unanimously elected major general of the resistance forces, and sixteen days later at Brownsville, he, according to Addison, advised a war for independence against the United States.[94]

As a matter of fact, Bradford, a successful lawyer and once a staunch Federalist, was the only excise opponent who was excepted from the government's general proclamation of amnesty. Never pardoned, he fled to Louisiana, then in possession of Spain, where he died.[95] But although Bradford was an officer of the Washington society, there is nothing to indicate that he acted in the interests of, or spoke for, the society during his opposition to the excise.[96]

The Pennsylvania Democratic Society in Philadelphia began its opposition to the excise in June, 1794, by appointing Benjamin F. Bache, editor of the *General Advertiser,* Peter Du Ponceau and A. J. Dallas as a committee of three to prepare for the coming Congressional election. The society intended to promote the election of men who would vote to repeal the excise law. The committee prepared a report, but the confusion engendered by the July incidents in western Pennsylvania prevented any action from being taken.[97] The society, disturbed by western violence, disapproved of any opposition that was not strictly constitutional.[98] In a message to the Washington society on August 14, 1794, the Philadelphians refrained from a clear expression of "sentiments" because of a lack of information. But they did hope that there would be no further bloodshed or property damage.[99] On September 11, 1794, they commended both Washington and Mifflin for using pacific means to restore order and resolved that if "the power of reason" failed, "the strength of the state" should be exerted.[100] When

Washington blamed the "self-created societies" for fomenting rebellion, the Philadelphians strenuously denied the charge and pointed out that several members of these societies had marched against the whiskey rioters.

But so great was Washington's influence and so respected was his judgment that his censure of the societies ruined them. His denunciation, coming after the Congressional elections in October, 1794, did not affect their outcome,[101] but his words discredited the organizations so effectively that their political promise was never fulfilled. His proclamation in 1792 had, in Hutchinson's opinion, injured the Republican campaign, and now a few words from him had balked any further formal political organization on the part of the administration's opponents. Before the elections of 1794, the Federalists had bitterly denounced the influence of Democratic Societies.[102] And when they were over, the President so emphatically aided the Federalist argument that the societies never again presented a challenge. But the Federalists must have been bitterly aware of the Republican strength in the Congressional elections of 1794, for in Philadelphia John Swanwick, a supporter of democratic clubs, defeated the ardent Federalist, Thomas Fitzsimons.

Expulsion of Westerners from the Assembly

Although Fitzsimons was defeated in Philadelphia, the city returned a Federalist delegation to the Pennsylvania House of Representatives. In fact, both branches of the legislature were predominantly Federalist, and when they convened in December, their mood in regard to the whiskey disturbance was definitely punitive. The session had hardly begun when Representative James Kelly, of York County, denied the right of the members from the counties of Westmoreland, Fayette, Washington and Allegheny to serve as assemblymen. It was his contention that the elections in that area of the State had been held during the insurrection and were therefore unconstitutional and void. After he had introduced a resolution to that effect on December 30, 1794,[103] Cadwalader Evans succeeded in having the resultant discussion postponed to permit Albert Gallatin and John Cunningham, of Fayette County, to argue the case of the western members. On the following day, Gallatin requested that the evidence allegedly substantiating the charge that the western counties were in a state of insurrection be placed before the House.[104] His request was granted.

On January 3, 1795, Gallatin made his greatest effort in defense of the right of the western members to sit in the lower house. In a very long speech he maintained that there was no violence in the four western counties after September 11, and certainly none on election day, October 14, 1794. The House had no constitutional right to determine contested elections; that was a duty to be delegated to a special committee only. "If this be a question of elections, I may perhaps perceive on this floor prosecutors, but I see no judges. If it is not a question of elections, what is it? It then can be nothing else than a disfranchising, retrospective act. If there exists anywhere a power to disfranchise the citizens of one-sixth part of the State, that power is, undoubtedly, of a legislative nature, and must be exercised by the legislature and not by a single branch."[105]

The House continued to discuss Kelly's resolution, and when its passage seemed inevitable Gallatin, on January 9, 1795, moved that the legislature adjourn for approximately a month. Such an adjournment would have allowed the four counties in question to hold another election and prevent their loss of representation. His resolution was defeated by a close vote.[106] A few minutes later, after the western members withdrew, Kelly's resolution passed by a vote of forty-three to twenty.[107] The members from the four western counties were thus expelled and one-sixth of the State was without representation in the House. The twenty members who voted against the resolution represented in whole or in part, nine counties. Philadelphia and all the eastern counties (with the exception of one vote in Philadelphia County) favored expulsion.

When the Senate also expelled its recently elected members from the western counties, the disfranchisement of the whole area was complete. Eleven representatives and four senators had been eliminated and the legislature calmly proceeded to do business for the entire State.

Benjamin Franklin Bache's *Aurora* reacted to the legislature's ejection procedure with outraged vigor. Having heard that the rump Assembly would do no business of importance until it again really represented the State, Bache suggested that it should be "contented to sit *gratis* or it will look as if they had an eye to the *loaves and fishes*."[108] He considered the expulsion a dangerous precedent that was dictated purely by factional interests. "Let the citizens of Pennsylvania examine the question abstracted from the influence of party, and they will never again delegate their confidence to men who have disfranchised citizens by *ex post facto* decisions, and without even the shadow of evidence. . . ." If the expulsion had not been dictated by party purposes, "an adjournment would have taken place immediately after the decision against the western members."[109]

William Findley considered the legislature's action a violation of the Constitution and an abuse of legal authority. "It was not conducted as a contested election by a committee nor was it done by Law, but by a summary vote of each house Separately. . . . No testimony was called for, no vouchers were produced, nor were there any facts stated."

Immediately after the expulsion, writs of election were issued to restore a western representation to the Assembly. Writing to Alexander Addison, William Findley expressed the wish that "all the expelled members who have attended should be returned again if they have not been offenders; this is the best way to contradict the unsupported presumption that the friends of Gov't durst not come out to vote."[110]

Findley's wish was fully satisfied. The voters in the four counties returned all the ousted members to the legislature, with the exception of one man, a senator who declined to run for re-election.[111] By the end of February, all had returned to their places. The voters had thus vindicated their original selections and rebuked the Federalists at the same time. The belief that the expulsion was a work of spite, revenge and party retaliation did not die among the Republicans. Echoes of their resentment were heard for years afterward. It was one more source of protest, one more charge of injustice that they could level against their opponents.

Political Consequences

In evaluating the political consequences of the excise disturbances, it is difficult to determine the concrete effect on the two contesting factions. Those who favored a strong central government could view with considerable approval the determined attitude taken by the administration in resisting and punishing violations of law. Their faith in the administration had been confirmed and justified. If so inclined, they could point to some of the western excesses as examples of unrestrained democracy and, by contrast, see in them a justification of the Hamiltonian concept of government. In the opinion of the staunch Federalist then, the administration had won a great victory from both a diplomatic and military viewpoint.

The Republican cause, at least during the troublesome years of excise resistance, suffered many disadvantages. Although their leaders could exploit public resentment against an unpopular law, no one of any responsibility or wide reputation could sanction violent resistance. And when it occurred they were embarrassed. The most important western leaders—Findley, Gallatin and Smilie—had to act and speak with extreme care. A failure to support their constituents would have been damaging locally, but a whole-hearted participation in the anti-excise movement, particularly after the Bower Hill incident and the stoppage of the United States mails, might have brought them under indictment for treason. Throughout the period of disturbance these men advised nothing but constitutional resistance. Their political enemies made strenuous efforts to implicate them in the more serious aspects of the disturbances—especially Findley—but without success. They continued to represent their sections in both the State and national legislatures.[112]

Mifflin's administration came through the troublous period with its political strength unimpaired. It received the sincere commendation of two such diverse groups as the Pennsylvania legislature and the Pennsylvania Democratic Society; and two years later was returned to office almost by acclamation. The Governor and his efficient secretary had done their utmost, "with delicacy," to prevent Washington from declaring that the western counties were in a state of rebellion.[113] Pleading lack of authority, they had refused to take independent action in calling out the militia. In both cases they did not alienate their Republican friends. But when Washington took determined action and called the militia in September, Mifflin used every available opportunity to exercise his not inconsiderable powers as an orator to excoriate the "seditious" westerners. At that time it was the popular thing to do. The friction that had developed between the Federal and State officials was carefully explained to the legislature in a way that made him appear as a champion of states' rights.[114] Undoubtedly, Mifflin acted throughout in a politically cautious and astute manner.

CHAPTER VII

PRESQUE ISLE

As an area Pennsylvania has been well endowed with valuable natural resources; and throughout most of her history their development has been marked by periods of intensive expansion and speculation. Before the discovery and wide usage of coal and oil, businessmen seeking sources for capital investment, made heavy speculative ventures into what was then the chief promotional field, a large and rich expanse of public lands.

In general outline the developmental procedure was relatively simple: the speculator merely bought large amounts of land at the lowest possible cost and then attempted to hold them until an influx of settlers raised the price. This general simplicity, however, was often complicated by factors extraneous to a simple business transaction. Since much of the land was bought outright from the State, the administration in power was often subjected to political pressure—on the one hand by speculators who constantly sought more and better opportunities, and on the other, by home seekers who claimed victimization through the land disposal system. Politics and land policies were thus bound together. In addition, problems attendant upon the development of large land tracts often involved ramifications of a national and even international nature. Finally, the projection of settled areas westward, through ambitious land purchasing and development schemes, occasionally irritated various Indian tribes and precipitated border trouble.

As an example of a development scheme that introduced problems of a general political and military nature, the attempted founding of a town at Presque Isle in 1794 affords an interesting and profitable case for study. In addition, it exemplified the friction that existed between the State and Federal administrations at a time when western excise disturbances had produced marked differences of opinion between the two administrations. Also, it precipitated questions as to the legitimate functions—their nature and extent—of the two governments. The newness of the national government, and the unprecedented issues involved in its impact on the States, lend a peculiar significance to this last aspect of the subject.

During the latter part of the eighteenth century, both the states of New York and Massachusetts claimed possession of a tract of land now generally known as the Erie Triangle. A section containing over two hundred thousand acres, it is bounded on the east by New York, on the northwest by Lake Erie and on the south by the forty-second parallel. After a long wrangle, the two contesting states ceded the disputed territory to the United States Government—New York in 1781, and Massachusetts five years later.

Pennsylvania had a natural interest in the territory, for possession of it would give her a wide and valuable frontage on Lake Erie. She, therefore, took steps to purchase it, first from the Indians and then from the United States. In January, 1789, her emissaries, John Gibson and Richard Butler, met various chiefs representing the Seneca, Cayuga, Tuscarora, Onondaga and Oneida tribes of the Six Nations and drew up articles of agreement concerning the area in question. According to these articles, the chiefs agreed to deed it for the sum of $2,000. to Pennsylvania at a future time.[1] The State thus attempted to protect its interest in the region until permanent title could be secured from the United States. Two years later, a complaint arose in the Seneca nation regarding boundaries of the recently purchased land. Determined to keep the agreement bright, Pennsylvania paid Chiefs Cornplanter, Half-Town and Big Tree $800.00 for a quit claim.[2]

Meanwhile, the State officials had been trying to buy the Erie tract from the United States. Negotiations, begun as early as 1789, had proceeded slowly, tempered by the fears of some speculators that New England men would move into the territory "and make a second Wyoming of it."[3] But finally the transaction was completed, in March, 1792, with the sale of the Erie tract to Pennsylvania for $151,640.25.[4] A few weeks later it was added to Allegheny County.[5]

At least a month before Mifflin sent the Assembly a copy of the "instrument of Conveyance," that body had been at work on a new law for the sale of vacant lands.[6] With purchase of a lake front, eminent Pennsylvanians became more interested in the Northwest lands. That a frontage on the lake might open the way to a greater participation in the lucrative fur trade was certainly not lost upon those who were interested in that business.

After considerable discussion, a bill for the sale of unsettled land was passed on April 3, 1792. It reduced the price of some lands east of the Allegheny and offered for sale all territory lying north and west of the Allegheny and Ohio rivers and Conewango Creek. Exception was made in the latter territory to lands set aside for public or charitable use. The land was offered only "to persons who will cultivate, improve and settle the same, or cause the same to be cultivated, improved and settled. . . ."[7]

The legislators were fully aware of the value of the Presque Isle area and they specifically reserved it for the use of the State. To prevent incursions into the section, they described the boundaries as follows: it was "formed by Lake Erie, the island or peninsula which forms the harbor and a tract extending eight miles along the shore of the lake, and three miles in breadth . . . and the whole of the harbor formed by the Presque Isle at the mouth of Harbor Creek which empties into Lake Erie, and along the shore of the Lake on both sides of said creek, two thousand acres."[8]

As a town site, the area at Presque Isle was indeed valuable, and this fact was not lost sight of by either the land speculators or the Assembly. It was thought that a development there would encourage settlement in the northwest and protect the frontier from Indian attack.[9] Most certainly, it would increase the value of the surrounding acres and open new commercial channels. In order to effect these objects the legislature, on April 8, 1793, empowered Mifflin to survey the area and lay out a town "at the most eligible place."[10]

The Governor, in carrying out his instructions, began by commissioning William Irvine and Andrew Ellicott to conduct the survey.[11] Very little was accomplished, however, before Mifflin asked the commissioners to delay their departure until frontier Indian disturbances had subsided sufficiently to permit the surveyors to work in safety.

Thus balked in his first attempt, Mifflin determined that by the next spring he would proceed with his plans in spite of the Indians. In December, 1793, he advised the Assembly that the completion of the Presque Isle project might involve the use of troops and that it would be well to prepare for such a contingency.[12] The legislature obliged, in an act of February 28, 1794, by authorizing the use of the militia to protect the surveyors.[13]

On March 1, 1794, the Governor had a very busy day. He appointed Captain Ebenezer Denny as officer in charge of a militia company which would be raised to carry out the legislature's orders and wrote him detailed instructions. Denny was ordered to establish his headquarters at Le Boeuf and protect the operations around Presque Isle. In addition, he was to guard the workmen engaged in building roads from Reading and French Creek to Lake Erie. The two projects, said Mifflin, were "intimately connected."[14] Second, he instructed the brigade inspectors of Washington, Westmoreland and Allegheny counties to assist

Denny in procuring soldiers.[15] Third, he notified commissioners Irvine and Ellicott that they would be assisted by a third commissioner, Albert Gallatin.[16] They were urged to begin work immediately. Mifflin reposed great confidence in General Irvine, regarding him as first in command of the Presque Isle project. In the matter of militia organization the Governor promised to ratify any plan the general advised.[17]

Denny experienced difficulty in securing enough men for his company. By May 2, 1794, he succeeded in procuring forty-seven militiamen and thirty volunteers. With these he set out for Le Boeuf.

In the meantime, reports of Indian unrest began to arrive in Philadelphia, and as the weeks went by they increased in number. In a series of letters to Mifflin, General John Wilkins warned that the British were inflaming the Six Nations Indians to action against Pennsylvania. He repeated rumors that the British would attack any troops going to Presque Isle and that the Indians would assist them.[18] General Israel Chapin, United States Superintendent of the Six Nations Indians, wrote in similar vein to Secretary of War Knox, and added that unless the Pennsylvania garrison at Presque Isle was made strong it would probably be attacked. He, too, was alarmed at British activity.[19]

When Dallas, in the absence of Mifflin, sent the letters from Denny and Wilkins regarding "possible" opposition to Knox on May 9, 1794,[20] the latter replied on the following day with the expressed doubt as to "whether any measures ought now to be urged, which are likely to produce disgust to our friends the six nations and to extend Indian Hostilities." In short, he intimated that the Presque Isle venture should be postponed. Mifflin did not reply directly to Knox's advice, but on May 23, 1794, he made clear his determination to go ahead with the Presque Isle development in spite of the Indians by issuing a call to the western brigade inspectors to enroll one thousand militiamen for active duty. They were to serve under General Wilkins and, if necessary, build block houses on the road to Presque Isle.[21] The Governor also notified Washington of his action.

Washington's reaction was immediate and decisive. Writing through Secretary Knox on May 24, he told Mifflin "to suspend for the present the establishment at Presque-isle."[22]

Mifflin was greatly disturbed and mortified at an "interference"[23] which he considered to be highly "impolitic, unpopular, and dangerous."[24] Although he did not express himself so forcibly to Washington, he did say that he very much regretted the lateness of the suspension notification. "I am apprehensive indeed," said the Governor, "that it is too late to prevent the execution of" the Presque Isle development. However, conceded Mifflin, he would obey the President "even at this late period," in order to "promote the views of the General Government" and avoid an extension of Indian hostilities. He would suspend the operation, now that the President had directly asked him to do so, but he could not have justified his action had he complied with Knox's "bare intimation" to Dallas on May 10, 1794.[25] In Knox's letter of May 24, in which he relayed Washington's suspension order, he had pointedly referred to his own warning of May 10, against any measures which might "disgust" the Indians. In spite of that Mifflin had then called for one thousand militia, a move that could quite conceivably cause "disgust." The censure was vaguely stated but unmistakable, and it irritated the Governor.

Washington's decision to suspend the Presque Isle operation was the result of a determination to keep the Six Nations Indians at peace. Information received in Philadelphia indicated that the Indians had become restive as soon as Pennsylvania began town and road-building operations in the northwest area. If the Indians were driven to desperation, it was anticipated that they would make common cause with disaffected western tribes already at war with the United States. Such an alliance was greatly to be feared, for the United States had been conducting campaigns into the west for several years.

Indeed, since its inception the national government had been trying, by means both forceful and conciliatory, to deal with the hostile Indians in the Wabash country. After two costly military expeditions had failed—one led by General Harmar and the other by Arthur St. Clair—Washington selected Anthony Wayne to make another attempt.[26]

While the energetic Wayne was marching westward, Washington, with the military man's caution regarding communication lines, was naturally much disturbed to hear that the Six Nations lying north of Wayne's route of march were dangerously restive.

The situation was made even more critical by reports of adverse British activity. Canada's Lieutenant Governor, John Simcoe, in clear violation of United States territory, had constructed a fort on the Miami River, sixty miles south of Detroit. Further, it was generally believed, and later research has proved, that the British were supplying the Indians with military equipment.[27]

The apprehension in Pennsylvania regarding British activity was not unwarranted, and most of it stemmed from the fact that the eight frontier posts the British had agreed to evacuate at the Treaty of

Paris in 1783 were still in their hands. Many men thought their presence encouraged the Indian raids and massacres that were being inflicted upon the frontiersmen. In addition, the forts, strategically located in the "Old Northwest," were so situated as to control the principal routes of communication and transportation.[28] All requests from the Federal government that the strongholds be relinquished were met with the complaint that the United States had not fulfilled its treaty obligations. But the real motive behind England's retention of the posts lay in the highly profitable fur trade.[29]

The Six Nations Indians inhabiting the area in question found themselves to be the victims of changing circumstances, for them not an unusual predicament. Before the Revolution, the land northwest of the Ohio had been recognized in solemn treaty as Indian territory. But when it was ceded to "their enemies, the Americans," in 1783, the Indians were at a loss to understand the change in sovereignty.[30] They naturally resented the change, for again the ownership of the region was subjected to negotiations between them and the white men. And from such conferences they often emerged as losers. To that even the youngest chiefs could testify.

Governor Mifflin was well aware of Indian hostility and of the presence of the British troops at the Miami rapids. The two combined threats, he thought, "must evince a hostile disposition, which cannot fail to command the most serious attention of the General Government."[31] Nevertheless, he was much irritated when the national government gave him convincing proof of the "serious attention" it was giving to the situation by stopping the Pennsylvania development scheme. And he did not hesitate to inform the national authorities of his annoyance at "the interference."

In a letter to Washington on May 25, 1794, he told the President that he had rescinded his orders to the brigade inspectors to draft a thousand soldiers and had stopped the commissioners from further work. Then he reminded Washington that the northwest territory had been purchased from both the Indians and the United States. As a result, Pennsylvania could hardly expect "that any hostile opposition would be made to her settling upon a property thus fairly acquired; or that the advancement of her peculiar interests in that respect would be deemed incompatible with the general interests of the Union."[32]

Mifflin's impatience at the continued delay was again made quite evident on June 13, 1794, in another letter to Washington in which he had enclosed, at the President's request, evidence of Six Nations' hostility.³³ To this Knox, who replied for Washington, made the obvious answer. Surely Mifflin, on the basis of the evidence he himself had submitted, could understand that the Presque Isle development "is an extremely delicate one, as it regards our peace with the Six Nations." Furthermore, it might possibly complicate the negotiations that were then under way between the United States and Britain.³⁴

On the same day that he received Knox's letter Mifflin replied to Washington in high dudgeon.³⁵ He had never felt that the Presque Isle project would be opposed by the Indians, but by the "machinating efforts of the agents of a foreign nation [Britain] in the neighborhood of the United States. . . ." And when he had asked for a thousand militia, it was his intention to use them in preventing a threatened foreign invasion. He resented Knox's statement, in a former letter, that it would be indeed fortunate if the "circumstances" that "had already occurred" (Mifflin believed Knox was referring to the militia draft) had not "matured the evil beyond the possibility of a remedy."

In this connection, however, Mifflin consoled himself with the recollection that Washington was "possessed of the law while the Legislature (whose power was alone competent to repeal it) was in Session; that you were seasonably apprised of every Step that was taken to carry it into effect; and that if, from information unknown to me, an earlier discontinuance of the Executive proceedings was deemed salutary, my conduct will evince the readiness with which I should have acquiesced in an earlier declaration of that opinion."³⁶ But on this score, Mifflin felt that he had little cause for worry or self-reproach. If the legislators chose to pass laws whose execution would endanger the peace, they were responsible for the consequences, not the executive.

Then he asked a very important and significant question: could the President of the United States really justify an act which suspended "the operation of a positive law of Pennsylvania? The Constitutional supremacy of the Laws of the Union will not be disputed. But may it not be asked what law of the Union does, nay, what power there is to pass a law which cou'd controul the Commonwealth in the legitimate exercise of her Territorial jurisdiction? Where there is no Law there can be no obligation; nor consistently with the principles of a Republican Government, can reasons of State or the admonition of circumstances (upon which the Secretary at War relies) furnish an Executive Magistrate with an authority to Substitute his opinions for Legislative institutions."³⁷ Mifflin loved to employ indirect and diplomatic language, but here the style certainly did not hide a very pointed implication: Washington, acting without authority from Congress (and its authority on the subject under consideration was at best questionable), was dangerously close to assuming an attitude of superiority to the law.

The Governor assured Washington that he had confidence in his patriotism and judgment, but, however consoling that was to him personally, he had to vindicate his conduct to the public. He was also confident that the national government would make every effort to remove "the temporary obstacles which exist." Then, with an eye to his own vindication, he explained the future adverse possibilities that the suspension might induce. "The bare suspension of our measures," he predicted, "will, probably, indeed, increase the difficulty of accomplishing them; and any great delay might eventually introduce a Controversy upon the right of doing so. The evil wou'd become irremediable by any peaceable process, if, taking advantage of the Circumstances which have already occurred, either the Six Nations, or any other ill-disposed neighbour, shou'd seize on the station which has been designated for our establishment.

"For these contingencies, however, and for the expense which the State has already incurred, I have no doubt the Justice of the General Government will satisfactorily provide."[38]

The Governor then ended his letter by promising that, come what might, he would continue to suspend the Presque Isle operation until Washington changed his opinion.

Why did Mifflin write such a controversial and censorious letter to Washington if he intended to conclude it by promising further acquiescence to the President's wishes? In parts it had been so provocative as to suggest an opposition which, when it failed to appear, made the ending definitely anticlimactic. Certainly Mifflin knew Washington well enough to realize that he could not be intimidated.

A partial explanation is found in the Governor's admission that he was motivated by certain political aspects of the Presque Isle delay that became evident shortly after the suspension.[39] Various powerful landowners and speculators protested vigorously. Mifflin was criticized in the daily press for tamely acceding to the Federal government, and confidential informants told him that he was the object of blame in many parts of the State. As a politician who was constantly alert and sensitive to public opinion, he realized that he needed to justify his action by placing his views on record. What could be better than a strong protest to Washington himself? In so doing he had questioned the President's right to suspend a State law, cast doubt on the power of

Congress to "controul the Commonwealth in the legitimate exercise of her territorial jurisdiction," and implied that should Pennsylvania suffer loss because of the suspension the Federal government would be expected to provide compensation. Finally, he had made it clear that he only worked for the State and that, in the last analysis, the legislature was responsible for any difficulties that had occurred. Should any vindication of his action be necessary in the future, he could always point to his letter. As a matter of fact, he fully intended to publish "the material parts" (that is, the sections that would serve to extenuate his conduct) of his entire correspondence with Washington.[40]

But in spite of his insistence that he had to carry out legislative orders, he failed to do so. He might argue with Washington, but he obeyed him.

The letter was written on June 14, 1794, but, strangely enough, it was not delivered to the President's office until June 17, 1794. Since Washington had departed for Mount Vernon on the morning of the seventeenth, he had not seen it. Secretary Knox, feeling that he knew Washington's sentiments on the subject, replied to Mifflin on June 21, 1794, in what he declared to be a spirit of cordiality and harmony.[41] Briefly but emphatically he answered the three primary points raised by Mifflin. First, the principal question at issue was not the "rights" of Pennsylvania or the "obligations which are urged to exist on the part of the United States in relation to them," but the protection of society as a whole. It was the practice in political communities to defer the "enjoyment of a right, or interest of a nation, to considerations respecting the safety or wellfare of the whole nation. The propriety then of a temporary suspension in the present instance must depend on the weight of the reasons which dictate it."[42] Second, it was "absolutely useless" for Mifflin to discuss Washington's justification for suspending the Presque Isle program as long as the Governor declared his willingness to obey orders. Third, Knox had never seen any evidence of hostility on the part of the Six Nations before Pennsylvania began her land development operations. Knox concluded by assuring the Governor that attempts were being made to remove the temporary obstacles which made the suspension necessary.

Taking his turn in this epistolary debate on June 24, 1794, Mifflin bowed to the amenities by reciprocating Knox's wish for harmony between the two governments.[43] Then he launched once more into the argument. He was not inclined to discuss Knox's doctrine regarding the primary interests of a nation as opposed to its parts, but he thought it obvious that the idea was least adaptable to circumstances which required its application through the discretionary powers of a state executive. Obviously, the Governor missed the point here and confused the issue, for Knox had not even hinted that any one part of a nation (in this case a state) possessed discretionary authority to determine what was or was not in the national interest. Such prerogatives were to be exercised only by the general government. But it is just possible that by the employment of circumlocutionary phraseology (to which he was occasionally addicted) the Governor meant to deny even the right of the Federal government to determine national interest when such determination was at the expense of a state. In any case, before embarking on such a significant move, the central government should consult the state legislature.

As to his determination to obey the suspension order, Mifflin assured Knox that his obedience was conditioned by Washington's assurances that the delay was of a temporary nature.

Then reverting again to the troublesome Indian question, Mifflin declared that Six Nations' hostility antedated the Presque Isle law. It had been induced by "some old grievances alleged to have been suffered from the Union . . . the constant machinations of British agents, and the corruption of British bribes. . . ."[44]

At this time events were occurring in the frontier regions which confirmed Knox's opinion regarding the attitude of the Six Nations. The Indians denied to Israel Chapin that they had sold the Erie tract to Pennsylvania,[45] and in the middle of June, at a huge council on Buffalo Creek, they insisted that Chapin go to Presque Isle and order all those who had settled there to move out.[46] When Chapin, accompanied by William Johnson, Indian agent for the British, and by a deputation from the Six Nations, reached Presque Isle on June 24, 1794, he found no one there. So, on the next day the delegation went to view the Le Boeuf garrison, which had arrived a few hours before. There the Indians told Captain Denny, officer in charge, that they considered the articles of agreement drawn up in 1789 as a treaty of peace and not as a bill of sale; the goods received were accepted as presents, and no money had changed hands.[47] Then they declared that if the garrison did not clear out of Le Boeuf at once, friendly relations would be severed. To this Denny replied that he had been ordered to occupy Le Boeuf and there he would stay until recalled.[48]

The bad western news only inspired Mifflin to greater activity. Fearful of an Indian invasion, he asked Knox for military supplies[49] and ordered General John Gibson to call more militia into service. Far from considering the prospect of a general Indian war as a deterrent to the land scheme, he took a completely opposite view. The extravagant demands made at Le Boeuf, he told Washington, were inspired by the British, more particularly by Johnson, their Indian agent. They were insulting to the State and deserved to be ignored. Now, more than ever, the safety of Pennsylvania and the preservation of its property are "involved in the immediate prosecution of our object; and I trust, that you will now find reason to concur in that opinion."[50]

But Washington did not concur. Instead, he still insisted on the suspension on the grounds that "the immediate prosecution" of the Presque Isle development would call the Six Nations Indians to arms against the United States.[51] He was of the opinion that a conference should be held on September 15, 1794, between the Six Nations and representatives of the State and national governments. The object would be "to adjust all discontents against the establishment at Presque Isle. . . ." Would Mifflin send a commissioner along with a United States representative to negotiate at such a conference?[52]

The Governor was now thoroughly disturbed and disgusted. His extended correspondence with Knox and Washington was not at all improving the situation or his disposition. As a matter of fact, "every addition to the correspondence" increased his "embarrassment."[53] No, he would not send a representative to confer with the Indians on September 15. It was his wish to cooperate with the government in an effort to conciliate the tribesmen, but he had no authority to send a commissioner.[54] He would furnish documents relative to the land controversy, but he wanted it "clearly understood that, on my part, no assent is given to any proposition that shall bring into doubt or controversy the rights of the State." There was no justice in the Indians, he said, or they would acknowledge the validity of a purchase that was fairly made.[55]

Mifflin had expected Washington to assume full responsibility for any consequences that might result from the suspension order. But this hope was blasted when Knox informed him that the President never intended to "carry his opinions upon the subject farther than to state them as strongly as they were conceived by him. It is with your Excellency to compare them with your constitutional and legal powers."[56]

Mifflin must have writhed in greater frustration when he read that, for during the past two months he had done little else than "compare" the suspension to his constitutional powers. And he had gotten nowhere. Now, to his dismay, he was informed that the full consequences of the delay would fall upon his shoulders. But the Governor had no inclination to accept the full burden.

Probably anticipating Knox's letter of the seventeenth and his consequent need for moral as well as legal support, Mifflin had asked Dallas to present the problem to Jared Ingersoll, land speculator and Attorney General for Pennsylvania. On July 14, 1794, Dallas asked Ingersoll if the Governor could legally justify the continued suspension beyond a period of time that would permit him to carry the law into effect.[57] The legislature had not specified a completion date, but it had offered land bounties to men who would settle in the area by May 1, 1795. Obviously, bounty promises would be worthless if the preliminary surveys were not finished in time. Further, the enlistment period of the soldiers recruited to protect the surveyors would expire in December, 1794. Mifflin interpreted these two conditioning factors as indications of the legislature's desire to have the surveys completed in 1794. Hence, his anxiety to have the suspension lifted as soon as possible.

Ingersoll answered Dallas' inquiry on July 18, 1794. Waiving every "consideration of Policy or Expediency," it was his opinion that the Governor had to conform to the law. That is, he had to complete the project in time to allow bounties for settlement. No delay could be justified beyond that time. "If it shall appear that measures of General Concern will be defeated by Pursuing the Line of Conduct pointed out by the Legislature, as the Governor has no dispensing Power, convening the Legislature is the only Remedy for the Inconvenience."[58]

Thus supported by Ingersoll's opinion, Mifflin was prepared to comment on his alleged responsibility for the consequences of the suspension. On July 18, 1794, he wrote Washington that if the President was "solicitous to avoid reproach for inattention, or a request to make full representations of any danger which is apprehended to the interest of the Union, a similar solicitude in the success of a particular Government to avoid reproach, either for transgressing the Constitutional boundaries of his authority, or for sacrificing the interests of the state, will be equally approved and indulged."[59] His "solicitude" had induced him to consult Ingersoll in an effort to "compare your opinions . . . with my constitutional and legal powers." He enclosed Ingersoll's opinion, and once more requested information as to how long the suspension would persist. If the obstacles were not shortly removed, he would have to do one of two things: direct the commissioners to proceed with the survey or call the legislature into special session. He would not take the latter step, however, unless Washington specifically requested it.[60]

That was the high point in the correspondence. When Knox replied for Washington on July 21, 1794, the Secretary's tone was mild and conciliatory.[61] Washington had never intended to embarrass Mifflin or infringe upon his constitutional powers, and for all consequences of the temporary stoppage Washington would accept full responsibility. But—the suspension was still in effect. It would continue until the campaign against the western Indians ended or until the Six Nations materially changed their attitude. Since neither Mifflin nor Ingersoll had "defined the period to which the suspension may . . . be legally continued," Knox thought that there would be sufficient time for the acquisition of land bounties after the projected September meeting with the Indians at Canandaigua. As for the expiration of the soldiers' enlistment period, it could always be extended.[62]

Mifflin disagreed with Knox. If the conference were held on September 15, 1794, he maintained, at least a month would be required to carry the report of its deliberations to Philadelphia. The commissioners could not possibly start to work for another three weeks, and by that time winter would have set in and the soldiers' enlistment period would have expired. He would suggest an earlier date for the conference, but according to his "sense of duty . . . the slightest interference" on his part would be improper.[63] But if the Indians remained hostile after the conference he would expect military aid from the national government, "not only to prevent any inconveniency that may arise from the expiration of the Pennsylvania enlistments, but effectually to subdue that resistance to the execution of the law of Pennsylvania which its suspension, by giving time and confidence to our ill disposed neighbors, must naturally increase."[64]

That ended the long interchange between Mifflin and Washington on the Presque Isle question. The Governor was in a difficult position throughout because he was being pulled in opposite directions by two powerful forces. He doubted Washington's authority to suspend the operation of a State law, but he obeyed the President on condition that the suspension would be only temporary. But therein lay the big question: how long could the delay continue and still be considered as of a temporary nature? The legislature had not specified a particular date for the project's completion. And the Governor, in an attempt to limit the suspension could only point to May 1, 1795, as the expiration date for bounty collections. Presumably, the surveys would have to be completed sometime before that date, else it would have been impossible for those entitled to bounties to receive them. Mifflin maintained that in order to satisfy that requirement the surveys would have to be completed before the winter of 1794. But this was debatable and Knox took advantage of it. The time element was therefore a principal factor in Mifflin's problem.

Another important aspect of the Governor's dilemma must not be neglected. Caught between the upper and nether millstones of presidential and legislative authority, Mifflin's problem was further aggravated by the pressure of public opinion. This aspect of the matter, previously adverted to in a discussion of Mifflin's letter to Washington on June 14, 1794, is of such consequence as to deserve further elaboration. It must not be forgotten that all during the correspondence Mifflin's letters had been written with the object of publishing them in justification of his deference to Washington's orders. It is quite likely that he could not forget for one moment his eligibility to stand for the governorship again in 1796.

If opposition to the suspension order in western Pennsylvania was as general and articulate as Mifflin's principal advisers said it was, then the Governor had cause for alarm. But even if his informants—many of whom had financial interests in the development—distorted or exaggerated conditions, Mifflin had to give them consideration. Their political weight and influence made any other course inadvisable. As soon as Mifflin announced the forced delay, they responded with outraged indignation.

General William Irvine, head commissioner, speculator and politician, protested with a vigor that was effective but not at all disinterested. For his valuable services in the Revolution he had been given a large tract of land below Presque Isle, afterwards known as Irvine's Reserve. He was one of those who strongly advocated the purchase of the triangle area from the United States.[65] When that had been effected, he, along with several others, joined Comptroller General John Nicholson in a vast speculation enterprise which was organized as the Pennsylvania Population Company. The organization was accomplished after Nicholson applied for three hundred and ninety land warrants in the triangle section. Also associated with the company was John Hoge, assemblyman and influential western Pennsylvania politician.[66]

During the first week of June, 1794, General Irvine gave forceful expression to his opinions in two letters to Mifflin. The Presque Isle establishment, he said, was exceedingly popular in the west, because most people thought it would end all presentiments of Indian outrage. But just when optimism was high, along came the suspension order which "occasioned a mixture of disgust resentment and fear."[67] It would benefit no one but the designing British, who doubted their ability to hold Presque Isle and the Miami Rapids at one and the same time. Now they could move in quietly to a strategic position and wait for war. Irvine was at a loss to understand how the British outmaneuvered Washington. Either the sources of his information were unreliable or it was falsified in transmission. Washington's "own head is clear & his heart pure, but I wish he may not have placed too much confidence in others, whose heads, at least are defective be their integrity as it may."[68] It was very unfortunate that Mifflin's order was delivered with such speed, for if it had arrived just two days later "the business would have been done" without fuss or friction. Truly, lamented Irvine, "a vast error" had been committed,[69] and "the interest and honor of the country [had been] sacrificed."[70] The whole western country was ready to aid in establishing a town at Presque Isle; but now anger and astonishment predominated.

Irvine gave Mifflin permission to relay his comments to Washington, comments which he thought were "more for you & your interest than against you. I am sure I mean it so, and hope I have not mistaken the point. It would not do perhaps, to have all the railings lavished on the General government without touching the state a little; it is most certainly a cursed business."[71] Completely disgusted, Irvine declared his intention to leave immediately for Philadelphia.

"Touching the state a little" educed a fervent disavowal of guilt from Mifflin. He assured Irvine that "no part of the blame can in justice be imputed to me; unless a cooperation in the measures of the General Government at a crisis be rendered a subject of condemnation."[72] Pained to hear that Irvine was coming east, he urged him to stay where he was, for the suspension was only temporary.

From David Redick, prothonotary in Washington County, came political news of an even more disturbing nature. Writing on June 5, 1794, he must have worried Mifflin considerably when he notified him that his "personal and political enemies [were], already beginning to turn this unhappy business to aid an opposition which had become hopeless by several defeats. Nor will your friends, unless other reasons beside the ostensible ones appear, be able to rebut. Besides, there is danger of a declention even amongst them, especially if the dreaded mischief [loss of life because of suspension] should unhappily take place."[73]

As to the legality of Washington's suspension order, Redick wanted to know what "in the name of common sense . . . could have induced the President to make such an unconstitutional request, or who could have counseled him to so ill timed, ill judged, and impolite interference. It never was his own head nor heart, else the American people had been surely mistaken in both." He had no authority to "prevent the execution of a State law, or to Interfere with the execution of it by a magistrate who is bound by the strongest obligations, both politic and moral."[74]

Like Irvine, Redick was certain that the British were responsible for all the trouble. Also like Irvine, his concern over the suspension was not disinterested: he planned to engage in the fishing business off the Erie shore.

Both Andrew Ellicott, Presque Isle commissioner, and General John Wilkins, supply contractor and land speculator in the Erie region, blamed the British for inciting the Indians to hostility. Ellicott presented Mifflin with two alternatives: either abandon all frontier posts down to Fort Franklin or build a fort at Presque Isle. Strongly advocating the latter measure, he was convinced that a strong post at Presque Isle would cut off the Six Nations from the western Indians and compel them to keep the peace.[75] The suspension would only make the Six Nations "more insolent than ever."[76] Furthermore, he pointed out, if the suspension continued, "the adventurers at Presq' Isle" who had already expended money would be in a "critical condition."[77]

It is possible that Ellicott's enthusiasm for the development scheme caused him to overestimate the strength of the garrison at Le Boeuf, the nearest post to Presque Isle. Writing from that place on July 19, 1794, he assured Mifflin that everything was in good order and the works strong enough to repel any number of Indians.[78] But Captain Ebenezer Denny, the officer in charge, took an entirely different view of the situation. He told General John Gibson, also on July 19, that the garrison was low on provisions. "If the Indians begin, the Lord knows how we'll make out. It will be from hand to mouth with us now."[79]

Several criticisms of the suspension order also appeared in Bache's *General Advertiser*. Washington's action was really a veto of a State law, an interference which reduced the states to the level of "corporations." Mifflin, in obeying Washington, had usurped legislative authority and played "with laws as boys play at ball." If Mifflin intended to become Washington's "High Constable," "we had better abandon our state governments, or *formally* delegate the legislative authority to the Governor."[80]

On June 21, 1794, a correspondent asked: "Have we become slaves to the will and to the menaces of a corrupt and vile British cabinet, that we dare not put ourselves in a condition to resist savage barbarities...."[81]

Although Bache lost no opportunity to castigate Washington, he did open his columns to "A Pennsylvanian" who took an opposite view of the matter. In a long and excellent letter he reviewed the history of the Presque Isle project and presented a strong defense of the President. It was his contention that the suspension was opposed chiefly by land speculators, who, in order to reap a profit, were willing to inflame the Indians into open hostility and sacrifice the interests of the Union. Only "the *private* interest of a few men is to be promoted by this settlement...."[82] But "A Pennsylvanian" was convinced that Mifflin would not be frightened by speculators' clamors into backing their schemes for the sake of a "local and partial popularity."

By the word "local" the writer referred to western Pennsylvania. But even in that section not everyone approved of the great emphasis Mifflin was placing on the land development scheme. When the Governor asked for the enrollment of one thousand militia in May, 1794, no less a figure than Presley Neville doubted the advisability of drafting so many men to pursue an object that was of only secondary importance. He was sure that the legislature "intended to assist and not distress" the western countries. The mobilization of a thousand men from the region would defeat the legislature's desires and harm agriculture. If the men were to be drafted, they should be called from all parts of the State.[83]

But approval of the suspension was a mere trickle compared to the flood of protest which poured into Mifflin's office. Had it been a simple matter of land development, the Governor's problem would have been less difficult. But unfortunately for him it involved a series of controversial issues which had agitated the minds of politicians for several years. Resentment at Britain's failure to relinquish certain frontier posts had increased when it was feared that she planned to extend her forts to Presque Isle and thus control the whole northwest region.

Those who had greeted the French Revolution with enthusiasm and sided with France looked with distrust on an administration which evidently wanted to appease the British. As one who had banqueted with Genêt and later proposed a toast to French success in the European war, Mifflin was expected to oppose any measure that favored British interests. And when his advisers repeatedly assured him that the suspension was just such a measure, he had to act accordingly. The western voters and their Republican leaders were important, and since the transmontane region was preponderantly anti-British in sentiment, Mifflin had to take their protests seriously.

Although he wanted to disregard the President's order, he could not have been unmindful of the possible consequences. Had he gone ahead with the Presque Isle establishment and precipitated a general Indian war, public opinion would have censured him severely. He could not afford to take that chance.

Up to the end of his long period of correspondence with Knox and Washington, Mifflin, aside from examining his conscience and his constitutional rights, had accomplished nothing. Only once, after receiving an opinion from Ingersoll on the illegality of continuing the suspension indefinitely, did he present Washington with a proposition of any finality. That occurred when he tried to force the President into a withdrawal of the suspension order under a threat of proceeding with the establishment unless the latter asked him to convene the legislature. That was a clever maneuver, for had Washington requested a special session of the Assembly, he would have thereby confirmed Mifflin's often expressed doubt as to his constitutional right to obey a presidential order at variance with legislative command. It was a nice point indeed. But circumstances made is unnecessary for Washington to take action on those alternatives.

Just as the Washington-Mifflin correspondence was reaching a climax, something happened in the troubled western counties of Pennsylvania which diverted the attention of both executives to a far more serious problem. On July 17, 1794, an enraged mob attacked the home of John Neville, one of many officers engaged in collecting an unpopular tax on whiskey. Ever since the passage of the national excise law in 1791, western farmers and distillers had protested against the collection of what they considered an unfair and discriminatory tax. Indignation meetings had been held, condemnatory resolutions passed and occasionally enforcement officers had been hampered in their attempts to register stills and collect the excise. The armed attack on Neville's house was by far the most violent incident that had occurred, and Washington was not disposed to regard it lightly. As a matter of fact he was convinced that the western opposition was so serious as to call for the employment of militia. Accordingly, on August 2, 1794, he asked Mifflin to send troops westward to enforce the law.

The request confronted the Governor with another dilemma. Was he legally authorized to use troops for such purposes? He could use them to fight Indians, but could he send Pennsylvania militia against western Pennsylvanians? After a careful search of the statutes he decided that he had no such specific authority, and therefore refused to comply with the request. However, when the President proclaimed an emergency on August 7, 1794, and asked for troops from various states, including Pennsylvania, Mifflin immediately cooperated by setting the State's draft machinery in motion. On the same day he asked the Assembly to meet in special session for the purpose of enacting legislation suitable to the emergency.

As events turned out then, neither Washington nor Mifflin found it necessary to convene the legislature to consider the Presque Isle question. That issue had been thrust into the background by the overshadowing importance of the excise disturbances.

But when Mifflin addressed the Assembly on September 2, 1794, he did not fail to include the troublesome subject in his remarks. After dwelling at some length on the whiskey riots he asked the lawmakers to make a decision on the suspension. They were competent to decide, he said rather bluntly, whether the "interest of the Union, requires in any degree, a sacrifice of the local interests of the State. . . ."[84]

Failing to reveal any signs of the vexation and perturbation that had marked Mifflin's views on the subject, the predominantly Federalist legislature unhurriedly and calmly took it into consideration. After some discussion it passed an act on September 23, 1794, which authorized the Governor to suspend the Presque Isle development.[85]

In the meantime, General Wayne had met the western tribes on August 20, 1794, and decisively defeated them at the Battle of Fallen Timbers. As a result, the possibility of conflict with the Six Nations was somewhat lessened. It was also thought that the victory had weakened the British influence over them.[86]

But the administration did not consider Wayne's triumph as a sufficient reason for removing the obstacles to the Presque Isle development. Although anxious to keep the Six Nations neutral for timely military reasons, Washington also wished to establish a more durable foundation for peace between them and the United States. It is not unlikely that a motivating factor behind this wish was anxiety regarding the delicate, if not precarious, relationship between Britain and the United States. No one could forget that the British still held forts on American soil which they had promised to vacate in 1783. These forts were definite threats to American security. Since the Six Nations were strategically located between the fringe of western settlements and these troublesome posts, the national government could not afford to ignore Indian complaints regarding land purchases. The seriousness of the complaints were accented by British maneuvers in the region. Actually it was a studied part of British frontier policy to create there an Indian buffer state or zone which under their tutelage would "shut off the United States from all contact with the Great Lakes and the St. Lawrence and would secure the strategic approaches to Canada."[87]

In an attempt to settle their grievances, some of which involved the Presque Isle establishment, the national government made arrangements to meet the Six Nations at Canandaigua in the autumn of 1794. (It will be recalled that Mifflin had declined an invitation to send commissioners to the proposed meeting.) The conference was held, and on November 11, 1794, a treaty was signed. For a satisfactory boundary settlement the United States paid $10,000 in merchandise and promised in addition to pay the Indians goods to the amount of $4,500 annually forever after.

When the Senate had ratified the treaty Timothy Pickering, then Secretary of War, notified Mifflin on January 27, 1795, "that the temporary obstacles to the establishment formerly contemplated by the State of Pennsylvania at Presqu' Isle are removed."[88] With the suspension lifted the Assembly on April 18, 1795, passed another act authorizing the survey of town sites at Franklin, Warren, Waterford and Presque Isle. The town at Presque Isle was to be called Erie. In the following December, Mifflin notified the legislature that all the surveys had been completed.[89] When lots in the various towns were later placed on sale the response was enthusiastic. At Carlisle, where sales exceeded expectations, some lots brought a price of over $300.

In conclusion, it should be said that the Presque Isle establishment, considered merely as one of the many land development schemes which dotted Pennsylvania history, is hardly deserving of the extended treatment received here. Its real importance, however, lies in the significant political and governmental question it presented. Although the whiskey disturbances made unnecessary a resolution of the problem regarding a conflict of authority between the State and national governments, the resentment engendered by Washington's suspension order played a notable role in the State's political development. However intangible were its results in terms of concrete election returns—it is impossible, for instance, to say what, if any, impression it had on the election of 1794—it was, nevertheless, integrally productive of a cumulative effect. As an example of executive interference in State functions it furthered opposition to the Federalist concept of strong central authority and gave the Republicans another weapon with which to attack their opponents. As an alleged encroachment on a State's authority, it was considered by some to be premonitory and symptomatic; and as such it fitted neatly into the slowing rising wall of Republican opposition.

In this instance government interference angered speculators and businessmen, a particularly influential group, for it included men like Wilkins, Redick, Ellicott and Irvine, all of whom were politically important. That Mifflin did not underrate their influence is evidenced by the solicitude and concern he showed in responding to their complaints. As far as Mifflin himself was concerned, no responsible group blamed him for his part in the suspension. He had come through with flying colors.

As a land development scheme the Presque Isle venture ended happily for all concerned—for all that is, except the Indians. At Fort Harmar, in 1789, they had sold their last remnant of land in Pennsylvania. In 1794 they had confirmed that sale at Canandaigua in return for goods and a guarantee of boundaries which would allow them to occupy certain lands elsewhere.

But less than two years later, in a speech at Fort Franklin, Cornplanter, Seneca chieftain, complained that in the summer of 1795 a "Gentleman from Albany" bought some of the lands allotted to the Six Nations. He predicted that the unjust purchases would continue "until they get all from us, and then we shall be left in distress." He preceded his revelation of the purchase by an eloquent appeal to the President: "Genl Washington, the Father of us all, hear what I have now to say, and take pity on us poor people. The Almighty has blest you, and not us. He has given you education, which enables you to do many things that we cannot do. You can travel by sea, as well as by land, and know what is doing in any other countries, which we poor people know nothing about. Therefore you ought to pity us."[90] Thus the savage to those whom "the Almighty has blest. . . ."

CHAPTER VIII

POLITICAL OPINIONS AND ELECTIONS
1793-1795

FROM 1793 TO 1795 the cumulative effect of the Genêt episode (expressing as it did the division of opinion in regard to France), the work of the Democratic Societies, the Whiskey Rebellion and Jay's Treaty was such as to produce two general bodies of opinion, Republican and Federalist. But had these events produced two political parties by 1795? The answer to that question requires an examination of the elections held during those years.

RE-ELECTION OF MIFFLIN

In 1793 Mifflin again went before the electorate as a candidate for the governorship. Renominated in the spring through the medium of a legislative caucus, he soon discovered that his most serious competitor was Frederick A. Muhlenberg,[1] a former Lutheran clergyman who had served with distinction in the Continental Congress, the State Assembly and the Congress of the United States.

Mifflin had been in office only a few months when Muhlenberg, thinking ahead to the next gubernatorial election, wrote to James Wilson that the Governor had already lost greatly in public favor.[2] He was convinced that, had he run in 1790, Mifflin would not have polled even a hundred votes in Berks County, Muhlenberg's own area. If Mifflin sought re-election, Muhlenberg assured his correspondent, he would lose not only Berks but Northampton and Montgomery counties as well. His prediction, possibly a bid for Wilson's future support, was to be proved completely wrong.

Candidate Muhlenberg had much in his favor. As a public figure he had a reputation for integrity and ability, and as the first presiding officer of the House of Representatives he had brought credit to himself and recognition to his State. His rather heavy face, with its prominent nose, pursed lips and double chins, was well known to America's leading politicians.[3] Of the candidate's excellent qualities his supporters did not lose sight, but considerable emphasis was placed on the fact that he was not "entirely immersed in party views."[4] An anonymous writer in the *General Advertiser* thought that he had been proposed only because he was a German, and that his candidacy indicated a strong disposition on the part of the Pennsylvania Germans to monopolize State politics and appropriate all the "loaves and fishes" to themselves. That they were adept at tilling the soil and saving money the correspondent readily admitted, but those attributes did not give them "the exclusive right to govern." The Constitution should be amended, he facetiously suggested, so as to permit each nationality to have its own Governor.[5] It is possible, incidentally, that the existence of the German Republican Society was as provocative of the writer's remarks as was Muhlenberg's candidacy.

Mifflin, as an incumbent seeking another term, was of course a much bigger target for his political enemies. Brought under attack by a writer who called himself "Anti-Janus," he was accused of making unwise judicial appointments, of enforcing the law in a haphazard manner, and of permitting citizens to be bullied out of their suffrage privileges during elections.[6] He had abused the pardoning power, said a correspondent, by freeing an inordinate number of persons for "electioneering purposes" and for "private emolument." Jobs had been created for no justifiable reason, unqualified men had been appointed to responsible positions, and "tories" had been "exalted to the first stations." Mifflin had turned Pennsylvania into a private estate with himself as lord of the manor.[7] Nor did the Governor's opponents fail to question the propriety of his association with "foreign emissaries" and factions.[8] Although no mention was made in this connection of Minister Genêt or of Mifflin's attendance at a Democratic Society pro-French celebration on August 8, 1793, the allusion was clear and the censure unmistakable.

Mifflin was also condemned for choosing Dallas as Secretary of the Commonwealth over "those whig characters" who had risked "fame, fortune and life" while fighting a country in which, at the time, Dallas held citizenship. To his political opponents Dallas, who had signed citizenship papers in 1783 and later became an active member of the Anglophobic Democratic Society, was still a "Briton" and a foreigner.

But if Mifflin had his detractors, he also had his champions. The ablest of these was "Atticus," who submitted letters to the *General Advertiser* in support of Mifflin's appointments and his exercise of the pardoning power. On August 8, 1793, he reproved Bache for publishing so many anti-Mifflin vilifications. "Is such abuse warrantable," he asked, "merely because the object is a public servant; are such accusations to be received merely because the party is an officer of the government?"⁹ To this "Anti-Janus" reacted with all the vigor of one who thought he saw an attack on the freedom of the press. Declaring Dallas to be the writer "Atticus," he condemned the presumption of an *"English subject"* in arraigning a native American printer for maintaining a free press.¹⁰

Bache, one year later to favor Frederick A. Muhlenberg for Congress, certainly did not discourage his anti-Mifflin correspondents. His paper bristled with their diatribes and "Atticus," whose first letter in defense of Mifflin was not published, submitted another merely to test Bache's impartiality. Certainly the editor made no effort to spare the feelings of his colleague in the Pennsylvania Democratic Society. Once he even violated custom by placing a letter accusing Dallas of being "Atticus" on the *Advertiser's* front page, an area usually reserved for advertising.¹¹

With the exception of the newspaper attacks on Mifflin and Dallas in July and August, 1793, the election offered little excitement and produced no innovations in campaign procedures. Although the Pennsylvania Democratic Society issued a circular letter in July, 1793, urging Republicans to organize county societies for election purposes, none acted on the suggestion.¹² Unlike the election of the preceding year, this one saw no committees of correspondence laboring assiduously to organize opinion. For this general apathy several reasons can be suggested: (1) The two leading candidates did not differ so widely in principle as to create either a wide divergence of opinion or a body of rabid partisans. Regardless of the outcome, neither the Federalists nor the Republicans had reason to fear startling or radical changes in the State government. The Governor's use of patronage had not created undue antagonisms because he had appointed men of both groups to office. Therefore, he could reasonably expect considerable bi-partisan support. Muhlenberg was not regarded as a strong party man, and if elected he could hardly be expected to dismiss large numbers of office-holders for partisan reasons. Generally, there was little evidence of party spirit during the campaign. Even the newspaper correspondents did not refer to either candidate as being representative of a particular group.

(2) The Genêt affair had not redounded to the Republicans' advantage, particularly after the French Minister's extravagant conduct tended to embarrass many who had received him with open cordiality. When, according to report, he threatened to supersede Washington's authority by appealing his cause to the people, it dismayed many who

revered the President as America's greatest hero. Genêt denied having made the threat but the damage had been done.[13]

It would have been political suicide for any man or group of men to vie with Washington in popular appeal. The effect on Philadelphia was, in James Hutchinson's opinion, so profound as to have "totally overturned the democratic interest."[14] It is quite possible, therefore, that Dallas and his associates hesitated to launch a Republican-sponsored campaign for fear that it would alienate many who might otherwise be disposed to forget that Mifflin had sat at a banquet table with the now discredited Genêt. It is almost certain that Dallas wanted to forget the whole episode, for it had burst on the political scene only because he had carried Genêt's alleged "appeal" threat to Mifflin, where it had not stopped. A more astute politician would not have acted in such haste.

(3) Also contributive to the election lethargy—at least in the Philadelphia area—was the yellow fever, a dread visitation that descended upon the city in the waning summer months. Thousands died and thousands more fled into the country. The newspapers, chief communicants of political propaganda, dwindled in size or suspended publication altogether.[15] Men thought of little else than the calamity which touched almost every home. At its height, just preceding the election, Philadelphians had little inclination to discuss politics or even to attend the polls.

With the State capital completely demoralized, the lethargic campaign dragged to a quiet close. When the returns were counted Mifflin was found to be an easy winner with 19,590 tallies to Muhlenberg's 10,700.[16] The Governor had a comfortable margin of approximately two to one, but it did not compare favorably to his almost ten-to-one victory over St. Clair in 1790. Muhlenberg won in only York and Bedford counties, but his record in all was much better than St. Clair's. In the Philadelphia area only 567 hardy souls voted. This was a loss of 1,285 compared to the gubernatorial election vote of 1790. Philadelphia and Bucks counties showed a combined loss of 1,852.

Election of 1794

In preparation for the Congressional election of 1794, the legislature, by an act of April 22, divided the State into twelve districts. The district composed of Bucks, Northampton and Montgomery counties was to select two representatives; the others were to choose one each. In accordance with former practice, representatives could be taken from the State at large.[17]

From the time work was begun on the bill in February, it was clear that most of the assemblymen favored the district system over an election at large. The chaotic election of 1792 was still fresh in their minds and it is quite possible that they wished to avoid another similar wave of factionalism. In the House, however, a minority of eighteen favored a general election, and because of their tactics the bill did not have a smooth passage. Their opposition was based on the following contentions: by implication the United States Constitution required an election "by the whole people, and not by any artificial subdivisions . . ."; the district method would leave fractions unrepresented because men would be inclined to "support the local interests . . ." rather than the interests of the State; the people did not request the new method. In their most interesting and significant objection they stated that even the Governor was chosen by "general suffrage." Yet by comparison his election "is not of half the consequence with the election of that body [the United States House of Representatives], on whose vote the right of Peace War, and all other great national questions may be finally suspended."[18]

When the House passed the district bill on February 27, 1794, by a vote of forty-five to eighteen, there was no indication of a factional division. The majority numbered members of both major groups, including such Federalists as Presley Neville, Cadwalader Evans, and Gerardus Wynkoop. In the minority were such politically diverse individuals as John Swanwick and Henry Kammerer, Republicans, and Jacob Hiltzheimer and Benjamin Morgan, Federalists, all from the Philadelphia area. Members in opposition came from various parts of the State, but most of them represented eastern counties.

With the abandonment of the general election system the Congressional campaign area was shifted from the State at large and placed within the confines of twelve districts. Gone was the necessity for State-wide nominatory procedure with its legislative caucuses, committees of correspondence and State conventions. The task of nominating thus devolved upon the county and district politicians.

In meeting the challenge, they had recourse to the usual haphazard methods of personal and semi-private nominations and to the customary general meeting held just before election day. But in Montgomery County an effort was made to provide a more representative mode of preliminary selection within the counties and districts. It was a method designed to give nominatory expression to small segments of the population bounded in this instance by township lines.

In accordance with resolutions passed at a meeting held at Norristown on August 12, 1794, the several townships selected two delegates each to attend a meeting for the purpose of electing a committee of five men, whose duty it would be to meet similar committees from Northampton and Bucks counties.[19] All three counties composed one Congressional district and were entitled to elect two Congressmen. The township representatives (chosen at the "usual township meeting places") met on August 30, 1794, and named a county committee. It was to collaborate not only with the counties in the Congressional district but with those in the Senatorial district of which Montgomery formed a part along with Bucks and Chester counties.[20] Information is lacking as to whether or not other counties followed Montgomery's lead, but in subsequent elections they were to do so.

As the candidates for Federal and State legislative offices were placed before the public, there was but little evidence of factional strife. The results of various nominating meetings held in the eastern counties were published in Bache's *General Advertiser,* Fenno's *Gazette* and Claypoole's *American Daily Advertiser,* and in no instance was specific mention made of political parties.

Generally speaking, the election was unrelievedly dull. Bache, ever alert to the ebb and flow of political tides, castigated the public for its "criminal indifference" at a time of "crisis." Everybody expected that the whiskey disturbances would bring a hotly contested election, he said, "but unless indeed matters are working in secret it would appear as if there would be no election."[21] In an effort to arouse the voters from the torpor which had apparently seized them, he pleaded for the election of men who favored a strict construction of the Constitution and the abolition of excise taxes. On October 13, 1794, he made a special plea for F. A. Muhlenberg, who was running for Congress in Philadelphia County. Muhlenberg's re-election was advocated because he had opposed the "extension of the excise system."[22]

But in spite of Bache's efforts, the public remained apathetic toward the election. It had been overshadowed by the whiskey disturbances. Thousands of men who might have enlivened the situation were marching over the mountains to punish the "whiskey boys." The presence of fifteen thousand armed men on Pennsylvania soil placed the election in the background.

In Philadelphia some interest was shown in the contest between Fitzsimons and Swanwick for the city's Congressional seat. Swanwick, abandoning the coyness expected of office-seeking politicians, made no secret of his intentions. He wanted to be a Congressman, and he had no desire to practice any genteel hypocrisy.²³ For such a violation of the accepted mode of conduct he was attacked by "T. T." in the *Gazette of the United States.* With obvious nostalgia "T. T." harked back to the days prior to 1792, when a candidate's friends worked privately in the interest of their choice while the candidate himself, "observing a reserve and decorum, evinced a becoming respect for public opinion and permitted it to take its own direction without an unfair bias." But all this had been changed by Swanwick, who "was the first to move forward in this new style." He was, declared "T. T.," an unstable, avaricious upstart who was unknown as a public figure until he "herded with its enemies [the public's enemies] and became their tool."²⁴ Here he was undoubtedly referring to Swanwick's association with the Pennsylvania Democratic Society and the anti-excise movement.

After Swanwick had been endorsed by a meeting at the German Lutheran schoolhouse on October 7, 1794, Fitzsimons' supporters took a counter action by announcing one of their own to be held on October 11, 1794.²⁵ When Bache mentioned the meeting in his paper, without directly identifying its sponsors, he deplored the practice of framing tickets before an election. But since such tickets were presented, he said, every man either had to make a choice "or throw away his vote." Therefore, in view of the influence exerted by prepared lists, he urged all Philadelphians to participate on October 11, as there would be little time to "modify" its result before election day.²⁶

When the citizens assembled at City Hall on October 11, 1794, at an hour too early for the convenience of "mechanics," Federalist Charles Biddle was elected chairman. After an exclusively Federalist list of names for State and Federal legislative offices was proposed, headed of course by Fitzsimons, it appeared for a moment as if "the republican spirit" would upset the calculations of the meeting's sponsors.²⁷ Despite the fact that the gathering "originated in a different interest," said the *General Advertiser,* "the nomination of John Swanwick was nearly confirmed and it was only after a second shew of hands that the chairman and judges could determine the question against him."²⁸

Although Fitzsimons had the endorsement of a general Philadelphia meeting and the unqualified support of the *Gazette of the United States,* he lost the election to Swanwick by a vote of 1,142 to 894. It is quite likely that Swanwick owed his success to the anti-excise sentiment, the "German" support and possibly to the Pennsylvania Democratic Society. In contrast to Fitzsimons' defeat it is of interest to note that all the assemblymen nominated by the Philadelphia meeting on October 11, 1794, were elected. To a writer in the *General Advertiser* the excise issue had been clear, and Swanwick's election was proof of the dominant anti-excise opinion in Philadelphia.[29]

When the election returns were all tabulated, the results, from the standpoint of partisanship, were rather inconclusive. The advantage, however, slight as it was, seemed to be with the Federalists. They elected Frederick A. Muhlenberg, John Richards, Richard Thomas, John W. Kittera, Thomas Hartley, Samuel Sitgreaves, and Daniel Hiester. The Republicans elected were John Swanwick, William Findley, Andrew Gregg, Samuel Maclay, Albert Gallatin and David Bard.[30]

As to the Federalist complexion of the new State legislature there was little doubt. With evident satisfaction the *Gazette of the United States* congratulated the voters on their wisdom in choosing "a great majority of Federal characters" to represent them in the Assembly. In the opinion of the *Gazette* the result indicated unequivocal "approbation" of the Federal administration. Indeed, the legislature soon displayed its Federalist character.[31] Shortly after organizing for the new session it elected Federalist speakers for both houses. Then, on February 26, 1795, it elected William Bingham, ultra-conservative Federalist leader in Philadelphia, to the United States Senate.[32]

Election of 1795 and Jay's Treaty

When Pennsylvania elected assemblymen again in 1795, the results were not greatly different from previous elections. Had Fenno's *Gazette* expressed an opinion on the returns, it would have been pleased to note that a majority of "Federal characters" had been selected once more. As only another "off-year" election it would not merit particular mention here had it not developed significant and important characteristics in the city and county of Philadelphia.

In those two districts, each of which was entitled to six Representatives,[33] the election produced a sharp and distinct partisan cleavage. Primarily the division sprang from resentment created by senatorial ratification of Jay's Treaty in August. Divided opinion on the subject manifested itself in the formation of "Treaty" and "Anti-Treaty" legislative tickets in the two districts.[34]

After a bitter campaign, the "Treaty Men" won in the city by approximately 400 votes, but in Philadelphia County they lost by over 250 votes.[35] Under ordinary circumstances the election would have been purely a matter of local interest, but when the influential *Aurora* threw its weight into the struggle it escaped local bounds. To Bache the contest was a golden opportunity to attack Jay's Treaty, and through it, the Washington administration. And as owner of one of the country's leading Republican papers, he could not be ignored.

As an issue the Treaty fitted neatly into his editorial hand. In his opinion, it was a vile and monstrous thing, and using it as a spalling hammer he attacked the whole Federalist conception of government. With vigorous and telling strokes he hacked away at the Federalist position and planted chink-forming wedges which, under constant pummelings, were to create serious fissures in the most conservative wing of the Federalist structure. The crevices were to appear a few months later in Pennsylvania when the State gave all but one of its electoral votes to Jefferson. As a master craftsman in the art of opinion building, the editor thus became the harbinger of the first significant Republican victory in Pennsylvania.

As a vehicle for Bache's opinions and those of the correspondents who fed its columns, the *Aurora* concentrated not only on the Treaty but on the alleged evils of the Washington administration which the Treaty supposedly epitomized. Both became targets for men who hated Britain and loved France;[36] both were deplored by all those who expressed fear of aristocratic principles and the overweening power of great wealth. Men in favor of the Treaty, declared pseudonymous "Cleon," were swayed by "British agents, old tories, the power of the Banks, and a long list of unprincipled speculators, who, like leeches, stick to our administration [national], because they fatten on its corruption. . . ."[37] In those few words "Cleon" admirably summarized Bache's position.

Of course, Bache's arguments against the Treaty did not go unanswered. John Fenno, editor of the *Gazette of the United States*, and William Cobbett, two journalists who supported the "Treaty Men" at every turn, were his ablest opponents. Both proclaimed the Treaty as being in the best interests of the United States, and Cobbett utilized it as an effective argument to deter the administration from making an alliance with France.[38] Cobbett, who was not to establish *Porcupine's Gazette* until 1797, at this time aired his trenchant views through the media of pamphlets. In one of his best efforts, a work entitled "A Little Plain English," written in August, 1795, he praised the Treaty as an instrument conducive to amity and better commercial relations between England and America.[39] But as one who feared the French Revolution and despised all "democrats" he could not discuss the Treaty's economic aspects without relating them directly to current political issues. And as he did so his abusive language often made him and his arguments extraordinarily vulnerable. When discussing the groups at loggerheads over the Treaty, for instance, he described those in opposition as being "almost the whole of that description of persons, who, among us royalists, are generally designated by the mob."[40] Such language was fuel for the *Aurora's* ever-burning fires.

Cobbett's influence on American public opinion is difficult to assess, but as a Francophobe and British propagandist it must have been considerable. In England his efforts were not unappreciated. There, in 1803, some years after the master polemicist left the American scene, at least one member of Parliament thought he deserved a "statue of gold" for "services" rendered to his country during "a most trying crisis in America. . . ."[41]

As an issue the Treaty was the best one that had been presented to the Pennsylvania Republicans. With its local, national and international ramifications, it presented a multi-faceted target for attack, and its timely interjection into the political stream climaxed a body of protest which had been developing over a period of years. But most important of all it was an issue which, in the hands of the Republicans, caused no embarrassment to its exploiters. In three previous attacks on Federalist policy the Republican schemes had gone awry. Their political weapons had developed an unfortunate habit of exploding instead of firing, and each instance of opposition had bred its own counter opposition. The enthusiasm for France produced a Genêt; the anti-excise protest created an insurrection; and the Democratic Societies had aroused the anger of Washington. But the opposition to Jay's Treaty did not boomerang.

The effect of Jay's Treaty on political development in Pennsylvania was such that, fifteen years later, a writer in John Binn's *Democratic Press* declared that "properly speaking the correct demarcation of parties in the state, ought to be dated from 1795, at the period when Mr. Jay's treaty was submitted to the senate. . . . The adoption of the British treaty accurately decided the fate of parties in this state, and from that period until 1805; there were only known democrats and federalists."[42]

Election of Senators by the Legislature

For a further examination of political development during the period from 1793 to 1795, some attention should be given to the election of United States Senators by the Pennsylvania legislature. Several were chosen during these years, and with the exception of Gallatin all were essentially conservative in their political opinions. Gallatin's election in 1793 really had its beginnings in 1789.

When the United States Senate first convened, it divided its membership into three distinct classes and allotted definite terms of office to each. This was in compliance with a specific constitutional order, the purpose of which was to prevent a complete change in Senatorial membership every six years.[43] In the drawing of lots to determine classification William Maclay was placed in that division of Senators whose terms expired on March 3, 1791.

Early in 1790 Maclay learned that "a certain set in Philadelphia" would oppose his re-election.[44] At the time it seemed to be an inconsequential matter, but as the months went by and the rumors grew more insistent, he began electioneering in his own behalf. Hoping for William Findley's valuable support, he paid the shrewd assemblyman a visit. The interview was not encouraging, and Maclay left in fear that Findley would work for John Montgomery of Carlisle.[45] He then went to Montgomery with the suggestion that the "agricultural interest of Pennsylvania" ought to unite to prevent the Philadelphians from driving a wedge of dissension between him (Maclay) and Findley. If this were effected, they would elect William Bingham. Montgomery agreed that such might be the case, but was otherwise noncommittal. Not disposed to neglect any opportunity, Maclay was the first to assist Thomas Hartley when this Representative fell and broke his arm. Maclay's quick solicitude was prompted by the suspicion that Hartley opposed his re-election.[46]

When the situation looked black, he could always console himself with his diary. "I can not help wishing myself honorably quit of the enviable station,"[47] he wrote on December 22, 1790. It had brought "calumny and detraction . . . slander and defamation . . ." and if he tried to defend himself, his enemies accused him of trying to collect votes. "What a set of vipers!"[48]

Seven days later, he was ashamed of himself for thinking so much about the election. Why did he want the office anyway? Was he not "blessed with affluence" and thoroughly domesticated? Did he not loathe Philadelphia and the "prevailing politics of the times"? Was he a "placeman, speculator, pensioner, or courtier" in need of a job? Why, he wrote, it is as "absurd for me to wish a continuance in Congress as to desire to walk among briers and thorns rather than on the beaten road."[49] But, however absurd the notion and thorny the path, he still wanted the senatorship. To be "honorably quit" of the office he would have to be elected for another term. The thought of defeat was unbearable. Convinced, however, that his cause was hopeless, he determined to have his mare saddled in readiness to leave immediately upon hearing that another man had been elected. Such, at any rate, was his expressed intention in December, 1790.

But if Maclay and his mare had waited for the dilatory legislature to choose a Senator, they would not have seen the Susquehanna for over two years. That much time was to expire before Pennsylvania would again have a full representation in the United States Senate.

Shortly after the legislature began discussion on the topic in August, 1791, it became evident that the method of selection would be the most difficult problem to solve. Briefly put, the question at issue was as follows: should the new Senator be chosen by a concurrent or joint vote of both houses? Of these two methods the House, under the speakership of William Bingham, was overwhelmingly in favor of the latter. That was conclusively demonstrated on September 10, 1791, when it approved a committee recommendation to that effect by a vote of fifty-seven to three.[50] But when a resolution favoring a joint vote went to the Senate it was promptly defeated. The summer session ended on September 30, 1791, with the houses still deadlocked on the issue.

Nor did they fare any better when the subject was again considered the following December. Then both houses prepared measures embodying their favorite means of selection. But bills and resolutions, amendments and counter amendments traveled back and forth with monotonous regularity, always returning to their place of origin bearing the anticipated irritants—"joint" for "concurrent" and *vice versa*. Unfortunately, the question did not lend itself readily to compromise, and both houses remained obdurate. The Senate even turned down a House suggestion that the dispute be submitted to a conference committee.[51] Instead, it displayed irritating intractibility by taking matters into its own hands. On February 23, 1792, it passed an arbitrary resolution which specified March 2 as the date on which it would choose a Senator. The House was requested to make its selection on the day following. If both houses agreed on the same man, everything would be satisfactory.

If not, concurrent elections would be held until agreement was reached.⁵²

The House did not look with favor upon such a proposal. Especially active against it was Albert Gallatin, of Fayette County, who had led House opposition to the Senate for the past year. On February 24, 1792, he persuaded the House to postpone action on the Senate resolution until further efforts could be made to secure a conference between the two branches.⁵³ A few days later the Senate withdrew its opposition to a conference and one was held. Its deliberations, however, produced no solution to the problem, and the session ended.

When the legislators returned in the following December, 1792, Mifflin decided to take notice of the stalemate. In his remarks on the question, so mildly phrased as almost to conceal a gentle reproof, he confessed to a feeling of mortification at Pennsylvania's weakened representation in the United States Senate. But he had no opinions to offer in the way of solution. He was satisfied to rely on the "wisdom" and "patriotism" of the assemblymen.⁵⁴

The legislators were prompt to exercise their "wisdom" by attacking the problem with the same methods they had used in the preceding session. Both houses passed bills similar to previous ones. The House, by a vote of forty-four to sixteen approved a measure for which John Swanwick and Albert Gallatin were chiefly responsible.⁵⁵ In the upper house, however, opinion was more evenly divided. Adhering to their original intention, those men who insisted on concurrent action forced through a resolution by a nine to eight vote which committed the Senate to an election on January 15, 1793.⁵⁶ The election was held according to schedule and James Ross was chosen as the Senate's Senator. But the eight minority members abstained from voting on the grounds that such action was unconstitutional, and that a legislative measure was necessary to determine a mode of selection.⁵⁷ The lower house, prompted by Swanwick and Gallatin, agreed with the dissenters and refused to "take any order" on the Senate's resolution. It was another deadlock.

But it was soon to be broken in a manner that surprised everyone but a few Senators. Realizing that the slight majority favoring concurrent action would remain adamant, the minority group of eight men waited patiently until the opposition was not at full strength in the Senate chamber. Their chance came on February 19, 1793, when only seven "concurrent" men appeared for the morning session. The others were absent on calls "to domestic life."⁵⁸ Quick to exploit such a fortunate circumstance the eight men, now the majority, hurriedly passed resolutions for which they had long contended. Before the noon recess, they triumphantly placed the Senate on record as favoring a joint *viva voce* election to be held on February 28, 1793.[59] The resolutions were then rushed to the lower house where they were approved on the following day.

The seven Senators who had been outvoted filed a dissent in which they maintained that the opposition had taken advantage of an "accidental majority" to infringe upon "the rights of the people."[60] A joint vote, they contended, prevented the legislative branches from checking each other. Such action was therefore clearly unconstitutional both from a State and national viewpoint. But the trick had been successful and the problem was solved. Nothing more could be done about it.

While the legislature had been engaged in its protracted quarrel over election methods, several aspirants to the office in question were anxiously awaiting its denouement. Arthur St. Clair, for instance, Governor of the Northwest Territory since 1787, wanted another job. He hated Cincinnati so much that even the thought of dying in that place was unbearable. If death, the "Grim Rascal," seized him there he would not rest comfortably in his grave. Of that he was certain. Then learning that he would receive some support for the senatorship, he came to the conclusion that the legislators would cease their bickering if they could agree on a suitable candidate. Perhaps he would be the man. So, when James Ross was proposed, St. Clair asked him if he would accept if elected. If Ross did not want the office he should so declare. Then their mutual friends would not be divided.

But Ross was also ambitious. After he and Alexander Addison had talked the matter over, they decided that St. Clair's optimistic supporters may have overestimated his chances of success. If that were the case, they reasoned, any attempt to elect him might end in the selection of someone less deserving than either of them. To avert such an unfortunate occurrence, Addison was authorized to announce Ross' candidacy if it seemed that St. Clair would fail of election. On January 20, 1793, Addison acquainted Albert Gallatin with the above turn of events and hinted that the "country members" should be informed of the situation. In Addison's opinion, no man could better "unite the general voice in his favour than Mr. Ross."[61] Apparently Judge Addison did not suspect that the man to whom he was writing would be the one to succeed in uniting "the general voice."

As election day drew near both Houses prepared lists of nominees. The Senate offered the names of James Ross, Colonel Henry Miller, William Irvine, Daniel Hiester and William Maclay. The House nominated the same men plus Gallatin, St. Clair, Peter Muhlenberg, Charles Thomson, William Bingham, William Smith, Edward Hand, H. H. Brackenridge, John Hannum and John Swanwick.[62] Such an array and variety of nominees would seem to indicate that the members were unorganized and hopelessly divided. But that was not the case.

When the election was held on February 28, 1793, it became evident that many candidates had been nominated by men who had no intention of voting for them. It also became evident that there had been much maneuvering behind the scenes. Of the fifteen men nominated, two, Henry Miller and Albert Gallatin, collected all but two of the total number of votes recorded. Gallatin was the winner over Miller by a vote of forty-five to thirty-five.[63] St. Clair and Irvine got one vote each and the anxious Maclay got none. Ross, despite the fact that he had once been the Senate's choice, received no support. The upper house's eighteen votes were divided evenly between the two leading candidates.[64] Although Gallatin received tallies from all sections, his heaviest support came from the western counties.[65] In the eastern part of the State twenty House members, representing an area covered by the city and the counties of Philadelphia, Bucks and Delaware, gave him only six votes.

When one considers the disadvantages under which Gallatin labored as a candidate, his success seems rather surprising. He had been a United States citizen for such a short time that he himself had doubted his eligibility on constitutional grounds when his name was proposed in a legislative caucus.[66] Also, as one who had resided in Pennsylvania for only a few years, he was lacking in family influence and long political associations.[67] Finally, and most important, Republican Gallatin belonged to the minority group in a legislature which was preponderantly Federalist. With unvarying consistency both branches had always elected Federalist speakers. This fact alone would make enigmatic his triumph over Henry Miller, a member of the dominant group. But along with these not inconsiderable handicaps were several conjunctively countervailing factors which served to operate in candidate Gallatin's favor.

As a legislator he displayed outstanding capacities from the very beginning of his career. A clever organizer of opinion, a shrewd and resourceful speaker, his abilities did not long go unrecognized. As a member of many important committees he distinguished himself in financial and parliamentary matters. And in the struggle over electoral procedures with the Senate he had played a vital role in defending the House's prerogatives.

Gallatin, then, was a person quite capable of transcending group alignments, weak and tenuously drawn as they were. This, at least, applied with particular force insofar as the country members were concerned. They knew him as an anti-excise man and a defender of agrarian interests. Fresh from bucolic pursuits and occasionally abashed by the polished debating smoothness of Philadelphia lawyers, they saw one of their own successfully match wits with the best that the city offered. Truly, a feeling of pride for Gallatin would have been for them a pardonable and not unnatural emotion.

Further, with Robert Morris already in the Senate, they were certainly not averse to selecting a man who would give western expression to the representation. And in this connection precedent favored them. The Senate had already shown a sectional desire to balance Pennsylvania's Senatorial membership when it abortively elected James Ross in January. In 1788 the Assembly had also demonstrated a geographic consciousness when it selected Maclay and Morris. If, therefore, it seemed advisable and expedient for the legislature to elect a westerner, and such appears to have been the case, the situation thus narrowed the field and worked in Gallatin's interest.

Although it is difficult to determine just how strong the Ross-St. Clair supporters were, it is just possible that many shared Addison's fear that they might neutralize each other and cause the election of another man, an easterner perhaps. Maclay, it will be recalled, had feared a similar split in the agrarian interest two years before. With the competition thus conveniently narrowed by geographic influences, Gallatin had some points of advantage. He was not handicapped by a disastrous military defeat, as was St. Clair, and among the assemblymen he was far better known than Ross. Maclay had many enemies, old and new, probably among them Findley who, although not an assemblyman, had considerable influence. Gallatin also had the support of Senator John Smilie—an able manipulator of opinion—, John Swanwick and Henry Kammerer. Although Kammerer nominated Muhlenberg he aided Gallatin.

Finally, some mention should be made of the possible relationship between Gallatin's election and the current pro-French sentiment which was at that time running high. His accent and his knowledge and appreciation of the great French political writers may have induced some to bestow upon him a vicarious approval of French Republican principles.[68] Although it is quite probable that all the above elements contributed to his election, it seems fairly certain that his success was not due to Republican strength in the legislature but primarily to the strength and personality of Gallatin himself.

Immediately after he was chosen on February 28, 1793, his certificate of election was rushed to the United States Senate. That august body, not at all disturbed by Pennsylvania's incomplete representation, waited one year before deciding by a twelve-to-four vote that Gallatin was not eligible to serve. Reference was made to Article I, Section 3, of the Constitution, which forbade Senatorial membership to anyone who had not been a citizen for nine years. Although Gallatin arrived in this country in 1780, one year before the Articles of Confederation conferred on "free inhabitants" the "privileges and immunities of free citizens in the several States," he had not taken the oath of citizenship (in Virginia) until 1785.[69] Therefore, according to a strict interpretation of the Constitution, an interpretation incidentally which would have barred all United States Senators from holding office in 1789, he was technically ineligible.

After Gallatin's expulsion in February, the Pennsylvania legislature was once again faced with the task of selecting a Senator. But this time there was no extended disagreement as to electoral method. Before the end of March, both houses decided to adopt the same procedure they had used the year previously. On April 1, 1794, they met in joint session and elected James Ross over Federalist Robert Coleman, of Lancaster County, by a vote of forty-five to thirty-five. With the exception of Samuel Sitgreaves, who got one Senate vote, no tallies were recorded for any other candidates.[70] Almost all the nominees came from the middle or western counties.

In later years it was asserted that Ross had been elected by a combination of westerners and "antifederal" men in other parts of the State.[71] In 1801 William Findley said Ross was mistakenly considered to be a Republican at the time, and that his election was an error.[72] However, if such an opinion was held in 1794, it is merely further proof of the confused partisan relationships then obtaining, for Ross' subsequent activities stamped him unmistakably as a Federalist.

As Robert Morris' term drew to a close, he resisted the importunities of his friends in the legislature and refused another term. After twenty years of public life he wished to devote his time to private concerns.[73]

When the legislature turned its attention to the selection of another Senator in February (Morris' term expired March 3, 1795), the electoral machinery worked with smooth efficiency. On February 26, 1795, the members, sitting in joint session, elected Federalist William Bingham over Republican Peter Muhlenberg by a vote of fifty-eight to thirty-five.[74] Judging from the list of nominees there seems to be little doubt that the legislature intended to choose a man from the eastern part of the State. For instance, the House proposed William Bingham, Peter Muhlenberg, Thomas Fitzsimons, Charles Pettit and William Irvine. With the exception of Irvine, who came from Carlisle, all resided in the Philadelphia area. Fitzsimons and Bingham were confirmed Federalists, the others were Republicans.

One year later, just a few days before Ross' abbreviated term ended in 1797, he was re-elected over Republican William Irvine by a vote of fifty-six to thirty-eight.[75] Peter Muhlenberg was again nominated but he received no votes. The election was carried off with decisiveness, for the majority had obviously agreed among themselves to support Ross. His western residence, plus the Federalist strength in the legislature, made his election almost inevitable.

Of all the United States Senators chosen by the Pennsylvania Assembly from 1788 to 1795, Gallatin alone had been an avowed Republican at the time of election. It is believed that the somewhat extensive treatment given to the election of a single individual is warranted from the standpoint of the indices it provides for a knowledge of legislative politics just following the rather indecisive Congressional election of 1792. There was as much evidence of political groping in the minds of the assemblymen as there had been in those of the men who drew up the Congressional ticket in the preceding year. And it is probable that the long quarrel over electoral methodology was induced partially, if not primarily, by a failure to agree on a candidate. Men did not yet know where they stood. But in a little over a year, three events occurred which served to mold opinion and limit boundaries: the Genêt incident, the Whiskey Insurrection and the rise of the Democratic Societies. The reaction from each of those occurrences was toward conservatism, and the legislature confirmed that tendency when it appointed two ultra-conservatives, Ross and Bingham, to the Senate. In short, the conservatives in the Pennsylvania Senate must have been so sure that a joint vote would not defeat a Federalist candidate that they withdrew their objection to the method. Such an assurance on their part prior to Ross' election in 1794 would have been incomplete because of the especially foggy political atmosphere. And it is here offered by way of explanation that the atmosphere was sufficiently cleared by public reaction to the above three events for party "managers" to make a general assessment of conservative strength.

It is not the intention here to state that factional lines in the legislature from 1793 to 1795 were gradually drawn so tight that the leaders could exert an iron discipline over party members. Such a conclusion, were it to possess validity, could only be posited on an evidential succession of consistent party divisions on controversial issues. Actually, one could search the legislative journals in vain for evidence of any such behavior during the period under consideration.

Summary, 1790-1795

Over a period of five years, from 1790 through 1795, the development of Pennsylvania politics showed certain characteristics which, at this point, should be brought under review.

Probably the most outstanding aspect of the general political behavior was the dependence local politicians placed on national issues as rallying points for the formulation of opinion. Under the circumstances though, such an outcome was almost inevitable. When the weak Confederation was replaced by a strong central government, a government whose powers were exercised by some of America's ablest men, the effect on Pennsylvania was profound. One of the first acts, it will be remembered, was to bring her Constitution into a closer relationship with the national document and confirm a slowly rising conservatism which had fed on Revolutionary reaction. Although it was a victory that tended to calm the internal broils of the past fifteen years, it was by no means an annihilating triumph. The new body of organic law was concessionary not retaliatory or vindictive; it was a compromise that was to last for almost fifty years. Under its liberal franchise provisions all eligible citizens could take an active part in government. And their first act was to elect a compromise Governor.

With most of the old issues dead (chiefly the constitutional one itself), the citizens could look upward to greater political heights, for that was the direction from which new issues came in an unending stream. And the voters did not have far to look or long to wait. The issues were being manufactured, for the most part, in the State itself, and to them Pennsylvanians reacted decisively. They paraded, argued, electioneered and even rebelled, but by 1795 the State was still conservative, even if by the slightest of margins. Washington was still the Great Leader and the majority followed him.

As various issues appeared the State's leaders failed to capitalize on them with telling results. That is, they did not effectually exploit public response by fully translating it into action at election time. Vital and exciting questions disturbed the public mind and created divisions of opinion which could be voiced only in a partial and haphazard fashion. A more adequate expression required the organization of responsible and integrated political parties.

But such organization was beset with many difficulties. In the first place parties were considered reprehensible and even dangerous by many public figures. Dallas, Findley and Mifflin decried factions and all their manifestations. So did Madison, Jefferson and Washington. They feared their rise and did not wish to be openly identified with them. This accounts in part for the rare appearance of general party labels as banners under which candidates were presented to the electors. Men might consider themeslves "Republicans" or "Democrats" or "Federalists," but they were reluctant to appear before the electorate under those headings. Most candidates were sponsored by the customary "meeting of respectable citizens," not by openly avowed partisan groups. To repeat a former caution, the terms Republican and Federalist, when here applied to men or groups, are still descriptive of a general body of opinion rather than of a tight party organization. Furthermore, there existed a general confusion in terminology. In the underlying and basic theories of government, Federalists and Republicans shared approximately the same views. That is, they both believed in the application of republican principles to the administration of a Federal government. To call a Republican an Anti-Federalist was to cast doubt on his loyalty. The confusion was bound to persist until, through the operation of clashing opinion-creating issues, each side adopted recognizable and antithetical positions.

As has been pointed out, the development of party machinery was retarded by the election of a compromise Governor and the use of the district system in Congressional elections. There was little object in devising nominatory procedure for the election of a person so widely recognized as Mifflin. Also, the general-election system was not employed in Congressional campaigns after 1792. So the biennial selection of national legislators no longer provided an opportunity for state-wide political organization. Such opportunities were indeed rare, for when

Washington and Mifflin were candidates, the result was almost a foregone conclusion. Campaigns in their behalf were unnecessary. The first real state-wide contest since 1792 was to come in 1796.

SECTION III
THE TRIUMPH OF REPUBLICANISM, 1796-1801

CHAPTER IX

SIGNS OF A RISING REPUBLICANISM

MIFFLIN ELECTED FOR THE THIRD TIME

WHEN MIFFLIN was returned to the gubernatorial chair in 1796, his election was not the result of any campaign or contest. It was reinstatement by acclamation. For when the politicians learned in January that he would "stand the pole for governor again," no competitor had a chance.[1] He was nominated all over the State with almost complete unanimity by Federalists and Republicans alike. Faintly and dimly seen in the background were Frederick A. Muhlenberg and Anthony Wayne. The critics of 1793 were no longer vocal against him and his path was virtually unobstructed.

On election day the citizens gave Mifflin a total of 30,020 votes as compared to 1,011 for Muhlenberg and 139 for Wayne. The Governor carried all counties with the greatest of ease, and in four of them—Bucks, Chester, Northampton and Allegheny—he got all the tallies polled. The counties of Lancaster, York and Northampton, with their heavy German populations, gave Muhlenberg a grand total of four votes. In 1793, it will be recalled, he had won in York County.[2]

Although Mifflin's undoubted popularity played an important role in the election, it would seem that an even more significant factor was chiefly contributive to his overwhelming success. That was the factor of suitability. He was considered unobjectionable by both the Federalists and Republicans at a time when the relative strength of the two major factions was gradually approaching equilibrium. Neither could risk the nomination of a decisive and frankly partisan candidate when the political balance was so delicate.[3] The reality of this political counterpoise was to be amply illustrated in the legislative and presidential elections.

CONGRESSIONAL ELECTION OF 1796

The Pennsylvania Congressional representation elected to the Fifth Congress was almost equally divided between the two major factions. The Republicans and the districts they represented are as follows: David Bard (Bedford-Franklin-Huntingdon), William Findley (Westmoreland-Fayette), Albert Gallatin (Washington-Greene-Allegheny), Andrew Gregg (Cumberland-Mifflin), Blair McClenachan (Philadelphia

County), John Swanwick (Philadelphia) and John A. Hanna (Dauphin-Northumberland-Lycoming). The Federalists were Samuel Sitgreaves and John Chapman (Bucks-Northampton-Montgomery), Thomas Hartley (York), John W. Kittera (Lancaster), Richard Thomas (Chester-Delaware) and George Ege (Bucks-Luzerne). As to party affiliations, these men have been classified, with one exception, in accordance with their voting record in the Fifth Congress;[4] they were frankly partisan and can be so listed with reasonable accuracy. The exception is George Ege, who resigned before he had a chance to vote on the controversial legislation passed during the months of July and August in 1798. However, in the light of his known affiliations two years later, it seems reasonable to assume that he would have voted for the Federalist measures in 1798, had he remained in Congress. For in 1800 he was nominated as a presidential elector by the Federalist State Senate.[5] Had there been the slightest doubt as to his partisan fidelity, he certainly would not have been nominated in that bitter contest.

The current topics of the day which inspired divisions of opinion came to the fore in the presentation of certain vigorous and positive individuals as candidates. In Philadelphia John Swanwick, running against Edward Tilghman for the city's one Congressional seat, was both praised and blamed for his anti-Treaty and pro-French opinions.[6] Two correspondents to the *Aurora*, "A Citizen" and "Polio," rang all the standard changes in his behalf. In the opinion of "A Citizen," all "Old Tories," British agents, aristocrats and speculators could be crushed only by the election of a man like Swanwick. A "certain party" that considered the mass of people as the "swinish multitude" had to be defeated in the interest of liberty and justice.[7] To "Polio" the issue was clear: men were now forced to decide whether they would rally to the cause of freedom or become "the mere tools of an arrogant and imperious faction. The Janus head of Aristocracy," he warned, "is overpowering the fair face of Republicanism. . . Fear not too strong a Republican (nay, to please the gentry of aristocracy, Democratic) body in your Congress."[8]

Merchant Swanwick's support was composed of a variety of elements. Lauded as a "commercial" figure who could best represent Philadelphia's businessmen,[9] he also appealed to the Francophiles and to those who had recently emigrated to the United States. On July 4, 1796, he celebrated American Independence as presiding officer of a celebration attended by the French Minister and Consul General. There he drank a toast to French success and to "our Republican Representatives in the Federal Legislature."[10] On October 5, 1796, he was elected president of the "Philadelphia Society for the information and assistance of persons emigrating from foreign countries."[11]

The Philadelphia race was a close one and, as it turned out, so was Swanwick's victory. He won by only seventy votes.[12]

Between the two opposing candidates in Philadelphia County the differences were clearly marked. There, Blair McClenachan, militant Republican and former president of the Pennsylvania Democratic Society, was opposed by Robert Waln, a confirmed Federalist.

In the transmontane election districts, candidates Findley and Gallatin were attacked for denying their participation in the whiskey disturbances.[13] Findley was also blamed for opposing Jay's Treaty and the ratification of the United States Constitution.[14]

There is no doubt that the spirit of partisanship was high and accentuated in Philadelphia and Philadelphia County. Both Republicans and Federalists presented distinct party tickets for both State and national legislative offices. The partisanship was recognized by Bache when he listed the election results in separate columns. For instance, when McClenachan defeated Waln by 272 votes, Bache announced it as a "majority for [the] Republican Candidates."[15] When all the county's Republican Assemblymen were elected by a majority of 520 votes, he announced a decisive victory for the "Republican ticket." In Philadelphia, however, where the Federalists won all of the Assembly seats by a margin of 642, Bache described the figure as the "Maj. against Republican Ticket," not, be it noted, as a *Federalist* majority.

This use of partisan terminology has a peculiar significance. It was the first time the *Aurora's* editor headed a list of winning candidates with the party term "Republican." But he did not use the word "Federalist" or "Federal" as descriptive of the Republican opposition. Indeed, it is almost certain that he thought it incorrect to apply those words to Republican opponents. When John Fenno, exulting over the election of an office-seeker in the Delaware election of 1795, referred to him as a "Federal" candidate, Bache, by implication, denied the appropriateness of the term.[16] He was probably in complete agreement with "A Federal Democrat" who declared that the "Aristocrats," foes of "Republican Government," insulted truth when they called "themselves Federalists."[17] Fenno, in his turn, showed an aversion to the use of "Republican." He would describe his political opponents as "Anti-

Federalists," whereas Bache would describe his as "Aristocrats." Both were terms of opprobrium.

But when Fenno referred to the success of a "Federal ticket" (in Delaware) in 1795, and Bache to the triumph of a "Republican Ticket" (in Pennsylvania), it would seem to indicate that the editors of the State's leading newspapers had recognized a party cohesiveness of sufficient strength to warrant the use of collective terms. Although no legislative candidates listed in the *Gazette of the United States* were described as being Federal or Anti-Federal, the terms did appear in connection with the presidential election. Briefly, both editors recognized the existence of partisan formations, and both occasionally referred to individuals as being "democratic" or "aristocratic." but neither headed legislative nominatory lists with party captions.[18] Actually, on the basis of the recorded minutes of various nominating meetings, they would have little reason to do so. None of the tickets presented to them for publication was sponsored by self-avowed party groups. This held true for election notices from the counties of Philadelphia, Montgomery, Westmoreland, Franklin, Bucks and Cumberland. Almost invariably the candidates were sponsored by the conventional "numerous and respectable meeting of citizens."[19]

Pennsylvania Favors Jefferson in 1796

The presidential election of 1796 loomed large in the evolutionary development of political factionalism in Pennsylvania. After almost eight years of interaction between the Federal and State governments, between a national authority and the people as individuals, the electorate at last had an opportunity to make a selection between two highly controversial candidates for the presidency. In two previous elections Washington's selection had been an almost foregone conclusion. Of heroic proportions in the eyes of the people, able, just and wise, he would have prevented the formation of parties, had it been humanly possible to do so. But the national policies adopted during trying and critical years had the inevitable effect of creating opposing bodies of opinion. And in few states had response to national action been as sharp and decisive (particularly over the excise law) as it had been in Pennsylvania. Thus, when Adams and Jefferson, two men whose opinions were well known to the politicians, appeared as rival candidates, the gage was down.

Long before anyone knew who the rival candidates would be, the Pennsylvania legislators began preparing for the election along partisan lines. Just as soon as the lower house started to work on a law for the selection of fifteen electors early in 1796, the Republicans, conscious of their minority position, advocated the district system of election. The Federalists, however, confident of their supremacy, favored a general election.

The progress of the electoral bill was attended by considerable wrangling over the two methods, and just as the winter session was nearing a close the question was resolved in three record votes: on March 29, 1796, John Smilie, leader of the Republicans, moved to recommit. The motion failed by thirty-three to thirty-three.[20] This was an important decision, for had the bill gone back to the committee, another dispute on method would have occurred. That, combined with later time-consuming wrangles in the House and Senate, might have prevented the passage of any law whatever. With the bill safe from recommitment, the Republicans, from lack of time and sufficient votes, had to accept the inevitable. The Federalists then succeeded in having it transcribed for a third reading, and one day later, it was passed by a vote of forty to twenty-five.[21] Mifflin signed it on April 1, 1796, three days before the legislature adjourned.

Several months after the bill became law, the Republican Committee of Correspondence, organized in Jefferson's behalf, declared that the district system of election had been championed by "the antirepublicans" in the legislature in order to give "full scope to their talents at intrigue and combination. . ." The committee lamented, "in common with their Republican friends throughout the State, that the advocates for fair election in the last legislature were unable to prevail in districting the State. . ."[22] According to the committee then, there had been a sharp partisan split in the legislature over the election law.

An examination of the above recorded votes lends some substantiation to that conclusion. Among the thirty-three men who voted for the bill's recommitment there were probably several who took advantage of an opportunity to register disapproval of a general election. But, since an apparently unalterable majority favored its inclusion, there was little object in refusing the bill a third reading. Moreover, the session was nearing a rapid close, and an electoral law of some sort had to be placed on the books if the State was to have a voice in the electoral college. It seems likely though, that the twenty-five men who held out to the bitter end would have preferred no law at all rather than countenance an abandonment of the district system. That the men in its favor were all Republicans, as the Republican Committee of

Correspondence later intimated,[23] or that the votes indicated a strict party division it is difficult to say. But this much can be said: all but three of the twenty-five men who stood firm on the final vote had a consistent record of opposition to the Federalist majority on all the partisan divisions which occurred during the session of 1795-1796.[24] There is little doubt that these men constituted a Republican nucleus. Further, it seems very probable that their intransigent stand was based on the supposition that the coming election would be a real partisan contest — not merely another confirmation of Washington — and that their general strength was not sufficient to carry a man of their choice.

The session ended on April 4, 1796. With the coming presidential election still uppermost in their minds the legislators, both Federalist and Republican, held meetings on the evening of the last day to nominate fifteen electors.[25] Unlike the Congressional nominatory gatherings of 1792 and 1794, these meetings were not characterized by confusion of purpose. Each group apparently knew the predilections of the men present, and each proceeded to nominate electors in a spirit of harmony. Not pure legislative caucuses, both meetings were attended by other interested citizens and, in the case of the Republican meeting, by national legislators.

The Federalist list of nominees, later captioned by the *Gazette of the United States* as the "Federal and Republican Ticket," was composed of men described as "the friends of *order and good government.*"[26] The nominated electors were representative of various sections of the State.[27]

The Republicans held their meeting at the State House. After nominating a ticket, headed by Thomas McKean,[28] they appointed a campaign committee to disseminate any important information which would "come to their knowledge at the seat of Government."[29] As chairman of this committee the meeting selected the indefatigable Michael Leib.

After the electoral lists had been prepared there ensued a period of anxious waiting. Would Washington run for a third term? That was the big question which agitated the minds of many Pennsylvania politicians. Evidently the President was in no hurry to enlighten the public, for month after month went by and his intentions remained a closely guarded secret. Knowing that Washington definitely planned to retire at the end of his term, Hamilton assured him that an announcement would not be necessary until approximately two months before the meeting of the electors.[30]

Washington then decided to make a statement on September 17, 1796, but four days before that date the *Aurora* scooped its rival journals by announcing that the President would definitely refuse to serve another term.[31] Having obtained the information through "respectable" channels, the enterprising Bache thought that because of its importance it should not be kept within the circle of Washington's confidential friends.

In the editor's opinion, no talent for "divination" was required to predict the rival candidates. "Thomas Jefferson and John Adams will be the men," the former "a steadfast friend to the Rights of the People," the latter "an advocate for hereditary power and distinctions. . ."[32] The electorate would have to choose between them.

Thus did Bache ring in the campaign and indicate the Republican style of attack which, incidentally, was maintained throughout the campaign. As a matter of fact, his words were so similar to those employed in the Republican State Committee's circular of September 25, 1796, that he very well could have been its author. The presidential contest, according to the circular, was a fight between "a tried republican and an avowed aristocrat." Thereafter, almost every issue of the *Aurora* repeated and amplified the above basis of distinction between the two candidates. Stressing the absolute necessity for strenuous effort on the part of all Republicans, Bache predicted that the election would determine not only the direction of politics but the existence of American independence. It would decide whether or not Americans would "continue to enjoy a Republican government or be brought under the yoke of a master."[33] The critical nature of the contest and the need for a heavy vote in Pennsylvania were also emphasized by the Republican committee. Anticipating that the states to the north and south would strike an almost even balance between the two candidates, the committee felt that it would be the role of Pennsylvania to cast the deciding vote.[34]

All through the campaign the *Aurora* spoke with a loud and strident voice. Bache's previous attacks on Federalist policies and their alleged anti-Republican tendencies were repeated with new emphasis and applications. Fearful of the rise of an aristocracy in the United States, he had, ever since the establishment of his paper, deplored all its "forerunners," such as honorary titles, presidential levees, the observance of officials' birthdays and high salaries.[35] Not sure that Washington himself would be able to resist the importunities of those who were said to prefer less and not more democracy, he often opened his columns to correspondents who criticized the President sharply. "Gracchus," for instance, thought that opinion had "so far consecrated the President, as to make it hazardous to say that he can do no wrong." Several of his acts "have been incompatible with the spirit of a free government and yet these acts have been regarded as right."[36] With gentle sarcasm, "A Farmer" described a case of mistaken identity. Told by his neighbor "Fribble" that Prince Edward could be seen driving along Philadelphia's streets in a cream-colored carriage drawn by six bay horses, "A Farmer" hurried to town to see the magnificent spectacle. But instead of seeing Prince Edward in the carriage he saw the "President of the United States! Ah thought I to myself, the times are changed, and have changed with them the *plain and republican General Washington* into a being, which my neighbor Fribble took to be a prince."[37]

For a two-year period, Bache had a valuable ally in Philip Freneau, a poet-journalist who established the *National Gazette* in Philadelphia in October, 1791. The new journal was designed to transcend local bounds and create Republican opinion in all sections of the country.[38] Until October, 1793, when his paper was discontinued for financial reasons, Freneau, who was as enthusiastically democratic as Bache, conducted a pro-French and anti-British campaign. He was vehement in his disapproval of the Hamiltonian program, the power of great wealth, speculation and all aristocratic principles.[39] As a republican crusader Freneau's influence on public opinion must have been considerable, for no less an authority than Jefferson declared that his paper saved the Constitution and "checked the career of the monocrats."[40]

As critical observers then, and as experts in the art of innuendo, sarcasm and invective, Freneau and Bache had materially assisted in creating an atmosphere of Republican opinion which, fully exploited by the latter, greatly aided Jefferson in 1796.

But Bache was not content to participate in the election as an editor alone. He also took active part in the more practical and mundane work of political organization.[41] Throughout the campaign he worked along with John Beckley, Michael Leib, William Irvine and Albert Gallatin, all of whom were ardent Jeffersonians. This group contributed greatly to Jefferson's victory in Pennsylvania.

Probably the most tireless worker of all was John Beckley, clerk of the House of Representatives and land speculator.[42] The energy and thought he devoted to the campaign are well illustrated in a series of letters he wrote to William Irvine, a political leader of wide interests and influence in the middle counties. On September 15, 1796, Beckley wrote Irvine that Washington had declined a third term and that notifications thereof had been sent to the Governors of each state, probably to be officially released about October 1, 1796.[43] The tardiness of the notice, Beckley believed, was calculated to "prevent a fair election. . ." But the scheme could be defeated if Pennsylvania exerted itself. The State really favored Jefferson and "a little exertion by a few good active republicans in each *county* would bring the people out, and defeat the influence of your little rotten towns such as Carlisle, Lancaster, York, etc.—a silent but certain cooperation among the country people may do much." Pennsylvania was the decisive State. If the Republicans carried it, Jefferson would be elected. Did Irvine have any "western friends" he could enlist in the fight? "What seems to be the sentiment, if any, in the country you passed thro? Cannot an effectual exertion be made? It is now or never for the republican cause."

On September 22, 1796, he sent Irvine the list of Republican electors that had been agreed upon in April, 1796. After Rittenhouse's death, Mifflin's name had been quietly substituted. The Governor, Beckley thought, was "as fully eligible as Judge McKean," and would help the ticket.[44] But the men who inserted Mifflin's name had apparently done so without securing the nominee's permission. For while Beckley was in the act of writing his letter to Irvine, he evidently learned that Mifflin had declined. He added this immediate item of news in a postscript, along with the prediction that either Charles Biddle or Thomas Barclay would be named as the fifteenth elector. When the list was complete, Beckley promised to send several copies to be "dispersed in a few judicious hands" and "scattered about in different neighborhoods."[45]

Not until October 4, 1796, did Beckley assure Irvine that Jefferson had "explicitly declared" his intention to serve if elected.[46] Along with this important information, he sent six copies of a Republican address to the people,[47] and a promise to forward one hundred more at the "first certain opportunity." To prevent any counter address, he suggested that the broadsides should be sent "over the mountain" before distribution in the central or eastern sections. They would not be scattered in Philadelphia until the rest of the State had been covered. This would give the Republicans the last printed word.

Beckley was well satisfied with the electoral list. Even the "aristocrats," he told Irvine, said it was the best and thought it would succeed.[48] It is quite evident that he placed a high value on the character of the electoral ticket, *i. e.*, on the prestige and influence of the men it presented to the public. And there is little doubt that they had chosen shrewdly and well. Chief Justice McKean, at the head of the list, was "respectable" and "sound." So was Jacob Morgan, banker and businessman. Jonas Hartzell, Peter Muhlenberg and Joseph Hiester would make a sincere appeal to those of German ancestry. In the middle counties William Maclay and Irvine were industrious, well known and influential. John Smilie could be depended upon to bring out the western vote. Had the Republican managers succeeded in running Mifflin, the ticket would have been even more popular. But it was strong enough without him.

Dallas, who had functioned efficiently with the inspiring James Hutchinson and Jonathan Sergeant in 1792, remained aloof from the elections in 1796. Although opposed to Jay's Treaty, he was not in favor of its use as an issue in the presidential election. On this point he was in sharp disagreement with Beckley, who thought of him as a "trimmer"[49] and as one undeserving of the confidence of Philadelphia "democrats."[50] But whatever his motive might have been for remaining in the background, Dallas had no part in the first real Republican victory in Pennsylvania.

During the months following Washington's declination of a third term, Federalist and Republican groups met throughout the State to approve and confirm the electoral nominations of April 4, 1796. If any efforts were made to substitute others for the ones first agreed upon, they were unsuccessful, for both of the original tickets (with exception of Boyd as a substitute for the deceased Rittenhouse) were presented intact to the voters on November 4, 1796.

In accordance with the law of April 1, 1796, each voter was required to write in the names of fifteen men.[51] Of course, he could copy verbatim the tickets prepared by the two parties, choose any electors presented by either party or write in the name of anyone else. However, so well publicized were the two tickets that no voter chose any man not included in the prepared lists.

The law also required that all returns were to be sent to the Governor's office within fourteen days of the election. Mifflin was then to announce the winners by proclamation. But at the end of the stated period (November 18, 1796) the Governor could not make an announcement of the electors chosen, because the counties of Fayette, Westmoreland and Greene had not been heard from. Mifflin was in a predicament, the critical nature of which was magnified by the closeness of the election, a fact already strongly indicated by the returns available. The law itself, offering at best only a dubious answer, required a discreet executive interpretation.

The section relative to the problem stated that duplicate election returns from each district were to be

> delivered to the prothonotary of the proper county, who shall file one of the said returns in his office, and shall forthwith transmit the other to the governor, so that the same may be delivered within fourteen days after the said election, and the governor shall enumerate and ascertain the number of votes given for each and every person so as aforesaid voted for, and shall thereupon declare by proclamation, the name of the persons duly elected and chosen to be delivered to the persons so chosen on or before the last Wednesday of the same month.[52]

The electors were then to meet at Harrisburg[52a] on the first Wednesday in December and discharge their functions. As a meeting place for the electors Harrisburg was more conveniently located than the capital.

The inadequacy of the law was clearly manifested in its failure to provide for all the contingencies that might arise. In their calm assumption that all the election results would be duly submitted within fourteen days, the legislators had ignored the realities of contemporary transportation difficulties, to say nothing of the oft demonstrated aberrations of local election officials. Then, when the apparently unanticipated situation arose, *i. e.*, when the fourteen-day period expired before all results were available, what action should be taken by the Governor? On the basis of the incomplete results, should he proclaim as elected the fifteen men who were leading at the moment? By so doing he would risk the possibility of issuing a false statement. Or, if he wished to postpone an announcement until all the statistics were at hand, how long could he so delay and still allow a period of time sufficient for the victorious electors to receive official notification and reach Harrisburg by December 7, the first Wednesday in the month? Worst of all, if he did not notify them until the "last Wednesday" in November, the thirtieth, Pennsylvania might go unrepresented in the electoral college.

The delicacy of Mifflin's problem was rendered even more extreme by the status of the two parties on November 18, 1796. On that day, Fenno added the figures already received from twenty counties and the city of Philadelphia and announced a "Federal" majority of 1064.[53] Obviously, if Mifflin were to proclaim the winners on that day, the Federalists would lead, despite the fact that the voters in the three western counties would be unrepresented. Finally, and this was an alarming possibility indeed, if those missing returns, when they did arrive, were so strongly weighted in favor of the Republicans as to reverse the official announcement, Mifflin could very well be a scapegoat of national, if not international, proportions.

Obviously, a decision of some sort was mandatory. But Mifflin, reluctant to decide the question independently, resolved to appeal to the judiciary. Accordingly, on November 18, 1796, Secretary Dallas placed the matter before the Supreme Court Judges, the President of the First District and the Attorney General.[54]

To the judges the situation was not without precedent. In fact, it was so similar to one that had occurred in the presidential election of 1792, as to be almost completely analogous. When the results in that year were not forthcoming within the time limit set by the legislature for their announcement, the judges ruled in effect that not less than fourteen days should elapse between the Governor's Proclamation of Election and the date set for the electors to meet in Harrisburg.[55] By applying the old rule to the present circumstances the jurists ordered that "the Governor should postpone any decision on the election of electors until the morning of Wednesday the 23rd inst."[56] That provided a two-weeks' period in which the electors could receive notification and travel to Harrisburg by December 7, 1796.

Obedient to judicial advice, Mifflin waited. But November 23, 1796, passed by and still none of the delinquent returns had arrived. On November 24, however, Westmoreland and Fayette counties submitted official counts,[57] and on that day, despite the absence of the Greene County returns, Mifflin announced the names of the fifteen electoral candidates who had received the highest number of votes.[58] On the following day, Secretary Dallas released an official statement which listed the thirty men voted for and the number of tallies received by each.[59] Of the first fifteen men, thirteen were Republicans, headed by Thomas McKean with 12,306 votes. William Maclay, with a total of 12,208, was the thirteenth Republican and numerically the last of the fifteen victors. The two successful Federalists were Robert Coleman and Samuel Miles, who polled 12,217 and 12,214 votes respectively.

The narrow margin of Republican victory was well illustrated by the small number of votes that separated McKean from Thomas Stokely, who polled the lowest vote of the Federalist list. Stokely's total of 12,071 was only 235 below McKean's. Further, the closeness of the election, as well as relative party strength, can be illustrated in another manner: for instance, an average of all the tallies recorded for both Federalists and Republicans reveals that the latter won by only eighty-six votes. As to the attention paid by the electorate to party tickets, it is interesting to note that the high-low differentials for the Republican and Federalist electors were 133 and 146 respectively.

The "Federal" majority of 1064, as stated by the *Gazette of the United States* on November 18, 1796, was based on figures received from Philadelphia and twenty counties. The parties had divided evenly, with ten counties each.[60] The city had favored the Republicans by 642, and that figure, combined with their votes in Philadelphia County, gave them a city-county majority of 2076.[61] In the transmontane area they carried the counties of Allegheny and Washington.[62] In addition, the Republicans were victorious in Berks, Northampton, Northumberland-Lycoming,[63] Mifflin, Cumberland, Bedford and Franklin. The Federalists won in Somerset, Huntingdon, Luzerne, Dauphin and the southeastern counties of Delaware, Chester, Bucks, Montgomery, Lancaster and York. The last named county was overwhelmingly Federalist by a vote of 3224 to 141.[64]

Immediately after Mifflin proclaimed the successful electors on November 24, 1796, correspondents to the *Gazette of the United States* registered a vigorous protest. It was contended that the Governor had violated the law by not announcing the winners on the basis of the results submitted within fourteen days of the election.[65] Fenno thought it "very probable" that the Fayette and Westmoreland returns were withheld "till it could be ascertained what number was wanted to turn the majority." Furthermore, Mifflin, Dallas and McKean, "decided friends of party" were declared to be responsible for the "scandalous business."[66]

The *Aurora,* taking a completely opposite view, charged that the mysteriously delinquent Fayette-Westmoreland returns had been delayed by those who wished to force the Governor into a premature announcement of the winners. The returns, said Bache, had actually arrived at the Greensburg post office less than a week after the election. But from that point they began to wander unaccountably. Having been carried toward Philadelphia they were arrested somewhere along the road and sent to Pittsburgh "by accident!"[67] It was a trick of the opposition, and Mifflin was to be warmly congratulated for not having been duped. "Never was a more barefaced attempt made upon the rights of the people, than on this occasion, and never were they resisted with a more dignified firmness, and just regard to principle."[68]

The odyssey of the ballots as told by Bache was not without foundation. On December 9, 1796, Mifflin promised the legislature that the circumstances behind the wanderings of the Westmoreland-Fayette returns between Greensburg, Pittsburgh and Philadelphia would be investigated "in the proper department."[69] In justification of his delayed proclamation, he said that had he "pursued a contrary course, the real voice of the people of Pennsylvania, fairly given, and accurately ascertained, would not have been announced."

Whatever may have been the real reason for the delayed returns, the fact remains that they arrived at Philadelphia in the nick of time. If they had been delayed much longer, Mifflin would have been forced to announce a Federalist victory.

Some time after Mifflin's proclamation of November 24, 1796, the returns of the election in Greene County arrived.[70] They increased the Republican vote by 210 and the Federalist by only forty-four.[71] Because of the delay, however, they did not officially alter the election's result. But had they arrived in time, all the Republicans would have been elected.

When the officially proclaimed electors met in Harrisburg on December 7, 1796, James Edgar and Jonas Hartzell, the two defeated Republicans, put in an appearance and demanded the right to vote on the grounds that the latest returns had placed them among the first fifteen candidates. But the assembled electors refused the request,[72] and proceeded to the business at hand. They gave Jefferson fourteen votes, Aaron Burr twelve, Thomas Pinckney three and John Adams one.[73] It was expected that the two Federalists would vote for Adams, but Samuel Miles upset the general calculation and cast his ballot for Jefferson.[74] Robert Coleman remained adamant for Adams.

A full Pennsylvania vote for Jefferson would not have made him President, but as it was, he failed by a very close margin. According to Edward Channing, Adams "owed his place in 1796 to three nameless electors; one in Pennsylvania [Robert Coleman], another a Virginian, and a third a North Carolinian. Why these electors, or any one of them voted for Adams is unknown; but he plainly was President by accident."[75]

The vote for Jefferson in Pennsylvania was a tribute to the organizing abilities of Republican managers and to the long anti-aristocratic campaign, led principally by editors Bache and Freneau. Realizing the value of publicity, they used it in a manner that far exceeded the imaginations of the Federalist editors. In summing up the Republican protest that had accumulated over the years, Bache gave it such emphatic direction that his readers could not fail to see the crucial nature of the election.

Geographically, the results showed Republican strength in the Philadelphia area and in the far western counties. Altogether, the Republicans carried thirteen counties to their opponents' ten. The Federalists had lost in the city of Philadelphia, but this was not the first time. John Swanwick had been successful there in two Congressional elections; and the victory, in each case, had followed an energetic, provocative campaign in which the Republicans, aided mightily by the *Aurora*, had gotten out the vote. Issues had been featured in each instance and they had been fully exploited by Swanwick's supporters.

The fact that Swanwick, wealthy merchant, and Jefferson, Virginia planter and Francophile, were the two men who could win in the normally Federalist metropolis, presents a nice point for speculation. This is of especial interest when it is noted that the prosperous agricultural counties of Lancaster and York, with their heavy German populations, defeated the great agrarian by large majorities. Although it is quite likely that the pro-French and anti-Treaty elements in Philadelphia city and county contributed much to Jefferson's victory, another group, the Quakers, should not be left out of consideration. Of course it is impossible to determine the extent of Jefferson's following in that sect, but in this connection an observation made by Fisher Ames, rabid New England Federalist, is worthy of record. Before the electors met in December, 1796, Ames, in a mournful letter to Christopher Gore, expressed the opinion that men who justified France were "wicked"; others were so "unspeakably mean" as to prefer a President who would "conciliate" that nation. "Some of the Quakers have supported the Jefferson ticket on that plea," he said. "I think the Yankee spirit higher and better; otherwise, I should wish to import a cargo of emancipated Dutchmen, to be the fathers of the next generation."[76]

Although the presidential election had brought victory to the Republicans in Pennsylvania, nothing suggested that the people, the "great beast," in Hamilton's opinion, had rushed to the polls in unprecedented numbers to cast a vote for the liberal Jefferson. The people had spoken, but not in a loud or compelling voice. As a matter of fact, it was rather weak. The average total vote for Adams was

12,162, for Jefferson, 12,258. If the combined total of 24,420[77] is set beside the more than 30,000 votes cast in each of the gubernatorial elections from 1790 to 1796, the contrast is immediately evident. It would therefore seem that more people were more interested in electing a Governor than they were in electing a President.

The reason for this might be attributed to the different methods employed in electing those two executives. In one instance the citizens were voting directly for a potential executive, the Governor; in the other they only gave a vote of confidence to intermediaries in whom they were expected to repose judgment, but in whose nomination they had little or no part. They were merely initiatory factors in a constitutionally enjoined process of indirection that intimated a lack of faith in the discernment of the general populace. Could they even be certain of the identity of the men who were running for the presidency? Here it will be recalled that Beckley, one of the inside managers in the Jeffersonian campaign, could not assure Irvine that their champion would serve until just a few days before the election. If those greatly interested politicians were forced to remain in the dark for so long, what of the great body of citizens who tended cattle and tilled the soil far in the hinterland? It was a murky business, and the comparatively low vote was hardly surprising.

To the Republicans, Jefferson's victory was a ray of hope and a challenge. If they could win with a deflated total vote, what might not be accomplished if the potential voting mass could be enticed to the polls in greater numbers? To the Federalists, the Republican victory should have been a warning. During the next two years the manner in which the two groups were to behave and the use each was to make of the lessons taught in 1796 were to determine in large measure the State's political pattern for years to come.

CHAPTER X

ELECTIONS, ISSUES AND LABELS

GROUP IDENTIFICATIONS IN THE ELECTION OF 1797

ALTHOUGH a majority of the legislators sent to the Pennsylvania Assembly during the elections of 1797-1798 were Federalists, there were increasing signs of growth in Republican strength and party consciousness. For instance, in assessing the assembly election of 1797, Benjamin Bache for the first time referred specifically to successful *Republican* or *Democratic-Republican* candidates. There is doubt, of course, as to whether the men so identified thought of themselves as candidates of the Republican *party,* but a significant step was taken toward party recognition when Bache felt confident enough of the existence of party cohesiveness to identify men whom he considered to be within its web. This editorial attempt at party classification strongly indicates that in Bache's mind at least the word "republican" was no longer solely an ideological descriptive, but was applicable to one who was ready to take open and avowed group action under a Republican banner. It had become more than a distinguishing title; it indicated that one who held definite Republican opinions in common with his associates would give open and concrete expression to them. In short, if a man were elected as a Republican—at least one so identified by Bache —he was expected to vote as a Republican in the legislature. As a case in point, Bache requested all the successful candidates for the House of Representatives to be present at the first sessions when a Speaker was chosen. That office was an important and powerful one, and the Republicans, he urged, should nominate a man for the position "when they can do it with every prospect of success."[1]

When the election returns came in during the months of October and November, 1797, Bache's mood was definitely jubilant as he pointed out the successful Republicans. Montgomery County had returned three of four, including Peter Muhlenberg, who was "a firm republican." Bache was not certain but he had "good reason to believe that" the two others "were worthy to be his colleagues."[2] In Northampton County there was a "great change." Three of four new members were "staunch republicans."[3] Samuel Maclay and Jacob Snyder, of Northumberland County, were "both democratic republicans."[4] There was "good authority for stating" that Joseph McClellan, Senator for the district of Chester, Montgomery and Bucks counties, would throw his weight "in the republican scale."[5] William Maclay and David Krause were elected to the Assembly in Dauphin County. "They are all right," exclaimed Bache.[6] In Washington County "the Republican Ticket . . . carried by a great majority,"[7] but in Allegheny the "anti-democratic" elements won.

In such fashion did Bache summarize some of the Republican victories in 1797. Regrettably enough, other Philadelphia editors did not follow his lead in attempting to classify candidates according to party. Andrew Brown, publisher of the *Philadelphia Gazette* was more interested in Europe, yellow fever, and the arrival and departure of the ships that sailed in large numbers across the first page of his paper, than he was in politics. The *American Daily Advertiser* and the *Gazette of the United States* were slow to present specific analyses of party affiliations. William Cobbett, however, in printing the results of the election in Philadelphia, forthrightly labeled the two opposing tickets as "Federal Republicans" and "Democratic."[8] A self-styled "Democratic Republican" nomination meeting had proposed a number of assembly candidates,[9] but Cobbett preferred to use the adjective alone. Ordinarily, his employment of the word "Democratic" was epithetical, of a linguistic force equal to "Jacobinical"; and between the two he made but faint distinction. He also applied the word "republican" to Federalists, as did others, and the use of the term "Federal Republican" was not uncommon in the Federalist press.

The elections in the Philadelphia area were closely fought, despite the yellow fever which was again scourging the capital. In the city's election for members to the House of Representatives the "Federal Republican Ticket"—to use Cobbett's term—was victorious over the "Democratic Ticket"[10] by approximately 300 votes. Of especial interest, however, was the contest for the Senatorial seat in the district composed of Philadelphia, city and county, and the county of Delaware. It is here set forth as being illustrative of the rapid rise of party spirit and temper.

In this Senatorial election, one marked by undoubted and unmistakable party divisions, Israel Israel, a confirmed Republican, was opposed by Benjamin Morgan, a talented young Federalist. Great efforts were made on both sides, and Israel managed to win, but by the narrow margin of only thirty-eight votes.[11]

In commenting on the city legislative elections, for both House and Senate members, Bache expressed great satisfaction at the results.[12] Although the yellow fever had driven many "aristocrats" from the city to their nearby country estates, they had "descended on the polls in crowds" on election day, as was their custom when the dread fever was rampant. The working classes, however, were not so fortunate. Having been forced to leave the city to make a living elsewhere, it was difficult if not impossible for them to return for the election. But despite the unfortunate circumstances, the Republicans had "trod closer on the heels" of their opponents than they had for many years. Most important of all, they had elected a Republican Senator, "a circumstance almost unprecedented."[13] Its significance was emphasized by the fact that Israel, as former vice president of the Democratic Society and an ardent Republican was generally held by his enemies to be "a bloody Jacobin, a fomenter of the western insurrection, everything in politics that is vile and violent." But he had won, and although he had been nominated by a small majority, the "union among the democrats" was such that on election day "there were not more than *two* or *three* scattering votes."[14]

To the Federalists, Israel's election as Senator was indeed a bitter defeat. In the opinion of William Cobbett, his success was not only "a complete triumph" of the Jews over the Gentiles but the triumph of the proprietor of the "Cross Keys Grog Shop."[15] It was a new step toward perfection in representative government, said Cobbett. "A public house is a most excellent stand for collecting the sentiments of the *sovereign people*, who never speaks his mind right freely, except when he's half drunk."[16]

But Israel's enjoyment of his victory was of short duration. On December 13, 1797, just eight days after he was sworn into office, the presiding officer of the Senate read a petition demanding an investigation of his election on the grounds that it was "unconstitutional and void."[17] Then, in conformity with a resolution already passed on the preceding day, a seven-man committee was selected to conduct an inquiry into the petitioners' allegations.

The committee's deliberations and hearings, extending over several weeks, were highlighted on January 24, 1798, by an impassioned appeal made by A. J. Dallas in defense of Israel. Consuming more than five hours in a speech that did not even then exhaust all his material, Dallas maintained that the committee's investigation had been dictated primarily by intemperate party spirit.[18] In support of this contention, he asked why irregularities had been found only in the senatorial election and not in the contests for the sheriff's office and places in the lower house. Were not all the offices important? Did not the same electors vote at the same time for all the officers? But his best efforts, not inconsiderable by any means, were unavailing. Benjamin Morgan's counsel produced the names of fifty-three voters who, it was stated, were unqualified to exercise the franchise. Dallas countered this array of names by declaring that at least three of the alleged voters had not even been at the polls.

But the committee attached great evidential weight to the fifty-three names, and on February 7, 1798, its chairman, Matthias Barton, announced before the Senate that Israel's election was "illegal and invalid" because "no enquiry was made as to the right of citizenship of any person who voted at the Northern Liberties and Southwark...."[19] Many unqualified persons had voted in those places, said Barton, and the number so voting "was greater than the difference in votes between the sitting member [Israel] and the person next highest in the vote [Morgan], thereby rendering it impracticable to ascertain who was the person duly elected by the qualified Freemen of the said district...."[20] The committee's report was accepted and that ended Israel's budding senatorial career. A special election was to be held on February 22, 1798, to fill the vacancy.

In an effort to redeem Morgan's October defeat, the Federalists launched an intensive attack on Israel, who was again the Republican nominee.[21] Deeming one campaign committee insufficient they selected two, a ten-man group with headquarters at Dunwoody's tavern and another of only five members at Ogden's.[22] In a series of broadsides they blamed him for participating in the Democratic Society movement which reputedly fomented the excise disturbances and cost the taxpayers a million dollars.[23] Furthermore, he was an avowed friend of France: to vote for him was to express a desire for "war and French influence."[24] In a broadside of February 21, 1798, "a Dutch man" accused Israel and his friends of spending "near Thirty thousand dollars"—some of it public money—to win the election while Morgan's supporters "were driven from their homes" by the fever. In addition, "a Dutch Man" justified the senatorial investigation committee: it deserved praise for magnanimously ordering a special election when in reality Morgan was entitled to his seat because he had a majority of the "legal" votes cast.[25]

The burden of the Republican campaign was carried by the *Aurora*. And although Israel's champions were effective—the old charges of aristocracy were reiterated—they could not match the volume of Federalist literature that appeared shortly before election day. The Federalists put forth a real effort to win, and they did so.

The results of the poll on February 22, 1798, favored Morgan by a majority of 357 votes.[26] He carried the city and Delaware County by comfortable margins, but in Philadelphia County he lost by 836. A comparison of the total votes cast (8,723) with those tallied in the same area during the presidential election of 1796 (5,498) shows the tremendous interest generated by the Morgan-Israel contest. Three thousand people were more interested in selecting a State Senator than they were in electing presidential electors. Actually the total vote was approximately one-third of the state-wide vote of 1796.[27]

Commenting on the narrowness of Morgan's victory, the *Aurora* said: "The issue of this election must strike terror into the hearts of the aristocrats: They know that every means lawful and unlawful, moral and immoral have been used to carry this point."[28]

The above account of assembly elections in the Philadelphia area has been presented primarily with the view of examining partisan strength and evidences of party nomenclature as shown in Pennsylvania's most influential newspapers. Prior to 1796, the use of party labels was rare. True there had appeared "Conferee," "Rights of Man," "Treaty" and "Anti-Treaty" tickets, but they lost currency with the disappearance of the particular issues or complaints which they represented. Broad, all-encompassing terms, when used at all, were vague and often somewhat meaningless. It was during the elections of 1796 and 1797, particularly the latter, that the terms "Federal" and "Republican" began to acquire more distinctive meanings.

Although a majority of the legislators sent to the Pennsylvania Assembly in 1797 were Federalists, there were increasing signs of a growth in Republican strength. The presidential election had been a revelation to them, and it seems quite likely that they seriously began to consider the possibilities of controlling the State. The growth in strength during the two years was important, but even more so were the recognizable evidences of an increased party consciousness which permitted that growth to be calculated and measured. That is, during those two years newspaper editors and correspondents showed an ever increasing inclination to use party labels in identifying candidates both individually and collectively. This is not to say that the practice of listing tickets under general labels suddenly became common or general: both Federalist and Republican editors still manifested a reluctance to concede formal recognition to the group they opposed by dignifying it with any inclusive identifying term that was not derogatory. Nevertheless, general party terms were beginning to creep into editorial phraseology.

Although the elections of 1797 occurred in an "off year," they did provide an opportunity to assess the continuing results of the political enthusiasm generated in 1796. In the following year Congressmen were again selected. Attention will now be directed to those elections in an effort to analyze the effect of national and international issues on the rising partisanship in Pennsylvania.

National and International Influences on the Elections of 1798

It was against a background of heightening international tensions that Pennsylvania conducted her Congressional and legislative elections in 1798. All through the political correspondence and journalistic literature relating to the elections, there ran thought currents replete with a consciousness of European developments and their possible effect on the United States. This preoccupation with a shifting imbroglio three thousand miles away becomes understandable only when due regard is paid to the intimate economic and ideological world interrelationships in which the country had become involved. Along her extensive littoral were a commercially-minded people that had hardly begun to throw off a dependence on European manufactured goods. Only at their peril, therefore, could they ignore a struggle which peeped out of almost every ship's log, determined the price of nails and brought widowhood to the wives of "neutral" sailors.

Previous eighteenth-century wars had conclusively proved that to fight with Britain was to fight on the ocean. The present struggle was no exception, and so vast was her empire and the theater of operations that almost every sailing ship, belligerent or neutral, played an integral part in the fray.

Although the United States was neutral by proclamation, her citizens could hardly avoid taking sides. And in making his choice the individual was necessarily influenced by the events during and subsequent to both the American and the French revolutions. Despite the violence of the latter upheaval, many Americans regarded France as a sister republic devoted to furthering the Rights of Man. Although their cause had received a setback through Genêt's conduct, it had probably been more than offset by Jay's unpopular Treaty. But in 1798 there occurred another episode which played directly into the hands of the Federalists and almost plunged the United States into war.

The unpleasantness between the United States and France that reached a peak in 1798 was the result of various circumstances and attritions that stemmed largely from Jay's Treaty, a document that was highly resented in France. Especially objectionable was one of its provisions which permitted the British to seize American supplies en route to France under the promise of future compensation.[29] The American Minister, James Monroe, suspected of inclining toward the French position, was removed on the advice of Washington's counsellors and replaced by Charles Cotesworth Pinckney. The new minister had British predilections, and when he arrived in France, he was virtually ignored by the French Directory. His treatment was given considerable publicity in the American press. When Adams became President, he appointed John Marshall and Elbridge Gerry as commissioners to work with Pinckney in an effort to adjust the differences between the two countries.

In the meantime, both England and France had issued more stringent rules in regard to neutral shipping. A British Order in Council had directed the capture of provision ships bound for European ports, and the French had retaliated by ordering the capture of American vessels sailing to or from British ports or carrying British goods. Both countries were enforcing their orders with such vigor that American insurance rates were almost prohibitory. This intolerable situation "inclined America to some sort of an agreement with France as she had with England."[30] Hence the appointment of Marshall and Gerry.

When the commissioners got to France in October, 1797, they announced their arrival to the French government and awaited a formal invitation to begin negotiations. But none came. Instead they were visited by mysterious individuals who suggested that the United States not only make a loan to France but "pay a douceur to the Directors and to their Minister of Foreign Affairs."[31] The Americans refused. Neither side would make concessions and the negotiations ended.

The unsatisfactory parleys were described in reports sent to Adams by the commissioners. And when they were eventually sent to Congress—with explanatory notes which substituted the letters X Y Z for the names of the French negotiators—the national reaction was one of intense excitement. Congress began to prepare for war and Washington was appointed commander-in-chief of the defense forces.

PENNSYLVANIA CONGRESSMEN AND THE LEGISLATION OF 1798

In the summer of 1798, when the United States reconsidered its old commitments with the French Republic and seriously began warlike preparations, its Congress enacted several laws which had interesting repercussions in Pennsylvania. In investigating this legislation the immediate purpose will be only to discover the position taken on it by Pennsylvania's delegation in the House of Representatives.[32] Its impact on the people and their State legislature will be discussed in subsequent chapters. Many of the laws passed are so well known that an extended discussion of them here—individually or *in toto*—would be out of place. Suffice it to say that the Federalist majority in Congress, fearful not only of France but of the administration's domestic opposition, enacted some hasty and generally unpopular legislation which eventually became ammunition for the Republican forces. Many Federalists had often winced under the lashings administered by the Republican press. To stop these attacks, they released a flight of arrows which did little damage and occasionally circled back to the bowmen. The American people were not ready to be deprived of the right to criticize their leaders.

The bills most resented were the highly controversial Alien and Sedition Acts. There were two Alien Acts, one approved on June 18, 1798, which increased the length of residence before naturalization from five to fourteen years, and one of June 25, 1798, which permitted the President to deport any aliens considered to be dangerous to the country.[33] The latter was considered to be particularly obnoxious, because of the arbitrary power it gave the executive.[34] When the House passed the second of these acts, on June 21, 1798, the Pennsylvanians divided four to six against it: voting for the bill were Chapman, Kittera, Sitgreaves and Thomas; in opposition were Gallatin, Gregg, Hanna, McClenachan, Bard and Hiester.[35]

The Sedition Act attempted to prevent any combination or conspiracy against the government or any publication defamatory to the President, Congress or the United States generally.[36] After it was given a third reading on July 10, 1798, the House passed it by the close vote of forty-four to forty-one. Six Pennsylvanians disapproved of the bill and five favored it. Those in the affirmative were Chapman, Hartley, Kittera, Sitgreaves and Thomas. The six opposed were Bard, Gallatin, Gregg, Hanna, Hiester and McClenachan.[37]

On July 6, 1798, when the House voted to abolish all existing treaties between France and America, the Pennsylvanians repeated their vote on the Sedition Act.[38] But on the bill authorizing Adams to "raise a Provisional army," the Pennsylvania delegation, although voting against it by six to five, experienced a change in alignment. Hanna voted in the affirmative (Thomas did not vote) and Findley joined the opposition.[39]

In not all instances, however, did the Pennsylvanians oppose the Federalist program. As a case in point they voted six to five against a resolution of July 3, 1798, requesting Adams to instruct Elbridge Gerry (who had remained in France after Marshall returned home) to open negotiations with the French "minister of Foreign relations" and conclude a treaty. Hanna's vote placed the Pennsylvania delegation in opposition to the resolution, but Bard, Gallatin, Gregg, Hiester and McClenachan still preserved a solid front.[40]

On the above legislation then, here presented because of its critical importance, the Pennsylvania delegation remained for the most part in opposition to the Federalist program.

The "Embassy" of George Logan

It was at the height of the Franco-American war scare that George Logan, a Pennsylvania Republican, made his widely publicized good will trip to France. Described by Edward Channing as one of "the curious by-products of combined Quakerism and Pennsylvania politics,"[41] Logan was an eminent Edinburgh-trained physician and a direct descendant of the more famous James Logan. Cultured and well informed, an intimate friend of Jefferson's, he was one of the very few men of whom the acidulous William Maclay had anything good to say. In Maclay's opinion (given in 1790), he not only professed democracy but practiced it.[42]

Greatly disturbed at the imminence of war, Logan decided to visit France in an effort to effect a reconciliation between the two countries. His trip had no official sanction, and when he arrived in France in August, 1798, he carried only a certificate of American citizenship, signed by Jefferson. Apparently that was sufficient introduction, for he had little trouble in opening negotiations with Talleyrand and some of the French Directors.[43] He then returned home firmly convinced that France wanted only peace with the United States. But his greatest difficulty as an "ambassador" occurred when he tried to get the American leaders to listen to his story. Washington gave him a cold and reluctant audience, listening only because Logan refused to leave until he had imparted his message.[44] The Federalist attitude toward Logan's "embassy" was derisive and scornful. He was a "daring usurper,"[45] a "mischievous creature"[46] whose mission should have been completely ignored.[47] His mission was not ignored by Congress, however. That body recognized it by passing a law making any similar future excursions a crime punishable by fine and imprisonment.[48]

Although excoriated by the Federalists, Logan was regarded by his Republican friends as a martyr and a successful negotiator.[49] The Republicans in Philadelphia County later elected him to the Assembly, an outcome mournfully anticipated by James Ross. Logan was entirely lacking in "talents," said Ross, he could only "babble and disorganize."[50]

Pennsylvania's reaction to these stirring national issues can be studied most directly by bringing under review the Congressional elections and the activities of the men selected. In both eastern and western Pennsylvania there occurred interesting party developments.

Congressional Elections in Western Pennsylvania

The dominance of Republicanism in western Pennsylvania was well illustrated in the Congressional elections of 1798. Of the five counties, only Allegheny favored the Federalists. In the Congressional district composed of Westmoreland and Fayette counties, the Republican supremacy was such that long before election time the Federalists doubted the advisability of even offering a candidate. The low estate to which the "friends of government" had fallen in that district was brought out sharply in a letter written by James Ross to Arthur St. Clair.[51]

St. Clair, still hoping to escape from his wilderness, had apparently asked Ross to estimate his chances of successfully contesting the Fayette-Westmoreland district. In his reply Senator Ross admitted that to defeat the "sans culottes" was an almost hopeless task. It could be accomplished, he thought, only if the dominant group should engage in inter-party strife and thus elect a "superior" man through spite. John Smilie was strong in Fayette, which had only a "small but firm . . . Federal party," but in Westmoreland County there was "no such thing as a Federal party."[52] In the latter area William Findley exercised control, and although he had declined to run in the current

Congressional race, the chances of electing a Federalist there had not improved, despite the number of Republicans already in hot pursuit of the office.[53] For no matter how energetically those candidates might "contend among themselves and scramble for power, they would all unite against the *government man*." Westmoreland County, said Ross bitterly, was a "mass of insurrectionary anti-federalism, Jacobinism, or whatever you please to call it." And that was the result of William Findley's "work." The "Federalist[s]" would probably have some friends there if there had been "any permanent, sensible leader, who could have organized and kept them in countenance against Findley." But there was no such Federalist leader in the vicinity, and as a consequence St. Clair's chances of election were slight indeed. But Ross did not pronounce the final word. That would have to come from Judge Alexander Addison who was then in Philadelphia. When he "comes home . . . I will consult him. . . . We will not commit you without a tolerable chance. . . ."[54]

But St. Clair was doomed to spend more time in his detested Cincinnati. Addison decided that it would not be advisable to contest the district.[55] So, with the field virtually in their own hands, the Republicans chose the stalwart John Smilie to represent the two counties in Congress.

In the district made up of Allegheny, Washington and Greene counties, the Federalists offered battle to Republican candidate Albert Gallatin, but by fighting among themselves they proved to be their own worst enemies. They were aggressive enough, but in their leadership they lacked the shrewd resourcefulness of a Findley and the practical brilliancy of the opposing candidate. Among them jealous ambition flourished mightily, cleverly aided and encouraged by H. H. Brackenridge. As a group, faced by an opponent as formidable as Gallatin, it could ill afford to dissipate its energies in internecine wrangling. Political warfare under such conditions was almost certain to end disastrously. And so it turned out.

The Federalist bark had hardly gotten under way when contrary winds began to blow; and throughout the campaign it was steered over a devious course. The trouble began when it was discovered that two strong candidates, Presley Neville and John Woods, wanted to sit in the same seat in the House of Representatives. General Woods had the active and open support of Alexander Addison, John and David Hoge and David Redick, but when they offered him as a candidate in John Scull's *Pittsburgh Gazette*, on August 25, 1798, the paper on the same day also carried the report of a meeting which had nominated Neville on August 13, 1798.[56]

The issue had been joined and the question then was: which candidate would retire in the interests of party harmony? To promote that necessary end, Addison and his confreres addressed an eloquent appeal to Neville on August 27, 1798.[57] The Congressional election, they said, was extremely important because of the delicate international situation. Gallatin would have to be defeated, and that could easily be accomplished if Neville's name had not been presented. Would he not therefore withdraw? All the confusion had been started by Brackenridge, they assured Neville. Through his intrigues he had created divisions "among the federal interest by setting you up in opposition to Mr. Woods. Mr. Gallatin's friends will stand by him against any federal character whatever, and your name being declared as a candidate can serve only to promote or rather ensure his election."[58] Brackenridge's real intention was to elect Gallatin by killing "two dogs with one stone."

The above letter appeared in the *Pittsburgh Gazette* on September 1, 1798, and Scull, with a good sense of editorial timing, published Neville's reply in the same issue, a scorching blast to the effect that, since he was the first candidate to appear, he fully intended to stay in the contest.

Brackenridge now entered the wordy fray with an acid quill. When he "took the field against John Woods" he "had no idea that Judge Addison was at the bottom of his nomination." In his opinion, and he was quite frank, it showed very bad taste on the part of a judge of Addison's importance to engage in the election at all. Addison could not let that go unanswered, and on September 17, 1798, he scolded Brackenridge severely for attacking him in the press.[59] They had been good friends for a long time, but—

This dispute raged on in issue after issue of Scull's paper. But enough has been said here to indicate that the Federalists in western Pennsylvania needed to put their house in order before attempting to meet a rising opposition. Neville did not withdraw from the contest until just before the election,[60] and by that time the rift had badly shattered the Federalist front.

While their opponents fought each other, the Republicans were working effectively and with much less bellicosity. They had only one candidate in the field, Albert Gallatin, of Fayette County. He had the support of William Findley and the enterprising John Israel, editor of the Washington *Herald of Liberty*. In Israel's opinion, Gallatin was badly needed to oppose the local "aristocratic junto" and to prevent a destruction of the "citizens' rights."[61] The Federalist attack on Gallatin centered around the allegation that he was so sympathetic toward France that in case of war he could not conscientiously sit in Congress.[62] Apparently the charge was not taken too seriously, for on election day Gallatin emerged as the victor over Woods. He lost in Allegheny County by 447 votes, but in Washington he beat Woods by a vote of 2,163 to 714.[63] This latter county, along with a comfortable majority in Greene, gave him a total majority of 1,740.[64]

Congressional Elections in the Philadelphia Area

The Congressional elections in eastern Pennsylvania were given an interesting partisan twist, when Governor Mifflin was considered as a candidate in both the city and county of Philadelphia. He was first named by a city group at Poor's schoolhouse, where the Republicans had met in the election of 1796, but before the nominators publicized the selection, they wisely asked Mifflin if he would serve.[65] When approached, the Governor cannily refused to give a direct answer and begged time to consider the matter. Then, on August 6, 1798, he declined because of ill health. But he held out a promise of future willingness to "renew his exertions" in the public service, after he had regained his health.[66]

The Federalists then nominated Robert Waln[67] and the Republicans named Samuel Miles,[68] the Federalist elector in 1796 who had voted for Jefferson. The latter's surprise action had not been forgotten, and a few days after his nomination he was berated as one who had been both "federal and anti-federal," and had for some reason "mistaken the true interests of his country."[69]

Mifflin's refusal to run in the city did not deter the Federalists in Philadelphia County. Apparently they thought his health would improve if they nominated him. But they were mistaken. As a group they had suffered severe reverses in both 1796 and 1797, and it is possible that they hoped Mifflin's name and prestige would carry their Assemblymen to victory. In addition, their sponsorship of Mifflin, assuming that he would serve, would stamp him as a Federalist. But whatever their motives they had nothing to lose, and the chance was worth taking. So on August 22, 1798, a meeting in the Northern Liberties drew up a list which included the Governor as a Congressional candidate. All the men were recommended because they were "attached to the federal government."⁷⁰ The ticket was well publicized in the newspapers, but Mifflin remained non-commital.⁷¹

To the *Aurora* it was merely a Tory trick. The "Tories" in Philadelphia County, knowing that only a Republican could be elected there, designed their nomination so as to pit "republican against republican." If the stratagem succeeded and Mifflin was elected but declined to serve, a special election would be necessary. That would give a chance to elect a Tory, "for it is well known that the republicans do not attend upon the election ground when a partial election only is to take place."⁷² Here Mifflin is definitely classed as a Republican.⁷³

The *Aurora* was not alone in holding this opinion on Mifflin's political affiliations. A writer in the *Gazette of the United States,* who styled himself "A Federalist," also held the same view.⁷⁴ Mifflin, said "A Federalist," justly deserved his country's thanks for his Revolutionary services. His impressive ability, if combined with greater moral strength, would have given him first rank in the nation. "But unfortunately for his country and himself, the materials of his mind were of too tender a nature to baffle the Demon of Corruption, ever on the watch for illustrious victims." The writer then linked Mifflin's "sensual appetites" to his association with the Republicans: ". . . flattered and carressed by Jacobins he became the dupe of their artifice" and "sunk to be an illustrious Chieftain of a despicable faction." However, there was still some hope for the Governor. If he were elected to Congress "by federal men," the correspondent was sure that his future conduct would "wipe away the disgrace of his past life."⁷⁴ᵃ

Partisan spirit could hardly go any farther. To "A Federalist" his party had almost become a religion, in the rites of which Mifflin could participate and thus receive absolution for sensual sins—sins, in this case, only assumed. As a leading politician, Mifflin had been exposed to relatively few attacks. Perhaps the scorching criticism at "A Federalist's" hands helped him to make up his mind on his nomination in Philadelphia County, for a few day later his refusal was made public.⁷⁵ It came shortly before election day and the Federalists had to cast about for a substitute. They quickly presented not one, but two, Benjamin Say and Anthony Morris,⁷⁶ despite the latter's refusal to serve.⁷⁷ With more unanimity the Republicans nominated Michael Leib,⁷⁸ who had little difficulty in beating Morris on October 9, 1798. The Republicans also elected their Assemblymen over a Federalist ticket headed by Frederick A. Muhlenberg. When they failed to elect a former Speaker of the United States House of Representatives to the Pennsylvania Assembly, the Federalists in Philadelphia County had indeed deteriorated. A well-known name was no longer enough to insure victory.

In Philadelphia the outcome was quite different. There the Federalists were still in the majority, and they experienced little difficulty in electing Robert Waln to Congress, all their candidates for the lower house of the legislature and Francis Gurney to the Senate. Gurney defeated the ever hopeful Israel Israel, once again the Republican nominee.[79] The election was marred by the yellow fever, which had again reached epidemic proportions. The vote was consequently low, the Federalist Assembly vote averaging 848 and the Republican only 313.[80]

Considering the Congressional elections from a state-wide viewpoint, it would seem that the Republicans fared quite well. They elected Michael Leib, Peter Muhlenberg, Robert Brown, Joseph Hiester, Andrew Gregg, Albert Gallatin, John Smilie and John A. Hanna.[81] Although Hanna occasionally voted with the Federalists in the Fifth Congress (1797-1799), he sided with the Republicans in several highly controversial issues during the Sixth Congress. On his voting record, therefore, it seems reasonable to place him in the Republican group. The Federalists sent to the Sixth Congress were Robert Waln, Richard Thomas, John W. Kittera, Thomas Hartley and Henry Woods.[82] In comparison to the election of 1796 (when seven Republicans and six Federalists were elected), the election of 1798 increased the Republican majority by three.

The Passing of Bache and Fenno

Philadelphia had another severe fever epidemic in 1798. It was at the height of this calamity that the city lost two of its most prominent editors, Benjamin F. Bache and John Fenno. When Bache died on September 11, 1798, Pennsylvania lost its leading Republican journalist. Ever since 1790, when the *General Advertiser* first appeared, he had worked assiduously to make his paper one of the country's best journals. But although active, alert and enterprising he was, like many of his contemporaries in the publishing field, constantly plagued by financial troubles. At the very first, when his paper was only a plan, he sought aid from Jefferson. But he was unsuccessful. Jefferson chose instead to help Freneau launch the *National Gazette* two years later.[83]

As a consequence, Bache was left for the most part to his own resources. At the time of his death he had, according to William Duane, spent more than twenty thousand dollars on his newspaper, the profits from which did not even pay his family's living expenses.[84] In the summer of 1798, when straitened circumstances made it impossible for him to retain Duane, whom he had hired earlier in the year, he obtained the necessary money to keep him on his staff "by a contribution of a number of republicans living in Philadelphia."[85] Thus was he assisted by the group he had so greatly aided and encouraged.

Despite the fever, the *Aurora's* presses continued to operate up to the day preceding Bache's death. After a brief suspension it reappeared on November 1, 1798, under the direction of Margaret Bache, the deceased editor's widow. On that day an editorial stated that, just before his death, Bache had asked that the paper be continued "with inflexible fidelity to the principles upon which it was founded and reared up."[86] Close at hand to carry on the work was William Duane, who later married Mrs. Bache and took complete editorial charge of the *Aurora*.

Born in New York state in 1760, young Duane had been taken to Ireland at the age of five by his widowed mother. There he was formally educated and taught the printer's trade. In 1787 he went to India and founded the successful and lucrative *Indian World* at Calcutta. But his prosperity ended when he denounced some practices of the powerful East India Company and championed the grievances of a group of army officers.[87] As a result, he was arrested, deprived of his property and deported without a trial. Smarting under such treatment, he went to England and made several attempts to secure the restoration of his property. After appealing through the courts and Parliament without success, he gave up and sailed for the United States.

Under his management, the *Aurora* soon reflected Duane's undoubted journalistic gifts and became "the most powerful organ of the Jeffersonians."[88] Tireless and fearless, a match for any contemporary in the publishing business, his abilities "made him the most effective journalist of his time."[89]

Bache's death received only bare and perfunctory notice in the *Philadelphia Gazette,* but when John Fenno died three days later the paper came out entirely surrounded by a heavy black border. "The friends of rational liberty and good government" deplore the loss of "their valuable fellow citizen."[90] Fenno's demise was a real loss to the Pennsylvania Federalists. Always had he supported the Hamiltonian program and violently opposed those who took issue with it. In his hands the *Gazette of the United States* was one of the most powerful opponents of the *Aurora* and all that it advocated. When it first appeared in April, 1789, financially aided by Hamilton and others of his persuasion, it was designed to be the sedate organ of the upper governmental circles.[91] But its dignity rapidly wilted under the pummelings soon to be administered by Freneau and Bache. The *Gazette's* delicate hauteur was engulfed by its more vigorous competitors and Fenno was then forced to enter the journalistic hurly-burly of scurrility and invective. But he never equaled Freneau's suave sarcasm or Bache's linguistic resourcefulness. After his death, the paper was continued under the editorship of his son, John Ward Fenno.

To one interested in Pennsylvania political development, the *Aurora's* suspension just at election time is a matter of real regret. Had Bache lived to analyze the election in the light of Pennsylvania's reaction to the critical legislation ground out by Congress during the summer, or had he listed the successful Republican candidates as he did the year before, it would have been of inestimable historical value. For he was more than an observant editor: having engaged personally in the practical business of harvesting votes he knew politics as well as politicians. No other Philadelphia publisher emulated his evaluative activities in 1797, and none made much of an effort to do so in 1798. The *American Daily Advertiser*,[92] rich, serene and little inclined toward controversy, paid scant attention to the political scene. But the *Philadelphia Gazette*, formerly somewhat indifferent to party warfare, now burgeoned forth with an unmistakable Federalist bias. And like its spiritual brother, the *Gazette of the United States*, it rarely mentioned either the word Federalist or Republican in identifying political figures.

The *Gazette of the United States* presented very few election returns, and when it did so, the successful candidates were almost invariably "friends to good government." In summarizing the election of 1798, it observed that with the exception of "a few local triumphs of the French faction, their cause may with truth be pronounced to be on the wane. The star of Jacobinism must soon cease to shed its malign influence; for shadows, clouds and darkness rest upon it."[93] To the *Gazette of the United States* the term "French faction"—one of several expressions it used to describe all those in opposition to "the federal interest"— was synonymous with "Democrat" or Democratic-Republican. No doubt, it was comforting to demolish the opposition in such brusque fashion, but in so doing, it ignored certain election returns which disclosed several "triumphs" other than of a purely local nature. But perhaps the observation merely reflected an unwillingness to portray more accurately a situation which, if publicized, may have proved disquieting. Also the paper may have been lulled into a state of well being by the vociferous protest that had greeted the cavalier treatment accorded to the "X Y Z" embassy.

Conceptions of Party Formation, 1797-1798

During the years 1797-1798, there appeared two statements regarding the existence and function of Pennsylvania political parties which happily throw considerable light on the political thought then current. The first to appear was an "Address to the Republicans of Northumberland County" by an anonymous "Republican" in the autumn of 1797.[94] This writer, with a remarkable and timely comprehension of the reality of party warfare and its consequences, enunciated a truly intelligent partisan creed. Concerned with the significance and potentialities of the two-party system, he saw the duties and obligations attendant upon factional strife. He did not deplore parties, but accepted them as he saw them, and offered a practical working philosophy for their utilization in discharging the work of government in a representative system.

Conspicuously absent from his "Address" were the shy and dissimulatory tactics so often employed at election time. Unblushingly practical and straightforward, his avowed purpose was to encourage a solidarity of opinion and action which would result in the election of the highest possible number of Republicans in Northumberland County. The arguments for a united Republican front were presented ably and clearly. As a group, he said, they enjoyed superior numbers in the county, and they must therefore capitalize on that fortunate condition. Certainly, when the Federalists were anywhere so favored, all the public officials spoke "their language." As a matter of self-protection then, the Republicans had to be equally "selfish" and elect men of their own persuasion. In a representative government, where the majority ruled, it was necessary for the minority to exert a constant vigilance in order to prevent that majority from becoming overbearing and repressive. Such action would tend to make the dominant group not only fairer and more just, but would serve as well to instill in it a fear that the minority might well attain the upper hand.

As "Republican" saw it, the chief problem in Northumberland County was nominatory. With but two assemblymen to be elected, it would be unwise for three Republicans to appear as candidates. That might very well have a schismatic effect and result in the election of Federalists. A similar rule applied to the office of sheriff. Only one Republican candidate should be selected and placed in the field; and once so designated, he warranted solid support. Anarchy should give way to disciplined cooperation and if the Republicans won, even by a narrow margin, they could not easily be deprived of their ascendancy.

The sententious writer then concluded his appeal by declaring that public business was carried forward "chiefly by the collision of parties." All citizens were therefore duty bound to vote, and it was clearly "immoral" for any Republican to evade his responsibility at the polls.[95]

As a disquisition on the purpose and practical functions of political parties and as a precursor of modern political conceptions and usage, the above "Address" was without a superior in the literature of the period. Bache had held it in such high regard that he used almost three columns of the *Aurora* to print it in full.

The principles and methods advocated by "Republican," principles specifically calculated to cement party structure and augment party spirit, were flatly opposed by A. J. Dallas in his speech before the Senatorial committee appointed to investigate Israel Israel's election in 1797.[96] In his view, party spirit deserved not cultivation but destruction. It was an unmitigated evil that had divided the country into groups, stimulated violent action, and disregarded "everything but its own gratification."[97] He lamented bitterly that party spirit, "active, restless, persevering, intemperate and intolerant," existed everywhere in Pennsylvania.

> ... let me ask whether in the present unhappy state of the community there is scarcely a department of government an act of civil society, not a place [in] the pulpit or forum, the theatre or the tea-table, that is not contaminated with this all pervading spirit; we have heard it in our streets and in our houses, in the public prints and on the floor of the Legislature, even within the walls of the National Councils: it has obtruded I say into every class of society, and goes nearly to annihilate the useful as well as the agreeable avocations of life. Unless an end is speedily put to this dreadful evil, no man will accept a situation in the public councils, it will be no longer safe, no longer honorable. Honor will retire to private stations, the dignity and energy of the government prostrate, private morals and enterprise will be undermined; and we shall be so abused as to suffer by a comparison with the aboriginal inhabitants of our Wilderness.

The above remarks by one of Pennsylvania's leading politicians would appear to be at strange variance with his known activities. Indeed, it is hard to reconcile his expressed attitude with the energy displayed by him during the Congressional election of 1792, and with his subsequent role in the election of Thomas McKean to the governorship. If Dallas' opponents during those elections had expressed curiosity as to what sort of activity he imagined himself to be involved in, such a reaction would have been quite understandable. Or, had he found all the evils of "party" to be resident exclusively in the opposing group, there would be no reason for puzzlement. There would then be no problem. But his censure was indiscriminate. All party spirit was a "dreadful evil."

By way of speculative explanation, it may be suggested that although Dallas, like many of his contemporaries, abhorred the symptomatic evidences of party strife—violence, public abuse and vituperation—he, nevertheless, accepted the inevitable when it became necessary to organize public opinion in support of a given object. Certainly, it was unpleasant to be libeled in the scurrilous press and to be loudly derided in the streets. Those were evils unquestionably, but in a governmental system that was based on majority rule some effort was necessary to search out, consolidate and give that majority effective expression. Detest party organization as he might, he had to use it nonetheless. The idealism of a Constitution that made no provision for party divisions was not borne out in fact. The concepts of "right" and "justice" were debatable, theoretically and practically, and they were not to be handed down arbitrarily by the educated and well born.

Further, it is quite possible that Dallas' attitude was a direct result of his experience as a politician. He had retreated from the Democratic Society when it underwent serious attacks; his participation in the Genêt episode had been unfortunate; he had recoiled from the use of Jay's Treaty as a political issue when Washington signed it; and then he had retired temporarily from political activity while Pennsylvania Republicans won their first real victory at the polls in 1796. He had been so often abused in the newspapers that he could indeed predict with genuine feeling that party strife would make it "no longer honorable" for a man to "accept a situation in the public councils. . . ."

An additional answer may be found in an examination of the possible future development of politics in Pennsylvania. Mifflin, the compromise Governor, had just about concluded his executive career. He had succeeded not as a "party man" but as one who had walked delicately between contesting groups, bowing to both right and left. His popularity and cleverness had enabled him to preserve a working balance. But in 1798 the political temper had changed in Pennsylvania. Too many passion-stirring events had occurred, and that they had not been without effect was demonstrated in 1796. A new and violently partisan force was being uncovered and rapidly energized. What might this new force accomplish or, more to the point, what might it destroy? What effect would it have on gentlemen lawyers, large land speculators and dignified councillors? It was enough to make a man pause. With another gubernatorial election in the offing, Dallas was undoubtedly giving it serious thought. That he would favor a "sound" man such as McKean would be likely. It comported with his past actions, utterances and associations. It is just possible therefore that his diatribe against party spirit was delivered in the hope that it would sufficiently dampen it to permit the election of McKean. It is also possible that Dallas' lengthy arraignment was calculated to perform the functions of a large red herring. True, his denunciation at times was general, but that he wished to place the onus of blame on the Federalists was unmistakable. Theirs was the true guilt, theirs the use of rabid party spirit to scourge the innocent Israel who had been fairly chosen in an honest election. And Dallas, an appointed public servant, presumably above the roils of partisanship, could denounce with heavy rhetoric the very evils in which he delighted to participate.

In contrast to "Republican's" positive program of method and purpose and Dallas' recognition and denunciation of parties, a Federalist correspondent to the *Philadelphia Gazette* displayed a singular naiveté and ignorance of the partisanship that was burgeoning lustily all about him.[98] Somewhere he had seen a "ticket" that advocated a complete turnover of Philadelphia's assemblymen. Such a proposed wholesale change, he thought, was disquieting and of doubtful wisdom. Some of the proposed men were admittedly able, but if the citizens wanted a change in personnel, "surely some persons would be placed on the ticket that had heretofore had some experience of the mode or manner of proceeding in the Legislature. . . ." It was very doubtful, he suggested, as to whether the proposed men were superior to those who had represented Philadelphia in the preceding year. Finally, he innocently inquired, since so many of our "fellow electors" had hastened from the city to avoid the prevailing fever, would it "look well to take advantage of their absence?" The disarming innocence of the appeal may have been calculated, but as electioneering propaganda it could not compare with the straightforward statement made by "Republican."

Shifting Loyalties

To the evidences of party crystallization that accumulated during the years 1797-1798, another should be added: shifting partisan affiliations. As the two major political groups continued to form behind more clearly recognizable banners, the individual politician had perforce to make a choice, and on the wisdom of that choice depended his political future. As a result, there was a good deal of shifting from one group to another.

An illustration of this occurred during the Philadelphia County elections for assemblymen. At the height of the controversy over Jay's Treaty in 1795, that county had elected a straight Anti-Treaty ticket composed of men who, with one exception, were, or became, ardent Republicans.[99] The exception was Richard Tittermary.

To anticipate an examination of parties in the Pennsylvania legislature (which occurs in the following chapter), it should be said here that Tittermary at first voted fairly consistently with his county colleagues. But as party borders became more evident, he began to favor the Federalists. In 1797, both county groups nominated Tittermary and a certain Thomas Forrest, the latter of whom also had Federalist inclinations.[100] At election time the popularity of the Republican ticket was illustrated in decisive victory. But the four men who ran with Tittermary and Forrest on the Federalist ticket polled only an insignificant number of votes. During the legislative session Tittermary's voting record showed that he was completely out of sympathy with the Republicans. He could not agree with their stand on national issues. As a result he was not included in their nominations in 1798. It would seem that in 1797 the Republicans either could not afford to omit him or else their discipline had not been sufficiently perfected to keep him out. Also, it is possible that they were not sure of him because they were not yet sure of themselves.

Two other instances of individual adaptation to shifting party alignments should be mentioned. They involve Tench Coxe and Samuel Miles. Coxe, a native Philadelphian, was a land speculator, a persistent office seeker and a facile writer on economic and political questions. In the early days of the Republic his Federalism was unquestioned. He advocated adoption of the national Constitution and, in 1790, was appointed Assistant Secretary of the Treasury.[101] Three years later he was made "Commissioner of the Revenue."[102] But although well launched on a government career, Coxe showed a lack of appreciation of the delicate balance between office tenure and political principles when he opposed Jay's Treaty of 1795 and favored Jefferson over Adams in the following year. The latter action ended his career under the Federalists.[103] He was dismissed from office in December, 1797, for no stated cause. Just why Coxe abandoned the Federalists is unknown, but after his dismissal he became an ardent Republican. His nomination for the Assembly by the "republican citizens" of Philadelphia in 1798 left no doubt on that score.[104]

Another man who changed allegiance during these formative years was Colonel Samuel Miles, a distinguished Revolutionary veteran. During the 1780's Miles had been associated with the Anti-Constitutionalists. In 1783 he spoke for that group in the Council of Censors and six years later he was elected alderman of Philadelphia along with several others who have been described as "old-line conservatives."[105] Although the *Gazette of the United States* said his career was "both federal and anti-federal,"[106] the Adams supporters reposed sufficient confidence in him to nominate him as an elector in 1796. Then he bolted the ticket and voted for Jefferson. By 1798 he had deserted the Federalists completely—or the opposite may have been true—when he accepted candidacy on the Republican Congressional ticket for the district of Philadelphia.[107]

The ascription of motives for the above shifts would be a hazardous and purely speculative undertaking. Whether these men thought they were changing from one "party" to another, would be a matter of question. But it seems fairly clear that they had abandoned one ideological group for another. This is emphasized by the fact that the changes of opinion as evidenced by Miles and Coxe were recognized by the Republicans when they nominated them for office. Both men preferred Jefferson to Adams, and after 1796, at least, that preference indicated something deeper than a mere recognition of difference in personality.

In concluding this study on the evidences of group formation that appeared during 1797-1798, it would appear reasonably safe to assume that by the latter year the two conflicting opinion groups had achieved recognizable borders, and that men within them were expected to act or speak in conformity with the broad conceptions which distinguished one from the other.

But what of the Pennsylvania legislature? What had been happening there? After considering elections during the period from 1796 to 1798 for evidence of divisional growth, it will be necessary to examine the activities of Pennsylvania's legislators with the same object in view.

CHAPTER XI

PARTY GROWTH IN THE PENNSYLVANIA HOUSE OF REPRESENTATIVES, 1795-1798

IN EXAMINING partisan trends in the legislature, special emphasis will be placed on the House of Representatives because the whole membership was subject to annual change. The votes herein listed as indicative of group formations and opinion alignments have not been selected from a wide variety for the simple reason that clear party divisions were few in number. Indeed, those presented are the only ones which show real signs of cohesiveness. The striking aspect of these groupings is that they occur rarely on questions of local interest. With few exceptions the issues which produced sharp divisions were of national or international significance.

1795-1796

As already indicated, Jay's Treaty was one of the most effective crystallizing agents to appear in the evolution of Pennsylvania's political formations. The State's reaction at the polls was somewhat inconclusive, but the response made to it by the legislators, both local and national, is more adaptable to concrete analysis. The national House of Representatives, to advert momentarily to that body for purposes of comparison, had no opportunity to vote on the acceptance or rejection of the controversial document. But it did put its opinions on record, if somewhat indirectly, when it passed a resolution on March 24, 1796, requesting Washington to provide the House with papers relating to the treaty. The Pennsylvania members favored the resolution by eight to four.[1] Although such action could hardly be interpreted as a blanket vote of disapproval, it did indicate that the Treaty was considered so questionable that it should be brought under review in the House.

The lower house of the Pennsylvania legislature also had an opportunity to express itself on the Treaty. In February, 1796, it received four proposed amendments to the United States Constitution which had been voted by the Virginia legislature in December of the preceding year. The Virginia Resolutions requested the following constitutional changes: all treaties would be submitted to the House of Representatives before ratification, and all those involving the Congressional powers stipulated in Section Eight of the First Article could not go into effect without House approval; impeachments were to be tried by a tribunal other than the Senate; Senators were limited to a three-year term; no Federal judge could hold any other appointment.[2] The Treaty amendments clearly reflected disapproval of the manner in which Jay's Treaty had been handled. These, in conjunction with the other recommended changes, indicated dissatisfaction with the duly constituted and basic concepts of the national government in the fields of international relations, senatorial tenure and the judiciary.

To the Anti-Treaty Pennsylvanians and to those who considered themselves as attached to the ideological concepts of Republicanism, the introduction of the Virginia Resolutions into the House afforded an opportunity to record a protest. To the "good government" and "rational liberty" men it was also an opportunity—but not for protest. They had a chance to justify the Constitution and give the national administration a vote of confidence. As it turned out, the latter group was in the majority.

The suggested Virginia amendments were read on February 24, 1796, and on the next day the legislators resolved that, since the American people had enjoyed liberty and prosperity under the document of 1787, it would be "unnecessary and improper" for the House to "take any measures" to alter it in the manner "proposed by the Commonwealth of Virginia."[3] The resolution, in definite support of the *status quo*, passed by a vote of 45 to thirty.[4]

As an indication of party affiliations, the vote would mean little, unless there were others of a generally similar nature on which to base a comparison or establish a criterion. Fortunately, for the purposes of analysis, other such opinion-determining votes occurred during the next three years. And to anticipate, it should be said here that the great majority of the men in opposition to the resolution of February 25, 1796, manifested a fairly consistent loyalty to the general principles embodied in the term Republicanism. They were the legislative center of Republican strength. Not all remained constant, of course: a few wavered, some were not re-elected, but a large number of them returned year after year. Among the thirty were several men who rarely deviated from broad Republican ideologies on controversial issues. They were Isaac Worrell, Michael Leib, Manual Eyre, William Linnard (all from Philadelphia County), David Mitchell (Cumberland), William Patterson (Bedford-Somerset), Michael Ruch and George Smith (Westmoreland), David Acheson (Washington), John

Smilie and John Cunningham (Fayette), and William Maclay (Dauphin).[5] Geographically, the thirty came from twelve different counties, with the majority in the western regions. The counties solidly opposed to the resolution were Philadelphia, Cumberland, Bedford-Somerset, Washington, Fayette, Dauphin and Mifflin.

In addition to the above, only two other votes occurred during the session which indicated cleavage along partisan lines. One appeared on January 29, 1796, when the House elected three directors of the Bank of Pennsylvania. Of the six candidates nominated, Charles Biddle, George Bickham and Jacob Morgan emerged as victors, with Richard Tittermary fourth highest. Tittermary was an "Anti-Treaty" man and he later joined the thirty on the Virginia amendments. Consequently, he could reasonably expect their support, and they gave it with hearty accord. For, with the exception of three men (one not voting), all those in the minority on February 25, 1796, voted for him. And all the assemblymen who favored him voted for Jacob Morgan, former member of the Pennsylvania Democratic Society and Jeffersonian elector in the following December.[6]

Other partisan splits occurred in March, when the House was concluding its work on a law prescribing the manner in which the State would elect presidential electors. Although the procedures involved in the final stages of the bill's progress through the House were discussed in chapter IX,[7] they must be reintroduced for purposes of comparison. More specifically, the immediate question is, how close was the relationship between the minorities on the election law and the Virginia Resolutions?

To recapitulate briefly, it will be recalled that the electoral law provoked a partisan quarrel over the methods to be employed in selecting presidential electors. The Federalists, because of their superiority, insisted on a general election. The Republicans, however, preferred the district system. On March 29, 1796, the two groups divided evenly by a thirty-three to thirty-three vote on a Republican motion to recommit. Later the bill was transcribed for a third reading by thirty-eight to thirty, and on the following day it was passed by forty to twenty-five.[8] On all these votes, a consistent Republican nucleus of twenty to twenty-five members stood firmly in the minority. Of the twenty-five who opposed the bill's final passage, no less than twenty-two favored the Virginia Resolutions. The similarity in groupings between these votes was so close as to be hardly accidental.

However, the cohesiveness displayed by the "Anti-Treaty" men was not apparent in other votes of a less controversial nature. For instance, the House elected a State Treasurer, Christian Febiger, by a unanimous vote.[9] But in such a case the Republican minority may well have questioned the advisability of challenging the office when the chances of winning were negligible.

1796-1797

When the House convened for the 1796-1797 session, it soon demonstrated an awareness of the intense partisanship engendered by the presidential election and of the growing misunderstanding between France and the United States. Its attitude on these matters was revealed in its response to a message from Mifflin on December 9, 1796.[10] The Governor was much perturbed at recent international events, and in his opinion, a "crisis" had arisen. This word he applied to the combined effect of two circumstances, "the President's retreat from public life" and the dissatisfaction "which the French republic had expressed at the conduct of our government."[11] At such a time, it behooved all to discourage "the ungenerous asperity of party spirit."

While the House was considering a dignified reply to Mifflin, Michael Leib, seconded by George Logan, moved a postponement to introduce some substitute paragraphs. One of these had its humorous aspects regarding party spirit:

> We most cordially unite with you in deprecating the acrimony of party spirit, and assure you that a feeling so illiberal, and unworthy enlightened Republicans, shall neither obtrude in our deliberations, nor give a cast to our proceedings. As it is our duty, so it will always be our inclination, to cherish harmony, and promote the happiness of our constituents.[12]

Coupled with this glib and somewhat dubious disavowal of partisan inclinations was a paragraph on Franco-American relations. It regretted the menacing nature of those relations, once so harmonious, and expressed a hope that "the good understanding once existing between the two countries would be completely restored."

But Leib was unsuccessful. The House refused to postpone its work in order to consider the substitute. Then Leib tried again. Seconded by John Smilie, he moved that just his material relating to France be included. That he was trying to obtain a House opinion favorable to an adjustment of the misunderstanding between France and America seems likely, but it is quite possible that he was also interested in procuring a record vote on the troublesome question.

At this juncture Cadwalader Evans, confirmed Federalist, moved to postpone consideration of Leib's last motion in order to introduce another paragraph for incorporation in the address. In Evans' proposed addition he regretted that France had taken exception "to the wise and prudent steps adopted by the President of the United States to preserve our own neutrality . . ." He hoped that the French would consider the government's action as "intended to preserve us from the horrors of war without an intention to infringe" upon the existing treaty.[13] The question then was: would the House postpone consideration of Leib's proposal in favor of Evans'. That produced a close record vote of thirty-three to thirty-two in favor of postponement.[14]

Since the whole question was dropped immediately after the vote (no mention was made of France or party spirit in the reply to Mifflin), it seems likely that all the jockeying over the material to be included was intended to secure the House's opinion on American foreign policy. The importance of such a fact-finding division was considerable, for a man's opinion on that question was as much a determinative of his general political affiliations as was his view on national executive authority or states' rights.

About six weeks later the House had another opportunity to express an opinion on national affairs generally and on Washington's administration in particular. This came when an address of acknowledgment and gratitude to Washington on his retirement from the presidency was proposed. Although the address passed easily by a record vote of forty-five to twenty-six, it is significant to note the large number in opposition.[15] When one considers the high regard in which Washington was held personally, it seems fairly safe to conclude that the dissenters, in refusing him a vote of thanks, possessed very strong feelings in regard to his administration. Perhaps it was merely another way of registering a formal protest against the administration's policies. By way of comparison it is of further significance to observe that, of the twenty-six dissenters, twenty-four of them had opposed Cadwalader Evans' motion to postpone discussion of Leib's substitute paragraph for the address to Mifflin on December 22, 1796.

These twenty-six men presented an almost united front on another highly controversial question which arose during the session. It involved the passage of a general election law which, although not concerned with broad national issues, did bear on one facet of Franco-American relations, namely, fear of alien influences on American life and government. Or, more specifically, it bore directly on the troublesome questions of citizenship, naturalization and the right of suffrage.

One of the recommendations Mifflin had made to the legislature in his message of December 9, 1796, stressed the need of a general election law which would more closely conform to the national and State Constitutions. With especial emphasis he dwelt on the necessity of a law which would prevent a recurrence of the confusion that had taken place during the late presidential election.[16]

During the first stages of the bill's passage through the House, it encountered surprisingly little opposition. At least, no divisions occurred similar to those on national questions. The closest vote was registered on March 28, 1797, when the first section of the bill was under consideration. This section denied the franchise to any man considered an alien under Federal law, unless he had been previously naturalized according to a United States law of 1795, or

> shall have been otherwise naturalized previous to that time, and shall produce a certification thereof, under the seal of the court wherein he has been naturalized, or, if otherwise naturalized before that time, then such certification or other written evidence thereof, as, from the nature of such naturalization, such person may reasonably be required to produce by any Judge or Inspector, or by any two electors qualified to vote at any such election.[17]

Fifty-one men favored the section and thirteen opposed it. Twelve of the latter group had a consistent record of minority opposition on controversial issues, but many of their colleagues joined the majority on that question. The minority, for the most part, remained steadfast when the bill had its third reading on April 1, 1797. But it could muster only fourteen to the opposition's forty-seven.[18] The bill was then sent to the Senate, where it received so many ultra-conservative amendments that it was strongly objected to by the Republicans when it was returned to the lower chamber. As the session was rapidly drawing to a close, the Republican objection was presented in the form of a motion by Leib to postpone consideration of the subject until the following September.[19] That brought on a record vote in which the motion to postpone was defeated by thirty-four to twenty-seven.[20] The House then passed the bill with all the Senate amendments, and sent it to Mifflin for approval. As to the unity and ideological kinship among the twenty-seven in disagreement, it is interesting to observe that no less than twenty-two of them had opposed both the address to Washington and Evans' motion to defer consideration of Leib's substitute paragraph in the House's address to Mifflin.

Judging from the above three votes, it seems fairly clear that the House minority group exhibited strong tendencies toward divisional uniformity. To "A Freeman," writing in the *Aurora,* there was no doubt whatever that the House had divided with an almost equal balance into two parties, the Republican and Aristocratic. In his opinion, the Republicans needed only six more members to become the dominant group. The election law passed in the closing days of the session was, in his opinion, definitely anti-republican.[21]

But the controversial law never went into effect. Mifflin vetoed it. His reasons for so doing were presented to the legislature when it convened again on August 28, 1797.[22] His principal objections dealt with the law's strictures on suffrage eligibility. He feared that some citizens might lose their votes for want of naturalization records that had been lost by public officials. Further, he questioned the reasonableness of demanding evidence that might have been established as far back as 1783. The law limited the vote to only those men whose names were on the county tax lists or to those who could secure two electors to swear that any particular individual had paid his taxes. Mifflin questioned the necessity of requiring testimony from *two* electors. One would be sufficient, he thought. Anyhow, why specify electors only? Why not permit anyone to so testify?[23]

After listening to the veto message, the legislators made no serious effort to write a new bill. In fact, they made little effort of any kind in this particular session, which lasted only a few days. Having met to complete some unfinished business remaining over from the preceding session, they had little inclination to do so. Philadelphia in those fever-ridden years was anything but salubrious. Furthermore, another election was in the offing.

1797-1798

When the new House of Representatives met in December, 1797, the one which had occasioned so much joy in the *Aurora* over the number of Republicans elected, it immediately ascertained partisan strength on a question involving international relations. In its reply to Mifflin's opening address, a committee appointed for that purpose had included a section which strongly approved the Federal government's conciliatory "spirit" in dealing with France. It was hoped that a similar attitude "on the part of the French Republic" would "lead to a speedy termination of all disputes, and rescue our commerce from further depredation."[24]

While the subject was under discussion in the committee of the whole on December 19, 1797, Michael Leib, seconded by Samuel Maclay, tried to substitute a paragraph in its stead which requested the Federal government to "revive that amity with the French Republic, which, as it is co-eval with our independence, every generous and sincere American must wish to find congenial with the spirit and reputation of our political institutions."[25] Leib's substitute had no chance of acceptance, and the record vote of forty-three to twenty-seven was strikingly similar in numbers to those of the preceding year.[26]

The only other sharp division that occurred during the session came in March, 1798, when William Maclay presented a resolution which, if successful, would have placed the House on record as opposing war "in any shape, or with any nation, unless the territories of the United States should be invaded, but more especially against a people with whom their hearts and hands have been so lately united in friendship."[27] The United States, Maclay contended, could not benefit from a war, nor could it stand the burdens war would impose.

The House did not vote on the acceptance or rejection of Maclay's resolution, but on whether or not it should "lie on the table." The question was decided in the negative by thirty-seven to thirty-three.[28] Two members, David Acheson (Washington) and Samuel Ainsworth (Dauphin), with a consistent minority record, did not vote.

The above are the only two examples of clear-cut partisan division to be seen in the House during the session of 1797-1798.

1798-1799

The representatives elected in the autumn of 1798 proceeded to business by electing Cadwalader Evans to the speakership. This betokened an unmistakable majority for the Federalists. As a matter of fact, their dominance was so impressive that even Senator James Ross was satisfied. It was to be regretted, he thought, that the membership lacked "merit and experience," but they would certainly "support" the national administration.[29] As to its lack of experience, the House no longer had the services of John Smilie, Michael Leib and Peter Muhlenberg—they had all been elected to Congress—but it is unlikely that Ross regretted their absence.

As in previous sessions, the House took early cognizance of the international situation. The dangerous tension between France and the United States was uppermost in every mind, and Mifflin, in his annual message, devoted much attention to it. America, he thought, had little to fear from "foreign ambition" because of her fortunate geographical position. As far as "external" outrages were concerned, the people were in a mood to meet any that might occur. But of real concern was domestic discord, which was everywhere apparent. And the reason for this: party politics! "The spirit of party, intolerant and vindictive, has evidently raged too long for the peace and reputation of our country; discolouring on the one hand, the current of public transactions, and, on the other, undermining that equal exercise of the rights of private opinion, which is, at once the proof and the preservative of a free constitution." [30] Confidence was needed, he said, mutual confidence between the people and their government. If that could be obtained, and if the "standard of political parties" would cease to be a measure for moral perfection, then would the republic continue "free independent, and powerful . . ."

The Governor's condemnation of the Federalists and the repressive legislation passed by Congress a few months before was unmistakable. But that a majority in the House disagreed with him was soon made evident. They had every confidence in Adams, and in a special address of December 20, 1798, they told him so. They were convinced that the French were trying to turn the people of the United States against their government. "The vilest arts of political seduction have been triumphantly employed in various governments, and especially in those of republican form." That last sentence led to a round condemnation of the then current and exciting *cause célèbre*, the "embassy" of George Logan. Not mentioning Logan by name, the indignant legislators found it deplorable that Americans had "daringly insulted our country, by an usurpation of powers not delegated to them, and by an obscure interference in our external concerns."[31]

With the country in a state of undeclared war, with the heroic Washington in command of the defense forces, with the citizens angrily discussing the Logan affair and the "XYZ" insult, it took courage to oppose the above address to Adams. But when it came to a vote on December 20, 1798, twenty-three Republicans did so. They were overwhelmed two to one, and when they explained their position on January 7, 1799, in a statement of dissent, the House forbade its inclusion in the *Journal* by a vote of 39 to 25.[32] The reason given for the dissent's exclusion: it contained "extraneous matter" and used "indecorous" language in its references to Adams.

There was no doubt of the Republicanism of the twenty-three men who opposed the laudatory address to the President. A great majority of them had served several terms in the legislature with consistent minority voting records. Some of the newer members in the group, men such as Nathaniel Boileau (Montgomery), Simon Snyder (Northumberland) and Isaac Weaver (Greene), were to become important Republican leaders. Geographically, the twenty-three represented eight counties or districts: Fayette, Philadelphia County, Northampton-Wayne (one legislative district), Washington, Northumberland, Greene, Berks and Mifflin. The full representations from the first six named voted solidly in opposition.

That was but the first division on issues involving national affairs. Several others were to occur before the session ended. During a two-day period, January 31 to February 1, 1799, three party votes were taken on a bill authorizing the Bank of Pennsylvania to lend the United States a sum not exceeding $500,000.[33] Two divisions, forty-one to thirty and forty-two to twenty-nine, were taken on two sections of the bill, and another of forty to thirty-one resulted in its passage. The Republicans were in the minority on all counts.[34]

A few days later the House had an opportunity to declare itself on the Alien and Sedition Acts, when the highly controversial and significant Kentucky Resolutions were brought under consideration. Born in Jefferson's shrewd political brain, the famous Resolutions had been carried to Kentucky in the fall of 1798 by John Breckenridge, a Kentucky state legislator. There most of them were sponsored by the legislature, along with an accompanying resolution which authorized the Governor to transmit them to other states.[35] Broadly speaking, the Resolutions presented the theory that the national government was the result of a compact which allowed it to exercise certain specific powers. The undelegated powers, or "the residuary mass of right," were reserved to the states. Therefore, when the national government assumed undelegated authority, its acts were automatically void. Within that category were the Alien and Sedition laws.[36]

For the Kentucky Resolutions a majority of the Pennsylvania House of Representatives had nothing but denunciation, and in a series of resolutions the Kentucky legislature was roundly condemned for unconstitutionally nullifying Federal laws. It was "a revolutionary measure." Only "the flagitious and designing" could find anything "terrifying" in the Alien and Sedition Acts, and the House was surprised to know that such opposition to them existed. The will of the majority should prevail.[37]

While the House was proceeding with its condemnatory resolves on February 8, 1799, the Republicans did everything possible to tone them down. Nathaniel Boileau tried to secure a postponement to consider a substitute which declared the Alien and Sedition laws to be obnoxious. Although it might be denied that a state could nullify United States law, said Boileau, it nevertheless had the right to request its Congressional representatives to repeal such laws, and Pennsylvania should so instruct its representatives.[38] Boileau's motion to postpone was defeated forty-two to twenty-six. Peter Frailey (Berks) then tried to obtain a postponement to consider a mild resolution which merely said that the House refused concurrence in the Kentucky Resolutions on the grounds of expediency. His motion was defeated thirty-nine to twenty-nine.[39]

In every instance but one the group so determined to condemn the Kentucky Resolutions was successful. The exception occurred on February 9, 1799, when a proposed amendment declared that the Resolutions were "evidently calculated to diffuse a spirit of discontent and dissatisfaction among the citizens of the United States, to weaken their confidence in the government of their choice, and to destroy every consideration of attachment and patriotism, which ought to bind a dutiful citizen to his country."[40] This was considered too harsh, and the Republicans, aided by a few who did not wish to go to such lengths, narrowly voted it down by thirty-three to thirty-one.

A month later, however, the House's reaction to the Virginia Resolutions was almost as strongly worded as the above unsuccessful amendment. When those Resolutions, similar to but milder than the ones from Kentucky, were considered on March 11, 1799, they were rejected by forty to twenty-nine, because they were "calculated to excite unwarrantable discontents, and to destroy the very existence of our government . . ."[41]

In such fashion, did the Federalist majority approve the Adams administration and the repressive legislation that was rushed through Congress in the summer of 1798. The Republican minority, averaging approximately twenty-seven members, had done its best, but it could not stem the tide. However, it had staunchly supported the Pennsylvania Republicans in Congress who had consistently placed the State's representation in opposition to the Alien and Sedition laws at the time of their passage.[42]

Sharp party division, so evident on issues of national import, appeared once again, as it did in 1797, when action was taken on another election law. Generally speaking, legislation of this character was a matter of local interest, and the only question which provoked a division concerned franchise privileges for naturalized citizens, a subject attended by overtones of national and even international significance.

After Mifflin's veto of the election bill, sent to him in the spring of 1797, the legislature made no serious effort to prepare another until the session of 1798-1799. Work on a new one was then promptly begun. Completed early in February, 1799, it was submitted to Mifflin, who approved it on February 15, 1799. The most important section of this large and comprehensive law dealt with franchise qualifications. Specifically, male citizens twenty-one years of age or over who, during a two years' residence had paid State or county taxes assessed at least six months before election day, could vote. All who claimed the right of suffrage, however, had to prove that they were citizens by birth, residence or naturalization. Anyone in the last category had to produce a court certificate in attestation.[43]

In connection with this last requirement, it will be recalled that Mifflin had vetoed the bill of 1797, because, among other things, it made no provision for those people who had lost their naturalization certificates. While the law of 1799 was being discussed in the House on January 13, an amendment proposed by Nathaniel Boileau on that very point brought on the only party vote that occurred during the law's passage. To make provision for anyone whose certificate had been "lost or mislaid," Boileau suggested that he should have the right to "be examined on his oath or affirmation respecting the same" by an inspector or judge of election.[44] But the Federalists disagreed, and the amendment was voted down by thirty-nine to twenty-five.

Traces of party cleavage on matters of purely local concern can be discerned in only two cases: a land law and an election for directors of the Bank of Pennsylvania. But in these instances the divisions were not completely partisan. The land law split occurred on March 29, 1799, while the House was considering an act to provide for the sale of reserved tracts in the northwestern section of the State. Isaac Weaver (Greene), interested in having the region settled with a minimum of speculation, proposed that the tracts should be sold only to those who would clear and cultivate them and build dwellings suitable for habitation. He would have the Land Office issue warrants only to those who promised to abide by the same regulations and strictures contained in the Land Act of 1792.[45] Weaver's proposal was defeated by forty-one to twenty-six, with the Republicans preponderantly in the minority.

A semi-partisan division also occurred when Bank directors were again elected. The candidates were George Bickham, Charles Biddle, Jacob Morgan and Samuel W. Fisher. The contest was between the latter two, Republican and Federalist respectively, and Morgan, supported by the great majority of the Republicans, was defeated.[46]

Conclusions

In summarizing this review of the activities of the House of Representatives from 1795 through the session of 1798-1799, certain conclusions seem to be warranted:

(1) From the first session on to the end of the period the record votes exhibited evidence of party division on national subjects. When those partisan votes were not the result of issues presented by other states, such as the Virginia and Kentucky Resolutions, they were forced upon the House, usually quite early in each session. It would appear then, that vital national issues served as convenient yardsticks with which to measure House sentiment and determine party strength.

(2) In only rare instances were party splits discernible on matters unrelated to national or international problems. By and large, the mundane work, the legislative hewing of wood and drawing of water, was ground out on a non-partisan basis. Public improvement and relief bills were not fundamental party matters.

(3) Sectionally, the two major groups were represented in all parts of the State. Generally speaking, however, the transmontane counties were preponderantly Republican and the easternmost were largely Federalist. The representations from the city of Philadelphia and the counties of Lancaster and York, with six representatives each, were almost solidly Federalist. So too, were Bucks and Chester, with four and five members respectively. Altogether, those five districts could be depended upon to send twenty-seven men who almost unanimously supported the national administration. Delaware, also Federalist, had only two representatives. Countering those, however, were the eastern counties of Philadelphia, Berks, Northampton and Montgomery. Although not always solidly Republican, they did send many anti-administration representatives to the House during the period under review. The five farwestern counties of Allegheny, Westmoreland,

Washington, Fayette and Greene elected a total of twelve members, the great majority of whom were Republicans. Although Allegheny had stronger Federalist inclinations than the others, one of her Representatives, Samuel Ewalt, voted with the Republicans on critical issues no less than five times. Generally, the western members and those from Philadelphia County united with a few active members from Berks, Northampton and Montgomery. They formed the nucleus of Republican strength in the House.

The group divisions manifested in the lower house supplemented and coincided with the State's general inclination, as indicated in the political urges and events already brought under review in the preceding chapters. There seems little doubt that by 1798 the stimulus of national and international issues had created two major opinion groups in Pennsylvania. This tendency toward cohesiveness had been somewhat vague and ill-defined prior to 1796. In that year, however, the appearance of two distinct and ideologically opposed presidential candidates had dramatically emphasized the cleavages inherent in the organization and subsequent operation of the national government.

With Adams' accession to the presidency, the delicate Franco-American situation rapidly reached a climax. And with it came a whole host of issues involving concepts of an explosive nature. While evolving a foreign policy and meeting the suspected French threat, the government took measures which emphasized the ever-sensitive question of national authority and power.

In this connection a question arises: were Federalist restrictive measures—such as the Alien and Sedition Acts—so severe as to threaten individual freedom? It was natural for some to think so, particularly those coerced or brought to book by the Sedition Act. Fearful of further repressive measures, many others predicted future encroachments by a government that forbade criticism of its chief executive and maintained courts that, to say the least, were arbitrary.

It is probable that if any one emotion dominated opinion on these matters it was fear. The newspapers of both political groups were full of gloomy forebodings and predictions of disaster. Innumerable were the charges and counter-charges of Jacobinism, anarchy and atheism on the one hand, and, on the other, aristocracy, monarchy, toryism and repression. Just how much of this mutually expressed apprehension was real or expediently feigned, it is of course impossible to say. But, whether or not the oft-repeated fears were genuine, they did help to consolidate the political groups. They had an appeal that calm reason could never excite.

Thinking men could not ignore those issues, and, in coping with them, they were often hopelessly divided. Politicians recognized the divisions and said so, as they inveighed against "party spirit." The remarks of Mifflin and Dallas on the reality and evils of party antagonisms have already been mentioned. Jefferson, probably the shrewdest politician in the country, also expressed himself positively on the existence of parties. In 1798 he said: "It is now well understood that two political sects have arisen within the United States, the one believing that the executive is the branch of our government which most needs support, the other that like the analogous branch in the English Government, it is already too strong for the republican part of the Constitution."[47] But while admitting the existence of parties, Jefferson had something illuminating to say about their composition: "both parties claim to be federalists and republicans, and I believe with truth as to the great mass of them; these appelations therefore designate neither exclusively."[48]

Undoubtedly, Jefferson was here interested in basic ideological distinctions. He was saying, in other words, that there were federal Republicans and republican Federalists. Although that cannot be gainsaid, and although neither wished to destroy constitutional government, it seems clear that in Pennsylvania the gulf between the two groups was broad enough to split the State into two sharply opposed factions. Surely the man who wrote the Kentucky Resolutions would have admitted the reality of that gulf had he read the House resolution which declared that only "the flagitious and designing" need be terrified by the Alien and Sedition Acts.[49]

Throughout the period then, between 1795 and 1798, opinion in Pennsylvania reached an advanced stage of crystallization. The years were formative ones for the Republicans, and in the next year they were to achieve a great victory.

CHAPTER XII

REPUBLICAN VICTORY

Fries' Rebellion, A Prelude to Victory

To the long list of Federalist measures and policies which produced adverse reactions and group divisions in Pennsylvania, one other should be added before turning to the Republican victory of 1799. This was a Federal tax law. The State's citizens, especially those in the western area, had already exhibited acute sensitivity in regard to levies in 1794, and now five years later riotous proceedings were to greet another tax. Although the Alien and Sedition Acts were resented because of their infringement of freedom of expression, they caused no organized violence. Writers and speakers were intimidated and some were arrested, but no one resorted to force. An attack on the purse was a different matter altogether, and to it some Pennsylvania citizens reacted in a series of disturbances known collectively, if somewhat grandiosely, as Fries' Rebellion.

While Congress was rushing through its belligerent anti-French legislation in the summer of 1798, it also made financial provision for a war which many, including Adams himself, thought imminent.[1] This hurried preparation took the form of two acts passed during the month of July, 1798. The first, passed on the ninth provided for the valuation of lands, dwelling houses and the enumeration of slaves.[2] For purposes of administration, commissioners were to be appointed to separate the states into districts and select assessors whose duty it was to collect enumeration lists. These lists were to "specify, in respect to dwelling houses, their situation, their dimensions or area, their number of stories, the number and dimensions of their windows" and the materials of which they were built.[3] The required enumeration of windows, incidentally, gave the assessment a popular name, the "window tax."

Toward this tax, the Pennsylvanians in the House took a favorable attitude, at least a majority of them voted for its final passage on June 13, 1798, by seven to two. In a non-partisan division, David Bard, Albert Gallatin, Andrew Gregg, John Hanna, John W. Kittera, Samuel Sitgreaves and Richard Thomas favored its passage, while only Joseph Hiester and Blair McClenachan disapproved.[4] Hiester, from Berks-Luzerne, and Sitgreaves, who with John Chapman represented the

Bucks-Northampton-Montgomery district,[5] came from areas in which the anti-tax disaffection was later most prevalent.

The second act, approved on July 14, 1798, laid a direct tax of two million dollars, to be apportioned among the several states. Pennsylvania's share was slightly in excess of $237,000. All this money was to be drawn in accordance with the evaluative assessments provided in the complementary law passed five days before.[6] When the direct tax bill, easily passed in the House on July 2, 1798, by sixty-two to eighteen, the Pennsylvania delegation split seven to three, with the majority in favor of passage.[7] Hiester and McClenachan were once more in the minority, but this time they were joined by Gallatin. Chapman, Hartley, Kittera and Sitgreaves, all Federalists, were joined by Bard, Hanna and Gregg. The Pennsylvania votes on these bills were non-partisan and more than two-to-one in favor of their passage. Whether or not Sitgreaves faithfully reflected the majority opinion in his district is a matter of doubt, but it is interesting to note that after his resignation he was replaced by Republican Robert Brown on December 4, 1798.

Opposition to the tax began in Berks, Northampton, Montgomery and Bucks counties when the assessors started to compile information. Several of the officials were attacked and deprived of their assessment rolls, and some of the citizens who were most bitterly opposed to the tax formed armed bands under the leadership of John Fries, a militia captain, auctioneer and confirmed Federalist.[8] To quell the disorders Richard Peters, Judge of the District Court at Philadelphia, ordered Marshal William Nichols into the disaffected region to arrest the insurrectionists.[9] Nichols succeeded in apprehending twenty-three men, whom he took to Bethlehem. There, on March 7, 1799, they were forcibly removed from his custody by a large band of horsemen led by the ubiquitous Fries.[10]

President Adams then took official notice of the disturbances by issuing a proclamation on March 12, 1799, in which he commanded the insurgents to disperse by March 18, and announced the necessity of calling out the militia.[11]

Governor Mifflin, although he had received no communication from Adams, brought the proclamation to the attention of the Assembly on March 14, 1799, with the recommendation that any measures taken to cooperate with the Federal government should be "devised and authorized by the Legislature."[12] The lower house responded by appointing a committee to consider the message.[13] Its report on March 20, was a severe denunciation of the "dishonorable" action taken by "combinations" to defeat a tax law which actually placed the heaviest burden on the wealthiest groups. Along with its report, the committee offered a resolution which promised the House's full cooperation in suppressing "unlawful and treasonable combinations" when the national government demanded it. But "as no such cooperation is now required, this House consider their interference at present as wholly unnecessary."[14]

On March 23, 1799, the committee's suggested resolution was adopted without a record vote. And shortly thereafter the Republicans essayed a partisan coup which failed badly. It came in the form of a resolution proposed by George Logan which requested the Governor to investigate the riots and report to the House with particular attention to "any circumstances which may be alledged or discovered, tending to shew the origin of the same in the agency of foreign incendiaries, or the seditious views of domestic traitors."[15]

Logan's proposal was a shrewd Republican maneuver. Ever since the Whiskey Rebellion and the Genêt affair they had been called revolutionists and Jacobins. Now they had an opportunity to invite investigation and thereby openly disavow any responsibility for the current disorders. The pressure, instead, was on the opposition. Fries, the leader of "treasonable combinations" was Federalist and so, too, was Bucks County, an area in which the disaffection was most intense.[16] If the Federalist majority in the House were to defeat the resolution, they could be accused of doing so in fear of an investigation of Federalists. They took that chance, however, and swamped it by a vote of forty-five to twenty-seven.[17] The exploitative possibilities of this vote were not ignored by the powerful *Aurora*. On April 11, 1799, it suggested that the majority feared an investigation would show that "federal politics and men were the cause" of the riots.[18] It was excellent political capital and in Duane's adroit hands it was used to good advantage.

Shortly after the issuance of Adams' proclamation, "almost all objection to the tax disappeared. Fries and his aiders and abettors submitted to the authorities, allowed their property to be assessed, and acquiesced in the law being carried into execution."[19] Nevertheless, the Secretary of War, on March 20, 1799, requested Mifflin to call out the militia. The Governor responded by ordering eight troops of cavalry and five hundred men to be ready for travel. They set out from Philadelphia on April 4 and during the next few days rigorously scoured the "hot water"[20] region and arrested many suspects. "These arrests," says the historian of Fries' Rebellion, "seemed to have been accompanied with unnecessary severity, and a veritable reign of terror existed while the troops were in the field. . . ."[21]

The alleged brutality of the militia, as it rounded up Fries and other rioters, was naturally given full space in the *Aurora*. It charged that captured suspects had been refused the right of bail, that homes had been illegally entered and that the whole anti-tax area had been terrorized. To support his accusations of violence Duane printed verbatim seven affidavits sworn to before Peter Nagle in the latter part of May, 1799.[22] He also published some unsigned letters which declared that the troops had been quartered free of charge.[23] This last accusation was vehemently denied in the *Gazette of the United States* on May 14.[24] But it also produced a more painfully direct and violent reaction one day later.

According to a signed editorial Duane declared that on May 15, 1799, a gang of armed bullies invaded his business establishment and demanded the identity of the correspondents who had accused the militia of bad conduct.[25] At gun point, the editor refused to comply, and he continued to refuse while the men lashed him severely and kicked him about through the shop. All the while he shouted duelling challenges to his tormentors, but none would accept.

The first man to strike him was Joseph B. McKean, son of Chief Justice Thomas McKean who had recently been nominated by the Republicans for the governorship. Joseph, said Duane, was a dupe of the Federalists who had incited him to the attack for electioneering purposes.

The editor was not so badly beaten as to be unable to publish his editorial one day after the assault. And in it he hurled defiance at all who sought to intimidate him. He was not afraid of any of them, "either collectively or individually." There is no doubt that he meant what he said, for he continued on undeterred and, if possible, in a fashion even more virulent than before. The Federalists had been embarrassed by the tax riots, and Duane exploited their discomfiture to the full. It was all capital grist for the Republican mill.

In April, 1799, a grand jury indicted the hapless Captain Fries for treason. He was brought to trial on the thirteenth and at its end was declared guilty.[26] Before sentence was pronounced, however, his attorneys succeeded in obtaining a new trial on the grounds of declared prejudice by one of the jurymen. His second trial, begun on April 29, 1800, was presided over by Richard Peters and the notorious Samuel

Chase. At the very beginning of the case Dallas and Lewis, Fries' lawyers, withdrew because the judges laid "down their opinions as to the law before hearing counsel."[27] Without the benefit of legal advice Fries was tried and found guilty. On May 2, 1800, he was sentenced to be hanged. The sentence was not carried out, however, for he was pardoned by Adams a few days later.

The Election of Thomas McKean

Amidst the exciting tensions created by the Alien and Sedition Acts, the international broils and the anti-tax sentiment, Pennsylvania began to prepare for another gubernatorial election. Party divisions had become so acute by this time that the Republicans and Federalists were belligerently determined to settle the matter of supremacy over the contest for the governorship. The temper of both was such that it was evident from the very start that the decision would not be made in the fashion which had characterized Mifflin's three elections. Certainly the unanimity with which the Governor had been selected in 1796 could not be repeated, for the times had changed. Mifflin, kindly, affable, without malice and generous to a fault, was undoubtedly the most popular man in the State. Impeccably honest, just and fair, he had devoted the greater portion of his life to a public service that left him insolvent.[28] And now, broken in health and fortune, he was almost at the end of his course.[29] Disliking violence and friction, he had handled Pennsylvania's citizens with gentleness and diplomacy. In his relations with the national government, however, he had not been so fortunate. As a matter of fact, most of his executive troubles had their origin in national policies. And on two occasions he had seen military forces ordered into action by presidential authority to preserve order in his State. In the second instance Adams had issued a military proclamation without even consulting him. But on neither occasion did he suffer any loss of prestige or popularity. Indeed, after the Whiskey Rebellion, he had been returned to office by almost unanimous consent. For years he had helped to preserve a balance between rising political factions. Toward the end of his last term, however, he inclined unmistakably toward Republicanism. Adept and experienced in testing political winds, he clearly saw which way they were blowing in 1799. The times had changed and he knew it.

Many others were also aware of change, at least in retrospect. In 1810 a number of Democrats prepared a general address which dwelt partially upon political alignments during Mifflin's three terms.[30] Then "parties were not marshalled against each other in all the strength and energy" which later became so evident. "Events" had relegated the Republicans to a minor position. The "political system . . . was but just going into operation" and Mifflin, famous as a "revolutionary character" had been accepted by the people as their candidate "at the instance of a few citizens casually assembled in Philadelphia."[31]

The changing times of 1799 were also remarked upon in a Republican "Address" of 1805. At the end of Mifflin's last term, it observed, "a new order of things required a new character of men."[32]

There is no reason to doubt the observations of these men who were actually on the scene. "A new order of things" did require a new type of politician. A man like Mifflin, equable and mollifying, was outmoded. Conflicting ideas and provocative events had combined to engender intense partisan rivalry and bitter hatreds that have seldom been equalled in the State's history. Party standard bearers would have to meet such conditions and carry the battle with aggressiveness and force.

The Republican leaders realized the need of such a man, and early in 1799 they took steps to select him. Within their ranks were several men who might have qualified. They were Dr. George Logan, Alexander J. Dallas, Judge Thomas McKean, General William Irvine and General Peter Muhlenberg.

Dallas' official duties had brought him into contact with many administrative functionaries throughout the State, and as a lawyer he was fairly well known. As to his chances of success, however, he himself thought they were remote because of his foreign birth and his lack of a "personal following among the voters. . . ."[33] But he wanted to continue on as Secretary of the Commonwealth under the new Governor, and he was therefore anxious to secure the nomination and election of a man who would be agreeable to such a suggestion.[34] Dallas was much in the Philadelphia social whirl and he needed the money. Further, the secretaryship afforded an excellent point of vantage from which to observe as well as to participate in the intimate political details of government. As a politician and as an attorney with an excellent clientele, these were considerations he could not ignore. Later, the Federalists, well aware of his ambitions, offered to retain him as secretary in return for support of their candidate. But, said Duane, who disclosed the proffered bargain, Dallas "*supurned* the temptation with promptness and indignation. . . ."[35]

George Logan, energetic, forthright and wholeheartedly Republican had been much in public notice since his controversial trip to France. As a gubernatorial nominee, it is quite likely that he would have been well supported by the many who hated Britain, war and John Adams. But in experience and practical political knowledge, he was not the equal of McKean, Irvine, or Muhlenberg. All were well known, all had excellent records as patriots during the Revolution. These three were being considered as candidates as early as January, 1799. By that time none of them had been determined upon, but it had already been decided to support only one of the three men.[36]

The choice was to be made in a series of gatherings held in Philadelphia during the next three months. Before any meetings were held, Peter Muhlenberg virtually eliminated himself as a candidate by telling William Findley "that he would not serve as governor and that he would do all he could to promote McKean's interest."[37] This information was given to Findley in strictest confidence, but since he was one of the foremost political figures in the State, and since Muhlenberg could very well have been a leading candidate for the nomination, the latter's declination made it much easier to select another man, particularly McKean. Muhlenberg, said Findley, wanted his refusal kept secret from his job-seeking relatives who were very anxious to see him in the Governor's chair. The secret, incidentally, did not leak out to either Muhlenberg's friends or to McKean. At least, Findley thought it had been kept from them up until the time he divulged the information to Israel in 1801. Findley said nothing about any others who might have known about it, and Israel was adjured to keep the matter confidential.

To select a candidate for the governorship, Republican Congressmen, State Representatives and other citizens started the delicate process by holding several meetings during the month of February, 1799. Several names were discussed, and to conduct a systematic canvass a standing "committee of nine from the western, middle and eastern counties, and one person from the city was appointed to consider the fitness and inquire into the public standing of the candidates."[38] The committee, headed by John A. Hanna, held many meetings and corresponded with interested people in various parts of the State.

Just before Congress adjourned, a large meeting was held on March 1, 1799, in Philadelphia.[39] Here private citizens and legislators, both State and national, met and once more considered all the candidates. Ballots were then taken and "it appeared that the opinions of a large majority were united in favor of Thomas McKean...."[40] The meeting then selected a corresponding committee to manage the Republican campaign. Its members were Peter Muhlenberg, William Irvine, Samuel Miles, Michael Leib, William Penrose, Tench Coxe and A. J. Dallas.[41]

The Republicans naturally stressed the amiability and cooperativeness which supposedly marked the work of the Philadelphia caucus. Also emphasized were the participation of men from all parts of the State and the great efforts made to consult all as to the best candidate.

These assurances, however, did not go unchallenged by the Federalists and some disgruntled Republicans. With obvious relish, John W. Fenno published a letter, supposedly written by a western Republican, which expressed dissatisfaction with the manner in which McKean had been nominated.[42] Far from being the choice generally, said the correspondent, the Chief Justice had been forced on the Republicans by turncoat Federalist intriguers who were motivated only by a desire to secure easy jobs for themselves. Dallas, "a man disposed to carry his talents to the best market," had been the chief schemer.

Many years after the election more light was thrown on the nomination caucus by the Philadelphia General Ward Committee, a Democratic organization.[43] In the Committee's opinion the people of the State were so overwrought by internal and foreign affairs in 1799 that they paid little attention to the means whereby McKean was placed in candidacy. The principal object "was to chose [sic] a person from the republican ranks; and hence very many supported the nomination, made in Philadelphia, in that year, by no more than thirty promiscuous and self-created organs of the public will, although they disliked both the manner of nomination and the person nominated."[44]

Although the nominating meeting was attended by politicians from various parts of the State (most of whom were legislators), it was in no sense a general convention. Its members were self-delegated, representative of the people only insofar as they had been selected as legislators. In brief, it was a small group of inner-circle partisans dominated, it would seem, by politicians from the Philadelphia area. Certainly that region was heavily represented in the State campaign committee by Miles, Dallas, Coxe, Penrose and Leib. The transmontane region was entirely ignored.

The only man appointed who did not live in the eastern section of the State was William Irvine, of Carlisle. The committee's work, however, must have been carried on largely without Irvine's assistance.

When its first circular letter appeared on April 9, 1799, his signature was missing.[45] He also failed to sign another important letter of August 7.[46] Of course, he could have advised from a distance; but there is strong reason to believe that he contributed little or nothing either to the committee's work or to McKean's campaign generally. Before the summer ended he was informed by John Beckley that he was "cuffed at by both parties and counted an enemy by both." Such a position was as "undesirable" as it was "unmerited." But, consoled Beckley, "it only remains to act with that consistent firmness, which has so conspicuously marked your character and conduct, by evidencing that without being, in the present tumult of struggle for the chair of Government, a party man, you are undeviatingly devoted to republican principles."[47]

Some Republicans charged that Irvine favored James Ross, the Federalist candidate, and even advocated his election.[48] Another correspondent, John Irwin, was so certain that Irvine favored Ross that he asked him to write letters in Ross' behalf.[49] But whether or not Irvine actually supported Ross, the Republicans were so suspicious of his conduct that he met opposition in his efforts to get a job after McKean was elected.[50]

With Irvine eliminated from the inner group of McKean's managers— and the evidence seems to warrant such an elimination—it limited the Republican committee membership to men who lived within the Philadelphia orbit. That gave the city group a disproportionate share in the planning of McKean's campaign. The strategists may have decided to concentrate chiefly on the most populous counties with the expectation that the western area, generally Republican, would fall automatically into line.

At the Republican caucus on March 1, 1799, six Philadelphians were in attendance, none of whom, of course, were either State or national legislators. Among them was A. J. Dallas, who apparently dominated the meeting and successfully championed McKean's nomination.[51] Leib and Duane, says Raymond Walters, created a division by holding out for Peter Muhlenberg's selection. They were suspicious of McKean's democracy.[52] The fight was so serious, says James Peeling, that "it sowed the seeds of future party dissension."[53] Under the circumstances though, both Duane and Leib were destined to wage a losing fight. Apparently, they were totally unaware of General Muhlenberg's conversation with Findley in which he voluntarily declared that he would refuse to serve.[54] If Muhlenberg really wanted the nomination, he hid his disappointment well, for he accepted a place on the State Committee and worked hard for McKean.

The membership of the Republican campaign committee could hardly have terrified the "rational liberty" men who dreaded an excess of democracy. A curious mixture of radical democracy and conservatism, with heavy emphasis on the latter, it was not calculated to frighten the "sound" and "respectable" groups in Pennsylvania. Indeed, Leib was the only democrat in the group who could be described as radical. Muhlenberg was a calm and discreet politician, not easily stampeded; Samuel Miles was a former Federalist and one of the richer men in the State; Penrose was an able merchant; Coxe was an old Federalist official, once strongly suspected of having loyalist sympathies. As to Dallas, no one would have called him a radical democrat.

The Federalist press naturally pounced on the committeemen with virulent gusto. With but one exception, said Fenno's paper, they were all "turn-coats." All could change their parties as easily as they could change their clothes.[55] Addressing himself to Dallas, "a True American" said the secretary could deceive no one as to his party loyalty. "No, Sir; both parties agree in this respect; both consider that you are an arrogant, assuming foreigner, and watch you as an artificial and dangerous character." How dare a foreigner recommend a Governor to the good people of Pennsylvania![56] The Federalists were very sure that they saw some Achilles' heels in the committee and they aimed many shafts at the most vulnerable spots.

But of course their biggest target was to be McKean himself. And he was not hard to hit. Indeed, it seems fairly safe to assume that, had they been permitted to choose their opponent, they could not have found one more susceptible to attack from so many quarters. Also, it is equally safe to assume that there must have been many surprised Republicans when the old Judge was announced as their candidate.

Born on March 19, 1734, the son of a tavernkeeper, McKean received his early education at Francis Allison's Academy in Chester County. From there he went to New Castle to study law. He applied himself with characteristic energy, and before he reached the age of twenty-one, he was admitted to the bar in the Three Lower Counties.[57]

All during the quarrels with Britain, from the Stamp Act Congress to 1783, McKean was a staunch and able patriot. The expression, "he was with us in '76"—or a variation thereof, so often used to describe the "boys of '76"—could sincerely be applied to him. And considering the number of times such labels were used to praise political aspirants, they must have been of considerable aid to any office seeker. His hard work and intense loyalty to the cause, at a time when Pennsylvania had more than its share of Tories and "sunshine patriots" would not be forgotten.

Consistent as he was to the Revolutionary cause, McKean by no means displayed that quality in his political affiliations. As an Anti-Constitutionalist he publicly opposed the State Constitution of 1776; but one year later, when offered the chief justiceship by the Bryanites, he "experienced a change of heart" and accepted "it from the hands of the enemy."[58] Years later, when most of the Constitutionalists disapproved of the proposed Federal Constitution, he attended the Pennsylvania ratifying convention and earnestly recommended its adoption.

There he expressed the firm conviction that the excellence of any government was to be found not in its form but in its administration: on that, said he, depended the "freedom, wealth and happiness of the people." And in his next sentence, apparently unaware of the contradiction in terms, he declared that "Despotism, if wisely administered, *is the best form of government invented by the ingenuity of man,* and we find that the people under absolute and limited monarchies, under aristocracies and mixed governments, are as contented and prosperous as we are, owing undoubtedly, to the wisdom of their rulers."[59]

Always distrustful of a government that exalted the legislative over the executive and judicial branches, he attended the Pennsylvania Constitutional Convention of 1790 and offered proposals that stamped him as being one of the most conservative, if not the most reactionary, man in the group. His advocacy of property qualifications for the franchise and for offices of Governor and Senator was at complete variance with the letter and spirit of the finished document. Altogether, his remarks on organic law were "evidence of his desire for a government exercised by men of property and education."[60]

During Washington's first administration, McKean gave every appearance of being a true Federalist, but in 1793 he showed strong sympathies for France. No good Federalist could condone that attitude. His opposition to Jay's Treaty, equally unforgivable, took him even farther from the fold, and when he appeared on the Jeffersonian electoral ticket in 1796, the break was almost complete. He was then a Republican.

At first blush the above account of McKean's chameleonic partisan behavior would seem to denote an unstable character, one prone to shift in every emotional breeze. But on closer examination one discovers that, although he changed parties often, he remained true to his nature and principles. He was aristocratic at heart, fearful of voting privileges for all, desirous of hedging democracy about with restrictive qualifications. After holding high and lucrative office under one of the most democratic state constitutions in the country, he could announce in 1787 that forms of government meant little, that administration was most important. And later, in the Pennsylvania Constitutional Convention he made it clear that the connection between wise administration and wealth was intimately close.

But shift and change as he might, the Chief Justice never miscalculated. All through a startling succession of political metamorphoses and governmental realignments, through war and rumors of war, through depression and recovery, he remained firmly in office. And he loved high station with a fierce devotion.

In 1799, then, McKean, from a partisan standpoint at least, was not a Federalist. In a strict party sense he may have been a Republican, but it is almost impossible to believe that he was ideologically either a democrat or a Jeffersonian Republican. Certainly he had nothing in common with the "liberty-pole" school of democracy.

Yet, despite the Judge's conservative background, he was not an anomaly among the Republican leaders in eastern Pennsylvania. With the exception of Leib and possibly of Muhlenberg, he fitted in rather neatly with his campaign committeemen. He had been nominated to win, not merely to stage a Republican demonstration, and his backers were shrewd enough to appraise correctly the advantages he had as a candidate. Some of them were by no means unaware of his background and his consequential susceptibility to attack. As an anonymous but obviously well-informed writer remarked in later years, "there was not merely a confirmed doubt, but a known certainty" as to McKean's "political opinion in regard to government . . . and before he was taken up it was contrived that he should be tested as to his future conduct and committed into such political declarations as would fix him in future or damn him for ever. . . ." Apparently McKean readily acceded, for he "required no coaxing."[61]

McKean's conservatism was by no means an unmixed evil, galling as it might have been to some of the old democrats who had followed George Bryan. It served to make him more acceptable to borderline Federalists, whose sleep would be undisturbed by Jacobinical nightmares if McKean were securely seated in the Governor's chair. Skeptical Republicans, on the other hand, could find consolation in the fact that the candidate had been "right" on many past issues. He had opposed Jay's Treaty and the Alien and Sedition Acts, and had expressed sympathy toward France. In addition, he had voted for Jefferson in 1796. That brought him within the aura of Republican opinion on national and international issues.

Of the men available to the Republicans, McKean was probably the most widely known. For twenty-two years he had traveled the circuit as judge, and in that time he had come into intimate contact with the State's most influential men. On the bench he had been capable, wise and learned, albeit occasionally arbitrary and domineering. Over sixty-five years of age, he was an arresting figure who would wear the mantle of high office with compelling dignity. Energetic, dynamic and aggressive, lean of countenance and penetrating of eye, he looked like the fighter he was and always had been. This undeniable quality of combativeness would be of invaluable aid to the Republican party. They needed a candidate who would carry the fight to the opposition, and in McKean they had such a man. Needful of a popular figure as well, they had the reassuring testimony of his record as an elector in the presidential contest of 1796. Then he had been accorded a higher vote than any other man in the field. No politician could ignore that.

As to the governorship itself, McKean had no illusions, either as to its advantages or disadvantages. After a few months in office, he was to tell John Dickinson that a Governor of Pennsylvania had heavier duties to perform than any other executive in the Union, not excluding the President. The office had, he believed, "as much power and patronage" as was necessary in a republican government, but the salary was inadequate "for a man worthy of the office." The cost of living had risen greatly and the Governor's salary of "two thousand pounds" was actually not more than one half of the same "sum ten years ago." Men in "inferior stations" were paid more.[62] Undoubtedly he was well aware of the Governor's duties and inadequacy of his salary long before he was nominated, but still he wanted the job.

While the Republicans were busily engaged in nominating activities, the Federalists had not been idle. At the same time they, too, were sponsoring informal discussion groups in Philadelphia in an effort to find a suitable candidate. After much conferring and speculating, it seemed that James Ross would be the most popular choice. Accordingly a committee composed of men from twenty-one counties was appointed to ask Ross if he would serve if elected. Ross was quite willing.[63]

His consent was reported to a caucus of State legislators and private citizens which met in Philadelphia on March 6, 1799. There he was formally and easily nominated. Apparently his nomination was merely confirmatory, for he was recognized as the candidate by the *Gazette of the United States,* one day before the caucus met.[64] The caucus then selected a correspondence committee, made up of Philadelphians, whose duty it was to coordinate the Federalist campaign.[65] In addition, the caucus appointed committees for every county in the State with the suggestion that they arrange for the formation of sub-groups in each township or district.[66] All these committees were to be interwoven by a web of correspondence, directed from Philadelphia. Thus the caucus left little to chance. Rather than depend upon the counties to organize their own committees they would relieve them of the task. The county politicians, however, were expected to add to their committees if local conditions required it. The list of county committeemen named by the caucus was not intended to be final or complete. The central Philadelphia committee, numbering ten men, was headed by Levi Hollingsworth, Robert Wharton and Benjamin Morgan.

Candidate James Ross and his opponent McKean had some qualities in common: both were lawyers and both, incidentally, were very good ones; both were ambitious and enamoured of public office; each maintained a high dignity of bearing, peculiar to his disposition. But in temperament Ross, smooth, polished and even-tempered was more approachable than the emotionally explosive McKean. In intelligence, ability and resourcefulness both were outstanding in the legal circles of the State.

Ross, born in York County in 1762, had the advantage of a Princeton education. After college he moved to Washington County where, after teaching school for a short time, he began the study of law under the encouragement of H. H. Brackenridge. An additional period of study in Philadelphia completed his legal education and he then returned to practice in Washington, where he lived until 1795. He then moved to Pittsburgh.[67]

His public career was auspiciously begun in 1789, when he was sent as a delegate to the Pennsylvania Constitutional Convention. In 1791 he became a member of the American Philosophical Society,[68] and in the same year he married into the prominent Woods family of Pittsburgh and Somerset.[69] His election to the United States Senate in 1794 placed him among the prominent Federalist political figures in Pennsylvania, and for twenty years he was to remain their acknowledged leader.⁷⁰ If many people shared William Findley's belief that Ross was a Republican in 1794,⁷¹ they were soon to be disillusioned. Shortly after going to the United States Senate he supported Jay's Treaty. His attitude on that highly controversial document was indicative of his future activities in the Senate, for he never deviated from the Federalist program. When elected in 1797 there was no doubt as to his partisanship. Undoubtedly conservative, he was reported to have said in 1799 that he saw "no good in any kind of election." Whether or not he actually expressed such an opinion, Jefferson took the story seriously enough to record it.⁷²

In selecting Ross as their standard bearer the Federalists had chosen well. They could justifiably anticipate strong support from the Federalists generally, and as a westerner their candidate would have a definite appeal in the transmontane region. He was, therefore, a formidable candidate, and the Republicans did not underestimate him.

The decision made at the Federalist caucus on March 6, 1799, to establish a network of committees which would affect every voter was elaborated upon by the State Committee. By May the Ross managers in Philadelphia were so impressed by the activities of the Republicans that they urged a further refinement of the committee method. The county as the basic unit was to be divided into election districts and these in turn into smaller divisions. No potential voter was to be neglected.⁷³

This plea for close and extensive organization did not go unheeded. The usual mode adopted was for the county committees, already appointed at Philadelphia, to select sub-groups which were to organize their localities and attend general county meetings. Several counties attempted to create such organizational machinery. Among them were Lancaster, Chester, Delaware, Cumberland, Huntingdon, Franklin, Allegheny and Montgomery. Minutes of the meetings held in the above counties were published in advocacy of Ross' election. At Easton he was nominated by an "assembly of respectable republicans."⁷⁴ In Cumberland County he was lauded for his "plain republican manners" and hailed as "the poor man's friend."⁷⁵

In prosecuting the Federalist campaign, the Philadelphia committeemen began by adopting a lofty attitude. According to a circular of May 27, 1799, their advocacy of Ross' election was prompted by a desire "to preserve the happiness and independence of their country; to suppress the spirit of anarchy and insurrection; to retain the true republican characteristics—equality of rights and subjection to the Constitution and laws established by the will of the whole society. . . ."[76] This declaration, incidentally, would have been endorsed with equal sincerity by their opponents. But as the summer wore on and the campaign grew hotter, a group of Federalists gathered at Dunwoody's tavern on August 13, 1799, determined to find a way to meet the Republican attacks. Then, with an air of injured and surprised innocence, it was discovered that their opponents had been so "illiberal" as to refer to James Ross with a reckless disregard for the truth. Retaliation was considered advisable and the group therefore prepared resolutions suggesting that the Philadelphia committee of correspondence collect and disseminate information on McKean and his followers. Promising full cooperation in such an effort, they recommended investigation of McKean's record as a judge and the utterances of his advocates, some of which they regarded as subversive of liberty, religion and the social order.[77]

The Philadelphia committee of correspondence, which actually performed all the organizing functions of a State campaign committee, had begun the contest mildly enough by eschewing "invidious comments" of a personal nature. However, it had permitted itself to observe that a Pennsylvania Governor should be young and vigorous, not a man in the decline of life who already had a lucrative and dignified position.[78] But after being prodded by the group at Dunwoody's tavern, it took a greater personal interest in the Republican nominee. On September 28, 1799, they accused him of having aided George Logan in his "insolent interference" in American negotiations with France by giving him a letter of introduction to the French authorities.[79] Further, at a time when America was faced with the "insulting aggressions of implacable" France, the committee thought it would be dangerous to elect a man who was possibly attached to that country.[80] Referring back to McKean's advocacy of property qualifications for State Senators, the committee expressed a profound skepticism of his sincere interest in securing equal rights for all. But Ross, they pointed out, had disapproved of McKean's proposal.[81]

Relatively speaking, the Philadelphia committee conducted its campaign with commendable restraint. In comparison to the verbal acid which flowed from the Federalist press, its observations were almost innocuous. Just as soon as McKean's nomination was announced, the newspapers began an attack on him which continued with increasing fury throughout the summer and autumn. Of the several weaknesses in his political armor—some of which have already been set forth—they were fully aware, and they exploited all of them with infinite variety.

The personal attacks may be summarized briefly as follows: McKean could remain true to no party or principle;[82] it was insinuated that he had proposed high property qualifications for the governorship at the Constitutional Convention in the hope of eliminating Mifflin who was financially embarrassed;[83] the "Jacobins," aware of his defects, hesitated to nominate him, but "the vain old man" persisted until he became the "Republican" candidate;[84] opposed to war with France he wanted to fight Britain in 1794;[85] as a judge he was "overbearing and aristocratical," not a "Republican" in any sense of the word;[86] he wanted to import "Twenty Thousand United Irishmen" into the country as men who understood "true liberty and the Rights of Man";[87] finally, he was a "vile old wretch" who canvassed votes on his judicial circuit and added new members to the population as he went along.[88]

The part played by rumor mongers, although not easily assessable, must have been considerable, for the Republican committee in Philadelphia went to the trouble of issuing a special letter to refute charges that McKean was a native-born Irish Catholic and prejudiced against his "German fellow citizens."[89] Knowing the critical importance of the German vote, both sides cultivated it assiduously. A story to the effect that the Federalists were soliciting support for Muhlenberg in the hope of splitting the Republicans was exposed in the *Aurora*.[90] Just a few days before the election, John Israel learned from William Barton of Lancaster that the Federalists there planned to circulate a report of McKean's death.[91] According to Duane, the ruse was actually employed.[92]

Throughout his long public career McKean had reacted angrily to libelous and defamatory remarks in the public prints. Those that were applied to him in 1799 must have rankled for a long time. But he was to retaliate, and with a vengeance, shortly after his election.

Aside from the slander, vilification and abuse which they employed with a rancor heretofore unequaled, the Federalists dwelt with grim seriousness on the dangers that supposedly threatened the country. Taking a stand exactly opposite from the one maintained by the Republicans, whose *bête noir* was Britain, they were sure that the greatest threat came from France. With "violence, perfidy, falsehood and intrigue" that country sought the ruin of America.[93] In such dangerous times Pennsylvania, one of the most powerful states in the Union, could ill afford to select a Governor who, inexperienced in military affairs and old in years, would be unable to meet French aggression. Men of vigor and resolution were needed to fight wars.[94]

A persuasive and able writer in the *Gazette of the United States* feared danger from another quarter—revolution and disunion within the country itself.[95] And should that be brought about through "the frantic and ungovernable ambition of our revolutionists . . . the influence of Pennsylvania in the scale of American consequence would be immense." Strategically located "between the clashing eastern and southern sections . . . she would become, in no small degree, the arbitress between them." The Governor of Pennsylvania with his great appointive, veto and military powers, if aided by "party spirit," was "almost above controul." He could, therefore, easily oppose the United States and "raise the banner of opposition to the federal administration."[96]

The Republicans started their campaign encouraged by the belief that French successes in Europe and the removal of the State capital from Philadelphia to Lancaster[97] would materially increase their chances of winning with McKean.[98] By June, 1799, electioneering, inspired and directed by the Philadelphia committee, was the order of the day everywhere in the State. The busy committeemen, to obtain propaganda for their circulars, directed inquiries to the leading politicians scattered throughout the Commonwealth. "We rely on the activity of all the men of property and influence in the Republican interest," Dallas told William Irvine. "Pray, how shall we fare in your county?"[99] Gallatin was asked for "certain and authentic information" on James Ross' activities during the Whiskey Rebellion.[100] The bits of information obtained were exploited by the committee and by Duane in the *Aurora*.

In western Pennsylvania McKean's campaign was publicized primarily by John Israel's *Herald of Liberty*. Earnest and sincere in his Republicanism, the young editor virtually turned his newspaper office into a western headquarters. From thence issued handbills, election tickets and requests for material to use in his columns.[101] The transmontane region was a critical one for the Republicans, and they needed all possible support there, despite many easy victories in the past. Ross, as a "native son," had a strong following. To counteract his popularity in Westmoreland County at least, William Findley was nominated for the State Senate in the hope that his prestige would be of assistance in carrying the entire ticket.[102] At the time Findley was unaware of his nomination—as a matter of fact he had declared his intention of retiring from politics—but to the Republicans his willingness to serve was of secondary importance. To place him before the electors as a Republican was the prime object.

Obviously, as Dallas had stated in his letter to Irvine, it was studied Republican strategy to concentrate their campaign around influential men, that is, recognized and popular leaders. The drafting of Findley was a good illustration of their intent. Apparently in line with such policy, this time with designs on those of German descent in eastern Pennsylvania, the *Aurora* printed a translation of a stirring letter to the Germans of Cumberland County.[103] After dwelling on the Federalist national legislation of 1798, the author declared that most of the Germans in Bucks, Northampton, Berks, Northumberland and Montgomery counties approved of McKean. Many of them had long favored the Federalist party, but at last its "hypocrisy and deceit" had been discovered. There followed a fulsome eulogy of Peter Muhlenberg, that staunch advocate of McKean who had fought both the British and the Sedition Act. Once more would he "come forward to defend our rights and to remove our grievances. He is the Moses of the German Israelites . . . who will lead the people out of the house of bondage. He calls on you in the name of McKean. Unite! Unite!"[104] In such fashion was an effort made to capitalize on General Muhlenberg's popularity.

To carry Pennsylvania for McKean, the Republicans based their campaign primarily on national issues, on the ills and dangers that, in their view, threatened the country as a result of Federalist policies. They deplored the increase in governmental expenses and the public debt, and the high Federal taxes and imposts such increase made necessary. They were alarmed at the "marked disregard of the national militia" and the "extensive establishment of land and naval forces. . . ."[105] They pointed to the dangers of a foreign war and feared the creation of a monarchy. Political affairs, it was maintained, had reached such a critical point that the country was faced with a crisis, the resolution of which would determine the fate of those principles so hardly won at the expense of blood and treasure in the Revolution.[106] If the people wanted monarchy, an established church, a standing army, and war, then they should support the "aristocrats."[107]

To William Duane the greatest threat to America came from Great Britain. He repeatedly charged that the *Gazette of the United States* was "a British paper," that Cobbett, of *Porcupine's Gazette,* was a "foreign emissary," that the "anti-Republican" party was British, and that they had all combined in an effort to destroy republican government in the United States.[108] To point up his argument, he used the bloody insurrection, then convulsing Ireland, as a horrible example of British tyranny and ruthlessness.[109] Undoubtedly his constant reference to the struggle in Ireland was not without effect on those of Irish descent in Pennsylvania.

While considering the Republican concentration on national and international affairs, one might wonder how they applied to a candidate for the State's chief executive position. The connection was made through Ross himself as a United States Senator and through his supporters, with emphasis on the latter. The best brief summary of the principal Republican issues and their bearing on Ross was presented by the *Aurora* on October 8, 1799.

> Do not the friends of James Ross associate with British emissaries, British pensioners, British merchants, old Tories, Refugees, Traitors, aristocrats, monarchists?
> Do not the friends of James Ross and James Ross himself *vote* for standing armies, Loans at Eight per centum . . . , High public salaries, Increase of Public Debt, Heavy taxes, Excises, Imposts, House tax, poll tax, window tax, hearth tax, Cattle and horse tax, land tax, Alien Bills and Sedition or Gag Bills to cram everything down your throats.[110]

On all of the above Duane dwelt at great length throughout the summer. And he did not forget to attack Ross personally. Ross, it was claimed, was "unknown," inexperienced and therefore unqualified.[111] Further, he was accused of having absented himself from the Senate when record votes were taken on various aspects of the Alien and Sedition Laws.[112]

The charge that Ross was a Deist was the one that the Federalists took most seriously.[113] It had its origin in a vote he had recorded at the Pennsylvania Constitutional Convention when Section 4 of Article IX was under consideration. Dealing with religious qualifications, the Section—finally adopted—barred no citizen from holding office who acknowledged the existence of God "and a future state of rewards and punishments. . . ."[114] Ross supported a motion to eliminate such a religious test, and for that he was assailed as a Deist and atheist.[115] To counteract the charge the Federalists went to considerable lengths. The Washington County committee of correspondence issued a letter of denial and secured numerous testimonials from men of "eminence and respectability." They were signed by clergymen and elders of the Washington Presbyterian church. All lauded Ross as a religious and God-fearing man and branded the rumors as malicious and false. The denials were published by the Philadelphia committee in a special broadside[116] and in various issues of the *Gazette of the United States* and the *Philadelphia Gazette*. It was the so-called Age of Reason, but the Federalists made every effort to prevent their candidate from being identified with one of its principal characteristics, Deism. Perhaps the connection between Deism and French liberal political thought was considered to be too close.

In the violent newspaper warfare which characterized the election, the Republicans were especially fortunate in the number of able men who used their pens in McKean's behalf. Editors Duane and Israel, alert and aggressive, laid down a constant barrage of propaganda; Dallas, Leib, Peter Muhlenberg, Miles and Coxe, as Philadelphia committeemen, issued several well written and cleverly timed broadsides that were given state-wide circulation. To this group should be added Thomas Cooper, a prominent English liberal who had come to America in 1794 to escape from what he termed "the most corrupt and corrupting government in Europe," the "British monarchy."[117]

In the summer of 1799 he contributed material in support of McKean that was used in the *Aurora*.[118] But of far greater aid to the Republican cause was his effort to define and clarify the multiude of party terms then current. It was during the spring of 1799, while he was serving as editor of the Northumberland *Gazette,* that Cooper wrote a series of articles which were later published in pamphlet form under the title *Political Essays*. In these he shrewdly analysed the contemporary *olla podrida* of labels, phrases and epithets and emerged with two general terms, Federalist and Republican. The gist of his evaluative efforts is to be found in two letters. These were signed, in order of their appearance, "Country Man" and "A Citizen."

In "Country Man" Cooper confessed bewilderment as to the "new fangled" political terms that were being bandied about and requests the editor (himself) to define them. "Country Man" stated his problem as follows:

> I will not pretend to define or describe an Aristocrat, a Democrat, a Jacobin, a Sans-culot, a Frenchman, an Anarchist, a Revolutionist, a Leveller, a Disorganiser, a Regicide, a Liberticide, etc. etc. etc. or even a Federal, an Antifederal, or a Friend of Government; for I am utterly unable to fix their boundary lines, or trace their shades of difference; and I make perpetual blunders when I attempt to apply them to my neighbors . . . All I can find out with certainty on this sub-

> ject is, that whatever the true meaning of these names may be, the most hot-headed, the most ignorant, the most interested, and those who have been suddenly raised from indigence to opulence are the most ready to apply them . . .
> Tell me, Mr. Editor, if a man be a good citizen, a good American, a good Republican, working his farm, supporting his family, obeying the laws, paying his taxes, and drinking his glass of whiskey in good humor with all the world, should he be hunted down as an Aristocrat, or sneered at as a Tory, or kicked out of company as a Jacobin, or have some of these hard favoured *Isms* thrown at his head if he cannot subscribe to the infallibility of his opponent? Some information on this subject would oblige a plain COUNTRY MAN.

With the problem thus outlined, Cooper proceeded to solve it in another letter to the editor, this time over the signature "A Citizen." He began with the terms Democrat, Jacobin and Anti-Federalist. The first two, said he, were borrowed, "with their modern significations, from the government party of England"; the last, once used to describe the minority group in the United States when the Constitution was adopted, was now mistakenly applied by the Federalists to all those who opposed them. They employed all three as terms of reproach, and intentionally confused Democrat with Jacobin. Actually, there was nothing opprobrious in the former word, for the Constitution itself was democratic. He then turned to a consideration of the two principal parties, "most improperly termed Federal and Antifederal," and then described them as follows:

> Those who think the power of the Executive ought rather to be encreased than diminished—who are fearful lest liberty should run into licentiousness, and would rather abridge than extend the rights of the people—who doubt about the practical expediency of a Republican Government, and begin to think a limited monarchy more tolerable than was heretofore supposed—who would strengthen the General at the expense of the State Governments, and stretch the meaning of the Federal Constitution to extend the powers of the President and Congress—who laugh at the efficiency of a militia—who are advocates for a standing army and a permanent navy as absolutely necessary, not only to repel aggressions from abroad, but to quell insurrections at home—who think the Commerce of the country of sufficient importance to be protected at the expence of a foreign war supported by taxes paid by the Farmer, on whom alone all taxes fall—who make (the executive officers of government who have jobs and places to bestow) synonimous with the Constitution, and con-

demn as enemies of the one, all who may disapprove the measures of the other—who think it dangerous to investigate the character and opinions of the public servants unless under the strong controul of sedition laws—who regard aliens, particularly republican aliens, with distrust, and are apprehensive that the best Constitution in the world is in perpetual danger from a handful of foreigners who come hither purposely to adopt it—such persons for the most part call themselves *Federalists*. Grades of difference there may be, but such are the leading features of the party so called.

Others there are, who are cautious of entrusting or extending power unless evidently necessary to the happiness of the people—who are jealous of reposing unlimited confidence in persons of superior station—who think the public character of every public man a fair object of discussion, of praise or censure—that restraint upon investigation, like the late sedition laws, imply a dread of it—that 'men love darkness rather than light, because their deeds are evil'—that a sincere friend of the Constitution and the Country, may sometimes, disapprove the opinions and measures of the officers of government—that the Commercial is not of equal importance with the Agricultural interest of America—that temporary depredations upon our vessels of trade by either of the contending powers, is not sufficient reason for plunging us into the evils of a foreign war, the domestic dangers of a standing army, the temptation to contest which a navy will induce, or the expence of any of them at a period of acknowledged poverty —who regard an alien flying from the tyranny of Europe as a friend, and rejoice in the accession of wealth and industry from whatever quarter it may come—who believe the best way to make a man, a good citizen, is to give him a stake and interest in the country—who love the principles of our own Constitutions, and rejoice at the downfall of political superstition in Europe—who neither adopt nor use political nicknames for party purposes, but glory in the appelation of Republicans. These persons are *usually* called Antifederalists.[119]

Cooper's description of the parties and issues was by far the best Republican statement to appear during 1799.

Obsessed by fear of war, monarchy, treason, revolution and each other—or so they led the citizens to believe—both sides made it appear that the very existence of the nation depended upon the proper selection of a Pennsylvania Governor. Ideologically, there was much stealing of thunder; the Republicans insisted that they were the true "federalists,"[120] and their opponents, while disavowing any support of "Royalty, Democracy or Jacobinism," declared with equal vigor that they were the "real republicans."[121] Of local issues there were practically none. The propagandists chose instead to deal in exciting generalities and slanderous obloquy.

As the bitter and feverish campaign drew to a close, the Philadelphia Republican Committee indulged in a few election predictions. After conceding every doubtful county to Ross and accentuating his majorities to the fullest, they forecast a Republican victory. They gave McKean a majority of 5,700 votes and sixteen counties. Ross, they thought, would carry nine counties and the city of Philadelphia. But, they cautioned, this happy outcome would be realized only if the Republicans equaled the Federalists "in zeal and exertion."[122]

When all the election returns were in and officially tabulated, it was discovered that the committee had overestimated McKean's majority by only 407 votes and his counties by six. In a total vote of 70,679, more than twice the number ever cast in any preceding gubernatorial contest, McKean, with 38,036 to his opponent's 32,643, had won by a margin of 5,393.[123] In carrying twelve counties, McKean was exceeded by Ross who won thirteen, plus the city of Philadelphia.

Contrary to the over-sanguine committee's expectations, the five western counties, recording a total of 11,307 votes, gave Ross a majority of 181. In Allegheny he was victorious by 2,106 to 976, in Greene by a little more than one hundred votes. McKean won in Washington, Westmoreland and Fayette, but in the latter by only 145.

In Berks, Northampton, Montgomery and Bucks, the counties most seriously affected by the "window tax" riots, McKean was given a thumping six-thousand-vote majority, more than double the total number cast for his opponent. Ross carried Bucks alone, but only by a mere 116. The validity of conclusions based on comparisons drawn between past performances and the election of 1799 may be questionable, but it should be pointed out that this was not the first time some of those counties favored the Republicans. In 1796 Berks and Northampton gave a majority to Jefferson, and during the next three years they elected to the legislature such firm Republicans as Peter Frailey, Baltzer Gehr, Peter Muhlenberg, John Coolbaugh, Jonas Hartzell, Charles Shoemaker and several others. From Montgomery had come two important Republican leaders: Nathaniel Boileau and Frederick Conrad. Although it was nothing new, then, for those counties to display Republican strength, it seems safe, nonetheless, to conclude that their emphatic repudiation of Federalist Ross reflected an adverse reaction to the national legislation passed in 1798. McKean lost in York and Lancaster counties, but in those two, plus Bucks, Northampton, Berks and Montgomery, comprising the region most heavily populated by citizens of German descent, he polled a majority of 4,322.

In addition to the counties already mentioned, Ross carried Chester, Franklin, Luzerne, Delaware, Somerset, Bedford, Huntingdon and the city of Philadelphia. But in all these last named areas his combined vote was a little more than a thousand under McKean's vote in Bucks, Northampton, Berks and Montgomery. Without belaboring the statistics further it seems fairly obvious that McKean's margin of victory came from the "window tax" counties. Just his majority in the three he carried was more than enough to elect him.

Had the Republicans depended on the western counties to carry the day they would have been sadly disappointed. There, McKean's touted democracy could not surmount Ross' popularity as a "native son." In carrying that area, the Federalists showed greater strength than they ever did before or after. All the western counties had favored Jefferson in 1796, but McKean was not Jefferson. Any similarity between his democratic proclivities and those of the great Virginian was largely expediential.

In organizational machinery the Federalists were not greatly inferior to their opponents. The Philadelphia Federalist committee met the exigencies of the situation capably, but their circulars lacked the force and ingenuity that characterized those issued by the Republicans.

The newspaper propagandists on both sides were able and equally scurrilous, but in timing and inventiveness Duane was without a peer. The cleverness with which he wooed the citizens of Irish and German extraction undoubtedly had much to do with the final result. One writer has said that he contributed most to the Republican cause.[124] Undoubtedly his services were of tremendous importance, but one must not ignore the support of Peter Muhlenberg, who enjoyed a great popularity in the area that contributed most to McKean's success. His name on the Republican circulars must have meant a great deal to many who floundered about in a welter of misleading slogans, sophistries, charges and counter charges.

If one wished to ignore McKean's background, his failure in western Pennsylvania and his method of nomination, his success might be described as a victory for positive democracy. But in the light of these three qualifying factors it would seem more likely that the democracy manifested in the results was a negative one, a revulsion of feeling from the Congressional excess of 1798, rather than a positive and emphatic affirmation of democratic constructiveness.

To the Federalists McKean's victory was a sour and bitter dose, a bad omen for the future. They did not know it then, of course, but never again would they control Pennsylvania politics. Already at hand was an epitaph, written not after their defeat but before the campaign began. In the preceding March, John Ward Fenno had surveyed his little world with jaundiced eyes, and from the depths of profound gloom delivered himself of the following:

> I no longer behold, when I look around me, any thing of much moment to struggle for. A country overrun by turbulence and faction, a government like a reed shaken by the wind; the people split into two deadly parties, whose impending collision must as surely produce bloodshed and misery, as that of flint and steel emits the spark. . . .
> The sun of federalism is fast retiring behind the clouds of turbulence and treason. Those who have so long been warmed by its genial influence, waste in stupid adorations, the allotted period of its salvation.[125]

But to an *Aurora* correspondent the future held not gloom but promise. Said he: "The genius of America is not dead, but only sleepeth."[126]

In the legislative elections the Republicans also fared well. By winning approximately forty-one seats to their opponents' thirty-five in the lower house, they enjoyed a clear majority for the first time.[127] They won solid representations in thirteen counties, including four in western Pennsylvania (Allegheny remained Federalist), and the "window tax" counties of Berks, Northampton and Montgomery. They even secured two members from York, a traditional Federalist stronghold; but they were unable to make a dent in the Philadelphia representation.

Along with the city, the Federalists received solid support from nine counties. With the exception of Fayette, they won either all or a majority of the seats in the counties that had favored James Ross.[128] Bucks gave them three of four and York four of six.

In the elections for State Senators, the Federalists were victorious, however, by the slightest of margins. Of the seven new members chosen, they elected four to the Republicans' three.[129] In the district composed of the city and county of Philadelphia and Delaware County, the two parties divided evenly by electing Benjamin Say, Republican, and John Jones, Federalist. The other two Republicans were William Findley (Westmoreland-Fayette) and Thomas Mewhorter (Northampton-Wayne). The other Federalists returned were Zebulon Potts (Chester-Bucks-Montgomery), James Ewing (York) and Thomas Johnston (Franklin). These Federalist Senatorial victories were to be of large significance in the approaching presidential election.

CHAPTER XIII

VICTORY AFFIRMED AND REAFFIRMED

The defeat of 1799 so disheartened the Federalists that they never recovered. Confused and dismayed, unable and seemingly unwilling to match the Republicans in appealing to the electorate and deprived of the French scare as an issue, they met serious reverses in the two following years. Their most stubborn resistance to the Republican tide came during the presidential election of 1800. The fight was not made at the polls, where their repudiation was unmistakable and emphatic, but in the upper house of the legislature. There a small majority of Senators prevented the selection of electors by an election at large, the method used on all previous occasions, and made it necessary for the legislature itself to choose them. In so doing, the lawmakers found themselves involved in a bitter contest that dragged on so long that the State just narrowly averted the loss of a voice in the presidential election. The battle well illustrated the intransigence of partisan groups in Pennsylvania and climaxed a struggle which had been steadily mounting in intensity since 1796.

Parties and the Presidency

Pennsylvania's role in the presidential contest of 1800 was begun in December, 1799, when the legislature divided on the old issue of election methodology. As a result of their recent successes, the Republican majority in the House of Representatives was convinced that an employment of the general-election method would enable them to choose either all or most of the fifteen electors to which the State was entitled. The Federalists, with a small but consistent majority in the Senate, apparently shared that conviction, for they held out stubbornly for a district election.

First to place itself on record, the Senate, by a vote of fourteen to nine on December 19, 1799, defeated a Republican motion to adopt an election law similar in basic essentials to the one used in 1796.[1] Since that law had provided for a general election, the issue was clear. The fourteen-to-nine vote, incidentally, was a true indication of the relative strength of the two parties in the upper house, for it was repeated over and over again throughout the session.

The Republican House of Representatives made its preference known on December 30, 1799, when it voted thirty-eight to thirty-four to "revive and continue in force" the law of 1796.[2] The Republicans had bitterly opposed that measure three years before, when they thought they were in the minority. But now, of course, the situation was quite different. With the battle thus joined there ensued a period of deadlock during which both houses exchanged, amended and re-exchanged diametrically opposed bills.

Finally, in the latter part of January, 1800, the controversy was placed in the hands of a conference committee. As an aid to solution that maneuver was a forlorn hope; it merely accented the disagreement. Both committees insisted on maintaining the stand taken by the houses they represented, and the stalemate continued.

In its report on March 12, 1800, the House committee of conference stated that the Senate not only adhered to the district system, but in addition it had devised a method of districting which would "produce an incorrect and unjust expression of the voice of the people."[3] In amplification of that the committee said:

> It will be found on examination, that the counties are so classed in forming those districts, that two thousand citizens opposed to the reputed opinions of the major part of the Senators, will be skillfully cast into a fruitless competition with two thousand five hundred citizens who adopt those opinions of a majority of the Senators . . . All the districts capable of such modifications are so arranged. The consequences would be obvious.[4]

Furthermore, the committee went on, where certain segments of the population were in heavy opposition to the majority of the Senators, the electoral districts were so apportioned that the segments "would be uselessly set against the small portions of citizens of the sentiments of the majority of the Senators, which were left undisposed of, by the first part of this scheme of election districts."

Although the committee studiously avoided mention of specific parties, preferring instead such clumsy phraseology as "major part of the Senators," etc., it unmistakably recognized their existence. But of greater significance was its recognition of party boundaries and groupings. Obviously, partisan geographic and population areas had become so clearly discernible to the Federalists that they sought to manipulate them advantageously in districting the State. As a matter of fact, the committee's criticism of the Senate's proposed districting system was an excellent description of an artful political device later to be known as "Gerrymandering."

After the conference committee dissolved in failure, there was little point in further belaboring the troublesome issue. The majorities in both houses were adamant, so the legislators concluded their work without making provision for an election or for the calling of a special session to try once more. Since they would not normally meet again until the latter part of December, when it would be too late to select electors, some interim action would have to be taken if the State was to have a voice in the selection of a president.

The vexing question was thus automatically shifted to Governor McKean. As early as March 7, 1800, before the conference committees had issued their reports, he had known that the Assembly would pass no election law. He had therefore decided to convene it again in August, and then, if the stalemate continued, there would be nothing left for him to do but issue a proclamation directing the manner in which the electors would be chosen.[5]

But after reconsidering the matter, McKean did not convene the Assembly in August. Had the legislators entertained any hope of reconciling their conflicting opinions in a summer session, he reasoned, they would have made arrangements for it. Surely they knew better than he what the results would be. Therefore, he decided, it would be an "abortive" and "expensive experiment" to call the same contestants back into the debating arena.[6] Consequently he determined to await the results of the October election before calling a special session.

The Election of 1800

In preparation for the election of a new House of Representatives and seven Senators, the party chieftains naturally utilized the presidential electoral issue that had been handed to them by the Assembly. The participation of Pennsylvania in the election of a President could very well depend on the outcome. Should either party secure a majority of both houses, it could send fifteen men of its own choosing to the electoral college. In effect, the citizens of Pennsylvania in choosing Assemblymen were indirectly nominating presidential electors. The emphasis placed on the national election during the campaign made that fact clear.

The Federalists repeated their old charges and dwelt fearfully on the "dreadful consequences" of "Jacobin" rule. They were sure a Republican victory would destroy the United States Constitution.[7] Religion was also introduced. To the *Gazette of the United States* Jefferson was an "infidel," and in numerous issues it exhorted its readers to ask themselves this "Grand Question: shall I continue in allegiance to God—and a Religious President; or impiously declare for Jefferson—and no God!!!"[8] France was still a bugaboo to the "rational liberty" men, but their oft expressed fears were not so effective as they had been in 1798; the tension between that country and the United States had perceptibly lessened.

The Republicans presented their numerous charges and complaints with vigor and aggressiveness. Their principal issues may be summarized as follows: The United States Constitution had been used by the Federalists to increase their wealth and power; the Pennsylvania Assembly should be controlled by men who would "assert the just authority of the individual states without impairing the rights of the union";[9] the Sedition Law was unconstitutional and subversive; partisan judges were more interested in electioneering than in dispensing equal justice; the Federalists had tried to provoke war with France for party purposes; loans had been obtained at excessive interest rates; oppressive taxes and imposts had enabled officials to fatten on the public treasury; an undefined common law in the hands of Federal judges threatened the life, liberty and property of all citizens.[10]

In short, the general theme of the Republican campaign was the harmful effect of Federalist rule. The people, it was said, had been shamefully victimized by a series of expensive and repressive measures which threatened the existence of republican government. The Federalists, although a minority group, were determined to retain control. This was amply demonstrated, the Republicans argued, by a willful and obdurate clique in the Senate which had thwarted the desires of a majority of Pennsylvania's citizens by holding out for an electoral law that would give unfair advantage to a minority group. To correct these evils and prevent their growth, the people had but to send a majority of Republicans to both branches of the legislature.

To all of the above the Federalists gave a categorical denial. The real wishes of the people had been enacted into national law by clear majorities, they said. In a republic the majority ruled. And the State Senators, in their insistence on a district election, were fairly representing their constituents and acting firmly on their constitutional rights.

The election, held on October 14, 1800, was a crushing defeat for the Federalists. Of the seven Senators elected they named only one,

Matthias Barton, district of Lancaster.[11] In the lower house they lost by over two to one. There they were represented by only twenty-three members to fifty-five for the Republicans.[12] In thus suffering their worst defeat to date, they won five of six seats in Philadelphia and carried the counties of Chester, Lancaster, Huntingdon, Delaware and Adams. All the rest were solidly Republican.

The Republicans were no less successful in the Congressional elections: by winning ten of the thirteen seats they emphatically established their numerical superiority in the State's representation in Congress.[13] Altogether, they had little difficulty at the polls in 1800. But the most crucial battle was yet to come, in the legislature.

Legislative Struggle Renewed

On October 18, 1800, four days after the election, Governor McKean issued a proclamation requesting the legislature to meet in special session on November 5, 1800.[14] Both the Federalists and Republicans then knew that for the first time the Assemblymen would have to choose electors, for there was not sufficient time to hold a general election. Both parties therefore began organizing their forces to bring pressure on the legislature, and from the very beginning it was recognized that the old and troublesome question of methodology would be the most vital point at issue.

Would the electors be chosen by a joint or concurrent vote of both houses? The determination of that question was all important, for despite the election of six Republican Senators the Federalists still possessed a majority in the upper house. A concurrent vote would bring inevitable disagreement, whereas a joint vote would place either all or a great majority of the fifteen electors in the Republican column.

Determined to elect Jefferson and Aaron Burr as President and Vice President respectively, the Philadelphia Republicans began their campaign on October 5, 1800, with the issuance of a memorial to the legislature requesting a joint ballot.[15] To encourage "temperate deliberation," the memorialists avoided any mention of the dispute which had resulted in the failure of the previous legislature to pass an election law. Appealing to all groups, they stressed the great evil that would befall Pennsylvania should it lose a presidential vote. For too long the State had been deprived of a "legitimate weight in the Federal councils and proceedings." But that would be rectified if the legislature used the joint-ballot system to "express the evident will" of the State's citizens.[16] A few days later, a Republican meeting at the State House endorsed the memorial and appointed committees to secure signatures in the city wards and in the county of Philadelphia.[17]

Putting great faith in the value of petitions, the Republicans in the metropolitan area induced large numbers of citizens from both parties to endorse the joint-ballot method. On November 7, 1800, John Beckley informed Dallas that they had secured 2448 signatures in the city alone and 2700 in the Northern Liberties, Southwark and the county of Philadelphia. Many others had been obtained in Delaware.[18] Beckley asked that special attention be paid to John Jones, who represented the district of Philadelphia city and county and the county of Delaware in the Senate. Jones had publicly declared that he would favor a joint vote if a majority of his constituents so demanded. That majority had been secured in writing, Beckley assured Dallas, so it would be advisable to demonstrate that fact to Jones by showing him all the petitions.

Throughout the special session the gathering of Republican memorials continued unabated, and they poured steadily into the Senate. On just one day, November 10, 1800, that house received petitions signed by 1907 joint-ballot advocates.[19]

The Federalists made no effort to engage in a war of petitions. Instead, they devoted their attention to the Senate. On November 5, 1800, when the legislature convened, it was believed that they could depend on a majority of two in the upper house.[20] To keep that majority firm, several eminent Philadelphia Federalists met on the same day at Dunwoody's tavern to plan a strategic pressure campaign.[21] There was nothing new in the resolutions adopted there: they merely reiterated the old contention that it was unconstitutional for the two branches of the legislature to vote jointly on any measure. (This despite the fact that the constitution specified a joint vote for the election of a State Treasurer.) Each house should exercise its functions separately, they insisted, for the more numerous House of Representatives could always outvote the Senate. To assist the Senate in maintaining its supposed constitutional rights, the meeting at Dunwoody's appointed a committee composed of Thomas Fitzsimons, William Lewis, William Rawle and other prominent Federalists. According to McKean, the committee kept in constant touch with the Federalist majority in the Senate throughout the special session. Letters of advice and encouragement were dispatched almost daily to Lancaster. And on one occasion, when it was feared that the majority would waver, the committee sent a special deputation to the capital which sponsored a dinner "to cheer their spirit and keep them steady."[22]

Two days after the special session began, McKean, in a sober and emphatic message, stressed the absolute necessity of appointing electors. To neglect such a duty, he said, would be as injurious to the Union as secession. They had definite authority to name electors—the legislatures of eight states did so—and in making their selection they should rise above "the suggestions of party" and disdain "a contest about forms."[23]

The Governor's suggestions fell on deaf ears, for during the next three weeks the deliberations of the legislators were characterized by little else than attention to "party" and "forms." Both houses quickly placed their members on record. On November 10, after defeating a Federalist resolution in favor of concurrent election by fifty-five to twenty-one, the House passed a joint-vote bill by fifty-six to twenty.[24]

When the House bill reached the Senate it was shorn of its joint-vote stipulation and amended so as to provide for a concurrent selection. Deferring to the more numerous House membership, the Senators were willing to allow it to select eight electors. Against strenuous opposition the amended bill passed the Senate on November 13, 1800, by thirteen to eleven, a vote that was a true measure of partisan strength, for it was to be repeated over and over again on all critical related divisions.[25]

The House received its drastically amended bill, refused to concur and promptly sent it back.[26] The Senate was equally obdurate and determined. With the thirteen Federalists holding firm, it refused to recede from its amendments. The legislature was thus deadlocked, and both sides were squared off for a long battle. McKean, awaiting the outcome with "inexpressible solicitude," notified the House on November 14, 1800, that the loss of Pennsylvania's vote would "be a vital stab to the Union" from which it would "never perfectly recover . . ."[27]

Thus prodded, the House appointed a conference committee and the Senate followed suit. But their deliberations were barren of results. Both committees insisted on maintaining the positions taken by the chambers they represented. The House committee, while holding out for a joint election in principle, thought that the real point at issue was the number of electors each house should elect. It was therefore willing to discuss the problem of apportionment; but the Senate committee refused.

When both parties had made their positions clear, the rabidly partisan newspapers in Philadelphia burst forth in violent abuse. There is little point in dwelling on the scurrility and vituperation that appeared in such papers as the *Gazette of the United States* and the *Aurora*. It is enough to say that each considered its opponents to be scoundrels and liars of the deepest dye; they said so almost every day in columns of lurid verbiage. However, the position taken by these papers, insofar as they were recognized as vehicles for the parties they championed, deserves brief mention.

The arguments of the *Aurora* were best summarzied in an account of a Republican meeting held at the State House on November 20, 1800, at which Duane served as secretary. Having been called to consider the legislative battle over methodology, the meeting adopted several resolutions condemnatory of the Senate majority. In their refusal to cooperate with the House of Representatives, it was declared, the thirteen Federalist Senators were guilty of "culpable conduct." They were ignoring the late election, which manifestly reflected a desire of the people for "a change of measures by a change of men . . ." Also, they were violating precedent: if joint voting was unconstitutional, then James Ross and William Bingham, elected by such a method, were not entitled to their seats in the United States Senate. For defying the clear wishes of the people, they "ought not to receive any place of profit, honour, or trust under this commonwealth."[28]

In the opinion of the *Gazette of the United States,* the thirteen Senators were to be commended for so nobly adhering to strict constitutional principles. They were "genuine Federal Republicans" and posterity would list their names "among the first of *American Patriots*—Who does not envy them the glorious title, which they merit,—what real American is there, who is not willing to hail them *Saviours Of Their Country?* They exhibit to their Sister States and to the World, an honourable example of Spartan Virtue."[29]

By the middle of November, 1800, when the vexing problem had been shunted into the hands of the conference committee, many Republicans had begun to suspect that the Senate majority was really motivated by a desire to prevent the State from having any presidential vote whatever, and not by a great love for the concurrent voting system. Peter Frailey, an experienced representative from Berks County, was one of the men who entertained such a suspicion. At the beginning of a week-end recess he was jouncing along the road between Lancaster and Reading, completely absorbed in the presidential-vote dilemma, when he was suddenly "struck" by an idea. "Suppose the Committee of Conference can not agree," he ruminated, "would it be out of order for a member in the House of Representatives to read a bill in his place predicated on the Principles for which the committee of the House now contend, to wit, a joint vote, and each house to nominate. Should it be rejected for want of form, I conceive it would show in a clear point of View, what the Senate now contend for—no vote for Pennsylvania."[30] Hoping that his "idea" might clear the air and force the Senate to admit that it was merely engaging in obstructionist and delaying tactics, Frailey hurriedly dispatched it to Dallas for his consideration.

Whether or not the scheme was originated solely by Frailey, it was seized upon as a possible solution. Accordingly, on November 20, 1800, the House of Representatives passed a bill which proposed that each chamber should nominate a certain number of electors, fifteen of whom were to be elected in joint session. The Senate was thus presented with a delicate problem: would it be feasible to withdraw its opposition to a joint vote? The obvious course of procedure was the shrewdest one, and it decided that it could do so without suffering any damage. Originally it had demanded the privilege of naming seven electors; now the House had made an offer which would permit it to do just that, but under the guise of a nomination.

Of course, the all-important question was: how many candidates should each House nominate? After a rapid exchange of amended and reamended apportionment figures it was discovered by November 22, 1800, that the House demanded the right to nominate nine, while limiting the Senate to six. The Senate, on the other hand, insisted that each house nominate eight.[31] The latter proposal would naturally end in the election of eight Republicans and seven Federalists. In consequence, since fourteen of the votes would be cancelled out, Pennsylvania would be given only one vote. Obviously, Frailey's little scheme had not worked out according to plan, and its only immediate result was another stalemate, which lasted for more than a week.

In the meantime, Republican leaders were anxiously watching the elections in other states. By the latter part of November, it was quite evident to all that the race between Adams and Jefferson would be very close. In fact, it was so close that Dallas, on November 28, 1800, was sure that the four electoral votes of Rhode Island would decide the issue. If Jefferson were defeated there, he predicted, Adams would be elected, for by that time he had abandoned all hope of securing a vote for Pennsylvania.[32]

Shortly thereafter, Dallas learned that Jefferson had lost in Rhode Island. He then calculated that if the Federalist electors remained faithful to their two candidates, Adams and Charles Cotesworth Pinckney, Adams would receive fifty-eight votes, Pinckney sixty-six and Jefferson sixty-five. Seeing an opportunity to cause a tie between Pinckney and Jefferson, Dallas hurriedly advised the Republicans in the House of Representatives "to take the single vote offered by the Senate."[33] That is, he counseled the House majority leaders to accede to the Senate's demands that each House nominate eight electors.

Evidently many others agreed that it would be more advantageous to choose one elector than none at all. At least McKean thought so, and just "when all expectations of an election for this state had ceased," he wrote to Jefferson, Senator William Findley was persuaded to try once more.[34] On November 23, 1800, he introduced a bill which the Senate promptly amended on the following day (Saturday) in conformity with its old demands.[35] When this bill was considered in the House on December 1, 1800, a majority of the members decided to capitulate. By a vote of fifty-three to nineteen they agreed to permit each house to nominate eight electors. Fifteen of the sixteen nominees would be chosen as electors by a joint vote.[36] The House had won on the joint-election issue, but the Senate had actually won the battle.

From that point on, events moved rapidly: the Senate promptly agreed, the bill was compared by a committee, signed by McKean and sixteen candidates were hurriedly nominated. At the election on December 2, 1800, all the nominees, with two exceptions, received no more than ninety-five nor less than ninety-four votes. The exceptions were Robert Coleman, a Federalist from Lancaster County, and Samuel Wetherill, the only Republican elected to the House from the city of Philadelphia. Coleman, who obtained only thirty-six votes to sixty-two for Wetherill, was eliminated. That resulted in the election of eight Republicans and seven Federalists.[37]

The members of both houses followed rigid partisan lines. In the Senate and House respectively Wetherill received ten and fifty-two votes to thirteen and twenty-three for Coleman. One Senator (Samuel Maclay) and three Representatives refused to participate on the grounds that the Senate had behaved in a manner contrary to former practice and in opposition to the will of a majority of the citizens.[38]

McKean lost no time in announcing the results. Shortly after the election he issued a proclamation requesting the electors to meet in Lancaster on the following day, December 3, 1800, and perform their duties.³⁹ Of course, no one was surprised to learn that they gave eight votes to the Jefferson-Burr ticket and seven to Adams and Pinckney.⁴⁰

The bitterness engendered during the month-long legislative contest which resulted in that vote threatened to agitate Pennsylvania politicians for years to come. The Republican members of the House of Representatives had been on the sharp horns of a very troublesome dilemma, and their surrender to the Senate was not pleasing to many of their constituents. Certainly the Representatives themselves were not satisfied either, but they had made what many conceived to be the best of a bad situation. William Penrose (Philadelphia County), whose thoughts on the matter no doubt closely resembled those held by his similarly harassed colleagues, explained his acquiescence to the Senate's demands in a letter to Dallas.⁴¹

> The stage has just arrived [he wrote after the election] & brought my colleague [William] Linnard. I have not seen him, but am informed his report is, that our republican friends in the City are outrageous [sic] at our conduct. if so I am sorry for it, but believe if our presidential Election depended upon a single Vote and we had refused to give it there would have been greater cause for censure—If they are dissatisfied with us they must supply our places next year with such men as *they believe will pay more attention to their interests.*

Governor McKean, seething with wrath and indignation, gave his version of the legislative squabble to Jefferson in a long letter of December 15, 1800.⁴² Three-fifths of Pennsylvania's citizens had favored Jefferson and Burr, he said. That was "known and admitted." Yet thirteen Senators had defied the general will and ignored every "honorable measure" the Republicans could devise. But they were "execrated by the Whigs" and punishment would be certain. Never would they "have the power to perpetrate the like mischief again . . ."

Aside from party considerations, McKean thought the "catastrophy" had been brought on principally by the ambitions and schemes of three Senators. John Woods (Washington-Greene-Allegheny), presiding officer of the Senate and brother-in-law of James Ross, favored the election of either Adams or Pinckney in the hope that he and Ross would receive appointments either in the Federal judiciary department or in the Northwest Territory. (Governor St. Clair was not "expected to live long.") McKean had also learned that Samuel Postlethwaite (Cumberland) favored Adams because he was told that his brother-in-law, Henry Miller, would be removed as State "Supervisor" if Jefferson were elected. The last man mentioned was Senator Dennis Whelen

(Bucks-Chester-Montgomery). He sought Adams' election, said the Governor, in the belief that his brother Israel would be retained as "Purveyor at Philadelphia." Those three men, McKean went on,

> governed their colleagues, all of whom are Anglo-Federalist. Indeed, the officers of the Customs at Philadelphia and all the officers under the Pres. of the U. S., with scarce an exception, have leagued against you, and evidenced as much malignity as they displayed in my election; some arts, calumnies & baseness have been practiced in both cases. Henry Miller, General [Edward] Hand, Robert Coleman etc. have been in this borough [Lancaster] almost constantly since the Legislature have been convened, keeping the thirteen firm to the party.[43]

Thus McKean to the Republican nominee. All the men he had listed as enemies, be it noted, were either motivated by a desire for office or by a desire to keep their friends in office. There seems to be little doubt that McKean was forehandedly sharpening a large axe wherewith to clear out the men who had long enjoyed Federal political plums in Pennsylvania. He and Jefferson shared their enemies in common, and these deserved punishment. And although he did not actually advise their castigation at that time, he unmistakably implied it.

If Jefferson himself experienced any great anger at the outcome of the Pennsylvania election, he did not reveal it when commenting on the subject in a letter to Benjamin Rush.[44] "Nothwithstanding the annihilation of the Pennsylvania vote," he mildly observed, "the Republicans seem to have obtained a majority of 8 in the late election. If so the vessel of the Union will be put on her republican tack and shew us how she works on that."

Jefferson was right. The new ship was indeed Republican, but the electoral college had failed to make clear the identity of the ship's captain. Of the 138 electoral votes, Jefferson and Burr received seventy-three each to sixty-five for Adams and sixty-four for Pinckney.[45] To break the tie between the two leading candidates, recourse was had to the Constitution, which, in Article II, Section I, provided that in case two majority candidates received an equal number of votes the House of Representatives, voting by states, should choose one of them as President. Since the House was Federalist, many Republicans awaited the outcome with apprehension.

When the first ballot was taken on February 11, 1801, Jefferson received only eight of the sixteen votes. Such a contingency had been foreseen,[46] and the Republicans were sure that they would be cheated out of the presidency. They therefore "formed a plan to surround the wilderness capital with militia in order to prevent fraud and hold the government till a new constitutional convention, called by Jefferson and Burr jointly could meet."[47]

But such drastic action was unnecessary, for the Federalists solved the problem in a more peaceful fashion. First, they "satisfied themselves that Jefferson would make no wholesale removals of Federalists from the lower ranks of the civil service . . ."[48] Then, strongly influenced by Hamilton, who distrusted Burr, they worked out an arrangement whereby a sufficient number of Representatives voted blanks to give Jefferson a majority of ten. That occurred on February 17, 1801, on the thirty-sixth ballot.

While the House of Representatives was taking vote after vote on the fate of the Republican candidates, the passionately interested Chief Executive of Pennsylvania was not standing passively by. Several days before the rumored tie vote had been recorded McKean assured Jefferson that if "bad men" dared "traiterously to destroy, or embarrass our general Government and the Union of the States, I shall conceive it my duty to oppose them at every hazard of life and fortune; for I should deem it less inglorious to submit to foreign than domestic tyranny."[49] He meant that, but at the time he thought no difficulties would occur. However, after learning of the stalemate in the House his apprehensions were aroused, and he began planning a series of "operations" he intended to carry out "in case of a certain unfortunate event in the decision of the House of Representatives."[50] His plan, which he thought the Federalists would consider "a bold stroke," was confided to several Republican Assemblymen who had agreed to continue the legislature in session until after March 4, 1801.[51]

As it turned out though, his planning was unnecessary. On February 20, 1801, while he was writing a detailed account of his scheme to Jefferson, the news of the Republican victory reached Lancaster. This naturally obviated the necessity of any action on his part, and he immediately destroyed the letter. But what was the "certain unfortunate event" he had feared? What was the "bold stroke" he had intended to deliver?

The answers to these questions he made clear in a letter to Jefferson on March 19, 1801.[52] Had the House of Representatives, he wrote, elected some one other than Jefferson or Burr as President (the "unfortunate event"), the Pennsylvania Republicans would not have submitted. They would have resisted strenuously, and McKean had determined to lead that resistance by implementing the following plan:

> A proclamation was framed by myself, enjoining obedience on all officers civilian military and the citizens of this State to you as President and Mr. Burr as Vice-President, in case you should so agree the matter between yourselves (as expected); a Resolution was also prepared for our House of Representatives to adopt, approving the proclamation and pledging themselves to support it, and an instrument to be signed by the eleven Senators, in case we could not prevail with one of the party in opposition, which would have made a majority in the Senate, as Mr. [Zebulon] Potts, belonging to them had left the House [Senate is meant] thro' indisposition; he is lately dead. The militia would have been warned to be ready, arms for upwards of twenty thousand were secured, brass field-pieces etc etc, and an order would have been issued for the arresting and bringing to justice every member of Congress and other persons found in Pennsyla. who should have been concerned in the treason. And, I am persuaded, a verdict would have been given against them, even if the Jury had been returned by a Marshall.[53]

Undoubtedly, McKean was ready to support Republican claims, by arms if necessary, but with the ringing of the victory bells and the prompt adjournment of the "electrified" Assembly on February 20, 1801, he assembled all his plans and committed them "to the flames."

Election of 1801

The Republican victory of 1799, positively affirmed one year later, was overwhelmingly reaffirmed in the legislative elections of 1801. This landslide, combined with the elections of the two preceding years, was of such proportions as to irreparably damage the Federalist cause in Pennsylvania and firmly establish Republican supremacy. In the elections for Assemblymen the Republicans won seventy-one of the eighty-six seats in the House of Representatives and nine in the Senate, the total number of vacancies.[54] Of the thirty-five counties the Federalists carried only six: Chester, Luzerne, Huntingdon, Delaware, Somerset and Adams. With the exception of Chester, none of them had more than two representatives. All the other heavily populated counties, which had contributed so largely toward Federalist control, had gone over to the Republicans. In Lancaster, a former stronghold, only one Federalist was elected.

Probably the harshest Federalist rebuff of all was the loss of Philadelphia. There, for the first time, the Republicans carried their ticket in its entirety. This included candidates for the legislature, the select and common councils and county commissioner.⁵⁵ Although the Republican majority was not large—in no case did it exceed 200 votes—a salient fact was clear: the citadel had at last been taken.

The Republicans were equally successful in the off-year Congressional elections, necessitated by the resignations of Albert Gallatin and Peter Muhlenberg. The two new Congressmen, William Hoge and Isaac Van Horne, were both Republicans.⁵⁶

The attitude of the Philadelphia Federalists, both before and after the debacle, was singularly phlegmatic. Although they must have been mortified at the defeat, they certainly did little to avert it. Their bitter last-ditch fight in the presidential contest seemed to have sapped their energies; and Jefferson's eventual victory was a rude jolt from which they could not easily recover. Now, in contrast to their opponents, they appeared to be dull and somnolent. At least, that is the impression one receives from reading the *Gazette of the United States* and the *Philadelphia Gazette.*

Both papers continued to scold the "Jacobins," with emphasis on McKean, Dallas and Duane, but as to positive practical programs they were almost silent. While the *Aurora* faithfully recorded and encouraged Republican campaign efforts, the Federalist journals had very little to report. Discouraged at the lethargy of its friends, the *Gazette of the United States* tried to goad them into action. "Federalists! How comes it that you are so inactive in this city?" it asked on August 17, 1801. Important elections are in the offing, so "rouse then from your torpor! It was not by inactivity your opponents gained their present superiority; it was by exertion and perseverance; and it is by these alone aided by your good cause, you can expect to do anything."⁵⁷

But this strident call evoked no immediate response. Another month went by before the paper could record any Federalist activity. Then, on September 29, 1801, it printed an account of a nomination meeting in Chester County. This was followed one day later by a report of another, held in Philadelphia. Evident in this latter meeting, which was held on September 29, were poor preparation and bad management, for the man nominated for the State Senate (Anthony Morris) refused to run. Seven days elapsed before he was replaced by another, James Ash. These two nominatory meetings were the only ones mentioned in the *Gazette of the United States.*

The *Philadelphia Gazette* had but little more to offer. Having no news of Federalist activity to report, it announced on July 15, 1801, that "fifteen 'Republicans,' or, in the cant of the times, the *people* of

Bucks, Montgomery, Northampton and Wayne," had nominated Isaac Van Horne for Congress.[58] Then, rather hopelessly, it conceded victory to Van Horne. Altogether, it carried not more than a half-dozen Federalist nomination notices, and just before the election a mass of advertisements (obtained in response to an offered twenty per cent. discount to all subscribing advertisers) drove almost all news of any kind out of the paper. Election day was allowed to pass unnoticed.

In sharp contract to Federalist lethargy, the Republicans were busily devising and perfecting a political *modus operandi*. Concomitant with their rise to dominance in the State, they sought the creation and improvement of nominatory methods within the counties which would more thoroughly represent the voters. To effectuate this, they utilized the townships as the smallest representative units and gave them a voice in county political activity. The will of the townships was expressed through elected delegates who attended general county meetings and constituted the membership of the county committee. Rapid strides had been made in this direction one year earlier in several counties, particularly Bucks and Chester,[59] but it was in 1801 that the system was considerably improved and extended. It functioned in several counties, but for purposes of illustration examples will be drawn only from Chester, Montgomery and Bucks.

As early as February 17, 1801, the Republicans in Chester County began preparing for the fall elections. On that date they held a general meeting in West Chester and formulated the following procedure. First, they appointed two-member corresponding committees for each township, whose function it would be to arrange for township elections on August 1, 1801. At that time each township would elect three men to serve on the county "Representative Committee." It would be the duty of this latter committee to meet on August 18, 1801, and make all nominations. Then a five-man "permanent" county committee was appointed to keep in touch with the township committees and all groups representative of other counties. To defray campaign expenses, collections were to be taken in each township, and all funds were to be cared for by a county treasurer.[60]

When the "Representative Committee" met on August 18, committeemen from thirty-three townships were present. They nominated candidates for the Assembly, one for Sheriff and County Commissioner, and two Directors of the Poor. Before doing so, however, the committeemen pledged themselves "Individually, each to the others" to support the general ticket and the will of the majority.[61]

In Montgomery County the nominatory methods were essentially the same as in Chester: two-man township standing committees (elected) represented their districts at general county nominating meetings.[62] The system, approved at a gathering in Norristown on May 13, 1801, was later hailed by "Thousands" in the *Aurora* as being "truly Republican," one that would give the people "an opportunity of controuling, and I hope of destroying the pernicious practices of certain characters (and every county has too many such) who arrogate to themselves a popularity to which their claim is at least questionable."[63] He hoped that all counties would emulate Montgomery in the interest of "internal harmony."

On June 18, 1801, the Montgomery County committee met and appointed five conferees to meet with those from Bucks and Northampton-Wayne, to select a candidate to represent the district in Congress. The conference was held later in the month and Isaac Van Horne was nominated.[64] For this they were accused of treachery by "A Citizen of Bucks," a correspondent to the *Aurora*, who maintained that according to custom only a public committee could choose a candidate; selection by a few individuals would "cast a reproach upon republicanism. . ."[65] In June, said "A Citizen of Bucks," the Bucks County townships had voted by ballot to select a Congressional candidate to be presented at the meeting of conferees. Joseph Clunn had been chosen, but the conferees had disregarded the voice of the people by nominating Van Horne. Such arbitrary methods would split the Republicans.[66]

Apparently the correspondent's real target was Van Horne, and not the method by which he was nominated, for later he charged that the candidate was a hesitant Republican in the legislative session of 1798, "when the balance of parties hung in awful suspense." He had not been among those who had voted against the laudatory address to John Adams in that year.[67]

At this time the Republicans feared disunity within their own ranks more than they did the Federalists. Apprehensive that the attack on Van Horne's nomination was calculated to create a division, Silas Hough, a county committeeman from Montgomery, took the charges seriously enough to answer them in a letter to the *Aurora*.[68] At a Bucks County meeting on May 5, 1801, said Hough, it had been agreed that the candidate to be selected by the conferees would receive solid support. When the conferees met they carried instructions from the various counties they represented. True, Joseph Clunn was the Bucks

County choice, but the men supporting him were only one-third of the conferees present. After the proposed candidates had been discussed, Van Horne was given a majority of the votes. Therefore, all the conferees, as well as all the Republicans in the district, were in duty bound to support him. The system was devised in the interest of unity and fair representation, and if one set of conferees refused to abide by the decision, there would have been no point in organizing the conference.

Although the above dispute was not of great importance, it has been introduced here to illustrate the operation of Republican party machinery and the opposition it encountered from those who objected to the demands of party discipline. Incidentally, the Bucks County committee met again on August 17, 1801, and approved the work of the conferees by a vote of fourteen townships to six. It also called for the election of a new county committee. When it met, all the township delegates presented their certificates of election and pledged support to the county and district tickets.[69] That maneuver, in effect a referendum, put the Republicans in Bucks County solidly behind Van Horne's candidacy.

During these two years the city of Philadelphia also experienced a growth in unit representation. In 1800 the legislature, by an act of March 1, increased the number of wards to fourteen and provided for the selection of two inspectors of election in each.[70] Quick to realize the advantages to be derived from organizing the wards as political units, the Republicans promptly arranged for the appointment of ward committees. They abandoned the old method of nominating candidates at a mass meeting held just a few days before election. Instead, the party members gathered in each ward and elected delegates to a general city committee. This committee nominated all candidates for city offices.[71] In 1801 the Federalists imitated the Republican method, but instead of selecting committees composed of several members—the Republican ward committees numbered five men—they named only one person to represent each ward.[72]

In 1801 the future looked black for the Federalists. For three years in succession they had been repudiated by the voters, and the last defeat was so annihilating that William Duane permitted himself only a brief moment of exultation. On October 15, 1801, with a condescension that must have been galling to his opponents, he called for an end of party strife in Philadelphia. The Republicans, he said, "now offer in the moment of success, the hand of friendship and conciliation." Unwilling, however, to forego the pleasure of lofty condemnation, he asked the Federalists to recall the harshness with which they had treated their opponents in former years and compare it to the "firm, dispassionate, disinterested, and tolerant" attitude now displayed by the Republicans. It was through union, said he, that the Republicans had won; they were aware of that and would not forget it in the future.[73]

CHAPTER XIV

McKEAN AND THE PATRONAGE POWER

WHILE RUNNING for the governorship in 1799, McKean had been subjected to a constant stream of virulent abuse. One month after the election, with the insults still rankling in his mind, he lashed out at his critics in an address to the Republicans in the Philadelphia area. The enemies who had combined against him, he said, were "traitors, tories, French Aristocrats, British agents, and British subjects, and their corrupt dependants, together with not a few apostate Whigs. . ." They lied and resorted to every practice to snatch votes, he continued, and, significantly enough, almost all the men holding office under the appointment of John Adams in Pennsylvania and neighboring states had joined the coalition against him.[1] There was no mistaking McKean's anger or the implied retaliation in this last remark, and if the Federalist office holders were not already stirring uneasily in their chairs they soon had cause to do so.

The patronage allotted to the Chief Executive of Pennsylvania was so extensive that even McKean was satisfied with it, and in doling out the plums at his disposal, he was, as usual, practical and realistic. Not wishing to act without advice, he called William Findley and some other leaders in for a consultation. When they asked him what his policy would be, he told them that he intended to remove incompetents and all those incumbents who had abused him personally.[2] But in other statements of policy he went much farther than that. Realizing that his appointive power could be used in the interest of partisan aggrandizement, he intended "to give a preference to . . . real republicans or whigs having equal talents and integrity, and to a friend before an Enemy . . ." He thought it "at least imprudent" to surround himself with hostile and spying officials.[3] To defeat the Federalists, he told Jefferson, they would have to be thrown out of office or, as he stated it, with Biblical allusions, they would have to "be shaven, for in their offices (like Sampsons locks of hair) their great strength lieth. . . The despisers of the people should not be their rulers, nor men be vested with authority in a government which they wish to destroy: a dagger," he continued, "ought not to be put into the hands of an assassin."[4]

The office holders of Federalist persuasion must have known that the Dionysian innuendoes in McKean's address to the Philadelphia Republicans had suspended a sword above many official chairs, but apparently determined to force the issue they held meetings in different parts of the State and decided against resignation. They would force the Governor to remove them.[5] The challenge was accepted with willingness and gusto; on December 18, 1799, McKean removed twenty-four officials with one blow.[6] In addition, he announced by proclamation that all holders of commissions would have to apply to him for their renewal within three months.[7] The twenty-four shorn "Sampsons" (prothonotaries, registrars and recorders) were curtly notified that they could save themselves trouble and expense by not applying for new commissions. McKean did not think the number dismissed was excessive. Indeed, a few months later he was sorry that he had not discharged "ten or eleven more."[8]

The Federalists were outraged at McKean's sweeping action. His exercise of arbitrary power was in imitation of the kings of England said the *Gazette of the United States*. According to his proclamation, all commissions not limited by law expired with the retirement of the Governor who granted them; such conduct would destroy republican government, for what man would accept public office "if the mere *will* of a governor" could deprive him of it?[9]

Day after day, lamentations of ousted Federalists appeared in the *Gazette*. One of the most typical came from John Arndt, Clerk of the Orphans' Court in Northampton County. In a pitiful farewell address Arndt recounted his past services: he had been a soldier in the Revolution (wounded in 1776), a Censor, a presidential elector, and a member of the Pennsylvania Constitutional Convention of 1790. But now, without regard for his many acts of public service, his official integrity, advanced age and large family, he was being dismissed. Why? Merely because he had electioneered for James Ross in 1799. Learning that his position was insecure after the election, he had gone to see McKean. But that "Patron of Equality," that "plain Republican" would not even talk to him. McKean was striking a mortal blow at the freedom of election, "for if the Governor is right, all minorities however, respectable for number or character, must be wrong and punishable."[10]

Since most of the office holders in Pennsylvania were Federalists, many Republicans greeted the removals with joy and a demand for more. The Federalists had established a precedent, said the *Aurora*, by dismissing men of Republican views; if McKean failed to follow their example, he would be committing an injustice to his supporters. Since all appointees under the national government were Federalists, then all

State officials should be Republicans.[11] To hungry office seekers the argument had an understandable appeal.

But to some Republican leaders the whole vexing problem of patronage was fraught with danger. Complete proscription, it was feared, would alienate many who might enter the Republican fold if a more lenient policy were followed. Jefferson was much concerned over the question, and after McKean asked him to dismiss some Federalist officials in Delaware, he advised caution. In his opinion the great majority of Americans held republican principles, including those who called themselves Federalists, the latter differing from the Republicans only in their conception of legislative and executive power. They had been "decoyed into the net of the monarchists by the XYZ contrivance," but they would desert that group and become "as one flesh" with the Republicans if the dominant group proceeded with moderation. They would not do so, however, if their "quondam leaders" were handled violently.[12]

McKean was inclined to approve of Jefferson's suggestions, yet he was convinced that the Federalist leaders would never relent. If they lost their followers they might become more "prudent," but they would always oppose Jefferson and himself.[13] Of that he was certain. Therefore, since the opposition would remain, its potency should be reduced. This could best be effected through the patronage, for if the Federalists had attained strength through their offices, the Republicans should emulate their methods. After the Republican success in Pennsylvania in 1800, he was certain that his use of the patronage power was correct, for he attributed that victory in part to a general approbation of his appointments and removals.[14]

After Jefferson's election, Dallas, with his usual caution and aversion to extreme measures, advised against a general proscription of Federalist officials. He was willing to let the Republicans have more than half of the offices, but not all of them. He was too realistic to expect that any course of procedure would produce a partisan coalition, but he was convinced—and in this he agreed with Jefferson—that a liberal policy would place enough Republicans in office as to either silence the opposition "or give a certainty of success in any future conflict." Dallas would conciliate all Federalists ("honest" or "mercenary"), "except the Anglo-Federalist, the Consolidator, and the monarchist . . . Adopt a different policy," he told Gallatin, "and the Parties will continue almost equally to divide the nation; every Federalist will become a conspirator;

every Republican will be a tyrant; and each general election will involve the hazard of a civil war."[15]

In theory McKean favored the expulsion of all enemies, but apparently he did not think all Federalists belonged in that category, for, according to William Findley, many Federalist officials who had voted for Ross were reappointed. In the five western counties, wrote Findley to Jefferson, only "two officers out of 15 were removed, and but three of the thirteen who were continued were republican or were known to have voted for" McKean. "The two removed were bad officers. In the whole state thirty-one officers were removed and thirty-two were continued." However, "the leading Germans in many instances insisted on and procured the removal of all in their respective counties."[16] It was Findley's belief that McKean's dismissals made him no new enemies, but many of his early appointments did—among the avid office-hunting Republicans. When McKean assumed office, said Findley, his task was made difficult by the number of poor officials inherited from the preceding administration. As president of a "public body," Mifflin was excellent, but he "had neither talent nor application for the responsibility he possessed" as Governor. During his three terms he had made no "scrutiny" of office holders, but McKean, on his trips through the State, had discovered many poor officials. Therefore, they had feared him and tried to prevent his election.[17]

To many Republican leaders in Pennsylvania, the general hunger for office was both surprising and embarrassing, particularly so after Jefferson's election. So many men sought the assistance of George Logan, a close friend of Jefferson's, that his wife Deborah was frankly amazed;[18] Duane was besieged in his home by a line of office seekers who requested his influence,[19] and Gallatin's mail was full of solicitations.[20]

These requests were troublesome for several reasons: since complete proscription might alienate many Federalists who could be enticed into the Republican camp by more lenient methods, it required a nice discrimination to weed out the die-hards and retain those who, if won over, might be influential enough to carry others in their train; further, care had to be exercised in selecting not only those Republicans most deserving of reward for faithful service, but also those who had sufficient influence and prestige to win support for the party at election time. Then, too, since disappointed office seekers could very well become a nucleus of dissension within the party, those who threatened to become most active and articulate would have to be appeased in some fashion.

These were important considerations, and added to them was uncertainty among some of the Pennsylvania leaders as to the patronage program Jefferson intended to follow. When several aspirants to officialdom asked William Duane for information and advice on this question of overall policy, he stated it as his opinion that "nothing would be done hastily, but upon due inquiry no man who had abused his trust to corrupt or persecuting purposes would obtain the confidence of the administration."[21] He had offered these assurances, Duane told Jefferson, to quiet some of the more importunate, and he also suggested, by way of mild warning to Jefferson, that many Pennsylvania Republicans were "discontented at the continuance in office of the three principal officers of the customs." In general, he thought that the "consolidation" of the party would depend in part "on the degree of countenance which the violent men in office met with," and he was sure that the dismissal of officials who had been "oppressors and persecutors" in Pennsylvania would produce a more "general adherence than even in the last general Election to the principles by which alone security can be obtained."[22]

As a practical and ambitious politician, Duane of necessity had to concern himself with patronage problems. Thorough and positive in this, as in most things, he prepared a list of the clerks in the national departments of government at about the time Jefferson became President. Opposite the names of the incumbents he placed descriptive epithets which well illustrate the multifarious shades of partisanship then current and the picturesque phraseology so typical of the Duanian style. He approved of a few, but in general he had a poor opinion of most of the clerks in office during Adams' administration. Following are some of the choice terms he used to describe them: "Hamiltonian," "Nothingarian," "Anythingarian," "Nincumpoop," "Democratic Executioner," "Adamite," "Ass," "Throatcutter," "Federalist," "So-So rather Dem," "High toned Fed," "decent," "Three Execrable Aristocrats," "Two paltry fools," "moderate," "Tory," "Hell-Hot," "O," "Raving Mad & Aristocrat."[23] It is quite likely that Duane prepared the list for the information of someone high in the federal administration. Whether he did it on request or on his own volition, it is difficult to say.

As the national leader, and therefore responsible for his party's strength and continuance, Jefferson was too astute either to underestimate the importance of Pennsylvania as a strong supporter of Republicanism, or to undervalue the solid contributions made by some of its political writers and leaders in the fight against Federalist control. Both he and McKean agreed that such stalwarts as John Beckley, Dallas, Thomas Cooper and Peter Muhlenberg, to mention just a few, should be rewarded for their efforts, and in their correspondence they exchanged suggestions as to how this could be done.

Several months before the election of 1800, Jefferson asked McKean to provide for Beckley, who had lost the clerkship of the House of Representatives.[24] The Governor promptly obliged by making him clerk of both the Mayor's Court of Philadelphia and the Orphans' Court of Philadelphia County.[25] Solicitous as to the welfare of Thomas Cooper, whom he considered to be one of "the first men in talents, virtue and republicanism," Jefferson asked McKean to "take care of" him.[26] No doubt Jefferson would have done something for Cooper himself, had not the "power" which controlled his nominations entertained "insurmountable prejudices against him."[27] Just what was the nature of the "power" which controlled his appointments Jefferson did not make clear, but apparently McKean was not hedged about by any such restrictions, for he promised to make Cooper a district judge. By so doing, wrote the Governor, "I shall imitate my friend, the late President Adams, in *securing* my friends offices, from which they cannot readily be removed . . ."[28]

McKean, in his turn, was desirous of buttressing the Republican party in Pennsylvania by securing federal jobs for prominent local leaders. As has already been mentioned above, he spent much time in persuading Jefferson to dismiss the Pennsylvania Federalists who held important federal positions within the State.

Of course, some of McKean's appointments caused dissatisfaction among a few disappointed Republicans. That was almost inevitable, for it was obviously impossible for him to satisfy everyone. By and large, however, his patronage policy met with success. Designed as an aid to partisan aggrandizement, it served as a reinforcing strand in the rope with which the Republicans were firmly trussing up the opposition and rendering it ineffectual.

CHAPTER XV

CONCLUSION

From 1776 to 1790 the people of Pennsylvania lived under one of the most liberal and democratic of all State constitutions. Subjected to attack from the moment of inception, this body of organic law survived without change until the latter year, when it was superseded by a more conservative but by no means drastically reactionary document. At the time of change, the State was almost evenly divided between conservative and liberal groups, and the new constitution, a compromise effort, went into effect without incident or turmoil. Designed to harmonize with the United States Constitution, it thus deferred to the new national government whose strong influence had already materially and peculiarly conditioned political behavior in Pennsylvania.

While the Constitution of 1776 existed, it was the focal point of controversy which split the State into two factions, most appropriately called Constitutionalist and Anti-Constitutionalist. With its demise, the loosely organized groups battling around it lost a vital cohesive impellant. The new circumstances called for realignment and reappraisal, and into this realignment each group carried ideological and psychological principles and fears. Generally speaking, the old liberal Constitutional faction entered the new period with an aversion to self-arrogated special privilege, aristocratic and monarchic tendencies and the influence of great wealth. Their conservative opponents, on the other hand, feared an excessive democracy which they thought would result in anarchy and revolution. That the apprehensions of both were often unfounded in fact was unimportant from the propaganda standpoint, that detracted not at all from their effectiveness when disseminated by the lurid press. When the United States government was established, many Pennsylvania liberals regarded it with uneasy foreboding, but to their opponents it offered hope for a sober and dignified future.

It was indeed a fortunate and happy day for Pennsylvania Federalists when Philadelphia became the national capital in 1790. The first three administrations were decidedly conservative, and to the city on the Delaware came great and influential figures who were a constant source of comfort to the local Federalist forces. Also, it seems reasonable to assume that the influence exerted on the Pennsylvania Assembly by Congress—functioning as they did in such close proximity—must have been considerable. While the national legislature was in session, Philadelphia donned a heavy cloak of conservatism, and the conditioning effect that may have had on the local lawmakers presents a nice problem for speculation. In connection with this question of atmosphere, it will be recalled that John Beckley saw greater hope for Republicanism when the State capital was taken out of Philadelphia and established in Lancaster.

Prior to the election of 1796, when the Republicans instituted activities which eventually resulted in a definite party organization, there occurred a series of events which produced broad divisions of opinion: the French Revolution, the Genêt episode, Jay's Treaty, the Whiskey Rebellion, the formation of Democratic Societies and the Presque Isle development project. All were highly controversial, and as they burst upon the political scene, men were forced to take sides in the passionate discussions which they produced. Both the Federalists and Republicans exploited these events to their own advantage. While the Republicans exulted in the principles and aims of the French Revolution, the Federalists dwelt with gloomy apprehension on the excesses that conflict produced and "viewed with alarm" their possible effect on "rational liberty" in the United States; if Genêt's mission inspired the Republicans to wild demonstrations, their opponents could point to them as examples of unrestrained democracy and Jacobinism; if the excise tax produced Republican anger, it also resulted in disturbances which strengthened the hands of the Federalist propagandists; if Jay's Treaty infuriated Anglophobes it also tended to console those who sought to establish friendly relations with Britain; finally, if the Democratic Societies promised much for Republicanism, they also provoked the wrath of the most highly respected man in the country.

So controversial were the above issues, and so intensive was the interplay of stimulus and response attendant upon their appearance that serious attempts were made to provide the resultant opinion groups with weapons of political aggrandizement. In brief, the hates, fears, hopes and aspirations they engendered needed the impetus and direction that could be obtained only through group organizations. By 1796 the cumulative effect of the above crystallizing factors was demonstrated in the divisions produced in the presidential election of that year. From that time the Federalists and Republicans fought for political control of the State along more disciplined lines, and by 1801 the latter had obtained complete supremacy.

Reasons for Republican Victory

The influences, events and forces which carried the Republicans to victory in Pennsylvania are numerous and varied. Many of them have been dwelt upon at considerable length in this study, but by way of summary and conclusion they may be restated as follows:

Leaders and Propagandists. It was the good fortune of the Republicans to have within their ranks a number of highly gifted political manipulators and propagandists. Some of them had the ability—rarely seen in the ranks of ordinary politicians yet so often characteristic of superior leaders—to not only see and analyze the problem at hand but to present it in a succinct fashion; in short, to fabricate the apt phrase, to coin the compelling slogan and appeal to the electorate on any given issue in language it could understand. Duane possessed that ability. So, too, did Gallatin and Cooper. Jefferson had it to an advanced degree. Since much of the political propaganda was inspired by international issues, the Pennsylvania Republicans were lucky in having the assistance of several Britons who had an excellent knowledge of the European situation, men such as Dallas, Joseph Priestley and Thomas Cooper. Duane, although born in America, was raised abroad, and he came to Philadelphia thoroughly imbued with democratic principles. Under his editorship, the *Aurora* was a tower of strength to the Republican forces.

Congressional Legislation of 1798. In addition to exploiting Pennsylvania's reaction to the Hamiltonian program, the whiskey tax, the condemnation of "self-created societies" and Jay's Treaty, the Republicans made very profitable use of certain laws passed by William Findley's "Mad Congress" in the summer of 1798. With frenetic haste the Federalist majority produced a body of legislation which, when its full effects were experienced, alienated a large section of the Pennsylvania electorate. Especially obnoxious were the Alien and Sedition Acts and the direct property tax. Undoubtedly, they contributed greatly to the defeat of Federalism.

Party Organization. In translating public opinion into effective political action, the Republicans were superior to their opponents. The mere expression of protest—in petitions, grumbling and the erection of liberty poles—was not enough: it had to be given point and direction at election time. In recognition of this fact the Republicans made serious efforts to carry the representative principle of government into nominating meetings, to convince the great mass of taxables (many of whom never bothered to vote) that change could be effected through concerted action. The Federalists did not seem to realize the magnitude and seriousness of the opposition to the ill-considered legislation of 1798, and before they could take effective counter action, it was too late.

Federalism in Pennsylvania was a belated expression of post-war reaction. Identified with and largely dependent on Federal leadership and stimulation, it was a mere dinghy attached to the national Federalist bark, captained by Hamilton, Washington and Adams. Producing no comparable leaders of its own, the Federalist group in Pennsylvania played a supporting role and basked in the reflected glory of those great national leaders who came to Philadelphia to conduct the nation's business. Actually, Federalism in Pennsylvania was at its height when there were no parties in existence. When Washington retired, it began to weaken. McKean's election dealt it a staggering blow and Jefferson's victory was its *coup de grace*.

General. Although the European wars somewhat retarded the flow of immigrants to the United States during the 1790's, the population of Pennsylvania increased from 434,373 in 1790 to 586,095 in 1800. The number of tax ratables was augmented by approximately 22,000 between 1793 and 1800, and over the period generally the number of ratables constituted about 19% of the population.[1] During the first three gubernatorial elections the average returns barely exceeded 32,000, but in 1799, because of intense partisanship and improved methods of gathering votes, the number exceeded 67,000, about one-half of the number of taxables.

As the population swelled and spread westward, administrative and electoral needs made it necessary to add to the number of counties. These increased from twenty-one in 1790 to thirty-five in 1801. By the latter year the House of Representatives had a membership of eighty-six and the Senate twenty-five, an increase since 1794 of eight and one respectively.

Concomitant with the growth of population in the western counties came demands that the State capital be placed in a more central location. In response to these requests, the legislature made several attempts to effect a removal from Philadelphia, but it was not until April, 1799, that the two houses finally agreed on Lancaster as the site of the new capital. The legislature was controlled by the Federalists at the time and the voting on the question was indicative of sectional, not partisan urges. In both houses the great majority of those in opposition to the bill represented the easternmost counties.[2] The selection of Lancaster was a concession to those who wanted to avoid miles of arduous travel, the yellow fever and the overweening influence of the great city on the Delaware.

In addition to its growth of population, the State increased its size by purchasing the "Erie Triangle," an area comprising 202,187 acres. The new territory afforded a valuable outlet to Lake Erie and gave Pennsylvania a second window to the westward. It was due in large measure to the income obtained from the sale of these lands and from others at the State's disposal that Pennsylvania was able to exonerate its citizens from payment of "every species of taxation . . . for a period of almost ten years."[3] While dwelling on that happy fact in his last address to the legislature, Mifflin regretted the necessity of recommending that a tax be imposed on "personal estate" and legal processes. During his administrations, revenue had been obtained from bank and United States stock dividends, land office receipts, duties on auction sales, and marriage and tavern licenses.

At the close of the eighteenth century the citizens of Pennsylvania could look back upon a thirty-year period which had been characterized by fairly definite political cycles. In 1780 the forces of rampant democracy were in full career, but ten years later they had been superseded by others of more conservative nature. These, in turn, had been swept away within another decade by the enthusiasm of Democratic-Republicanism. Pennsylvania, along with her sister states, had shown that republican government was possible. The cycles had not been completed without the display of passion and fear, but at no time had the bayonet supplanted the ballot.

NOTES—Chapter I

1. W. F. Dunaway, *A History of Pennsylvania*, 203.
2. Allan Nevins, *The American States During and After the Revolution*, 149.
3. *Ibid.*, 132.
4. J. Paul Selsam, *The Pennsylvania Constitution of 1776*, 1.
5. *Ibid.*, 256; James H. Peeling, "The Public Life of Thomas McKean, 1734-1817" (Unpublished doctoral dissertation, University of Chicago, 1929), 41-42.
6. Dunaway, 211.
7. John H. Fertig, comp., *Constitutions of Pennsylvania*, 247.
8. Selsam, 211.
9. William Findley, "An Autobiographical Letter," *Pennsylvania Magazine of History and Biography*, V (1881), 443. Hereafter this magazine is cited as *PMHB*.
10. Fertig, 249. There was doubt as to the authorship of the section on the council. But it was ascribed to George Bryan and James Cannon. See H. M. Jenkins, *Pennsylvania, Colonial and Federal*, II, 104.
11. Findley, "Autobiographical Letter," 443.
12. *Proceedings Relative to Calling the Conventions of 1776 and 1790*, 69. Unless otherwise indicated this description of the Council of Censors' meeting is based on this work, hereafter cited as *Proceedings*.
13. *Ibid.*, 124.
14. Robert L. Brunhouse, *The Counter-Revolution in Pennsylvania, 1776-1790*, 155.
15. *Ibid.*, 197.
16. *Ibid.*, 206
17. *Pennsylvania Packet*, March 26, 1789.
18. *Proceedings*, 136; Brunhouse, 221-224.
19. Thomas McKean to John Adams, April 30, 1787, quoted in Peeling, "Thomas McKean," 130.
20. Brunhouse, 205.
21. Peeling, "Thomas McKean," 30.
22. Findley, "Autobiographical Letter," 443.
23. *Pennsylvania Packet*, November 25, 1789.
24. William Rawle, "Sketch of the Life of Thomas Mifflin," *Memoirs of The Historical Society of Pennsylvania*, II, pt. 2, 121.
25. Alexander Graydon, *Memoirs of a Life Chiefly Passed in Pennsylvania*, 324.
26. Russell J. Ferguson, *Early Western Pennsylvania Politics*, 102-103.

27. Graydon, 317.
28. Thomas Fitzsimons to Benjamin Rush, August 20, 1789. Miscellaneous Manuscripts, American Philosophical Society. Hereafter referred to as APS.
29. *Ibid.*
30. Findley, "Autobiographical Letter," 445.
31. *Ibid.*
32. *Ibid.*, 446.
33. Ferguson, 105.
34. *Proceedings,* 153
35. *Ibid.*, 151.
36. Callista Schramm, "William Findley in Pennsylvania Politics," 52, cited in Ferguson, 107.
37. *Proceedings,* 10. Thomas McKean, who wanted a government controlled by the educated and propertied classes, would have restricted the suffrage to those who owned an estate of £50 value or had an annual income of £3. Peeling, "Thomas McKean," 147.
38. Findley, "Autobiographical Letter," 446.
39. Graydon, 318.
40. Ferguson, 107. Ferguson does not mention Graydon's *Memoirs.* "Hambden" in an election broadside of October 9, 1792 (HSP), attributed Lewis' defeat on the senatorial issue to Wilson. Hinting at apostasy Lewis had referred to Wilson as "a *jay* in borrowed plumes."
41. Graydon, 320.
42. Peeling, "Thomas McKean," 147.
43. Fertig, 189-211.
44. *Ibid.*, 209-211.
45. Sanford W. Higginbotham, "Frontier Democracy in the Early Constitutions of Tennessee and Kentucky, 1772-1799" (Unpublished thesis, Louisiana State University, 1941), 75-76.
46. *Ibid.*
47. Eugene E. Doll, "American History as Interpreted by German Historians." Published in *Transactions of the American Philosophical Society,* XXXVIII, pt. 5, June, 1949.

NOTES—Chapter II

1. *United States Census, 1790, Population,* 9-11.
2. Excellent descriptions of western Pennsylvania can be found in Ferguson's *Early Western Pennsylvania Politics,* and in Leland D. Baldwin, *The Whiskey Rebels.*
3. Dunaway, 234.
4. Report of the State Supreme Court, signed by Justices Thomas McKean, George Bryan and Jacob Rush, December 20, 1790. Copy in Manuscript Collections, Library Company of Philadelphia. Hereafter referred to as Library Co.
5. *Ibid.*
6. *Ibid.*
7. *Ibid.*
8. Burton Alva Konkle, *Life and Times of Thomas Smith, 1745-1809,* 191.
9. See above p. 7.
10. Brunhouse, 208.
11. Paul Leicester Ford, *The Origin, Purpose and Result of the Harrisburg Convention of 1788,* 16.
12. J. B. McMaster and F. D. Stone, eds., *Pennsylvania and the Federal Constitution, 1787-1788,* 561.
13. *Ibid.*
14. *Ibid.*
15. Ford, *Harrisburg Convention,* 40.
16. James McLene to William Irvine, September 12, 1788, Irvine Papers, X, 14. HSP.
17. Nevins, *The American States,* 294.
18. George D. Luetscher, *Early Political Machinery in the United States,* 129.
19. *Statutes at Large,* XIII, 140-145.
20. Luetscher, 128.
21. *Ibid.*
22. Elizabeth K. Henderson, "Some Aspects of Sectionalism in Pennsylvania, 1790-1812" (Unpublished doctoral dissertation, Bryn Mawr, 1937), 17.
23. Charles A. Beard, *Economic Origins of Jeffersonian Democracy,* 101.
24. McLene to Irvine, September 12, 1788; Brunhouse, 216.
25. Ephraim Blaine to William Irvine, October 2, 1788, Irvine Papers, X, 16.

26. David Redick to William Irvine, October 2, 1788, Irvine Papers, X, 17.
27. Edgar S. Maclay in the Preface to the *Journal of William Maclay,* xvii.
28. *See* Charles A. Beard's Introduction to Maclay's *Journal,* v.
29. Ellis P. Oberholtzer, *Robert Morris,* 234.
30. *See* Oberholtzer's sketch of Morris in the *Dictionary of American Biography,* XIII, 219-223. Hereafter cited as *DAB*.
31. *Ibid.*
32. *Annals of Congress,* 1 Cong., 1 Sess., 113
33. Maclay, *Journal,* 52.
34. *Ibid.,* 29.
35. *Ibid.,* 173.
36. *Ibid.,* 223.
37. *Ibid.,* 285.
38. Beard, 185
39. *Ibid.,* 133
40. *Ibid.,* 139.
41. *Ibid.,* 270.
42. *Ibid.,* 298.
43. *Ibid.,* 73.
44. *Ibid.,* 341
45. *Ibid.,* 188.
46. Thomas Fitzsimons to Benjamin Rush, August 28, 1789, Misc. Mss., APS.
47. Philip S. Klein, ed., "Jonathan Roberts, Memoirs of a Senator from Pennsylvania, 1771-1854," in *PMHB,* LXI (1937), 473.
48. Bernard Faÿ, "Early Party Machinery in the United States," in *PMHB,* LX (1936), 381.

NOTES—CHAPTER III

1. Maclay, *Journal,* 187.
2. *Ibid.,* 195.
3. *Ibid.*
4. *Ibid.,* 206.
5. E. P. Oberholtzer, *Robert Morris,* 215
6. Possibly John Patton, from Berks County
7. Maclay, *Journal,* 235.
8. *Ibid.,* 265.
9. *Ibid.,* 249.
10. James Hutchinson to Albert Gallatin, June 11, 1790, Gallatin Papers, IV, New-York Historical Society.
11. Samuel Bryan to Albert Gallatin, May 13, 1790, Gallatin Papers, V.
12. Fitzsimons to St. Clair, n. d., [1790], in W. H. Smith, ed., *The St. Clair Papers,* II, 192. The letter was probably written within a very few days of the convention's adjournment. Fitzsimons had not attended the caucus and according to what he told St. Clair he did not know the names of any of the men who had made the nomination.
13. Broadside, 1790, Broadsides Collection, HSP. It is likely that the appeal came out around the middle of September, for mention of the caucus' nomination appeared in a letter to the *Packet* on September 18, signed by some of the men who had written the broadside, with the addition of William Nichols and George Latimer.
14. *DAB,* XVI, 293-295.
15. *Ibid.,* XII, 606-608.
16. Francis Vinton Greene, *The Revolutionary War,* 16.
17. McMaster and Stone, 702.
18. Bernard Faÿ, *The Two Franklins,* 151.
19. Bernhard Knollenberg, *Washington and the Revolution,* 75.
20. William Rawle, "Sketch of the Life of Thomas Mifflin," 125.
21. *Ibid.,* 124.
22. *Pennsylvania Packet,* September 6, 18, 29, 1790.
23. *Ibid.,* September 9, 1790.
24. Thomas Fitzsimons to Samuel Meredith, September 24, 1790, Ferdinand J. Dreer Collection, HSP.
25. *Ibid.*
26. Arthur St. Clair to Thomas Fitzsimons, October 12, 1790, Autograph Collection of Simon Gratz, HSP

27. *Ibid.*
28. *Ibid.*
29. William Findley to William Irvine, n. d., Irvine Papers, X, HSP. The letter was written sometime after Findley returned home from the Constitutional Convention in September. He mentioned a near famine condition due to a late spring and early fall.
30. *Journal of the Pennsylvania House of Representatives, 1790-1791,* 28. Hereafter cited as *Pennsylvania House Journal.*
31. *Ibid.,* 28; *Pennsylvania Packet,* December 20, 1790.
32. Samuel Bryan to Albert Gallatin, December 18, 1790, Gallatin Papers, IV.
33. Charles Biddle, *Autobiography,* 244
34. *Ibid.,* 245.
35. *Ibid.*
36. *Ibid.*
37. Samuel Bryan to Albert Gallatin, December 18, 1790, Gallatin Papers.
38. *Ibid.*
39. Raymond Walters, *Alexander James Dallas,* 25.
40. Fertig, *Constitutions,* 149. Dallas was commissioned on January 19, 1791. His salary was £500 per year. (*Pennsylvania Archives,* 9th Ser., I, 73.)
41. Walters, *Dallas,* 26.

NOTES—Chapter IV

1. *Statutes at Large,* XIII, 140-145.
2. Thomas Fitzsimons to Arthur St. Clair, 1790.
3. *Pennsylvania House Journal, 1790-1791,* 82.
4. The remaining votes came from Chester (2), Montgomery (3), Delaware (2), Berks (1), Dauphin (1), and Luzerne (1).
5. Dunaway, 234.
6. *Pennsylvania House Journal, 1790-1791,* 152.
7. *Journal of the Senate of Pennsylvania, 1790-1791,* 124. Hereafter cited as *Pennsylvania Senate Journal.*
8. *Ibid.,* 148.
9. *Statutes at Large,* XIV, 20-23.
10. Frederick A. Muhlenberg to Thomas Fitzsimons, September 12, 1791, Gratz Collection.
11. *Ibid.*
12. See *General Advertiser,* October 10, 1791.
13. Andrew Gregg to Albert Gallatin, September 27, 1792, Gallatin Papers, IV.
14. *Pennsylvania Packet,* February 3, 1789.
15. E. P. Allison and Boies Penrose, *Philadelphia, 1681 to 1887,* 61.
16. *Pennsylvania Packet,* February 3, 1789.
17. A. J. Dallas, comp., *Laws of Pennsylvania, 1781-1790,* II, 658; and Allison and Penrose, 61.
18. Krout and Fox, *The Completion of Independence,* 17.
19. *Ibid.,* 51.
20. E. P. Oberholtzer, *Philadelphia, a History of the City and Its People,* I, 397.
21. Charles Campbell to William Findley, February 22, 1793, quoted in Callista Schramm's "William Findley in Pennsylvania Politics," *Western Pennsylvania Historical Magazine,* XX (1937), 37.
22. *Pennsylvania House Journal, 1791-1792,* 284.
23. *Ibid.,* 300.
24. *Pennsylvania Senate Journal, 1791-1792,* 237
25. *Statutes at Large,* XIV, 271-274.
26. *Annals of Congress,* 2 Cong., 1 Sess., 1359.
27. Biddle, *Autobiography,* 255.
28. *Ibid.,* 251.
29. Maclay, *Journal,* 379.

30. *Ibid.* Maclay entered his criticism in his journal shortly after he had met Hutchinson at Boyd's tavern in 1791, a hostelry much frequented by westerners when they came to Philadelphia for legislative sessions.
31. A. J. Dallas to Albert Gallatin, November 8, 1793, Gallatin Papers, IV.
32. *DAB,* XVI, 589-590.
33. Baldwin, *Whiskey Rebels,* 44.
34. Ferguson, *Early Western Pennsylvania Politics,* 114.
35. Circular letter, issued by Conferees, 1792, Broadsides Collection, HSP.
36. *Ibid.; General Advertiser,* July 31, 1792.
37. Circular letter issued by Conferees, 1792, Broadsides Collection, HSP.
38. Minutes of the July 27 meeting as reported by its secretary, William Smith, *General Advertiser,* July 31, 1792.
39. "A Citizen," *General Advertiser,* July 30, 1792.
40. *Ibid.*
41. *Ibid.*
42. "Freedom of Election," in the *General Advertiser,* August 1, 1792.
43. James Hutchinson to Albert Gallatin, August 19, 1792, Gallatin Papers, IV.
44. "Freedom of Election," *General Advertiser,* August 1, 1792.
45. *Ibid.*
46. *Ibid.*
47. *General Advertiser,* August 4, 1792.
48. Circular letter, issued by Conferees, 1792, Broadsides Collection, HSP.
49. *Ibid.*
50. *General Advertiser,* August 1, 1792.
51. James Hutchinson to Albert Gallatin, August 19, 1792, Gallatin Papers, IV.
52. *Ibid.*
53. *Ibid.*
54. Circular letter issued by Conferees, 1792, Broadsides Collection, HSP.
55. *Ibid.*
56. *Ibid.*
57. James Hutchinson to Albert Gallatin, August 19, 1792, Gallatin Papers, IV.
58. Circular letter issued by Correspondents, August 3, 1792; *General Advertiser,* August 4, 1792.
59. "A Pennsylvanian," *General Advertiser,* July 31, 1792.

60. "Sydney," *General Advertiser*, August 9, 1792.
61. Broadside, October 9, 1792, HSP.
62. William Findley to Albert Gallatin, August 20, 1792, Gallatin Papers, IV.
63. Broadside, signed "Mentor," 1792, HSP.
64. "Common Sense, Jun.," *General Advertiser*, August 14, 1792.
65. *General Advertiser*, September 5, 7, 14, 1792.
66. "Cerberus," *General Advertiser*, September 5, 1792.
67. *Ibid.*, September 14, 1792.
68. "A Friend to Good Government," *General Advertiser*, October 2, 1792.
69. James Hutchinson to Albert Gallatin, August 19, 1792, Gallatin Papers, IV.
70. Same to Same, September 14, 1792, Gallatin Papers, IV.
71. This John Barclay was a merchant, not the former Mayor of Philadelphia.
72. James Hutchinson to Albert Gallatin, September 14, 1792, Gallatin Papers, IV.
73. *Ibid.*
74. Thomas Hartley to William Irvine, August 29, 1792, Irvine Papers, XI, 24.
75. John Montgomery to William Irvine, August 28, 1792, Irvine Papers, XI, 23.
76. Same to Same, September 17, 1792, Irvine Papers, XI, 29.
77. John Wilkins, Jr., to William Irvine, August 31, 1792, Irvine Papers, XI, 26.
78. William Findley to William Irvine, September 28, 1792, Irvine Papers, XI, 30.
79. Andrew Gregg, to Albert Gallatin, September 27, 1792, Gallatin Papers, IV.
80. *Pennsylvania Archives*, 2d Ser., IV, 31.
81. Gallatin Papers, XV, 185.
82. John Wilkins, Jr., to William Irvine, August 31, 1792, Irvine Papers, XI, 26.
83. James Hutchinson to Albert Gallatin, September 14, 1792, Gallatin Papers, IV.
84. William Findley to William Irvine, September 28, 1792, Irvine Papers, XI, 30.
85. *General Advertiser*, September 27, 1792; September 26, 1792.
86. Luetscher, *Early Political Machinery*, 132.
87. *General Advertiser*, September 26, 1792.
88. *Ibid.*, September 15, 18, 1792.
89. *Ibid.*, September 22, 1792.

90. *Gazette of the United States,* September 26, 1792.
91. *General Advertiser,* September 25, 1792.
92. Dallas to Gallatin, September 25, 1792, Gallatin Papers, IV.
93. Hutchinson to Gallatin, September 25, 1792, Gallatin Papers, IV.
94. Thomson withdrew in the very last stages of the campaign, but he polled a considerable vote in Philadelphia. Hutchinson to Gallatin, October 24, 1792, Gallatin Papers, IV; *General Advertiser,* November 1, 1792.
95. *Pennsylvania Archives,* 4th Ser., IV, 227.
96. He here made reference to a proclamation Washington had issued during the summer regarding the excise meetings in western Pennsylvania.
97. Hutchinson to Gallatin, October 24, 1792, Gallatin Papers, IV.
98. *Ibid.*
99. *General Advertiser,* November 8, 1792.
100. Citizens at Redstone Fort to Committee of Correspondence at Philadelphia, September 17, 1792, Gallatin Papers, IV.

NOTES—CHAPTER V

1. Samuel F. Bemis, *Jay's Treaty*, 136.
2. J. S. Bassett, *The Federalist System*, 87-88.
3. Bassett, 91. According to Bemis (p. 146), Genêt sent only two privateers out of Charleston.
4. Bernard Faÿ, *The Two Franklins*, 175
5. Proclamation, April 22, 1793. Select Federal Communications, I, 3. Public Records Division, Pennsylvania Historical and Museum Commission, Harrisburg, Pennsylvania
6. *General Advertiser*, May 17, 1793.
7. *Ibid.*
8. *Ibid.*, May 21, 1793.
9. Faÿ, 179.
10. The paper did not come out under the name *Aurora* until November 8, 1794.
11. Faÿ, 123.
12. *General Advertiser*, May 17, 1793.
13. *Ibid.*, October 1, 1794.
14. Adams to Jefferson, June 30, 1813. Cited in James H. Peeling, "The Public Life of Thomas McKean, 1734-1817," 192.
14a. *Ibid.*
14b. Graydon, *Memoirs*, 335.
15. *Gazette of the United States*, November 18, 1794. This was a term used by a "Peter Penitent."
16. Bassett, 91.
17. Jefferson to Genêt, unsigned draft, June 5, 1793, Jefferson Papers, LXXXVII. For extended correspondence on this subject, *see* Jefferson Papers, particularly the volume cited.
18. Hamilton to Rufus King, August 13, 1793. John C. Hamilton, ed., *The Works of Alexander Hamilton*, V, 574. Hereafter cited as Hamilton, *Works*.
19. *Ibid.*
20. *Ibid.*, 575.
21. Paul L. Ford, ed., *The Writings of Thomas Jefferson*, I, 252. Hereafter cited as Jefferson, *Writings*.
22. Bemis, 146.
23. Quoted in W. O. Lynch, *Fifty Years of Party Warfare*, 36.
24. Hamilton, *Works*, V, 576.
25. King to Hamilton, November 26, 1793, *ibid.*, V, 589.
26. Walters, *Dallas*, 49.

27. Pertinent section quoted in Walters, *Dallas*, 49.
28. Dallas to Gallatin, November 8, 1793, Gallatin Papers, IV.
29. Deborah Norris Logan, *Memoir of Dr. George Logan*, 151.
30. Luetscher, 32.
31. Jefferson, *Writings*, VI, 326. It should be noted that by "monocrats" Jefferson did not mean Federalists. He was always careful to distinguish between the two.
32. Bassett, 99.
33. Washington to Charles Cotesworth Pinckney, July 8, 1796. Worthington C. Ford, ed., *Writings of George Washington*, XIII, 238. *See also* James A. James, "French Diplomacy and American Politics, 1794-1795," *Annual Report of the American Historical Association for the Year 1911*, I, 153.
34. Minutes, Society for Political Inquiries, HSP.
35. E. Vale Blake, *History of the Tammany Society*, 21.
36. *Ibid.*, 19.
37. Eugene P. Link, *Democratic-Republican Societies*, 15. Link says a total of forty-one societies originated in the United States from 1793 to Jefferson's election to the Presidency in 1800.
38. William Miller, "The Democratic Societies and the Whiskey Insurrection," *PMHB*, LXII (1938), 324.
39. *Gazette of the United States*, November 24, December 29, 1794.
40. Luetscher, 35.
41. Faÿ, 187.
42. Link, 205.
43. Jefferson, *Writings*, I, 253.
44. John Bach McMaster, *A History of the People of the United States*, II, 109. "The real object of the society . . . was to control the politics of Pennsylvania and re-elect Governor Mifflin." Luetscher, 35.
45. Link, 6.
46. *General Advertiser*, April 15, 1793.
47. *Ibid.*
48. Minutes of the Pennsylvania Democratic Society, HSP. Subsequent pages have also been torn out of the Minutes
49. *Ibid.*
50. Biddle, *Autobiography*, 252.
51. Edward Ford, *David Rittenhouse, Astronomer Patriot, 1732-1796*, 190.
52. Minutes, Pennsylvania Democratic Society.
53. William Barton, *Memoirs of the Life of David Rittenhouse*, 410.
54. Biddle, *Autobiography*, 252.
55. *House Journal*, 4 Cong., 2 Sess., 625.
56. *Annals of Congress*, 4 Cong., 2 Sess., 2050.

57. *Ibid.*, 1885.
58. Minutes, Pennsylvania Democratic Society.
59. *General Advertiser*, May 11, 1794.
60. *Ibid.*, May 10, 1794.
61. Minutes, Pennsylvania Democratic Society.
62. *Ibid.*
63. *Ibid.*
64. Link, 206.
65. Bemis, 23.
66. *Ibid.*, 24.
67. Edward Channing, *A History of the United States*, IV, 137.
68. *Aurora*, July 24, 1795.
69. *Ibid.*, August 15, 1795.
70. *Ibid.*, October 9, 1795.
71. *Ibid.*, November 18, 1795.
72. *Ibid.*, April 30, 1796.

NOTES—Chapter VI

1. *Annals of Congress,* 1 Cong., 3 Sess., 1884. Voting affirmatively were George Clymer, Thomas Fitzsimons, and Henry Wynkoop. In the negative were Thomas Hartley, Daniel Hiester and Peter Muhlenberg.
2. Maclay, *Journal,* 81; Hugh Henry Brackenridge in his *Incidents of the Insurrection in the Western Parts of Pennsylvania in the Year 1794,* II, 6-9, discusses the traditional hate of Pennsylvania for excise taxes. He attributes much of it to the European heritage of the English, Scotch and Irish.
3. Maclay, *Journal,* 375-376.
4. *Pennsylvania House Journal, 1790-1791,* 109; *Pennsylvania Archives,* 2d Ser., IV, 19.
5. Brackenridge, III, 16.
6. *Pennsylvania House Journal, 1790-1791,* 535.
7. Jenkins, *Pennsylvania, Colonial and Federal,* II, 40.
8. *Pennsylvania Archives,* 2d Ser., IV, 21.
9. William Findley to William Irvine, August 17, 1792, Irvine Papers, XI, 21.
10. Gallatin Papers, XV, 185.
11. *Pennsylvania Archives,* 2d Ser., IV, 30.
12. B. M. Rich, "Washington and the Whiskey Insurrection," *PMHB,* LXV (1941), 334-352.
13. *Ibid.*
14. Hamilton, *Works,* IV, 247, quoted in Rich.
15. Rich, "Washington and the Whiskey Insurrection."
16. Mifflin's informants on the prosecution in Allegheny County were mistaken, for on November 9, James Brison of that county reported to the Governor that no prosecutions "for Riots or breaches of the peace committed in direct opposition to the collection of [excise] Revenue" had been instituted there. *Pennsylvania Archives,* 2d Ser., IV, 44-45.
17. Findley to Mifflin, November 21, 1792, Provincial Delegates Papers, IV, 88, HSP.
18. George Clymer to Edward Hand, December 13, 1792, Gratz Collection, Old Congress, HSP.
19. *Pennsylvania Archives,* 4th Ser., IV, 231
20. *Ibid.,* IV, 230.
21. Link, *Democratic-Republican Societies;* H. H. Brackenridge to Tench Coxe, August 8, 1794, *Pennsylvania Archives,* 2d Ser., IV, 143.
22. Baldwin, *Whiskey Rebels,* 3
23. *Ibid.,* 10.

24. Brackenridge to Coxe, August 8, 1794, *Pennsylvania Archives*, 2d Ser., IV, 143.
25. Resolves for a Pittsburgh meeting of September 7, 1791. *Pennsylvania Archives*. 2d Ser., IV, 20
26. Rich, 338.
27. John Gibson to Thomas Mifflin, *Pennsylvania Archives*, 2d Ser., IV, 69.
28. *Ibid.*, IV, 78-79
29. *Ibid.*, IV, 173.
30. *Ibid.*, IV, 69.
31. *Ibid.*, IV, 82.
32. *Ibid.*, IV, 140.
33. H. H. Brackenridge to Tench Coxe, August 8, 1794, *Pennsylvania Archives*, 2d Ser., IV, 140-144. Brackenridge asked Coxe to publish his letter.
34. *Pennsylvania Archives*, 2d Ser., IV, 76-77
35. *Ibid.*, IV, 145.
36. *Ibid.*
37. Mifflin to Washington, August 5, 1794, Pennsylvania Collection, I, 16. Library of Congress.
38. *Ibid.*
39. Wilson to Washington, August 4, 1794, Pennsylvania Collection, I, 14. It should be noted that Wilson named only two counties.
40. Rich, 340.
41. Hamilton to Washington, August 5, 1794, *Pennsylvania Archives*, 2d Ser., IV, 103.
42. E. Randolph to Mifflin, August 7, 1794, *ibid.*, IV, 119.
43. Mifflin to Washington, August 12, 1794, *ibid.*, IV, 148.
44. *Ibid.*, IV, 151.
45. Mifflin to Washington, August 22, 1794, *ibid.*, IV, 194.
46. Because of this reluctance to use troops, Mifflin has been accused of timidity. *See* Basset, 109.
47. In 1792, Hamilton said in a letter to Washington: "As to the idea of a war upon the citizens to collect the impost duties, it can only be regarded as a figure of rhetoric." (Rich, 336.)
48. Hamilton, *Works*, IV, 575. Cited in Rich, 340.
49. *Pennsylvania Archives*, 2d Ser., IV, 126.
50. *Ibid.*, IV, 122.
51. *Ibid.*, IV, 134.
52. *Ibid.*, IV, 130.

53. E. Randolph to Jasper Yeates, August 8, 1794, Wallace Papers, III, 35. HSP. Many original papers dealing with the work of the commissioners are to be found in Volumes I and II of the Pennsylvania Collection of the Library of Congress.
54. Randolph to James Ross, August 7, 1794, Ross-Woods Papers, Western Pennsylvania Historical Society.
55. Mifflin to Washington, August 5, 1794, *Pennsylvania Archives*, 2d Ser., IV, 109.
56. *Ibid.*, IV, 110.
57. Edward Shippen to Jasper Yeates, August 6, 1794, Gratz Collection, Supreme Court of Pennsylvania.
58. United States Commissioners to E. Randolph, August 17, 1794, *Pennsylvania Archives*, 2d Ser., IV, 164.
59. Hamilton to Mifflin, September 9, 1794, *ibid.*, IV, 267.
60. Washington, through Randolph, to the United States Commissioners, September 29, 1794, Ross-Woods Papers.
61. *Pennsylvania Archives*, 2d Ser., IV, 274.
62. Report of A. J. Dallas to Pennsylvania Senate, September 10, 1794, *Pennsylvania Archives*, 2d Ser., IV, 280-282. In a report of January 16, 1795, Dallas ascribed Pennsylvania's poor showing principally to imperfections in the militia law, *ibid.*, IV, 506-521.
63. Speech at Lancaster, September 26, 1794, *ibid.*, IV, 375.
64. Message of Governor to Pennsylvania Assembly, September 17, 1794, *ibid.*, IV, 312.
65. *Pennsylvania House Journal, 1794-1795*, 49; *Pennsylvania Archives*, 2d Ser., IV, 327.
66. *Ibid.*, IV, 389.
67. Findley to William Bradford, September 16, 1794, Wallace Papers, III, 38-39.
68. *Ibid.*
69. *Ibid.*
70. Brackenridge to Coxe, September 5, 1794, *Pennsylvania Archives*, 2d Ser., IV, 301-303.
71. James Ross to Richard Peters, October 12, 1794, Peters Manuscripts, X, 28, HSP.
72. James Ross to William Bradford, October 12, 1794, Wallace Papers, III, 40.
73. Rich, 345, 348.
74. William Findley, *History of the Insurrection in the Four Western Counties of Pennsylvania*, 169. For Findley's account of the interview, see pp. 169-189
75. Rich, 344.
76. *Aurora*, November 10, 1794.
77. *Pennsylvania Archives*, 2d Ser., IV, 445.

78. Rich, 349.
79. Baldwin, 244-248.
80. Rich, 349.
81. *Pennsylvania Archives,* 9th Ser., II, 1005-1007.
82. *Aurora,* November 10, 1794; George M. Dallas, *Life of Alexander James Dallas,* 47. "This disproportionately huge military movement against the western malcontents," says George M. Dallas, "had an unforseen tendency to augment the bitterness of political strife. Although the jealous friends of liberty could rejoice in the bloodless restoration of order, they perceived, for the first time, with amazement and alarm, the immense power placed by the federal constitution practically in the hands of the leading advisers of the executive. Such a power was unsafe while lodged with men, some of whom were believed to incline towards a rule of force, rather than one of opinion; of rank and wealth, rather than of simplicity and equality."
83. James Veech, *The Monongahela of Old,* 144.
84. *Gazette of the United States,* November 15, 1794.
85. Rich, 350.
86. *Gazette of the United States,* November 22, 1794.
87. William Findley to Alexander Addison, November 28, 1794, Mss. Collection, Darlington Library, University of Pittsburgh.
88. *Abridgement of the Debates of Congress, 1789-1856,* I, 533.
89. *Ibid.,* I, 540.
90. *Ibid.*
91. Miller, "Democratic Societies," 331.
92. Brackenridge, *Incidents,* III, 25. Brackenridge gives an interesting explanation of the motives behind the society's organization: "Some of the leaders in it, had been disappointed in their wishes to be justices of the peace, or to be upon the bench, as associate judges; others were harrassed with suits from justices and courts, and wished a less expensive tribunal [they tried suits between their members]; others favored it, as an engine of election for county offices, or for the state legislature; others, from a desire natural to men of being conspicuous."
93. Link, 147.
94. Deposition of Alexander Addison, *Pennsylvania Archives,* 2d Ser., IV, 391. In a letter to Mifflin on October 4, 1794, Bradford declared that at Brownsville he urged a submission to the laws and had always done so, *ibid.,* IV, 396.
95. *Ibid.,* IV, 111.
96. Miller, "Democratic Societies," 345.
97. Luetscher, 55-56.
98. Minutes, Pennsylvania Democratic Society, 131.
99. *Ibid.,* 135.
100. *Ibid.,* 145.

101. William Miller, "First Fruits of the Republican Organization: Political Aspects of the Congressional Election of 1794," *PMHB*, LXIII (1939), 138.
102. *Ibid.*, 162.
103. *Pennsylvania House Journal, 1794-1795*, 61.
104. *Ibid.*, 62.
105. Henry Adams, *Writings of Albert Gallatin*, III, 44. Hereafter cited as Gallatin, *Writings*.
106. *Pennsylvania House Journal, 1794-1795*, 76.
107. *Ibid.*, 80.
108. *Aurora*, January 14, 1795.
109. *Ibid.*, January 20, 1795.
110. Findley to Addison, January 9, 1795, Mss. Collection, Darlington Memorial Library.
111. Gallatin, *Writings*, III, 67; *Aurora*, February 18, 1795.
112. Findley to Addison, January 9, 1795.
113. Dallas to Irvine, August 7, 1794, Irvine Papers, XII, 79.
114. Mifflin's Message to the Legislature, September 2, 1794, *Pennsylvania Archives*, 2d Ser., IV, 247-258.

NOTES—Chapter VII

1. *Pennsylvania Archives*, 2d Ser., VI, 730-731.
2. *Ibid.*, 627.
3. Maclay, *Journal*, 120.
4. *Pennsylvania Archives*, 2d Ser., VI, 630. Apparently the land was worth seventy-five times as much to the United States as it was to the Indians.
5. *Statutes at Large*, XIV, 239.
6. *Pennsylvania Archives*, 4th Ser., IV, 225.
7. *Statutes at Large*, XIV, 233. The detailed settlement provisions of this bill led to a controversy that has been described in Elizabeth K. Henderson's "The Northwest Lands of Pennsylvania, 1790-1812," *PMHB*, LX (1936), 131-160
8. *Statutes at Large*, XIV, 239
9. *Ibid.*, XIV, 395.
10. *Ibid.*
11. Mifflin to Irvine and Ellicott, April 15, 1793, Secretary of Commonwealth Letter Book, III, 341. Public Records Division, Pennsylvania Historical and Museum Commission, Harrisburg, Pennsylvania.
12. Mifflin to Washington, May 25, 1794, *Pennsylvania Archives*, 2d Ser., VI, 669-671.
13. Irvine Papers, XII, 59; *Pennsylvania Archives*, 2d Ser., VI, 631.
14. Mifflin to Ebenezer Denny, March 1, 1794, *ibid.*, VI, 636-638.
15. Circular Letter, Mifflin to Brigade Inspectors, March 1, 1794, *ibid.*, VI, 631.
16. Mifflin to Presque Isle Commissioners, March 1, 1794, *ibid.*, VI, 635. Ellicott and Irvine were also the commissioners in charge of the construction of a road from Reading to Presque Isle.
17. Dallas to Brigade Inspectors of Westmoreland and Washington counties, May 9, 1794, Irvine Papers, XII, 39; Mifflin to Brigade Inspectors of Westmoreland, Washington, Allegheny and Fayette counties, May 23, 1794, Irvine Papers, XII, 44.
18. Wilkins to Mifflin, May 11, 1794, *Pennsylvania Archives*, 2d Ser., VI, 658.
19. Israel Chapin to Knox, May 6, 1794, *ibid.*, VI, 656.
20. Dallas to Knox, May 9, 1794, *ibid.*, VI, 659.
21. Mifflin to Brigade Inspectors, May 23, 1794, Irvine Papers, XII, 44.
22. Knox to Mifflin, May 24, 1794, Irvine Papers, XII, 49.

23. Mifflin to Presley Neville, June 13, 1794, *Pennsylvania Archives*, 2d Ser., VI, 696.
24. Mifflin to John Wilkins, June 13, 1794, *ibid.*, VI, 698.
25. Mifflin to Washington, May 25, 1794, *ibid.*, VI, 669-671.
26. George D. Harmon, *Sixty Years of Indian Affairs*, 35.
27. *Ibid.*, 36. Professor Harmon says: "As a result of the Battle of Fallen Timbers some members of the Detroit Volunteers were captured, and there is no doubt but that the British at Detroit furnished at this time arms and ammunition to the Western tribes." *See also*, Bemis, 178.
28. Bemis, 3.
29. *Ibid.*, 5.
30. *Ibid.*, 8.
31. Mifflin to Irvine, May 23, 1794, Irvine Papers, XII, 43.
32. Mifflin to Washington, May 25, 1794, Irvine Papers, XII, 59; *Pennsylvania Archives*, 2d Ser., VI, 669-671.
33. Mifflin to Washington, June 13, 1794, *ibid.*, VI, 699.
34. Knox to Mifflin, June 14, 1794, *ibid.*, VI, 700; and Society Collection, HSP. The Secretary of War was here referring to the mission of John Jay to England. Jay had been sent over to make a treaty, and since the United States was already suffering under disadvantages which made negotiations difficult, the administration tried to avoid any action which would magnify those disadvantages. It was felt that an open break with the British at that time would be disastrous.
35. Mifflin to Washington, June 14, 1794, *Pennsylvania Archives*, 2d Ser., VI, 701-705.
36. *Ibid.*, VI, 704.
37. *Ibid.*
38. *Ibid.*, VI, 704-705.
39. Mifflin to Irvine, June 14, 1794, Irvine Papers, XII, 56.
40. *Ibid.*
41. Knox to Mifflin, June 21, 1794, Irvine Papers, XII, 64; *Pennsylvania Archives*, 2d Ser., VI, 712-713. The letter is incorrectly dated June 25 in the *Pennsylvania Archives*.
42. *Pennsylvania Archives*, 2d Ser., VI, 713.
43. Mifflin to Knox, June 24, 1794, *ibid.*, VI, 714-715
44. *Ibid.*, VI, 714.
45. *Ibid.*, VI, 725-727
46. Israel Chapin to Knox, June 26, 1794, *ibid.*, VI, 715.
47. Ebenezer Denny to Mifflin, June 29, 1794, *ibid.*, VI, 725.
48. Ebenezer Denny to Mifflin, July 4, 1794, *ibid.*, VI, 739.
49. Knox to Mifflin, July 7, 1794, *ibid.*, VI, 740. Knox complied but insisted that the equipment had to be replaced in kind or paid for.
50. Mifflin to Washington, July 15, 1794, *ibid.*, VI, 742.

NOTES—CHAPTER VII

51. Knox (writing for Washington) to Mifflin, *ibid.*, VI, 744.
52. *Ibid.*, VI, 745.
53. Mifflin to Washington, July 18, 1794, *ibid.*, VI, 746.
54. *Ibid.*, VI, 747
55. Mifflin to Washington, July 22, 1794, *ibid.*, VI, 752.
56. Knox to Mifflin, July 17, 1794, *ibid.*, VI, 744.
57. Dallas to Ingersoll, July 14, 1794, *ibid.*, VI, 741.
58. Ingersoll to Dallas, July 18, 1794, *ibid.*, VI, 746.
59. Mifflin to Washington, July 18, 1794, *ibid.*, VI, 747.
60. *Ibid.*
61. Knox to Mifflin, July 21, 1794, *ibid.*, VI, 751-752.
62. *Ibid.*
63. Mifflin to Washington, July 22, 1794, *ibid.*, VI, 753.
64. *Ibid.*
65. C. W. Butterfield, ed., *Washington-Irvine Correspondence*, 69.
66. Daniel Agnew, *A History of the Region of Pennsylvania North of the Ohio and West of the Allegheny River*, 129.
67. Irvine to Mifflin, June 3, 1794, Irvine Papers, XII, 52.
68. *Ibid.*
69. *Ibid.*
70. Irvine to Mifflin, June 4, 1794, *Pennsylvania Archives*, 2d Ser., VI, 683.
71. *Ibid.*
72. Mifflin to Irvine, June 14, 1794, Irvine Papers, XII, 56.
73. Reddick to Mifflin, June 5, 1794, *Pennsylvania Archives*, 2d Ser., VI, 678-680.
74. *Ibid.*
75. Ellicott to Mifflin, July 19, 1794, *ibid.*, VI, 748.
76. Ellicott to Mifflin, June 5, 1794, *ibid.*, VI, 680.
77. *Ibid.*
78. Ellicott to Mifflin, July 19, 1794, *ibid.*, VI, 749.
79. Ebenezer Denny to Gibson, July 19, 1794, *ibid.*, VI, 750.
80. *General Advertiser,* June 24, 1794.
81. "From Correspondents," *General Advertiser,* June 21, 1794.
82. "A Pennsylvanian," *ibid.,* August 1, 1794.
83. Presley Neville to Irvine, June 2, 1794, Irvine Papers, XII, 51.
84. *Pennsylvania House Journal, 1794-1795,* 15.
85. *Ibid.,* 65.
86. Wilkins to Mifflin, October 10, 1794, *Pennsylvania Archives,* 2d Ser., VI, 781.
87. Bemis, 109.

88. Pickering to Mifflin, January 27, 1795, *ibid.*, VI, 799.
89. *Pennsylvania House Journal, 1795-1796*, 13.
90. Speech of Cornplanter, March 8, 1796, *Pennsylvania Archives*, 2d Ser., VI, 825.

NOTES—Chapter VIII

1. Luetscher, 133. The legislative session ended on April 11. *See Pennsylvania House Journal, 1792-1793*, 386.
2. Frederick A. Muhlenberg to Wilson, May 13, 1791. Papers of James Wilson, III, 32, HSP.
3. *See* picture of Muhlenberg in Gratz Collection, HSP.
4. *American Daily Advertiser*, August 14, 1793.
5. *General Advertiser*, July 5, 1793.
6. "Anti-Janus" in *General Advertiser*, July 9, 1793.
7. *Ibid.*
8. "An American," *American Daily Advertiser*, August 14, 1793.
9. "Atticus," *General Advertiser*, August 8, 1793.
10. "Anti-Janus," *ibid.*, August 21, 1793.
11. *Ibid.*, August 4, 1793.
12. Walters, *Dallas*, 46.
13. Genêt to Washington, August 13, 1793, in *American Daily Advertiser*, August 24, 1793.
14. Walters, *Dallas*, 48.
15. Bache suspended publication from September 26 to November 26. See *Aurora*, September 26, 1796.
16. These totals are exclusive of the vote in Allegheny County, which did not appear in the official list presented to the legislature. *Pennsylvania House Journal, 1793-1794*, 39.
17. *Statutes at Large*, XV, 171-174.
18. *Pennsylvania House Journal, 1793-1794*, 226-227.
19. *General Advertiser*, August 15, 1794.
20. *Ibid.*, September 4, 1794.
21. *Ibid.*, October 7, 1794.
22. *Ibid.*, October 13, 1794.
23. It will be recalled that when the legislature was considering a Congressional election law, Swanwick favored the election-at-large method. As an anti-excise man it is possible that he considered his chances would be much better in a general election than in the Philadelphia area, where Fitzsimons had a considerable following. Such an assumption is valid, of course, only if Swanwick was at the time a candidate.
24. "T.T.," in *Gazette of the United States*, October 11, 1794.
25. *General Advertiser*, October 10, 1794.
26. *Ibid.*, October 11, 1794.

27. *Ibid.*, October 14, 1794.
28. *Ibid.*
29. *Ibid.*, October 18, 1794.
30. Election proclamation, February 28, 1795, *Pennsylvania Archives,* 4th Ser., IV, 330; Wold, *Biographical Directory of the American Congress,* 57.
31. *Gazette of the United States,* October 30, 1794
32. *Pennsylvania House Journal, 1794-1795,* 207.
33. This was in accordance with the provisions of a law passed April 22, 1794, which gave the House a membership of seventy-eight and reapportioned the districts. *Statutes at Large,* XV, 158-161.
34. The "City Treaty Ticket" was composed of George Latimer, Jacob Hiltzheimer, Lawrence Seckle, Francis Gurney, Benjamin Morgan and Robert Waln. The "Anti-Treaty" men in Philadelphia County nominated Richard Tittermary, Blair McClenachan, Michael Leib, Isaac Worrell, Manuel Eyre and William Linnard. See *Aurora,* October 5, 1795.
35. *Ibid.*, October 15, 1795. On October 15, Bache twitted John Fenno who had attempted to minimize the anti-treaty strength: "Citizen Fenno! Let those laugh who win. It is true, that the influence of wealth and industry of religious sectaries prevented a total change in the representation from the city and county of Philadelphia for the ensuing Legislature: but maugre that unprecedented industry and in the teeth of that influence, half of the representatives have been changed—Is this nothing, Citizen Fenno?"
36. "A Constitutionalist," *Aurora,* October 15, 1795.
37. "Cleon," *Aurora,* October 24, 1795.
38. "A Bone to Gnaw for the Democrats," in John M. and James P Cobbett, eds., *Cobbett's Political Works,* I, 37-52.
39. *Ibid.*, I, 52-85
40. *Ibid.*, I, 53.
41. *Ibid.* The tribute to Cobbett was made by Windham in a debate in the House of Commons, August 5, 1803.
42. "Franklin," in *The Democratic Press,* July 31, 1810.
43. United States Constitution, Section III.
44. Maclay, *Journal,* 170.
45. *Ibid.*, 337.
46. *Ibid.*, 347.
47. *Ibid.*, 343.
48. *Ibid.*
49. *Ibid.*, 350.
50. *Pennsylvania House Journal, 1791-1792,* 497.

51. John Smilie moved to accept the House's offer but Richard Peters, Speaker of the Senate, broke an eight to eight tie on the resolution by voting in the negative. *Pennsylvania Senate Journal, 1791-1792,* 51.
52. *Pennsylvania House Journal, 1791-1792,* 166.
53. *Ibid.,* 169.
54. Mifflin's Address to the Legislature, December 7, 1792. *Pennsylvania Archives,* 4th Ser., IV, 233.
55. *Pennsylvaina House Journal, 1792-1793,* 59. None of the House votes was close. The opinion there in favor of joint action was overwhelming.
56. *Pennsylvania Senate Journal, 1792-1793,* 67.
57. *Ibid.,* 70. The eight dissenters were William Montgomery, John Moore, John Hanna, Abraham Smith, Thomas Kennedy, Joseph Hiester, John Smilie and Robert Brown. None of them came from the city of Philadelphia or the four eastern counties of Philadelphia, Delaware, Bucks and Chester.
58. *Pennsylvania Senate Journal, 1792-1793,* 136.
59. *Pennsylvania House Journal, 1792-1793,* 191.
60. *Pennsylvania Senate Journal, 1792-1793,* 136. The seven Senators were Lindsay Coats, John Edie, John Hoge, Thomas Jenks, Anthony Morris, John Sellers and Richard Thomas. With the exception of John Hoge, who came from the Washington-Fayette district, all of the seven represented districts located east of the mountains.
61. Addison to Gallatin, January 20, 1793, Gallatin Papers, IV.
62. *Pennsylvania House Journal, 1792-1793,* 214, 217.
63. *Ibid.,* 220.
64. With the exception of John Hoge (Washington-Fayette district), all the Senators who favored concurrent action voted for Miller. The opposition voted for Gallatin.
65. This despite the fact that the influential David Bradford, of Washington County, voted against him. The remainder of the Washington delegation—three men—favored Gallatin. *Pennsylvania House Journal, 1792-1793,* 214
66. Henry Adams, *The Life of Albert Gallatin,* 98.
67. James Veech, *The Monongahela of Old,* 170.
68. *Ibid.*
69. Adams, *Gallatin,* 119
70. *Pennsylvania House Journal, 1793-1794,* 311.
71. "An Elector," *Aurora,* August 27, 1799.
72. William Findley to Israel Israel, February 25, 1801. Dreer Collection, American Statesmen, II.
73. Morris to Pennsylvania House of Representatives, January 12, 1795, *Pennsylvania House Journal, 1794-1795,* 85.

74. *Ibid.*, 207. In the Senate Bingham won by sixteen to four, in the House by forty-two to thirty-one.

75. *Ibid., 1796-1797*, 208. Ross got fifteen votes in the Senate and forty-one in the House. Irvine recorded eight in the Senate and thirty in the House.

NOTES—Chapter IX

1. William Findley to Alexander Addison, January 3, 1796, Mss. Collection, Darlington Memorial Library.
2. *Pennsylvania House Journal, 1796-1797*, 34
3. Raymond Walters in his biography of Dallas makes an interesting generalization on Mifflin's easy election: "This time the Federalists, recognizing Mifflin's tight hold on the masses throughout the state, declined to oppose him even though they realized that Dallas had made a thorough-going Democratic-Republican of the affable old general." (p. 74).
4. For details on those records, *see* pp. 182-183.
5. *Pennsylvania Senate Journal, 1800-1801*, 66.
6. *Aurora*, September 21, 1796; *Gazette of the United States*, July 12, 1796.
7. "A Citizen," *Aurora*, September 17, 1796.
8. "Polio," *Aurora*, October 7, 1796.
9. "A Citizen," *Aurora*, September 17, 1796.
10. *Gazette of the United States*, July 12, 1796.
11. *Ibid.*, October 8, 1796.
12. *Aurora*, October 13, 1796.
13. *Pittsburgh Gazette*, August 27, 1796.
14. *Ibid.*, September 3, 10, 1796.
15. *Aurora*, October 13, 1796.
16. *Ibid.*, October 12, 1795.
17. *Ibid.*, October 9, 1795.
18. Fenno, for instance, referred to "democrats in Congress." *Gazette of the United States*, December 29, 1796.
19. A perusal of Andrew Brown's dull *Philadelphia Gazette* failed to produce even one party label. With its emphasis on foreign news and shipping advertisements, Brown's paper rarely mentioned matters of local political interest in 1796.
20. *Pennsylvania House Journal, 1795-1796*, 429. According to a House rule all motions were lost in the event of a tie vote.
21. *Ibid.*, 433.
22. Republican State Committee Circular, signed by Michael Leib, chairman, September 25, 1796, Broadsides Collection, HSP.
23. *Ibid.*
24. See *pp.* 199-202 for a discussion of partisan votes.
25. *Aurora*, October 24, 1796; *Gazette of the United States*, November 4, 1796.

26. *Ibid.*
27. Federalist electors, listed in *Aurora*, October 25, 1796:
    Israel Whelen (Philadelphia)
    Samuel Miles (Montgomery)
    Henry Wynkoop (Bucks)
    John Arndt (Northampton)
    Valentine Eckhart (Berks)
    Thomas Bull (Chester)
    Robert Coleman (Lancaster)
    John Carson (Dauphin)
    William Wilson (Northumberland)
    Samuel Postlethwaite (Cumberland)
    Jacob Hay (York)
    Benjamin Elliott (Huntingdon)
    Ephraim Douglas (Westmoreland)
    John Woods (Allegheny)
    Thomas Stokely (Washington)
28. Republican electors:
    Thomas McKean (Philadelphia)
    Jacob Morgan (Philadelphia County)
    James Boyd (Chester)
    Jonas Hartzell (Northampton)
    Peter Muhlenberg (Montgomery)
    Joseph Hiester (Berks)
    William Maclay (Dauphin)
    James Hanna (Bucks)
    John Whitehill (Lancaster)
    William Irvine (Cumberland)
    Abraham Smith (Franklin)
    William Brown (Mifflin)
    John Piper (Bedford)
    John Smilie (Fayette)
    James Edgar (Washington)

David Rittenhouse was on the original list prepared at the State House meeting, but after his death in June, 1796, his name was replaced by that of James Boyd.

29. Republican State Committee Circular, September 25, 1796.
30. Lynch, *Fifty Years of Party Warfare*, 59.
31. *Aurora*, September 13, 1796.
32. *Ibid.*
33. *Ibid.*, October 28, 1796.
34. Republican State Committee Circular, September 25, 1796.
35. *General Advertiser*, December 7, 1792.
36. *Ibid.*, February 10, 1794.
37. "A Farmer," in *ibid.*, January 29, 1793.
38. Lewis G. Leary, *That Rascal Freneau*, 196.

39. *Ibid.*, 199.
40. *Ibid.*, 233; Samuel E. Forman, *Political Activities of Philip Freneau*, 245-246
41. At a Republican nominating meeting at Poor's schoolhouse in Philadelphia on November 2, he acted as secretary. *Gazette of the United States*, November 4, 1796.
42. Faÿ, "Early Party Machinery," 383. *See also* the same author's *Two Franklins*, 299
43. Beckley to Irvine, September 15, 1796, Irvine Papers, XIII, 112.
44. Same to same, September 22, 1796, *ibid.*, XIII, 113.
45. *Ibid.*
46. Same to same, October 4, 1796, *ibid.*, XIII, 115.
47. This was probably the broadside printed on September 24.
48. Beckley to Irvine, October 4, 1796.
49. Walters, *Dallas*, 73.
50. Link, 202.
51. *Statutes at Large*, XV, 428-430.
52. *Ibid.*
52a. *Pennsylvania Archives*, 4th Ser., IV, 356-358; *Aurora*, December 12, 1796.
53. *Gazette of the United States*, November 18, 1796.
54. Dallas "To the Chief Justice, and the Associate Judges of the Supreme Court—the President of the First District—and the Attorney General of Pennsylvania," November 18, 1796. *Philadelphia Gazette*, November 21, 1796.
55. *Ibid.*, November 18, 1796.
56. Edward Shippen, Thomas Smith, Jared Ingersoll, & James Biddle to Thomas Mifflin, November 18, 1796, *ibid.*, November 21, 1796.
57. *Aurora*, November 25, 1796.
58. Governor's Proclamation, November 24, 1796. *Pennsylvania Archives*, 4th Ser., IV, 356.
59. *Gazette of the United States*, November 26, 1796.
60. *Ibid.*, November 18, 1796. In Fenno's paper the parties were described as "Federal" and "Anti-Federal."
61. *Philadelphia Gazette*, November 18, 1796.
62. When the returns from Westmoreland, Fayette and Greene finally reached Philadelphia, it was found that they, too, had favored the Republican ticket.
63. Lycoming was listed with Northumberland and a single return covered both areas.
64. *Philadelphia Gazette*, November 18, 1796.
65. "Pennsylvaniensis," in *Gazette of the United States*, November 25, 1796.

66. *Ibid.*, November 25, 1796.
67. *Aurora*, November 25, 29, 1796.
68. *Ibid.*, November 30, 1796.
69. Governor's Address to the Legislature, December 9, 1796. *Pennsylvania Archives*, 4th Ser., IV, 361.
70. Fisher Ames to Christopher Gore, December 3, 1796, in Seth Ames, ed., *The Works of Fisher Ames*, I, 205. Ames said it was rumored that Mifflin, on the strength of the Greene County vote, would issue a new proclamation and certify all the Republicans. See *Aurora*, December 12, 1796.
71. *Ibid.*, November 29, 1804.
72. *Ibid.*, December 13, 1796. As to the right of Edgar and Hartzell to vote, Bache had observed on December 12, that "it may probably be made a question in the proper time and place, whether the voice of the people ought to be frustrated, owing to trifling informalities, by the rejection of the votes of those two persons." See *ibid.*, December 12, 1796.
73. *Gazette of the United States*, December 10, 1796.
74. *Ibid.*, September 24, 1798.
75. Channing, IV, 217.
76. Ames to Gore, December 3, 1796. Ames was almost in despair over the French influence in America. "To celebrate French victories may be right for Jacobins; but *we* should cease to celebrate the Fourth of July." Overcome with gloom he predicted the calamity that would befall the United States if Jefferson became Vice-President: "Party will have a head responsible for nothing, yet deranging and undermining everything, and France would have a new magazine of disorganizing influence. . . . I own I am ready to croak when I observe the gathering of the vapors in our horizon."
77. These figures are approximate and do not include the "uncounted" returns from Greene County

NOTES—Chapter X

1. *Aurora*, October 14, 1797.
2. *Ibid.*
3. *Ibid.*, October 19, 1797.
4. *Ibid.*
5. *Ibid.*, October 14, 1797.
6. *Ibid.*, October 20, 1797.
7. *Ibid.*, November 6, 1797.
8. *Porcupine's Gazette*, October 12, 1797.
9. *Philadelphia Gazette*, October 7, 1797.
10. *Porcupine's Gazette*, October 12, 1797.
11. *Aurora*, October 13, 1797.
12. *Ibid.*, October 14, 1797.
13. *Ibid.*
14. *Ibid.*
15. *Porcupine's Gazette*, October 16, 1797.
16. *Ibid.*
17. *Pennsylvania Senate Journal, 1797-1798*, 22.
18. *Aurora*, January 31, and February 3, 1798. In these two issues the paper devoted a total of twelve full columns to Dallas' speech.
19. *Pennsylvania Senate Journal, 1797-1798*, 111.
20. *Ibid.*
21. *Aurora*, February 19, 1798.
22. Broadside, n. d., HSP.
23. Broadside, February 21, 1798, HSP.
24. Broadside, n. d., HSP.
25. "A Dutchman," broadside of February 21, 1798, HSP.
26. *Aurora*, February 26, 1798.
27. In the presidential election of 1796, the vote in the area under consideration was a little less than one-fifth of the total for the State at large.
28. *Aurora*, February 26, 1798. Morgan did not serve out his term, resigning in 1799. See *Aurora*, April 16, 1799. Perhaps all they wanted to do was to make the "point."
29. Channing, IV, 177.
30. *Ibid.*, IV, 187.
31. *Ibid.*

32. Pennsylvanians elected to the Fifth Congress in 1796: David Bard (Rep.), Samuel Sitgreaves (Fed.), John Chapman (Fed.), William Findley (Rep.), Albert Gallatin (Rep.), Andrew Gregg (Rep.), John A. Hanna (inconsistent voting record), Thomas Hartley, George Ege (Fed.), John W. Kittera (Fed.), Blair McClenachan (Rep.), John Swanwick (Rep.), Richard Thomas (Fed.). Because of death and resignations the following changes occurred in the Pennsylvania delegation during the Fifth Congress: Samuel Sitgreaves resigned in 1798, and was replaced by Robert Brown (Rep.) on December 4, 1798; George Ege resigned in October, 1797, and was replaced by Joseph Hiester (Rep.) on December 1, 1797; John Swanwick died on August 1, 1798, and was replaced by Robert Waln (Fed.) on December 3, 1798.

33. Writing to Jefferson in 1813 John Adams declared that he had not applied this act "in a single instance." (F. M. Anderson, "The Enforcement of the Alien and Sedition Acts," *Annual Report of the American Historical Association for 1912*, 115.

34. Bassett, *Federalist System*, 258.

35. *Annals of Congress*, 5 Cong., 2 Sess., 2028; *House Journal*, 5 Cong., 2 Sess., 346.

36. *Annals of Congress*, 5 Cong. (1797-1799), appendix, 3776-3777.

37. *Annals of Congress*, 5 Cong., 2 Sess., 2171.

38. *House Journal*, 5 Cong., 2 Sess., 373.

39. *Ibid.*, 301.

40. *Ibid.*, 366.

41. Channing, IV, 202.

42. Maclay, *Journal*, 346.

43. Deborah Norris Logan, *Memoir of Dr. George Logan*, 23; Channing, IV, 202.

44. *Ibid.* In the words of the *Gazette of the United States* for November 15, 1798, Logan "had the *unpardonable effrontery* to wait upon General Washington. Upon his introduction he offered his polluted hand to the General, who declined returning his fraternal salutation." Logan's invitation to visit Stenton, his home, was refused by Washington "in a mingled tone of indignation and contempt. . . ."

45. *Gazette of the United States*, November 12, 1798.

46. James Ross to George Stevenson, December 14, 1798, Ross-Woods Papers.

47. David Redick to William Irvine, February 11, 1799, Irvine Papers, XIV, 70.

48. *Memoir of Dr. George Logan*, 23.

49. *Ibid.*

50. James Ross to George Stevenson, December 14, 1798. He was elected to the Assembly to replace John Huston who resigned.

51. James Ross to Arthur St. Clair, July 5, 1798, in W. H. Smith, *Life and Public Services of Arthur St. Clair*, II, 422-426.

52. *Ibid.*, II, 423.

53. Senator Ross eschewed the word "Republican" and did not use it in the letter here discussed. He much preferred the term "Jacobin" which occurred with great frequency in his correspondence during the years 1798-1800. *See* Ross-Woods Papers.

54. Ross to St. Clair, July 5, 1798, *Life and Public Services of Arthur St. Clair*, II, 422-426

55. Editor's note, in *ibid.*

56. With the encouragement of Brackenridge, the *Pittsburgh Gazette* was founded by John Scull and Joseph Hall in July, 1786. After Hall's death, which occurred a few months later, Scull continued the paper alone. He was a strong Federalist, but he believed a newspaper should represent the community as a whole, and for several years he followed a nonpartisan policy and avoided controversy. During John Adams' administration, however, he closed his columns to any criticism of the Federalists and regarded the Jeffersonian group as a "treasonable" combination. *See* Alston G. Field, "The Press in Western Pennsylvania to 1812," *Western Pennsylvania Historical Magazine*, XX (1937), 232-234, 259.

57. *Pittsburgh Gazette*, September 1, 1798.

58. *Ibid.*

59. Alexander Addison to H. H. Brackenridge, September 17, 1798, Mss. Collection, Darlington Memorial Library.

60. Ferguson, 147.

61. John Israel to Albert Gallatin, September 23, 1798, Gallatin Papers, V

62. *Pittsburgh Gazette*, August 25, 1798.

63. *Ibid.*, October 20, 1798.

64. *American Daily Advertiser*, October 30, 1798.

65. *Philadelphia Gazette*, August 8, 1798.

66. *Ibid.*

67. *Ibid.*, August 25, 1798.

68. *Ibid.*, September 18, 1798.

69. "A Federalist" in the *Gazette of the United States*, September 24, 1798.

70. *Philadelphia Gazette*, August 24, 1798.

71. See the *Aurora*, August 27; *American Daily Advertiser*, September 4; and *Gazette of the United States*, September 24, 1798.

72. *Aurora*, August 27, 1798.

73. *Gazette of the United States*, September 24, 1798.

74. *Ibid.*

74a. The "Demon of Corruption" referred to here is the "Demon Rum." There seems little doubt that in an age characterized by heavy drinking, both public and private, Mifflin was quite at home, and in the face of the available evidence one is inclined to suspect that some of his "illnesses" were those common to the tippler. Some of Mifflin's contemporaries have commented on this aspect of his career. One has stated that the Governor, while commanding the Pennsylvanians at Carlisle during the Whiskey Rebellion, unwisely issued orders that almost precipitated a battle between his own men and the New Jersey troops. Mifflin "was charged with being in a shameful state of intoxication, and was obliged publicly to ask pardon of some officers and make that excuse." (David Ford, *Journal of an Expedition Made in the Autumn of 1794, Proceedings of the New Jersey Historical Society*, VIII, 85-86). In his memoirs Jonathan Roberts describes him as "a worn out debauchee" whose face showed signs "of deep dissipation." (Philip S. Klein, "Memoirs of Jonathan Roberts," *PMHB*, LXII (1938), 89.) Another contemporary, Oliver Wolcott, told Hamilton that the Governor was drunk every day and that "Dallas and Judge McKean possess[ed] the efficient powers of government." (Wolcott to Hamilton, April 1, 1799, Hamilton, *Works*, VI, 106, cited in Peeling, "McKean," 204.) Finally, in reference to Mifflin's death, a Pennsylvania historian has flatly stated that he "drowned himself in drink," (Ferguson, *Early Western Pennsylvania Politics*, 211). Wolcott's statement, that Mifflin was unable to conduct the affairs of government because of drunkenness, is the most damaging. As to its truth or falsity, the present writer must admit that the evidence does not warrant either categorical denial or affirmation. It is undoubtedly true that the Governor was seriously ill during his last year of office (when Wolcott made his accusation) and that much work fell to the capable hands of Dallas, but it is another matter indeed to assert that McKean and Dallas conducted the administration because Mifflin's habitual drunkenness made it impossible for him to do so.

75. *American Daily Advertiser*, September 28, 1798.
76. *Ibid.*
77. *Ibid.*, October 1, 1798.
78. *Philadelphia Gazette*, October 1, 1798.
79. *American Daily Advertiser*, October 11, 12, 1798.
80. *Ibid.*
81. Wold, ed., *Biographical Directory of the American Congress*, 66; *Pittsburgh Gazette*, November 10, 1798
82. The above Representatives have been classified as to party adherence according to their voting record on certain controversial measures and resolutions which appeared during the course of the Sixth Congress. Thomas Hartley's name does not appear. He died before the votes recorded below were taken, but his record in the Fifth Congress definitely placed him in the Federalist group.

On February 10, 1801, the House, after a first reading, voted on the rejection of a bill which would continue the suspension of commerce between France and the United States. Pennsylvanians voting to reject: Brown, Gallatin, Gregg, Hanna, Hiester, Leib, P. Muhlenberg, Smilie, and John Stewart. Republican Stewart was elected to replace Thomas Hartley who died December 21, 1800. Voting in the negative were: Thomas, Waln, and Woods. See *House Journal,* 6 Cong., 2 Sess., 793.

On January 23, 1801, a resolution was offered which requested the "Committee of Revisal and Unfinished Business" to prepare a bill continuing in force "an Act in addition to the Act, entitled 'An Act for the punishment of certain crimes against the United States,'" The House divided evenly by a 48 to 48 vote, which tie was broken in favor of the resolution by the Speaker. Voting in the affirmative were Kittera, Thomas, Waln and Woods. For the negative were Brown, Gallatin, Gregg, Hanna, Hiester, Leib, P. Muhlenberg, and Smilie. (*House Journal,* 6 Cong., 2 Sess., 772.)

Probably most indicative of party split was the division on a resolution of March 3, 1801, which offered Theodore Sedgwick, Speaker of the House, a vote of thanks for his services. Voting for the resolution: Kittera and Woods. Against it were Brown, Gallatin, Gregg, Hanna, Hiester, Leib, P. Muhlenberg, and Smilie. *Ibid.,* 847.

83. Faÿ, *Two Franklins,* 150.
84. *Aurora,* August 11, 1802.
85. *Ibid.*
86. *Ibid.,* November 1, 1798.
87. *DAB,* V, 467-468.
88. *Ibid.*
89. *Ibid.* Another writer has this to say of Duane: ". . . it is no doubt true that he was overbearing and violent, factious, most scurrilous and insolent, no respecter of character or position, and not very scrupulous as to the fairness of the methods he used; but it should never be forgotten that he had been the sufferer from more than one disgraceful instance of gross wrong perpetrated on him by members of the very class who plumed themselves on their superiority and their high honor." William M. Meigs, "Pennsylvania Politics Early in This Century," *PMHB,* XVII (1893), 463.
90. *Philadelphia Gazette,* September 15, 1798.
91. Krout and Fox, 158.
92. This newspaper also lost one of its key figures in the autumn of 1798. Septimus Claypoole, one of the proprietors, died at Elkton, Maryland, on October 15 (*American Daily Advertiser,* October 20, 1798).
93. *Gazette of the United States,* October 23, 1798.
94. "Republican," in *Aurora,* September 20, 1797.

95. *Ibid.*
96. *See* pp. 177-178.
97. *Aurora,* January 31, 1798.
98. *Philadelphia Gazette,* October 9, 1797. For a similar appeal see *Porcupine's Gazette,* October 9, 1797.
99. "Anti-Treaty Ticket" in Philadelphia County in 1795: Blair McClenachan, Richard Tittermary, Michael Leib, Isaac Worrell, Manuel Eyre, William Linnard (*Aurora,* October 15, 1795).
100. "Democratic-Republican Ticket" in 1797: Richard Tittermary, Michael Leib, Thomas Forrest, Isaac Worrell, Manuel Eyre, William Linnard (*Aurora,* October 12, 1797).
101. When Coxe arrived in New York on May 7, 1790, to take up his treasury duties, William Maclay observed that he was "affected" with the "Cacocthes scribendi." In that connection, however, the caustic Senator from Pennsylvania paid him a grudging compliment. "He [Coxe] has persevering industry in an eminent degree. These are the qualities that have recommended him to this appointment. Hamilton sees that the campaign will open against him in the field of publication, and he is providing himself with gladiators of the quill, not only for defense but attack." (Maclay, *Journal,* 252.)
102. *DAB,* IV, 488-489.
103. Harold Hutcheson, *Tench Coxe,* 39.
104. *Philadelphia Gazette,* September 18, 1798.
105. Brunhouse, 221.
106. *Gazette of the United States,* September 24, 1798.
107. *Philadelphia Gazette,* September 18, 1798.

NOTES—Chapter XI

1. *Abridgement of the Debates of Congress, 1789-1856,* I, 692. Pennsylvanians in favor of the resolution: David Bard, William Findley, Albert Gallatin, A. Gregg, S. Maclay, F. A. Muhlenberg, John Richards, John Swanwick. Those in opposition: Thomas Hartley, J. W. Kittera, Samuel Sitgreaves and Richard Thomas. Daniel Hiester did not vote.
2. *Pennsylvania House Journal, 1795-1796,* 269.
3. *Ibid.,* 272.
4. *Ibid.,* 273.
5. *Ibid.,* 269-273.
6. *Ibid.,* 172-177.
7. See pp. 162-164.
8. *Pennsylvania House Journal, 1795-1796,* 428-434.
9. *Ibid.,* 101.
10. *Pennsylvania Archives,* 4th Ser., IV, 358-374.
11. *Ibid.,* IV, 373.
12. *Pennsylvania House Journal, 1796-1797,* 55.
13. *Ibid.,* 57.
14. *Ibid.*
15. *Ibid.,* 201.
16. *Pennsylvania Archives,* 4th Ser., IV, 359-360.
17. *Pennsylvania House Journal, 1796-1797,* 369.
18. *Ibid.,* 407.
19. *Ibid.,* 422.
20. *Ibid.,* 422-423.
21. "A Freeman," in *Aurora,* October 2, 1797.
22. When the preceding legislature was on the point of adjournment, Mifflin had notified it on April 5 that because of the limited time at his disposal he would keep the election law "under advisement." *Pennsylvania Archives,* 4th Ser., IV, 380.
23. *Pennsylvania House Journal, 1796-1797,* 9-13.
24. *Ibid., 1797-1798,* 39.
25. *Ibid.*
26. *Ibid.*
27. *Ibid.,* 306.
28. *Ibid.*
29. James Ross to George Stevenson, December 14, 1798. Copy in Ross-Woods Papers.

30. Mifflin's address to the General Assembly, December 7, 1798, *Pennsylvania Archives,* 4th Ser., IV, 422.
31. *Pennsylvania House Journal, 1798-1799,* 58.
32. *Ibid.,* 90.
33. *Ibid.,* 172-176.
34. *Ibid.*
35. Channing, IV, 255.
36. *Ibid.,* IV, 226.
37. *Pennsylvania House Journal, 1798-1799,* 199.
38. *Ibid.,* 191.
39. *Ibid.,* 192.
40. *Ibid.,* 199.
41. *Ibid.,* 289.
42. *See* pp. 182-183.
43. J. Bioren, publisher, *Laws of Pennsylvania,* III, 340-352.
44. *Pennsylvania House Journal, 1798-1799,* 106.
45. *Ibid.,* 367.
46. *Ibid.,* 138-143.
47. Quoted in Luetscher, 45.
48. Quoted in Channing, IV, 216.
49. *Pennsylvania House Journal, 1798-1799,* 199.

NOTES—Chapter XII

1. Adams to Washington, June 22, 1798, Gratz Collection, Administrations, 3-4. "My administration," Adams wrote, "will not certainly be easy to myself. It will be happy, however, if it is honourable. The prosperity of it to the country will depend upon Heaven, and very little on anything in my power. I have no qualifications for the martial part of it, which is like to be the most essential."
2. *Annals of Congress*, 5 Cong., 2 Sess. (Appendix), 3758.
3. *Ibid.*, 3763.
4. *House Journal*, 5 Cong., 2 Sess., 335.
5. Chapman did not vote.
6. *Annals of Congress*, 5 Cong., 2 Sess. (Appendix), 3378-3786.
7. *House Journal*, 5 Cong., 2 Sess., 362.
8. F. M. Eastman, *Fries' Rebellion*, 72; *Aurora*, April 11, 1799.
9. *Gazette of the United States*, March 11, 1799.
10. *Ibid.*
11. *Pennsylvania House Journal, 1798-1799*, 311; Dunaway, 418.
12. Governor's message to Legislature, March 14, 1799, *Pennsylvania Archives*, 4th Ser., IV, 424-425.
13. *Pennsylvania House Journal, 1798-1799*, 330.
14. *Ibid.*
15. *Ibid.*, 344.
16. Eastman, 72.
17. *Pennsylvania House Journal, 1798-1799*, 345.
18. *Aurora*, April 11, 1799.
19. Eastman, 74.
20. The anti-tax disorder is also known as the "Hot-water Rebellion." See Dunaway, 418.
21. Eastman, 75.
22. *Aurora*, May 24, 1799.
23. *Ibid.*, April 11, 1799.
24. *Gazette of the United States*, May 14, 1799.
25. *Aurora*, May 16, 1799.
26. John Beckley to William Irvine, May 10, 1799, Irvine Papers, XIV, 84. "Fries is convicted of high treason," writes Beckley, "and I presume must hang if it were only to prove the infallibility of presidential proclamations."
27. Eastman, 80.

28. Joseph Reed to William Irvine, January 25, 1800, Irvine Papers, XV, 5. Reed and Irvine were two of the three executors Mifflin had appointed in his last will. In notifying Irvine of his appointment, Reed said: "I believe there will be but little trouble, as I am afraid the Estate he has left, is very inconsiderable."

29. John Beckley to William Irvine, January 2, 1799, Irvine Papers, XIV, 63. "Mifflin," wrote Beckley, "has been *very* ill, and not yet absolutely safe."

30. Democratic Address, signed by Thomas Leiper, *Aurora*, September 3, 1810.

31. *Ibid*.

32. A Republican Address, June 10, 1805, in George M. Dallas, *Life and Writings of Alexander James Dallas*, 225.

33. Walters, *Dallas*, 88.

34. *Ibid*.

35. *Aurora*, December 20, 1799.

36. John Beckley to William Irvine, January 2, 1799, Irvine Papers, XIV, 63.

37. William Findley to Israel Israel, February 25, 1801, Dreer Collection, American Statesmen, II.

38. *Aurora*, April 25, 1799.

39. A Democratic Address of August 30, 1810, *Aurora*, September 3, 1810, signed by Thomas Leiper. In his thesis, "The Public Life of Thomas McKean," 206, James H. Peeling says that this meeting was held in Lancaster. Walters (*Dallas*, 89) also places it in that town. The documents available to the present researcher, however (and he has seen those cited by both authors), fail to confirm this. There seems little reason to question the address signed by Leiper which places the meeting in Philadelphia. In addition, a letter to the *Aurora* specifically stated that all the nominatory meetings, including the one of March 1, "have been held in Philadelphia." "Many" in *Aurora*, April 25, 1799.

40. *Aurora*, April 25, 1799.

41. Republican Circular of April 9, 1799, printed in *Aurora*, April 16, 1799.

42. *Gazette of the United States*, August 6, 1799.

43. Democratic Address, signed by Thomas Leiper, *Aurora*, September 3, 1810.

44. *Ibid*.

45. *Aurora*, April 16, 1799.

46. *Ibid.*, August 15, 1799.

47. John Beckley to William Irvine, August 23, 1799, Irvine Papers, XIV, 96.

48. Matthew Irwin to William Irvine, January 22, 1800, Irvine Papers, XV, 4; *Gazette of the United States,* August 7, 1799.
49. John Irwin to William Irvine, September 13, 1799, Irvine Papers, XIV, 97.
50. Matthew Irwin to William Irvine, January 22, 1800.
51. Walters, *Dallas,* 89; Peeling, 206
52. Walters *Dallas,* 89.
53. Peeling, 206.
54. *See* page 221.
55. *Gazette of the United States,* August 6, 1799.
56. *Ibid.,* September 11, 1799.
57. Peeling, 3-7.
58. Brunhouse, 35.
59. *Pennsylvania Packet,* December 3, 1787. Quoted in McMaster and Stone, *Pennsylvania and the Federal Constitution, 1787-1788.*
60. Peeling, 146.
61. Anonymous letter entitled by Duane "Pennsylvania Politics, November—1803," in the *Aurora,* August 7, 1805. The letter was written in 1803.
62. Thomas McKean to John Dickinson, June 23, 1800, McKean Papers, III, 35.
63. Federalist Circular, March 6, 1799, *Aurora,* April 11, 1799. Duane in publishing the circular, claimed that he was exposing a Federalist secret.
64. *Gazette of the United States,* March 5, 1799.
65. Broadside, May 27, 1799, Morris of Fairhill Mss., 76, HSP.
66. Federalist Circular, March 6, 1799.
67. James I. Brownson, *The Life and Times of Senator James Ross,* 1-3.
68. Certificate of Membership, in Ross-Woods Papers, WPHS.
69. Baldwin, 51.
70. *Ibid.*
71. William Findley to Israel Israel, February 25, 1801, Dreer Collection, American Statesmen, II.
72. Brownson, 19.
73. Ross Circular of May 27, 1799, *Philadelphia Gazette,* August 8, 1799.
74. *Ibid.,* August 9, 1799.
75. *Oracle of Dauphin,* October 7, 1799.
76. Ross Circular, May 27, 1799.
77. *Pennsylvania Gazette,* August 21, 1799.
78. Broadside, May 27, 1799, Morris of Fairhill Mss., 76, HSP.

79. Letter of the Philadelphia Committee of Correspondence for Ross, *Philadelphia Gazette,* September 28, 1799.
80. *An Address to the Freemen of Pennsylvania* (Pamphlet prepared by the Philadelphia Committee of Correspondence for Ross), n. d., HSP.
81. *Ibid.*
82. *Gazette of the United States,* March 5, 1799.
83. *Ibid.,* August 16, 1799.
84. *Philadelphia Gazette,* August 17, 1799.
85. *Ibid.,* August 20, 1799.
86. *Oracle of Dauphin,* August 21, 1799.
87. *Ibid.*
88. William Cobbett, *Porcupine's Works,* VII, 300, 333, as quoted in James H. Peeling, "Governor McKean and the Pennsylvania Jacobins," *PMHB,* LIV (1930), 323.
89. Letter of the Philadelphia Republican Committee, *Aurora,* August 7, 1799.
90. *Aurora,* June 29, 1799.
91. John Israel to A. Gallatin, October 5, 1799, Gallatin Papers, V.
92. *Aurora,* October 11, 1800.
93. *An Address to the Freemen of Pennsylvania.*
94. *Philadelphia Gazette,* August 20, 1799.
95. "Anti-Janus," *Gazette of the United States,* March 5, 1799.
96. *Ibid.*
97. A law to move the capital to Lancaster had been passed in the spring of 1799. *See* page 272.
98. John Beckley to William Irvine, April 26, 1799, Irvine Papers, XIV, 82.
99. A. J. Dallas to William Irvine, June 14, 1799, Irvine Papers, XIV, 88.
100. Tench Coxe to Albert Gallatin, August 2, 1799, Gallatin Papers, V.
101. John Israel to Albert Gallatin, October 5, 1799, Gallatin Papers, V.
102. William Findley, "An Autobiographical Letter," *PMHB,* V (1881), 449; Ferguson, *Western Pennsylvania Politics,* 152.
103. "A Citizen of Dauphin," *Aurora,* July 30, 1799.
104. *Ibid.*
105. Republican Committee Circular, *Aurora,* April 16, 1799; Stacy Potts to an unidentified person, August 8, 1799, Society Collection, HSP. Potts, a Quaker merchant and extensive landowner, took a practical view of the election and its possible consequences. Disagreeing with those men who thought public debts and high taxes salutary—

men he identified as Ross' supporters—he preferred instead to have "so great a stock in the State Bank & Treasury as will relieve the Citizens from the Expenses of the State Government. . . ." Large armies he conceived to be unnecessary if reliance were placed on "strict Justice" and the militia.

106. Republican Resolution at a Philadelphia County meeting, *Aurora*, August 16, 1799.
107. *Aurora*, April 30, 1799.
108. *Ibid.*, April 25, 26, 29, 1799.
109. Scattered issues of the *Aurora* throughout the summer of 1799. *See* especially, that for August 13, 1799.
110. *Ibid.*, October 8, 1799.
111. "Robert Slender," in *Aurora*, April 23, 1799.
112. *Aurora*, September 25, 1799.
113. *Ibid.*, June 28, 1799.
114. John H. Fertig, comp., *Constitutions of Pennsylvania*, 205.
115. Brownson, 7-8.
116. Broadside, August 28, 1799, HSP.
117. Thomas Cooper, *Political Essays*, 28.
118. *Aurora*, September 11, 1799; Dumas Malone, *The Public Life of Thomas Cooper*, 103.
119. Cooper, *Essays*, 27-32.
120. *Aurora*, July 24, 1799.
121. Philadelphia Committee of Correspondence for Ross; *An Address to the Freemen of Pennsylvania*.
122. Letter of the Philadelphia Republican Committee, September 25, 1799.
123. All statistics used in this summary were obtained from the *Pennsylvania House Journal, 1799-1800*, 35, 40.
124. William M. Meigs, "Pennsylvania Politics Early in This Century," *PMHB*, XVII (1893), 462.
125. *Aurora*, March 5, 1799.
126. *Ibid.*, May 20, 1799.
127. Peeling, "McKean," 210; *Aurora*, November 1, 1799. The *Aurora*, by listing Isaac Van Horne (Bucks) as a Federalist (his past voting record probably warranted such a listing at that time), recorded only forty members for the Republicans. But since Van Horne later voted with the Republicans and was subsequently chosen by them as a presidential elector in 1800, it would seem that he more properly belonged in the Republican column. John Beckley estimated the number of Republicans in the House at 42. John Beckley to William Irvine, October 25, 1799, Irvine Papers, XIV, 98.
128. *Aurora*, November 1, 1799.
129. *Pennsylvania Senate Journal, 1799-1800*, 3-4.

NOTES—CHAPTER XIII

1. *Pennsylvania Senate Journal, 1799-1800*, 35.
2. *Pennsylvania House Journal, 1799-1800*, 69.
3. *Ibid.*, 384.
4. *Ibid.*, 386.
5. Thomas McKean to Thomas Jefferson, March 7, 1800, Jefferson Papers, Vol. 106, p. 18210.
6. Governor's message to the Senate, November 19, 1800, *Pennsylvania Archives*, 4th Ser., IV, 457-458.
7. *Gazette of the United States*, October 13, 1800; *Philadelphia Gazette*, July 25, 1800.
8. *Gazette of the United States*, September 16, 1800.
9. Address issued by a Philadelphia Republican meeting of July 23, 1800, in *Aurora*, July 28, 1800.
10. Philadelphia County Republican meeting of August 9, 1800, *Aurora*, August 16, 1800.
11. *Gazette of the United States*, November 1, 1800; *Pennsylvania Senate Journal, 1800-1801*, 4-5. The Senators and the districts they represented are as follows: John Pearson (Philadelphia City and County and Delaware County), William Rodman (Chester-Bucks-Montgomery), Matthias Barton (Lancaster), William Reed (York-Adams), Christian Lower—or Laur (Berks-Dauphin), James Harris (Luzerne-Northumberland-Mifflin-Lycoming), John Hamilton (Washington-Allegheny-Greene).
12. *Gazette of the United States*, November 1, 1800; *Aurora*, November 4, 1800. In their party captions the two papers differed. The *Aurora* referred to its opponents as Federalists and Monarchists, while the *Gazette of the United States* preferred "Federal Republican" for its chosen party and "Democrat" for the opposition. Both agreed as to the partisan totals.
13. The Pennsylvania Congressmen elected and the districts they represented are as follows:
   Federalists: Joseph Hemphill (Chester-Delaware), Thomas Boude (Lancaster), Henry Woods (Bedford-Somerset-Franklin-Huntingdon).
   Republicans: William Jones (Philadelphia), Michael Leib (Philadelphia County), Peter Muhlenberg and Robert Brown (Bucks-Montgomery-Northampton-Wayne), Joseph Heister (Berks-Luzerne), John A. Hanna (Dauphin-Northumberland-Lycoming), John Stewart (York-Adams), Andrew Gregg (Cumberland-Mifflin-Centre), John Smilie (Westmoreland-Fayette), Albert Gallatin (Washington-Greene-Allegheny-Crawford).
   Pennsylvania Archives, 4th Ser., IV, 472-473; *Gazette of the United States*, November 1, 1800.

14. *Pennsylvania Archives,* 4th Ser., IV, 452-453.
15. *Aurora,* October 25, 1800.
16. *Ibid.*
17. *Ibid.,* November 1, 1800.
18. Beckley to Dallas, November 7, 1800, Dallas Papers, A. J. Dallas Box, HSP.
19. *Pennsylvania Senate Journal, 1800-1801,* 14-15.
20. *Gazette of the United States,* November 5, 1800.
21. *Aurora,* November 10, 1800.
22. McKean to Jefferson, December 15, 1800, Jefferson Papers, Vol. 108, p. 18496.
23. Governor's message to the Legislature, November 7, 1800, *Pennsylvania Archives,* 4th Ser., IV, 454-456.
24. *Pennsylvania House Journal, 1800-1801,* 20-21. On this latter vote John Hopkins, a Federalist from Lancaster, sided with the Republicans. *Aurora,* November 12, 1800.
25. *Pennsylvania Senate Journal, 1800-1801,* 20-21; *Pennsylvania House Journal, 1800-1801,* 31. The partisan division in the Senate was as follows: Federalists (in favor of a concurrent vote): Matthias Barton, Abraham Carpenter, James Ewing, Francis Gurney, Thomas Johnston, John Jones, Samuel King, Joseph McClellan, Samuel Postlethwaite, Zebulon Potts, Richard Smith, Denis Whelen, John Woods, Speaker; Republicans (in favor of a joint vote): William Findley, John Hamilton, James Harris, John Kean, Christian Lower, Samuel Maclay, Thomas Mewhorter, John Pearson, William Reed, William Rodman, Benjamin Say.
26. *Pennsylvania House Journal, 1800-1801,* 31.
27. *Ibid.,* 36.
28. *Ibid.*
29. *Gazette of the United States,* November 14, 1800.
30. Peter Frailey to A. J. Dallas, "Sunday Morning," 1800, Dallas Papers, A. J. Dallas Box.
31. *Pennsylvania House Journal, 1800-1801,* 58-70; *Pennsylvania Senate Journal, 1800-1801,* 33-42.
32. Dallas to McKean, November 28, 1800, McKean Papers, III, 41.
33. Same to same, December 1, 1800, *ibid.,* III, 42.
34. McKean to Jefferson, December 15, 1800, Jefferson Papers, Vol. 108, p. 18496.
35. *Pennsylvania Senate Journal, 1800-1801,* 56-59.
36. *Pennsylvania House Journal, 1800-1801,* 92; for election law see *Statutes at Large,* XVI, 493-495.
37. *Pennsylvania House Journal, 1800-1801,* 100-106.

38. *Aurora,* December 4, 1800; William Penrose to A. J. Dallas, n. d. [1800], Dallas Papers, A. J. Dallas Box.

39. *Pennsylvania Archives,* 4th Ser., IV, 465-466.

40. *Aurora,* December 6, 1800; Channing, IV, 234-235. Channing is of the opinion that the electoral vote "probably represented public opinion in the State." This conclusion is based in part on a mistaken belief that the Republicans had only a small majority in the House of Representatives.

41. William Penrose to A. J. Dallas, n. d. [1800], Dallas Papers, A. J. Dallas Box.

42. McKean to Jefferson, December 15, 1800. *See also* McKean Papers, III, 44, for a copy of the letter.

43. *Ibid.*

44. Jefferson to Benjamin Rush, December 14, 1800, Jefferson Papers, APS.

45. Bassett, *The Federalist System,* 290.

46. McKean to Jefferson, January 10, 1801, McKean Papers, III, 46. McKean was told that the Federalists "intended to so manage as to keep the States [the sixteen states represented by one vote each in the House] equally divided, in order that Congress may in the form of a law appoint a President for us until a new election shall take place." But it was his belief that the Federalists would not do so, and that Jefferson would receive a unanimous vote in the House.

47. Bassett, 292.

48. *Ibid.,* 293. Bassett does not make clear the identity of the person or persons who assured the Federalists that Jefferson would respect the tenure of their office holders. Senator James Ross heard the promises with considerable skepticism. He had been assured by Jefferson's "confidential" friends that their candidate would "heal divisions, remove no man from office, discountenance the turbulent, and beckon modest merit from the shade. These have been called siren songs and I feel like those who listen to the sirens, we shall first see the fields whitened with bones of the deluded and then add our own to the melancholy spectacle." His real opinion was that it would be better to have "any Constitutional legal President rather than none. Besides we have little prospect of electing a Federal man were the election to be tried again in the coming autumn . . . Pennsylvania would be unanimously against us. . . ." *See* James Ross to George Stevenson, February 19, 1801, copy in Ross-Woods Papers.

49. McKean to Jefferson, January 10, 1801, McKean Papers, III, 46.

50. Same to same, February 20, 1801, Jefferson Papers, Vol. 109, p. 18758.

51. *Ibid.*

52. McKean to Jefferson, March 19, 1801, McKean Papers, III, 50 (copy).

53. *Ibid.*

54. *Aurora,* November 16, 1801. An election law of February 27, 1801, increased the membership of the House to 86 and of the Senate to 25. Based on the number of taxable inhabitants this reapportionment provided a ratio of 86 to 1350 and 25 to 4670 for the House and Senate respectively. See *Statutes at Large,* XVI, 583-586.

55. *Gazette of the United States,* October 14, 1801; *Aurora,* October 15, 1801.

56. *Aurora,* November 16, 1801. Van Horne represented the Northampton-Bucks-Montgomery district and Hoge the district composed of the counties of Washington, Allegheny, Greene and Crawford.

57. *Gazette of the United States,* August 17, 1801.

58. *Philadelphia Gazette,* July 15, 1801.

59. *Aurora,* July 30, 1800; Luetscher, 78-79.

60. *Aurora,* May 28, July 16, 1801.

61. *Ibid.,* September 19, 1801.

62. *Ibid.,* May 15, 1801.

63. *Ibid.,* June 25, 1801.

64. *Ibid.,* June 22, August 28, 1801.

65. *Ibid.,* July 22, 1801.

66. *Ibid.,* August 5, 1801.

67. *Ibid.,* August 29, 1801. *See also* p. 207.

68. *Aurora,* August 10, 1801.

69. *Ibid.,* October 1, 1801.

70. Bioren, *Laws of Pennsylvania,* III, 412-415.

71. *Aurora,* September 3, 1804.

72. *Ibid.,* October 1, 1801.

73. *Ibid.,* October 15, 1801.

NOTES—Chapter XIV

1. *Aurora,* November 12, 1799.
2. Findley to Jefferson, received March 14, 1804, Jefferson Papers.
3. Thomas McKean to Thomas Jefferson, January 10, 1801, McKean Papers, III, 46.
4. Thomas McKean to Thomas Jefferson, July 21, 1801, Jefferson Papers, Vol. 114, p. 19677.
5. Thomas McKean to Thomas Jefferson, January 10, 1801, McKean Papers, III, 46.
6. Alexander J. Dallas, Circular Letter to Twenty-four Office Holders, December 18, 1799, Nead Papers, HSP.
7. *Gazette of the United States,* January 21, 1800.
8. Thomas McKean to Thomas Jefferson, January 10, 1801, McKean Papers, III, 46.
9. *Gazette of the United States,* January 21, 22, 1800.
10. *Ibid.,* February 20, 1800.
11. *Aurora,* February 18, 1800.
12. Thomas Jefferson to Thomas McKean, July 24, 1801, Jefferson Papers, Vol. 114, p. 19694.
13. Thomas McKean to Thomas Jefferson, August 10, 1801, Jefferson Papers, Vol. 115, p. 19809.
14. Thomas McKean to Thomas Jefferson, January 10, 1801, McKean Papers, III, 46.
15. Alexander J. Dallas to Albert Gallatin, June 14, 1801, Gallatin Papers, V.
16. William Findley to Thomas Jefferson, received March 14, 1804, Jefferson Papers.
17. *Ibid.*
18. Deborah Logan, *Memoir of Dr. George Logan,* 105.
19. William Duane to Thomas Jefferson, June 10, 1801, "Letters of William Duane," *Mass. Hist. Soc. Proceedings,* 2 Series, XX, 265.
20. Gallatin Papers, *see* Volume V.
21. William Duane to Thomas Jefferson, June 10, 1801, "Letters of William Duane," 265.
22. *Ibid.*
23. The list, a booklet, is labeled "1801, Clerks in Offices given by W. Duane," Gallatin Papers, V.
24. Thomas Jefferson to Thomas McKean, January 9, 1800, McKean Papers, III.
25. Thomas McKean to Thomas Jefferson, March 7, 1800, Jefferson Papers, Vol. 106, p. 18210.

26. Thomas Jefferson to Thomas McKean, March 9, 1801, McKean Papers, III, 49.
27. *Ibid.*
28. Thomas McKean to Thomas Jefferson, March 19, 1801, McKean Papers, III.

NOTES—Chapter XV

1. Luetscher, 12, 24-25.
2. *Pennsylvania House Journal, 1798-1799*, 391; *Pennsylvania Senate Journal, 1798-1799*, 259.
3. *Pennsylvania Archives*, 4th Ser., IV, 43.

BIBLIOGRAPHY

I

1. Manuscript Sources

American Philosophical Society
    Jefferson Papers
    Miscellaneous Manuscripts

Darlington Memorial Library, University of Pittsburgh
    Miscellaneous Manuscripts
    Nisbet Papers

Girard College, Philadelphia, Pennsylvania
    Girard, Stephen, Papers

Historical Society of Pennsylvania
    American Manuscripts
    Berks County Papers (Miscellaneous)
    Church and Meeting Collection
    Conarroe Collection
    Dallas Papers (A. J. Dallas Box)
    Dreer, Ferdinand, Collection
    Etting Collection
    Gilpin Papers
    Gratz Collection
    Hand, Edward. Papers
    Irvine, William. Papers
    Lea and Febiger Collection
    McKean, Thomas. Papers
    Nead Papers
    Norris Papers
    Parker, Daniel. Papers
    Pennsylvania Democratic Society, Minutes
    Peters Papers
    Provincial Delegates Collection
    Rawle, William. Family Papers
    Shippen Papers
    Society Collection
    Society for Political Inquiries, Minutes
    Stauffer Collection

    Wallace Papers
    Wayne, Anthony. Papers
    Wilson, James. Manuscripts
    Yeates Papers

Library Company of Philadelphia
    Dilwyn Papers
    Miscellaneous Manuscripts
    Rush, Benjamin. Manuscripts
    Smith Collection

Library of Congress
    Jefferson Papers
    Pennsylvania Collection
    Personal Papers (Miscellaneous)

New-York Historical Society
    Findley, William. Papers
    Gallatin Papers

Pennsylvania Historical and Museum Commission, Public Records Division
    Governors' Papers (Mifflin and McKean Administrations)
    Miscellaneous Papers
    Secretary of the Commonwealth, Letter Books

Western Pennsylvania Historical Society
    Miscellaneous Papers
    Ross-Woods Papers

2. Newspapers and Broadsides

American Daily Advertiser (Dunlap)
Aurora-General Advertiser
Gazette of the United States
Oracle of Dauphin and Harrisburg Advertiser
Pennsylvania Packet
Philadelphia Gazette
Pittsburgh Gazette
Porcupine's Gazette
Broadsides Collection. Historical Society of Pennsylvania

3. Official Documents

Abridgement of the Debates of Congress, 1789-1856, New York, 1858. Vols. I and II.

Abridgement of the Laws of Pennsylvania from the Year 1700 to the Second Day of April, 1811; with references to reports of judicial decisions in the Supreme Court of Pennsylvania, John Purdon, comp., Philadelphia, 1811.

Century of Population Growth from the First Census of the United States to the Twelfth, 1790-1900, Washington, 1909.

Constitutions of Pennsylvania, John H. Fertig, comp., Harrisburg, 1926.

Debates and Proceedings in the Congress of the United States, Second to Fifth Congress, Washington, 1849-1851. Generally referred to as *Annals of Congress.*

Election Laws of Pennsylvania, Digested and Arranged, with Notes and Judicial Decisions . . . to 1868, Harrisburg, 1868.

Federal and State Constitutions..., Francis N. Thorpe, comp., 7 vols., Washington, 1909.

Journal of the Pennsylvania House of Representatives, 1790-1801, Philadelphia, Lancaster, and Harrisburg, 1790-1932.

Journal of the Senate of Pennsylvania, 1790-1932, Philadelphia, Lancaster, and Harrisburg, 1790-1932.

Laws of Pennsylvania, 1700-1808, republished by M. Carey and J. Bioren, 8 vols., Philadelphia, 1803-1808.

Laws of Pennsylvania, 1781-1790, Alexander James Dallas, comp., 2 vols., Philadelphia, 1790.

Pennsylvania Archives, 2d Ser., vols. IV and VI, Harrisburg, 1876 and 1877; 4th Ser., vol. IV, Papers of the Governors, 1785-1817, Harrisburg, 1900; 9th Ser., 10 vols., Harrisburg, 1931. This last series is known as "Minutes of the Executive Department."

Proceedings Relative to Calling the Conventions of 1776 and 1790; Minutes of the Convention that Formed the Present Constitution of Pennsylvania, Harrisburg, 1825.

State Trials of the United States during the Administrations of Washington and Adams with References, Historical and Professional, and Preliminary Notes on the Politics of the Times, Francis Wharton, comp., Philadelphia, 1849.

Statutes at Large of Pennsylvania, 1682 to 1801, James T. Mitchell and Henry Flanders, comps., Harrisburg, 1908.

4. Contemporary Writings

a. General Collections

Ames, Fisher, *The Works of Fisher Ames,* edited by Seth Ames, 2 vols., Boston, 1854.

Cobbett, William, *Letters from William Cobbett to Edward Thornton, written in the years 1797 to 1800,* edited by G. D. Cole, New York and London, 1937.

———, *Porcupine's Works,* 12 vols., London, 1801.

———, *Selections from the Political Works of William Cobbett; being a complete abridgement of the 100 volumes which comprise the writings of "Porcupine" and the "Weekly Political Register,"* edited by J. M. Cobbett and J. P. Cobbett, 6 vols., London, 1835.

Duane, William, "Letters of William Duane," in *Proceedings of the Massachusetts Historical Society,* ser. 2, XX (Boston, 1907), 257-394.

Hamilton, Alexander, *The Works of Alexander Hamilton,* edited by John C. Hamilton, 7 vols., New York, 1851.

Jefferson, Thomas, *The Works of Thomas Jefferson,* edited by Paul Leicester Ford, 12 vols., New York, 1904-1905. Known as the Federal Edition.

———, *The Writings of Thomas Jefferson, 1760-1826,* edited by Paul Leicester Ford, 10 vols., New York, 1892-1899.

Logan, Deborah Norris, *Memoir of Dr. George Logan of Stenton,* edited by Frances A. Logan, Philadelphia, 1899.

Washington, George, *The Writings of George Washington,* edited by Worthington C. Ford, 14 vols., New York, 1889-1893.

———, *Washington—Irvine Correspondence,* edited by C. W. Butterfield, Madison, 1882.

b. Individual Works

Biddle, Charles, *Autobiography of Charles Biddle, Vice-President of the Supreme Executive Council of Pennsylvania, 1745-1821,* edited by James S. Biddle, Philadelphia, 1883.

Brackenridge, Hugh H., *Incidents of the Insurrection in the Western Parts of Pennsylvania in the Year 1794,* Philadelphia, 1795.

Cobbett, William, *History of the American Jacobins*, Philadelphia, 1796. Reprinted as an appendix to William Playfair's *History of Jacobinism*.

———, "A Bone to Gnaw for the Democrats," 1795. A pamphlet published in *Select Pamphlets*, printed by Mathew Carey, Philadelphia, 1796.

Cooper, Thomas, *Consolidation, an Account of Parties in the United States from the Convention of 1787 to the present Period*, Columbia, S. C., 1824.

———, *Political Essays, Originally Inserted in the Northumberland Gazette*, Northumberland, 1799. In a preface to the little volume Cooper noted that many of the essays were written while he was editor of *The Sunbury & Northumberland Gazette*. Others had been added when he wrote the preface; the additions were marked with asterisks. The essays considered in the discussion of the election of 1799 were originally published in the *Northumberland Gazette*. However, since Cooper's preface was written at Northumberland on July 10, 1799, all the articles in that volume could have affected McKean's election. Cooper started to edit the *Gazette* in April, 1799. He continued to the first week in July of that year.

———, *Political Essays*, 2d edition, Philadelphia, 1800. Of this edition, Cooper wrote, "I have omitted some and substituted others in their room."

Findley, William, *History of the Insurrection in the Four Western Counties of Pennsylvania*, Philadelphia, 1796.

———, "An Autobiographical Letter," in the *Pennsylvania Magazine of History and Biography*, V (1881), 440-450. This letter was written on February 27, 1812.

Graydon, Alexander, *Memoirs of a Life Chiefly Passed in Pennsylvania*, Harrisburg, 1811.

Maclay, William, *The Journal of William Maclay*, edited by Edgar S. Maclay, New York, 1927. An intimate account of the First Congress by Senator Maclay. He is bitter, discerning, and deplores the Federalist trends.

Rawle, William, "Sketch of the Life of Thomas Mifflin," in *The Memoirs of The Historical Society of Pennsylvania*, vol. II, part 2, Philadelphia, 1827.

Roberts, Jonathan, "Memoirs of a Senator from Pennsylvania: Jonathan Roberts, 1771-1854," edited by Philip S. Klein, in the *Pennsylvania Magazine of History and Biography*, LXI and LXII (1937-1938). The material useful for this period appears in LXII, 64-97.

II

Secondary Sources

Adams, Henry, *History of the United States of America*, 1801-1817, 9 vols., New York, 1890-1891.

————, *The Life of Albert Gallatin*, Philadelphia, 1879.

————, *Writings of Albert Gallatin*, Philadelphia, 1879.

Agnew, Daniel, *A History of the Region of Pennsylvania North of the Ohio and West of the Allegheny River*, Philadelphia, 1887.

Allison, E. P., and Penrose, Boies, *Philadelphia, 1681-1887: a History of Municipal Government*, Baltimore, 1887.

Alton, James, "French Diplomacy and American Politics, 1794-1795" in *Annual Report of the American Historical Association for the Year 1911*, Washington, 1913, vol. I, pp. 151-163.

Anderson, Frank Maloy, "The Enforcement of the Alien and Sedition Acts," in *Annual Report of the American Historical Association for the Year 1912*, Washington, 1914, pp. 115-126.

Baldwin, Leland D., *Whiskey Rebels*, Pittsburgh, 1939.

Barton, William, *Memoirs of David Rittenhouse*, Philadelphia, 1913.

Bassett, J. S., *The Federalist System, 1789-1801*, vol. XI of *The American Nation*, New York, 1906.

Beard, Charles A., *Economic Origins of Jeffersonian Democracy*, New York, 1927.

Bemis, Samuel F., *Jay's Treaty, A Study in Commerce and Diplomacy*, New York, 1924.

Blake, E. Vale, *History of the Tammany Society from Its Organization to the Present Time*, New York, 1901.

Bridenbaugh, Carl and Jessica, *Rebels and Gentlemen: Philadelphia in the Age of Franklin*, New York, 1942.

Brownson, James I., *The Life and Times of Senator James Ross*, Washington, Pennsylvania, 1910. Some useful material on Ross' career in the United States Senate, 1799-1803.

Brunhouse, Robert L., *The Counter-Revolution in Pennsylvania, 1776-1790*, Harrisburg, 1942.

Buck, Solon J. and Elizabeth H., *The Planting of Civilization in Western Pennsylvania*, Pittsburgh, 1939.

Channing, Edward, *A History of the United States*, Vol. IV, New York, 1917.

Clark, Mary Elizabeth, *Peter Porcupine in America: The Career of William Cobbett, 1792-1800*, Philadelphia, 1939.

Dallas, G. M., *Life and Writings of Alexander James Dallas*, Philadelphia, 1871.

Davis, W. W. H., *The Fries Rebellion: 1798-1799*, Doylestown, 1899.

Dictionary of American Biography, edited by Allan Johnson and Dumas Malone, 21 vols., New York, 1928-1936.

Doll, Eugene E., "American History as Interpreted by German Historians, 1770-1815," *Transactions of the American Philosophical Society*, XXXVIII, pt. 5, June, 1949.

Dorpalen, Andreas, "The German Element in Early Pennsylvania Politics, 1789-1800," in *Pennsylvania History*, IX (1942), 176-190.

Dunaway, W. F., *A History of Pennsylvania*, New York, 1935.

————, "Pennsylvania as a Distributing Center of Population," in the *Pennsylvania Magazine of History and Biography*, LV (1931), 134-169.

Eastman, Frank M., *The Fries Rebellion*, New York, 1922.

Egle, William H., *Historical Register: Notes and Queries, Historical and Genealogical, Relating to Interior Pennsylvania*, 2 vols., Harrisburg, 1883-1884.

————, editor, *Notes and Queries, Historical and Genealogical*, Harrisburg, 1894-1900. There are 15 volumes with this title in the Library of Congress. They are compilations of articles, some of which appeared in newspapers. All unsigned items are written by Egle.

Evans, Paul D., *The Holland Land Company*, Buffalo, 1924.

Faÿ, Bernard, "Early Party Machinery in the United States: Pennsylvania in the Election of 1796," in *Pennsylvania Magazine of History and Biography*, LX (1936), 375-390.

————, *The Two Franklins*, Boston, 1933.

Ferguson, Russell J., "Albert Gallatin, Western Pennsylvania Politician," in *Western Pennsylvania Historical Magazine*, XVI (1933), 183-195.

————, *Early Western Pennsylvania Politics,* Pittsburgh, 1938.

Field, Alston, "The Press in Western Pennsylvania to 1812," in *Western Pennsylvania Historical Magazine,* XX (1937), 231-264.

Flanders, Henry, "Thomas Fitzsimons," in *Pennsylvania Magazine of History and Biography,* II (1878), 306-314.

Ford, Edward, *David Rittenhouse, Astronomer, Patriot, 1732-1796,* Philadelphia, 1946.

Ford, Paul L., *The Origin, Purpose and Result of the Harrisburg Convention of 1788,* Brooklyn, 1890.

Forman, Samuel E., *Political Activities of Philip Freneau,* Johns Hopkins University Studies in Historical and Political Science, ser. 20, nos. 9-10, Baltimore, 1902.

Goodman, Nathan, *Benjamin Rush,* Philadelphia, 1934.

Greene, Francis Vinton, *Revolutionary War and the Military Policy of the United States,* New York, 1911.

Harmon, George Dewey, *Sixty Years of Indian Affairs, Political, Economic and Diplomatic,* 1789-1850, Chapel Hill, 1941.

Henderson, Elizabeth K., "Some Aspects of Sectionalism in Pennsylvania, 1790-1812" (Unpublished doctoral dissertation, Bryn Mawr, 1935).

————, "The North-Western Lands of Pennsylvania, 1790-1812, *Pennsylvania Magazine of History and Biography,* LX (1936), 131-160.

Higginbotham, Sanford W., "Frontier Democracy in the Early Constitutions of Tennessee and Kentucky, 1772-1799" (Unpublished thesis, Louisiana State University, 1941).

Hutcheson, Harold, *Tench Coxe: A Study in American Economic Development,* Baltimore, 1938.

Jenkins, H. M., *Pennsylvania, Colonial and Federal, 1608-1903,* 3 vols., Philadelphia, 1903.

Knollenberg, Bernard, *Washington and the Revolution,* New York, 1940.

Konkle, Burton Alva, *Life and Times of Thomas Smith, 1745-1809,* Philadelphia, 1904.

Krout, John A. and Fox, Dixon Ryan, *The Completion of Independence, 1790-1830,* volume V of *A History of American Life,* New York, 1944.

Leary, Lewis, *That Rascal Freneau: A Study in Literary Failure*, New Brunswick, 1941.

Link, Eugene Perry, *Democratic-Republican Societies, 1790-1800*, New York, 1942.

Luetscher, George D., *Early Political Machinery in the United States*, Philadelphia, 1903.

Lynch, W. O., *Fifty Years of Party Warfare, 1789-1837*, Indianapolis, 1931.

McMaster, John Bach, *A History of the People of the United States*, New York, 1887. Volume II only.

———, and Stone, Frederick D., editors, *Pennsylvania and the Federal Constitution, 1787-1788*, Lancaster, 1888.

Malone, Dumas, *The Public Life of Thomas Cooper, 1783-1839*, New Haven, 1926.

Marsh, Philip M., "Philip Freneau and His Circle," *Pennsylvania Magazine of History and Biography*, LXIII (1939), 36-59.

Meigs, William M., "Pennsylvania Politics Early in this Century," *Pennsylvania Magazine of History and Biography*, XVII (1893), 462-490.

Miller, William, "The Democratic Societies and the Whiskey Insurrection," *Pennsylvania Magazine of History and Biography*, LXII (1938), 325-349.

———, "First Fruits of Republican Organization: Political Aspects of the Congressional Election of 1794," *Pennsylvania Magazine of History and Biography*, LXIII (1939), 118-143.

Muhlenberg, H. A., *The Life of Major-General Peter Muhlenberg*, Philadelphia, 1849.

Nevins, Allan, *The American States During and After the Revolution*, New York, 1924.

Newlin, C. M., *Life and Writings of Hugh Henry Brackenridge*, Princeton, 1932.

Oberholtzer, E. P., *Philadelphia, a History of the City and Its People, a Record of 225 Years*, 4 vols., Philadelphia, 1911.

———, *Robert Morris, Patriot and Financier*, New York, 1903.

Ostrogorski, M., "The Rise and Fall of the Nominating Caucus, Legislative and Congressional," *American Historical Review*, V (1899), 199-283.

Peeling, James H., "Governor McKean and the Pennsylvania Jacobins, 1799-1808," *Pennsylvania Magazine of History and Biography*, LIV (1930), 320-354.

————————, "The Public Life of Thomas McKean, 1734-1817" (Unpublished doctoral dissertation, University of Chicago, 1929).

Rich, Bennett M., "Washington and the Whiskey Insurrection," *Pennsylvania Magazine of History and Biography*, LXV (1941), 334-352.

Richards, Henry Melchoir Muhlenberg, *Governor Joseph Hiester*, Lancaster, 1907.

Rossman, Kenneth, "Thomas Mifflin, The Revolutionary Patriot from Pennsylvania," (Unpublished doctoral dissertation, University of Iowa, 1940).

Schramm, Callista, "William Findley in Pennsylvania Politics," *Western Pennsylvania Historical Magazine*, XX (1937), 31-40.

Selsam, J. Paul, *The Pennsylvania Constitution of 1776*, Philadelphia, 1936.

Smith, W. H., editor, *Life and Public Services of Arthur St. Clair*, 2 vols., Cincinnati, 1882. The author has as a general heading of his book *The St. Clair Papers*. Over half of the first and all of the second volume are devoted to letters and documents.

Society for Political Inquiries, "Report of the Committee appointed to examine the Minute Book of the Society for Political Inquiries," in *Memoirs of the Historical Society of Pennsylvania*, Philadelphia, 1827, II, pt. 2, pp. 45-51.

Thomas, E. Bruce, *Political Tendencies in Pennsylvania, 1783-1794*, Philadelphia, 1938.

Veech, James, *The Monongahela of Old; or, Historical Sketches of Southwestern Pennsylvania to the Year 1800*, Pittsburgh, 1892.

Walters, Raymond, Jr., *Alexander James Dallas . . .*, Philadelphia, 1943.

Wold, Ansel, compiler, *Biographical Directory of the American Congress, 1774-1927*, Washington, 1928.

Woodbury, Margaret, *Public Opinion in Philadelphia, 1789-1801*, *Smith College Studies in History*, volume V, nos. 1 and 2, Northampton, Mass., 1920.

INDEX

Acheson, David, 200, 206.

Adams, John, 272; appoints commission to France, 1797, 181; commended by Pennsylvania Assembly, 207; and election of 1800, 261-255, *passim;* electoral votes, 1796, 172, 173-174; on Genêt, 77; on his administration, 315; issues proclamation against tax rioters, 1799, 216; McKean on appointments of, 268; William Maclay's opinion of, 28; pardons Fries, 219; Presidential candidate, 1796, 162, 165.

Addison, Alexander: on David Bradford, 108; in Constitutional Convention of 1790, 13; and Senatorial election, 1793, 148, 150; supports Woods for Congress, 1798, 185-186.

"Address to the Republicans of Northumberland County," 192-193.

Ainsworth, Samuel, 206.

Alien and Sedition Acts, 215; Assembly approves, 208; influence party growth, 212-213; vote of the Pennsylvania Representatives on, 182-183.

Aliens, definition of, 1797, 204.

Allegheny County, 299; in election of 1790, 40; Federalists in, 1792, 54; Whiskey riots in, 289.

Allegiance, oath of, required of Assemblymen, 3, 6.

American Daily Advertiser, 191.

American Revolution, Pennsylvania groups supporting, 2.

Ames, Fisher: on French influence, 306; on Presidential election, 1796, 306; on Quakers, 173.

Anatomical Hall, Philadelphia, Republican meeting at, 61.

Anti-Constitutionalists, 4; and Constitutional Convention of 1790, 7-17; and Council of Censors, 1784, 5-6.

Anti-Federalists: Congressional ticket, 1788, 23, 24; Thomas Cooper explains, 236; definition of, 31; as party label, 1796, 162; and United States Constitution, 22-23. *See also* Republicans.

Anti-Treaty Party: ticket, in election, 1795, 142-144; in Philadelphia County, 300, 312; supports Virginia Resolutions, 200.

Aristocracy, Republican fears of, 165-166, 172.

Armstrong, James, 107; and election of 1792, 65, 66.

Armstrong, John, 25.

Arndt, John, 5, 264.

Ash, James, 257.

Assembly of Pennsylvania: address to George Washington, 203-204; apportionment of representation, 2, 5-6; approves Alien and Sedition Acts, 208; authorizes militia call, 103; authorizes Presque Isle suspension, 131; branches of, 13; concurrent *vs* joint election, 1791-1792, 146-149; in 1800, 247-252; denounces tax rioters, 1799, 216-217; election of members to, 1795, 142-143; 1797, 175-180; 1798, 180; 1800, 245-247; 1801, 256-261; elects United States Senators, 1791-1795, 145-153; expels western members, 1795, 109-111; growth of political parties in, 1795-1798, 199-213; McKean's address to, 1800, 249; membership, 272; Mifflin addresses, 1796, 202; Mifflin reports on excise disturbances, 93-94; opposes Kentucky Resolutions, 208-209; opposes Virginia Resolutions, 199-200, 209; and Presidential election, 1800, 243-253; reception of United States Constitution in, 22; repeals excise law, 91; reply to Governor's address, 1796, 1797, 202-203, 205-206; Republicans in, 1799, 240; Senators elected to, 1800, 321; special session of, 1794, 124, 130, 131; 1800, 247-252; votes complimentary address to Adams, 207.

Assumption, Pennsylvania Congressmen and, 27-28.

[339]

Aurora: announces Washington's decision on third term, 165; champions Israel, 1798, 179; on delayed election returns, 1796, 171-172; Duane editor of, 190; on Federalist nomination of Mifflin, 1798, 188; on Jay's Treaty, 89-90; lists party members in Assembly, 319; makes political capital of tax riots, 217-218; opposes Washington administration, 143; party labels used in, 1796, 161-162; 1797, 175; 1800, 321; political propaganda in, 136-137; presents campaign issues, 1799, 234; in presidential election, 1796, 165-166, 172-173; publication suspended, 1796, 299; 1798, 190, 199; publicizes Genêt, 77; on selection of Presidential electors, 1800, 250; title first used, 285. *See also General Advertiser.*

Bache, Benjamin F., 108, 191; criticizes Presque Isle suspension, 128-129; on delayed election returns, 1796, 171-172, 306; on election of 1797, 175-176, 177, 179; on election tickets, 141; estimates of, 189-190, 191; and Genêt, 77; on Jay's Treaty, 89; member of Pennsylvania Democratic Society, 84; member of Society for Political Inquiries, 81; opposes expulsion of westerners from Assembly, 110-111; on Presidential candidates, 1796, 165; prints "Address to the Republicans of Northumberland County," 193; publishes letters critical of Mifflin, 136-137; supports Frederick A. Muhlenberg for Congress, 137, 140; supports Republicans, 1796, 165-166, 172-173; twits John Fenno, 300; uses Jay's Treaty as election issue, 143; uses party labels, 1796, 161-162; 1797, 175.
Bache, Margaret (Mrs. B. F.), 190.
Baker, Hilary, and election of 1792, 57, 58.
Baltimore Republican Society, 107.
Bank of North America, 7.
Bank of Pennsylvania: directors elected, 1796, 201; 1799, 210, 211; in party politics, 1799, 208.
Barclay, John, 283; and election of 1792, 57, 58, 61, 62, 66.
Barclay, Thomas, 167.
Bard, David, 142, 313; elected to Congress, 1796, 159; favors tax laws, 1798, 215; favors treaty with France, 183; opposes Alien and Sedition Acts, 182, 183.
Barton, Matthias, 178, 247, 321.
Barton, William, 231.
Beard, Charles, opinion of William Maclay, 26.
Beckley, John; advice to Irvine, 1799, 223; favors Lancaster as State capital, 270; on Fries, 315; opinion of Dallas, 168; in Presidential campaign, 1796, 166-168, 174; receives political office, 268; on Republicans in General Assembly, 319; and selection of Presidential electors, 1800, 248.
Bedford County, 6.
Berks County, Republicans in, 238.
Bickham, George, 201, 211.
Biddle, Charles, 141, 167; Director of Bank of Pennsylvania, 201, 211; and Genêt, 76, 77; and gubernatorial election of 1790, 38, 41; hostility toward Mifflin, 41-42; opinion of James Hutchinson, 53; and Pennsylvania Democratic Society, 84.
Big Tree, 114.
Bingham, William, 38, 46, 146, 250; elected to United States Senate, 1795, 142, 152, 302; and election of 1792, 65; on political parties, 30; residence attacked, 89; sketch of, 34; United States Senatorial candidate, 145, 149.
Boileau, Nathaniel, 208, 238; opposes Alien and Sedition Acts, 209; on suffrage qualifications, 1799, 210.
Bourne, Benjamin, 107.
Bower Hill, burned, 95, 96, 112.
Bowman, Ebenezer, 61.
Boyd, James, 51, 304; Presidential elector, 1796, 168.
Boyd's Tavern, Philadelphia, 282.

INDEX 341

Brackenridge, Hugh Henry, 148, 228; in Congressional election, 1798, 185-186; on excise disturbance, 96; on excise law, 91; on Mingo Creek Society, 108; on origin of Democratic Societies, 292; and *Pittsburgh Gazette,* 309; on use of militia in excise riots, 103, 104.
Braddock's Field, anti-excise meeting at, 95, 108.
Bradford, David, 301; opposes excise law, 92, 95, 108; not pardoned for excise violations, 108.
Bradford, William, Commissioner on excise riots, 100.
Breckenridge, John, 208.
Brison, James, 289.
British, activities of, and Presque Isle, 116, 117, 119, 123, 127, 128, 129, 131-132.
Brown, Andrew, 176, 303.
Brown, Robert, 216, 301; elected to Congress, 1798, 189.
Bryan, George, 4, 8, 11, 226; Council of Censors ascribed to, 275; delegate to Harrisburg Convention, 22; and gubernatorial election of 1790, 35-36.
Bryan, Samuel: and gubernatorial election of 1790, 35-36, 40; member of Pennsylvania Democratic Society, 84; seeks appointment as Secretary of the Commonwealth, 1790, 42-43.
Bucks County: in election of 1790, 40; representation in Assembly, 2; Republican nomination procedures in, 1801, 259-260; and Whiskey Insurrection, 102.
Buffalo Creek, Indian council at, 122.
Burr, Aaron, 172, 253-256, *passim.*
Butler, Richard, 114.

Canandaigua, conference at, 123, 125, 132, 133.
Cannon, James, Council of Censors ascribed to, 275.
Canon, John, opposes excise law, 95.
Capital, United States, location of, 28-29.
Carlisle, militia assembles at, 104-105.
Caucuses, 1796, 164; Federalist, nominates Ross for Governor, 228, 229; Republican, nominations, 1799, 221-222, 223.
Channing, Edward, on Presidential election, 1796, 172.
Chapin, Israel: at Indian council, 122; reports on Indian unrest, 116.
Chapman, John, 215, 216; elected to Congress, 1796, 160; supports Alien and Sedition Acts, 182.
Charlestown, S. C., Genêt's reception in, 76.
Chase, Samuel, presides at Fries' trial, 219.
Chester County: in election of 1790, 40; nomination meeting in, 257, 258; representation in Assembly, 2; and Whiskey Insurrection, 102.
"City Treaty Ticket," 300.
Clarkson, Matthew, 55.
Claypoole, Septimus, death of, 311.
Clunn, Joseph, 259.
Clymer, George, 4, 25, 289; and assumption, 28; elected to Congress, 1788, 24; on excise disturbances, 93; favors excise law, 91; favors protective tariff, 27; and gubernatorial election of 1790, 33.
Coats, Lindsay, 301.
Coats, William: and election of 1792, 62; member of Pennsylvania Democratic Society, 84.
Cobbett, William: influence on public opinion, 144; on Israel's election to Senate, 1797, 177; supports Jay's Treaty, 153-144; uses party labels, 1797, 176.

INDEX

Coleman, Robert, 254; nominated Presidential elector, 1800, 252; Presidential elector, 1796, 170, 172; Senatorial candidate, 151.
Committee of Commerce and Manufactures, 85.
Committee of Conference, and election of 1792, 55-56, 57-59, 60, 64-65, 67.
Committee of Correspondence, and election of 1792, 57-68 *passim*.
Conferees. *See* Committee of Conference.
Congress, United States: debates issue of Democratic Societies, 107; influence on Pennsylvania Assembly, 270; Pennsylvanians in, 27-29, 47-48, 321.
Congressmen, Pennsylvania, 1796, party affiliations of, 308; party votes of, 1801, 311.
Conrad, Frederick, 238.
Conservatism, in Senatorial elections, 1788-1795, 152-153.
Constitution of 1776: opposition to, 4; as party coalescent, 269; provisions of, 3-4.
Constitution of 1790, 1-17; character of, 153; influence of, 17.
Constitution, United States: opposition to, 7; ratification of, 22.
Constitutionalists, 4; in Constitutional Convenion of 1790, 10-11; and Council of Censors, 1785, 6; opposition to United States Constitution, 7; Senatorial candidates, 1788, 25; support American Revolution, 6.
Coolbaugh, John, 238.
Cooper, Thomas, 271; *Political Essays* of, 235-237; receives political office, 268.
Cornplanter, 114, 133.
Correspondents. *See* Committee of Correspondence.
Council of Censors, 3, 5-6.
Counties, election committees in, 1792, 55; Federalists organize, 1799, 229; organization of, western Pennsylvania, 20.
Courts, Federal, and excise adjudication, 93, 94, 95, 100-101.
Coxe, Tench: and assumption, 28; Maclay's opinion of, 312; party allegiance of, 196-197; Republican committeeman, 1799, 222, 224, 235.
Craig, Isaac, 55.
Crime: decrease of, 20; in Philadelphia, 48.
Cunningham, John, 109, 201.

Dallas, Alexander James, 89, 108, 257, 268, 271, 310; acts against excise rioters, 96; appointed Secretary of the Commonwealth, 1790, 43-44; attacked in press, 136-137; attends conference on excise disturbances, 97; Samuel Bryan's opinion of, 43; consults Jared Ingersoll on Presque Isle suspension, 124; defends Israel's election, 1797, 177-178; and delayed election returns, 1796, 170; and Democratic Societies, 82, 84; dominates Republican caucus, 1799, 223; and election of 1792, 53, 54, 55-56, 57, 61, 62, 65, 68; on evils of political parties, 178, 193-195; and Genêt, 76, 78-79, 138; and governorship of Pennsylvania, 1799, 220; and McKean's election, 232, 233; on militia law, 291; opposes use of militia against excise rioters, 103; political activity of, 194; on Presidential election, 1800, 251-252; Republican committeeman, 1799, 222, 224, 235; sketch of, 43; takes no part in election of 1796, 168; on use of patronage powers, 265-266; withdraws as Fries' attorney, 219.
Dauphin County, and Whiskey Insurrection, 102.
Deism, Ross charged with, 234-235.
Democrat, 236.
"Democratic-Republican," defined, 176.
"Democratic-Republican Ticket," 1797, 312.
Democratic-Republicans. *See* Republicans.
Democratic Societies, 81-87; H. W. Brackenridge on origins of, 292; and growth of political parties, 152-153; influence on Pennsylvania politics, 270; number of, 286; and Whiskey Insurrection, 107-109.

Democratic Society, Canaan, New York, 107.
Democratic Society, of Washington, N. C., 107.
Democratic Society, Washington, Pennsylvania, 86, 108.
Denny, Ebenezer, commands militia for Presque Isle, 115-116, 122, 128.
Duane, William, 250, 257, 271; attack on, 1799, 218; edits *Aurora,* 189-190; and McKean's election, 232, 233, 235, 239; opinion of, 311; and patronage problem, 266-267; on Republican victory, 1801, 260-261; sketch of, 190; supports P. Muhlenberg for Governor, 1799, 223.
Dunwoody's Tavern, Philadelphia, 178, 230, 248.
Du Ponceau, Peter Stephen, 76, 108.

Edgar, James, 172.
Edie, John, 301.
Ege, George: elected to Congress, 1796, 160; resigns Congressional seat, 308.
Election districts, 1794, 138-139; manipulation of, 1800, 244-245.
Election laws: 1788, 23; 1791, 45-47; 1792, 51; 1794, 138-139; 1796, 163-164, 168-169, 201; 1797, 203-204, 205, 210, 1799, 210; 1801, 324.
Election returns, delayed, 1796, 168-171, 305.
Elections: apathy toward, 1793, 137-138; issues in, 1799, 233-234; significance of, 1799, 239-240; special Senatorial, 1798, 178-179.
Elections, Assembly: 1797, 175-180; 1798, 180; 1800, 245; 1801, 256-261.
Elections, Congressional: 1788, 23-25; 1791, 45-48; 1792, 51-68; 1794, 109, 138-142; 1796, 159-162; 1798, 180-182, 184-189; 1800, 247.
Elections, district *vs* general, 138-139, 154, 163-164, 243-244.
Elections, presidential: 1792, 170; 1796, 170-171, 172-174, 179, 270-271; 1800, 243-256.
Electors, Presidential, in 1792, 66; 1796, 164, 304; 1800, 243-252.
Ellicott, Andrew, 133; advocates fort at Presque Isle, 128; commissioned to survey Presque Isle, 115, 116, 128.
Epple's tavern, Philadelphia, 58.
Erie. *See* Presque Isle.
Erie Triangle, 114, 118, 123, 273.
Evans, Cadwalader, 45, 109, 139, 203-204.
Ewalt, Samuel, 212.
Ewing, James, elected to State Senate, 241.
Executive Council, 3, 6.
Excise laws: and election of 1792, 63, 67; 1793, 142; opposition to Federal, 91-112; Pennsylvania's repealed, 91.
Excise taxes: H. H. Brackenridge on Pennsylvania's dislike of, 289; influence on Pennsylvania politics, 270.
Eyre, Manuel, 200, 300.

Fauchet, Minister, 87.
Fayette County, 6, 10; in election of 1790, 40; election returns delayed, 1796, 168-171.
Febiger, Christian, 202.
"Federal Republican," defined, 176.
Federalism, in Pennsylvania, 272.
Federalist, as party label, 1796, 161-162.
Federalist campaign committee, 1799, 228, 229-230, 239.

Federalists: accused of manipulating election districts, 1800, 244-245; in Allegheny County, 1792, 54-55; in Assembly, 1795, 109; 1797, 175-180; 1798, 206; 1799, 240; attack McKean's partisan appointments, 264; attack Republican committeemen, 224; bring pressure on State Senate, 1800, 248-249; causes of defeat, 271-272; defeated, 1800, 246-247; definition of, 31, 52, 53; described by Thomas Cooper, 236; elected to Congress, 1788, 24; 1792, 66; 1794, 142; 1796, 160; 1798, 189; 1800, 321; and election of assemblymen, 1795, 142; election propaganda, 1799, 230-232; 1800, 245-246; exploit Whiskey Insurrection, 111; factors favoring rise of, 269-270; favor district elections, 1800, 243-244; ideology of, 71-73, 154; in legislative election, 1801, 256-261; legislative program of, 1798, 182-183; lethargy of, 257; nominate Mifflin for Congress. 1798, 187-188; opinion of Democratic Societies, 82, 84, 86, 87, 106; oppose Gallatin for Congress, 1798, 185; oppose Israel for State Senate, 1798, 178-179; oppose Virginia Resolutions, 200; organize Philadelphia wards, 260; in Philadelphia, 1792, 55-59; in Presidential election, 1796, 164, 171, 173, 304; 1800, 243-253; scornful of Logan's "embassy," 184; and Senatorial elections, 25, 149, 152; support Adam's administration, 207, 209; and tax rioters, 1799, 217; victory of, 1788, 24; in Western Pennsylvania, 1798, 184-187.

Fell, Jesse, 61.

Fenno, John, 300; death of, 189, 190; reports election results, 1796, 169, 171; supports Jay's Treaty, 143; uses party labels, 1796, 161-162.

Fenno, John Ward, 191; gloomy prophecy of, 240; publishes attack on McKean, 222.

Ferguson, Russell J., quoted, 15.

Findley, William, 4, 8, 42, 107, 112, 142, 263, 271, 313; in Constitutional Convention of 1790, 8, 9, 11-14; and constituents, 50; criticizes Mifflin's appointments, 266; elected to Congress, 1791, 47, 48; 1796, 159, 161; and election of 1792, 53, 54, 60, 61, 63, 65; 1793, 145, 150, 151; on excise disturbances, 93, 103, 104, 105; favors district elections, 45; on McKean's use of patronage, 266; on P. Muhlenberg and the governorship, 1799, 221, 223; nominated for State Senator, 1799, 232-233, 240; opposes expulsion of westerners from Assembly, 111; opposes provincial army, 183; and Presidential election of 1800, 252; James Ross on, 184-185; on James Ross, 229; supports Gallatin, 1798, 186; supports Mifflin for Governor, 1790, 39-40.

Fisher, Samuel, director, Bank of Pennsylvania, 211.

Fitzsimons, Thomas, 5, 248, 289, 299; and assumption, 28; Congressional candidate, 1794, 141; and Constitutional Convention of 1790, 11; elected to Congress, 1788, 24; 1791, 47; and election of 1792, 65, 66; and gubernatorial election of 1790, 33, 34, 35, 36, 39, 41; favors excise law, 91; member of Society for Political Inquiries, 81; opposes Democratic Societies, 107; on political parties, 30; and protective tariff, 27; Senatorial nominee, 1795, 152.

Forrest, Thomas, 196.

Forts, British, in northwest, 117-118.

Forts, United States, in Presque Isle area, 128.

Frailey, Peter, 238; and Kentucky Resolutions, 209; and selection of Presidential electors, 1800, 250-251.

France, trade with, 88.

Franchise. *See* Suffrage.

Franco-American relations, Assembly's view of, 202-203, 205-206; influence party growth, 212-213; influence on Senatorial election, 1793, 150-151.

Franklin, Benjamin, 4, 25; President of Society for Political Inquiries, 81.

French Revolution, Pennsylvania's reaction to, 75, 80, 87, 270.

Freneau, Philip, 191; and Jefferson, 189; supports Republicans, 166, 172-173.

Fries, John, 216, 217, 218; convicted of treason, 315.

Fries' Rebellion 215-219.

Fur trade, in northwest Pennsylvania, 114, 118.

INDEX 345

Gallatin, Albert, 42, 112, 142, 166, 257, 266, 271, 301, 313; in Constitutional Convention of 1790, 8, 9, 10, 13-14, 15; delegate to Harrisburg Convention, 22; denied seat in United States Senate, 151; elected to Congress, 1796, 159, 161; 1798, 185-187, 189; elected to United States Senate, 145, 148, 149-150; and election of 1792, 53, 54, 62, 63, 64, 66; favors tax laws, 1798, 215; favors treaty with France, 183; and McKean's election, 232; opinion of Genêt, 79; opposes Alien and Sedition Acts, 182, 183; opposes concurrent election of United States Senators, 147; opposes excise law, 92; opposes expulsion of westerners from Assembly, 109-110; sketch of, 149-150; support Mifflin for Governor, 1790, 40; and survey of Presque Isle, 116.
Gates, Horatio, 38.
Gazette of the United States, in Congressional election, 1794, 141, 142; election propaganda in, 1800, 246; 1801, 257; under Fenno's editorship, 190-191; on Logan's "embassy," 308; on McKean's use of patronage, 264; on Samuel Miles, 197; use of party labels, 305, 321; reports election results, 1796, 169, 171; 1798, 191; on selection of Presidential electors, 1800, 250.
Gehr, Baltzer, 238.
General Advertiser. See Aurora.
Genêt, Edmond, and Democratic Societies, 82; ministerial appointment of, 75; and Pennsylvania politics, 270; recalled, 79; reception in Philadelphia, 76-78.
Genêt affair, 75-81; and growth of political parties, 137-138, 152-153.
German Republican Society, 82, 83-84, 107, 136.
Gerry, Elbridge, 181, 183.
Gibson, John, 114, 122, 128; on anti-excise riots, 96.
Giles, William, 107.
Governor, election of, 1790, 33-34; patronage powers, 263; powers of, 14.
Graydon, Alexander: on Constitutionalists, 1790, 10; on election of Senators, 14-15; on fear of national government, 10; on Genêt, 77.
Greene County, election returns delayed, 1796, 168-171, 172.
Gregg, Andrew, 107, 142, 313; elected to Congress, 1791, 48; 1796, 159; 1798, 189; and election of 1792, 61, 63, 66; favors tax laws 1798, 215, 216; favors treaty with France, 183; opposes Alien and Sedition Acts, 182, 183.
Gurney, Francis, 38; 300; elected to State Senate, 1798, 189.

Half Town, 114.
Hall, Joseph, edits *Pittsburgh Gazette*, 309.
Hamilton, Alexander, 78, 87, 164, 272; censures Pennsylvania officials, 1794, 98, 99, 100; and Democratic Societies, 82; discusses assumption plan with Morris, 28; distrust of Burr, 255; drafts proclamation against excise rioters, 92; exploits Genêt incident, 79; and Fenno, 191; on use of militia in excise collections, 290.
Hamilton, John, 321.
Hammond, George, residence attacked, 89.
Hand, Edward, 93, 149, 254.
Hanna, John A., 301; elected to Congress, 1796, 160; 1798, 189; favors tax laws, 1798, 215, 216; heads Republican committee, 1799, 221; opposes Alien and Sedition Acts, 182, 183; opposes negotiation of treaty with France, 183.
Hannum, John, 149.
Harmar, Josiah, 100, 102, 117.
Harris, James, 321.
Harrisburg, Presidential electors meet in, 1796, 169, 170, 172.
Harrisburg Convention, 1788, 22-23, 31.
Hartley, Thomas, 5, 107, 142, 145, 289, 310, 313; elected to Congress, 1791, 47; 1796, 160; 1798, 189; and election of 1792, 61, 63, 65; favors protective tariff, 27; favors tax laws, 1798, 216; opposes assumption, 28; supports Sedition Act, 183.

Hartzell, Jonas, 172, 238.
Hegewisch, Dietrich Hermann, on Constitution of 1790, 17.
Hiester, Daniel, 107, 142, 149, 289, 313; Congressional candidate, 1788, 23, 24; elected to Congress, 1791, 47; and election of 1792, 61, 65, 66; favors treaty with France 183; opposes assumption, 28.
Hiester, Joseph, 301; elected to Congress, 1798, 189; opposes tax laws, 1798, 215, 216; Presidential elector, 1796, 168.
Hiltzheimer, Jacob, 38, 139, 300.
Hoge, David, supports Woods for Congress, 1798, 185.
Hoge, John, 51, 301; land speculation of, 126; supports Woods for Congress, 1798, 185.
Hoge, William, elected to Congress, 1801, 257.
Hollingsworth, Levi, Federalist committeeman, 228.
Hopkins, John, 322.
Hopkinson, Francis, member of Society for Political Inquiries, 81.
Hough, Silas, on need for party discipline, 1801, 259-260.
House of Representatives, United States, election of Jefferson in, 1800, 254-255.
Howell, Governor, 105.
Huston, John, resigns from Assembly, 308.
Hutchinson, James, 42, 168; and Democratic Societies, 82, 84; and election of 1792, 53-68 *passim;* on excise protest, 1792, 63, 66; and Genêt, 76, 77, 79, 138; sketch of, 53-54; supports Mifflin for Governor, 1790, 35-40.

Indian wars, and Presque Isle, 115-117, 118-119, 123, 130.
Ingersoll, Jared, 96; attends conference on excise disturbances, 96; and election of 1792, 57; on legality of Presque Isle suspension, 124, 130.
Irvine, William, 25, 107, 149, 302; commissioned to survey Presque Isle, 115, 116; commissioner on excise riots, 101; correspondence with Beckley, 1796, 166-168, 174; and election of 1792, 60, 61, 65; executor of Mifflin's estate, 316; and governorship of Pennsylvania, 1799, 220, 221; and McKean's campaign, 1799, 222-223; Presidential elector, 1796, 168; protests Presque Isle suspension, 126-127, 133; Senatorial nominee, 1785, 1797, 152.
Irvine's Reserve, 126.
Irwin, John, 223.
Israel, Israel, 193, 195; candidate for State Senate, 1798, 178-179, 189; elected to State Senate, 176-178; member of Pennsylvania Democratic Society, 84, 85, 86.
Israel, John, 231; supports Gallatin, 1798, 186-187; supports McKean, 1799, 232, 235.
Issues, national, in Pennsylvania politics, 153-154.

Jackson, Samuel, 62.
Jacobin, 236.
Jacobs, Israel, elected to Congress, 1791, 47.
Jay, John: accuses Dallas of friendship with Genêt, 79; negotiates treaty, 1794, 88-89, 296; and neutrality proclamation, 76.
Jay's Treaty, 87-90, 181, 197; crystallizes parties in Pennsylvania, 199; in election of 1795, 142-144; 1796, 161, 168; influence on Pennsylvania politics, 270.
Jefferson, Thomas, 271; and Democratic Societies, 82-83; and election of 1800, 247, 251, 254; electoral votes, 1796, 172, 174; and Freneau, 189; and Genêt, 78-79; George Logan, friend of, 183; notes existence of party groups, 1798, 213; Pennsylvania votes for, 1796, 143, 162-174; praises *National Gazette,* 166; on Proclamation of Neutrality, 80; Quaker support for, 1796, 173; rewards Pennsylvania Republicans, 267-268; on use of patronage power, 265.
Jenks, Thomas, 301.
Johnson, William, British Indian agent, 122, 123.

Johnston, Thomas, elected to State Senate, 241.
Jones, John, 248; elected to State Senate, 240.
Judiciary, provision for in Constitution of 1790, 16.

Kammerer, Henry, 139; and German Republican Society, 83; and Senatorial election of 1793, 150.
Kelly, James, 109, 110.
Kennedy, Thomas, 301.
Kentucky Resolutions, Assembly's vote on, 208, 209.
King, Rufus, 79.
Kirkpatrick, Abraham, 55.
Kittera, John W., 107, 142, 313; elected to Congress, 1791, 47; 1796, 160; 1798, 189; and election of 1792, 61, 65; favors tax laws, 1798, 215, 216; supports Alien and Sedition Acts, 182, 183.
Knox, Henry, 78; correspondence on Presque Isle suspension, 116-126; requests militia to quell excise rioters, 100.
Krause, David, elected to Assembly, 1797, 176.

Lake Erie, roads to, 115.
Lancaster, and Congressional election of 1792, 59, 62, 64-65; State capital in, 232, 272-273.
Lancaster Convention, 1788, 24.
Lancaster Convention, in election of 1792, 64-65.
Land bounties, granted at Presque Isle, 124, 125, 126.
Land laws, 1792, 114-115; 1799, 210-211.
Lands, public, Presque Isle development, 113-133 *passim.*
Latimer, George, 279, 300; and election of 1792, 58, 64.
Le Boeuf, Fort, 115, 122, 123, 128.
Lee, Governor, 104, 105.
Leib, Michael, 200, 206, 300; chairman of Republican campaign committee, 1796, 164, 166; Congressional candidate, 1798, 188, 189; and democratic societies, 83-84; deplores party spirit, 1796, 202; favors nomination of P. Muhlenberg, 1799, 223; and general election law, 1797, 204; Republican committeeman, 1799-222, 224, 226, 235.
Lenox, David, and enforcement of excise law, 95.
Lewis, William, 248; in Constitutional Convention of 1790, 8, 12, 13, 14; and election of 1792, 58, 60, 65; jibe at James Wilson, 276; supports St. Clair for Governor, 1790, 36; withdraws as Fries' attorney, 219.
Linnard, William, 200, 253, 300.
Little Democrat (Little Sarah), 78, 79.
Logan, Deborah, 266.
Logan, George, 266; deplores party spirit, 1796, 202; "embassy" of, 183-184, 207; Federalists attack, 230; and governorship of Pennsylvania, 1799, 220, 221; member of Pennsylvania Democratic Society, 84; newspaper criticism of, 308; proposes resolution on tax riots, 217.
Lower, Christopher, 321.
Lycoming County, 305.

McClenachan, Blair, 54, 89, 300; elected to Congress, 1796, 159, 161; favors district elections, 45; favors treaty with France, 183; member of Pennsylvania Democratic Society, 84, 85; opposes Alien and Sedition Acts, 182, 183; opposes tax laws, 1798, 215, 216.

MacFarland, James, 95.
Maclay, Samuel, 142, 313; elected to Assembly, 1797, 175; motion on Franco-American relations, 206; refuses to vote for Presidential electors, 252.
Maclay, William, 201; on John Adams, 28; admires George Logan, 183; and assumption, 27, 28; elected to Assembly, 1797, 176; elected to United States Senate, 25; on gubernatorial election of 1790, 33-35; *Journal* of, 26; and location of United States capital, 28-29; opinion of Tench Coxe, 312; opinion of James Hutchinson, 53; opinion of George Washington, 29-30; opposes excise law, 91; Presidential elector, 1796, 168, 170; and protective tariff, 27; resolution opposing war, 206; Senatorial candidate, 1790-1793, 145-146, 148, 149, 150; sketch of, 25-26.
McClellan, Joseph, elected to Assembly, 1797, 176.
McKean, Joseph B., leads attack on Duane, 218.
McKean, Thomas, 8, 89, 257, 310; on Adams' appointments, 268; address to Assembly, 1800, 249; attends conference on excise disturbances, 96, 97; calls meeting of Presidential electors, 1800, 252-253; calls special session of Assembly, 247; commissioner on excise riots, 101; compared with Ross, 228; considers special session of Assembly, 1800, 245; in Constitutional Convention of 1790, 8, 9, 11, 12, 13-14, 15; elected Governor, 1799, 219-241; and election of 1792, 56, 57, 59; on Federalist propaganda, 1800, 248; on Federalist tactics in Presidential election, 1800, 323; and Genêt, 79; on Governor's office, 227; and patronage power, 263-268; plans in case of Jefferson's defeat, 1800, 255-256; political philosophy of, 225-226; Presiential elector, 1796, 164, 167, 168, 170; and Presidential election, 1800, 252; proposes suffrage restrictions, 276; sketch of, 224-227; on selection of Presidential electors, 1800, 253-254; supported for governorship by Dallas, 194, 195; votes received, 1799, 238-239.
Manufacturers, and Pennsylvania Democratic Society, 85-86.
Marshall, James, opposes excise law, 92, 95, 108.
Marshall, John, 181.
Massachusetts, claims Erie Triangle, 113-114.
Matlack, Timothy, 4.
Mewhorter, Thomas, elected to State Senate, 240.
Mifflin, George, 37.
Mifflin, Thomas, 4, 313; effect of Whiskey Insurrection on administration of, 112; appointments criticised, 136, 266; appoints commissioners on excise riots, 101; appoints Dallas Secretary of the Commonwealth, 44; to Assembly on Fries' Rebellion, 216; attempts to quell excise disturbances, 92-93, 97, 98; attends conference on excise disturbances, 96; and Charles Biddle, 41-42, 44; Samuel Bryan and, 42-43, 48, calls out militia in excise riots, 100, 102-103; calls out militia in Fries' Rebellion, 217; charged with drunkenness, 310; in Constitutional Conventon of 1790, 9-10, 11; correspondence on Presque Isle suspension, 116-126; correspondence on Whiskey Insurrection, 98-99; declines to run for Congress, 1798, 187-188; and delayed election returns, 1796, 169-171; deplores party spirit, 202, 207; on election of United States Senators, 1792, 147; Fitzsimons' opinion of, 34; and general election law, 1797, 204, 205, 210; and Genêt, 76, 77, 78, 79; Governor, 34, 35-36, 37-40, 135-138, 159, 303; illness of 316; member of Society for Political Inquiries, 81; message to Assembly 1796, 202; 1798, 206-207; Newspaper opinion of, 188; opposition to election of, 1793, 136-137; pardons Whiskey Rebels, 105; political career described, 219-220; political qualities of, 72, 194-195; proposed as Presidential elector, 1796, 167, 168; proposes toast to French Republic, 86-87; recommends tax on property, 273; reports to Assembly on excise disturbances, 93; sketch of, 37-38; on states rights in Presque Isle suspension, 119-122, 131; will of, 316.
Miles, Samuel, 5, 34; Congressional candidate, 1798, 187; party allegiance of, 196-197; Presidential elector, 1796, 170, 172; Republican committeeman, 1799, 222, 224, 235.
Militia: called out in Fries' Rebellion, 217-218; ordered to Presque Isle, 115, 116, 117, 118, 119, 123, 129; in Whiskey insurrection, 96-106 *passim*, 112, 131.
Militia law, A. J. Dallas on, 291.

INDEX

Miller, Henry, 149, 253, 254, 301.
Mingo Creek Society, 86, 108.
Mitchell, David, 200.
"Monocrats," Jefferson's use of term, 286.
Monroe, James, 181.
Montgomery, John, 62; and Senatorial election, 1790, 145.
Montgomery, William, 107, 301; and election of 1792, 61, 66.
Montgomery County: and Congressional election of 1792, 59, 64; nomination procedures in, 1794, 139-140; 1801, 259; Republicans in, 238.
Moore, John, 301.
Morgan, Benjamin, 58, 139, 300; candidate for State Senate, 1797, 176-179; Federalist committeeman, 228; resigns as State Senator, 307.
Morgan, Jacob: director of Bank of Pennsylvania, 201, 211; and election of 1792, 62; member of Pennsylvania Democratic Society, 84, 85, 86; Presidential elector, 1796, 168.
Morris, Anthony, 257, 301; Congressional candidate, 1798, 188.
Morris, Robert, 4, 55, 57, 58; and assumption, 28; and gubernatorial election of 1790, 33-34, 35, 36, 41; and location of United States capital, 29; member of Society for Political Inquiries, 81; and Arthur St. Clair, 34; sketch of, 26; United States Senator, 25, 150, 151, 152.
Muhlenberg, Frederick A., 5, 27, 313; candidate for Governor, 1793, 135, 137; 1796, 159; Congressional candidate, 1788, 23, 24; 1791, 47; defeated for Assembly, 1798, 188-189; and election of 1792, 61, 65, 66; and gubernatorial election of 1790, 34, 35, 36; and location of United States capital, 29; on Thomas Mifflin's candidacy, 1793, 135; sketch of, 135-136.
Muhlenberg, Peter, 87, 107, 206, 238, 257, 268, 289; Congressional candidate, 1788, 23, 24; 1798, 189; elected to Assembly, 1797, 175; and election of 1792, 61, 65; Federalists seek support of, 231; and German Republican Society, 83; and governorship of Pennsylvania, 1799, 220, 221, 223-224; opposes assumption, 28; Presidential elector, 1796, 168; Republican committeeman, 1799, 222, 224, 226, 235; Senatorial candidate, 1793, 1795, 149, 150, 152; supports McKean, 1799, 233, 239.

Nagle, Peter, 218.
National Gazette, Republican policy of, 166.
Naturalization, required for voters, 204, 210.
Neutrality, proclamation of, 80.
Neville, John: Bower Hill attacked, 130; and enforcement of excise law, 95; sketch of, 54-55.
Neville, Presley, 55, 139; Congressional aspirant, 1798, 185-186; opposes militia call for Presque Isle, 129.
New York, claims Erie Triangle, 113-114.
Newspapers: coverage of French Revolution, 75; Federalist, attack Republican committeemen, 224; political propaganda in, 136-137, 212-213, 230-232, 249-250; report elections, 1797, 175-176, 179; support Jefferson, 1796, 165-166, 172-173; support McKean, 1799, 235; use of party labels by, 1797-1798, 176, 179, 180; *See also under names of papers.*
Nichols, William, 279; ordered to arrest tax rioters, 1799, 216.
Nicholson, John, land speculation of, 126.
Nomination procedures, 1788, 24-25, 34; in Congressional election, 1791, 47; 1792, 52, 55-62, 64-65, 67; 1794, 139-140; "Republican" on, 1797, 192-193.
Northampton County, Republicans in, 238.
Northumberland County, representative in Executive Council, 6.
Northumberland Gazette, Cooper's political essays in, 235.

Oberholtzer, Ellis P., opinion of William Maclay, 26.
Ogden, Samuel, in Constitutional Convention of 1790, 14.
Ogden's Tavern, Philadelphia, 178.
Orders in Council, 1793, 88.

Paine, Thomas, member of Society for Political Inquiries, 81.
Parkinson's Ferry, anti-excise meetings at, 101, 103, 104, 105.
Party labels, 309; 1795, 154; 1796, 161-162; described by Thomas Cooper, 1799, 235-237; in elections of 1797, 1798, 175, 176, 179, 180.
Party machinery, 1795, 154; Federalist and Republican, 1799, 228, 229, 239.
Patronage: McKean's use of, 263-268; Mifflin's use of, 136, 137; as party weapon, 263, 265; problem of, 266-267.
Patterson, William, 200.
Pearson, John, 321.
Pennsylvania: in 1790, 19-21; favors Jefferson in 1796, 162-174; relations with Federal government, 21-26.
Pennsylvania Democratic Society, 82, 83-87; aids Swanwick, 142; in election of 1793, 136, 137; and Whiskey Insurrection, 108-109.
Pennsylvania Germans: anti-Jefferson, 1796, 173; in election, 1793, 142; 1799, 231, 233, 239; favor partisan appointments, 266; in politics, 136.
Pennsylvania Population Company, 126.
Penrose, William: on Jefferson's election, 1800, 253; Republican committeeman, 1799, 222, 224.
Peters, Richard, 301; and Fries' Rebellion, 216, 218.
Pettit, Charles, Senatorial nominee, 1795, 152.
Philadelphia: carried by Republicans, 1801, 256-257; description of, 1789, 49-50; in elections of 1790, 40, 41; 1792, 48-68; 1794, 141-142; 1795, 142-144; 1797, 176-179; 1798, 187-189; Genêt in, 76-78; government under charter of 1789, 48-49; influence in McKean's election, 222, 223; influence on political parties, 269-270; Jefferson carries in 1796, 173; population, 1789, 49; social life, 1790's, 49; wards organized by Federalists and Republicans, 260.
Philadelphia City Committee, 1776, arranges for Provincial Convention, 3.
Philadelphia Gazette, 191; election propaganda in, 1801, 257, 258; short on political news, 303.
Philadelphia "Junto," 33, 36, 39, 40, 41, 42.
Pickering, Timothy, 132.
Pinckney, Charles Cotesworth, 181, 253, 254.
Pinckney, Thomas, 172.
Pittsburgh, anti-excise meetings at, 92, 103; and election of 1792, 62-63; population of, 1790, 20.
Pittsburgh Gazette, in election of 1798, 185-186.
Political parties: in 1790, 30-32; in 1792, 52-53, 67; in 1798, 213; changing spirit of, 220; concepts of, 1797, 1798, 192-196; Democratic Societies and, 81, 82; in elections of 1790, 38, 40-41; 1792, 52-68 *passim;* 1796, 270-271; 1797, 175-180; 1800, 243-256; Franco-American relations and, 202-203, 204, 205-206; French Revolution and, 80; growth of in Pennsylvania, 1793-1795, 135-155 *passim;* in 1796, 162-174; 1795-1798, 199-213; Jay's Treaty and growth of, 144; lack of organization in, 154; national issues promote growth of, 211, 212; opposition to, 154, 178, 193-195, 202, 207; party discipline, 1801, 258, 259, 260; relative strength, 1796, 171; sectionalism and, 211-212; shifting allegiances in, 196-198; use of party names, 154, 161-162, 176, 179, 180, 235-237, 309; in Western Pennsylvania, 1798, 184, 185; Whiskey Insurrection and, 106, 111-112.

Poor's Schoolhouse, Philadelphia, 305.
Population, in Pennsylvania, 1790, 1800, 20, 272; of Philadelphia, 1789, 49.
Postlethwaite, Samuel, 253.
Potts, Stacy, 318.
Potts, Zebulon, 256; elected to State Senate, 241.
Powell, Samuel, 51, 55, 56, 58.
Presque Isle: boundaries of, 115; political aspects of suspension of survey, 120, 126, 129-130; price of lots at, 132; and states rights, 113-133 *passim;* survey ordered, 115, 132.
Priestley, Joseph, 271.
Privateers, Genêt and, 76, 78-79.
Public lands, revenue from, 273.
Public opinion: Cobbett's influence on, 144; on Presque Isle suspension, 120, 126, 128-129.

Quakers, object to Constitution of 1790, 16; support Jefferson, 1796, 173.

Randolph, Edmund, 97, 98, 101.
Rawle, William, 248; and election of, 1792, 58; on Mifflin, 38.
Redick, David, 25; protests Presque Isle suspension, 127-128, 133; reports to Washington on excise riots, 103, 104, 105; resigns from Washington Society, 108; supports Woods for Congress, 1798, 185.
Redstone Old Fort, meeting at, 101.
Reed, Joseph, executor of Mifflin's estate, 316.
Reed, William, 321.
Republican, as party label, 1796, 161-162.
Republican Society of the Yough, 86, 108.
Republicans: aid Bache, 190; attitude toward Logan's "embassy," 184; campaign committee, 1799, 222, 224, 238; Committee of Correspondence, 1796, 163, 164, 165; Congressional ticket, 1792, 61-62; Thomas Cooper's definition of, 237; definition of, 52-53; effect of Genêt affair on, 80; elected to Assembly, 175-180, 200-201, 240, 319; elected to Congress, 142, 159-160, 189, 321; and election of 1792, 54-66 *passim;* election propaganda, 1796, 167; 1799, 232, 233-235; 1800, 246; favor general elections, 163-164, 243-244; favor joint election of Presidential electors, 1800, 247-252; favor partisan appointments, 264-265; growth of party strength reviewed, 179; hurt by Whiskey Insurrection, 111-112; ideology of, 71-73, 154; make Jay's Treaty political issue, 89-90, 144; nominate Mifflin for Congress, 1798, 187; nominating procedures, 1801, 258-260; oppose address to Adams, 1798, 207-208; oppose Alien and Sedition Acts, 209; organize Philadelphia wards, 260; party discipline, 1801, 258, 259-260; party leaders, 1799, 220; plan to ensure Jefferson's election, 1800, 254-255; in Presidential elections, 1796, 170-171, 173; 1800, 243-253; Presidential electors, 1796, 164, 167, 168, 304; reasons for victory of, 271-272; seek political offices, 264-265, 266; select candidate for Governor, 1799, 220-223; and Senatorial elections, 149, 152; support Virginia Resolutions, 200; supported by *Aurora,* 1796, 165-166; win legislative election, 1800, 247; 1801, 256-261 *passim.* See also under Anti-Constitutionalists.
Richards, John, 142, 313.
"Rights of Man Ticket," 64.
Rittenhouse, David, 304; and Genêt, 76, 79; and Pennsylvania Democratic Society, 84; proposed as Presidential elector, 1796, 167, 168.
Roads to Lake Erie, 115; Reading to Presque Isle, 295.
Roberts, Jonathan: on Mifflin, 310; on political parties, 31.
Rodman, William, 321.

Ross, James, 250, 264; candidate for United States Senate, 1793-1794, 148, 149, 150; charged with Deism, 234-235; commissioner on excise riots, 100; compared with McKean, 228; in Constitutional Convention of 1790, 14; elected to United States Senate, 147, 150, 151, 152, 302; Federalist candidate for Governor, 1799, 223, 227-230; on Jefferson's election, 323; opinion of George Logan, 184; use of party labels, 309; on parties in Western Pennsylvania, 1798, 184-185; political ambitions of, 253; sketch of, 228-229; on use of militia in excise riots, 104; votes received, 1799, 238-239.
Ruch, Michael, 200.
Rush, Benjamin, 28; member of Pennsylvania Democratic Society, 84; supports St. Clair for Governor, 1790, 36.

St. Clair, Arthur, 5, 117, 138, 184, 185, 253; candidate for Governor 1790, 34, 36-37, 38, 39, 40, 41; candidate for United States Senate, 148, 149, 150; on Constitutionalists, 39; sketch of, 37.
Say, Benjamin: Congressional candidate, 1798, 188; elected to State Senate, 240.
Scott, Thomas, 24, 107; and election of 1792, 65, 66; opposes assumption, 28.
Scull, John, edits *Pittsburgh Gazette,* 185, 186, 309.
Seckle, Lawrence, 38, 300.
Secretary of the Commonwealth: candidates for, 1790, 42-44; duties of, 44.
Sectionalism: in Pennsylvania Assembly, 208, 211-212; in elections, 1791, 46; 1792, 51; 1793, 149, 150, 152; 1796, 173; in Pennsylvania, 1790, 19-20; and removal of capital to Lancaster, 273.
Sellers, John, 301.
Senators, Pennsylvania, election of, 15. *See also under* Elections.
Senators, United States, elections of in Pennsylvania, 25, 145-153. *See also under* Elections.
Sergeant, Jonathan D., 168; and Democratic Societies, 82, 84; and election of 1792, 53, 54, 61, 62, 66; and Genêt, 76, 77, 79; sketch of, 54.
Shoemaker, Charles, 238.
Simcoe, John, 117.
Sitgreaves, Samuel, 142, 313; in Constitutional Convention of 1790, 8, 9; elected to Congress, 1796, 160; and election of 1792, 65; favors tax laws, 1798, 215, 216; resigns Congressional seat, 308; Senatorial candidate, 151; supports Alien and Sedition Acts, 182, 183.
Six Nations: conference at Canandaigua, 123, 125, 132; hostility toward Presque Isle development, 121, 122, 123, 125, 128, 131-132; and purchase of Erie Triangle, 114, 118, 122, 123.
Smilie, John, 4, 23, 107, 112, 163, 201, 202, 206, 301; in Constitutional Convention of 1790, 8; elected to Congress, 1798, 185, 189; and election of 1792, 60, 61, 63, 66; opposes excise law, 92; Presidential elector, 1796, 168; and Senatorial election of 1793, 150.
Smith, Abraham, 301.
Smith, George, 200.
Smith, William, 149.
Snyder, Jacob, elected to Assembly, 1797, 175.
Snyder, Simon, 208.
Society for Political Inquiries, 81, 82, 83.
Spotswood, William, 43.
State House, political meetings at, 55-58, 250.
States rights: Presque Isle development and, 113-133 *passim;* Whiskey Insurrection and, 112.
Stokely, Thomas, 170, 172.

Suffrage: McKean's views on, 225, 276; qualifications in colonial Pennsylvania, 2; qualifications in Constitutions of 1776, 3; of 1790, 16; qualifications in election laws, 1797, 204-205; 1799, 210.
Swanwick, John, 89, 139, 142, 173, 313; Congressional candidate, 1794, 141-142; death of, 308; elected to Congress, 107, 160-161; favors elections-at-large, 299; member of Pennsylvania Democratic Society, 84, 85, 86; and Senatorial election, 1793, 147, 149, 150.

Tammany, Sons of, 81.
Tammany Society, New York, 81.
Tariff, protective, advocated by Pennsylvania Representatives, 27.
Taverns, Philadelphia, 49. *See also under names of taverns.*
Tax laws: provoke Fries' Rebellion, 215-216; vote of Pennsylvania Representatives on, 1799, 215-216.
Taxes, in Pennsylvania, 273.
Test Laws, 6.
Thomas, Richard, 142, 301, 313; elected to Congress, 1796, 160, 1798, 189; favors tax laws, 1798, 215; supports Alien and Sedition Acts, 182, 183.
Thomson, Charles, 40, 149; and election of 1792, 61, 62, 66, 284.
Tilghman, Edward, Congressional candidate, 1796, 160.
Tittermary, Richard, 196, 201, 300.
Townships: in county politics, 258; in election of 1794, 140.
Trade, West Indian, 88.
Treason: Fries guilty of, 218-219; trials in Whiskey Insurrection, 105.
"Treaty" ticket, in election of 1795, 142-144.

Uniontown, anti-excise, meeting at, 103.

Van Horne, Isaac: elected to Congress, 257-260, *passim;* party affiliation of, 319.
Veto, and executive power, 12, 13, 16.
Virginia Resolutions, vote on in Assembly, 199-200, 209.

Waln, Robert, 300; Congressional candidate, 1796, 161; 1798, 187, 189; and election of 1792, 58, 65.
War, William Maclay's resolution against, 206.
Wards, Philadelphia, organized by Republicans and Federalists, 260.
Washington, George, 154, 272; address of Assembly to, 203, 204; appoints commissioners on excise riots, 100-101; aristocratic tendencies criticized, 165-166; calls conference on excise disturbances, 96-97; condemns Democratic Societies, 87, 106, 109; corresponds with Mifflin on excise riots, 98-99; correspondence on Presque Isle suspension, 116, 118-126; favors Federalists, 80; and George Logan, 184; Maclay's opinion of, 29-30; and Mifflin, 37-38; pardons Whiskey Rebels, 105; popular estimate of, 162; proclamation against excise rioters, 92, 100; receives Genêt, 78; and Republican party in Pennsylvania, 81; sends John Jay to England, 88; signs Jay's Treaty, 89; signs neutrality proclamation, 76; third term question, 164-165, 167.
Washington County: in election of 1790, 40; representation in Executive Council, 6.
Washington County Committee, denies Ross' Deism, 234-235.
Wayne, Anthony: candidate for Governor, 1796, 159; leads expedition against Indians, 117, 131.
Weaver, Isaac, 208; and land law, 1799, 210, 211.
Wells, Richard, 38, 58.

West Indies, trade with, 88.
Western Pennsylvania: causes of unrest in, 94-95; Congressional elections in, 1798, 184-187; in election of 1799, 239.
Westmoreland County: in election of 1790, 40; election returns delayed, 1796, 168-171; representation in Executive Council, 6.
Wetherill, Samuel, nominated Presidential elector, 1800, 252.
Wharton, Robert, Federalist committeeman, 228.
Whelen, Dennis, 253.
Whelen, Israel, 254; and election of 1792, 58.
Whiskey Insurrection: affects Congressional election, 1794, 140; George M. Dallas on, 292; effect on Democratic Societies, 107-109; and growth of political parties, 152-153; political consequences of, 111-112; and Presque Isle development, 130; prosecutions in Allegheny County, 289; punishment of rioters, 105; significance of, 105-106; Washington calls conference on, 96-97.
Wilcocks, John, 58.
Wilkins, John, 133; on anti-excise riots, 95, 96; attributes Indian hostility to British, 128; reports on Indian unrest, 116.
Wilkins, John, Jr., 62.
Willing, Anne (Mrs. William Bingham), 34.
Wilson, James, 4, 135; in Constitutional Convention of 1790, 8, 11-12, 13, 14-15; and election of 1792, 57, 58; William Lewis on, 276; member of Society for Political Inquiries, 81; reports on excise disturbances, 96, 97, 98, 100; supports St. Clair for Governor, 1790, 36.
"Window Tax," 215; and election of 1799, 238-239.
Wolcott, Oliver, on Mifflin, 310.
Woods, George, 55.
Woods, Henry, elected to Congress, 1798, 189.
Woods, John: Congressional candidate, 1798, 185-187; political ambitions of, 253.
Worrell, Isaac, 200, 300.
Wynkoop, Gerardus, 139.
Wynkoop, Henry, 24, 27, 289; and assumption, 28; Congressional candidate, 1791, 47; and election of 1792, 65, 66.

"XYZ Affair," 181, 207.

Yeates, Jasper, commissioner on excise riots, 100.
Yellow fever, in election of 1793, 138; 1797, 176, 177; 1798, 189.
York County, and election of 1792, 65.